AF208180

ORIGINAL & COPY

L'ART DE LA COPIE

KÖNEMANN

© 2020 koenemann.com GmbH
www.koenemann.com

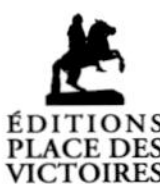

ÉDITIONS
PLACE DES
VICTOIRES

© Éditions Place des Victoires
6, rue du Mail – 75002 Paris
www.victoires.com

ISBN : 978-2-8099-1656-0
Dépôt légal : 4e trimestre 2020

Concept, project management: koenemann.com GmbH
Text: Edwart Vignot
Translations into English, German, Spanish, Portuguese and Dutch by
koenemann.com GmbH
Layout: Mathilde Decorbez

Picture credits:
Bridgeman images except pp. 4-5, 27, 29 (31), 54, 72, 103, 115, 119, 121,
196, 204, 211, 215, 218 (220) : akg images gmbh, pp. 39 (41) : Artothek
pp. 12, 13, 25, 33, 37, 47, 57, 81, 61 (63), 75, 77, 85, 133, 153, 157, 188, 213,
226, 229 : photos Julien Pépy © Private collection, p. 93 : https://commons.
wikimedia.org/wiki/File:Lille_Jordaens_vaches

Colour separation: Nord Compo, Villeneuve-d'Ascq

ISBN: 978-3-7419-2504-7 (international)

Printed in China by Shyft Publishing / Hunan Tianwen Xinhua Printing Co., Ltd.

pp. 4-5 :

Venus of Urbino

Vénus d'Urbin

Venus von Urbino

La Venus de Urbino

Vênus de Urbino

Venus van Urbino

Tiziano Vecellio (1489-1576)

———

1538, Oil on canvas/Huile sur toile,
119 × 165 cm, Galleria degli Uffizi, Firenze

pp. 6-7 :

Olympia

**Édouard Manet
(1832-1883)**

———

1863, Oil on canvas/Huile
sur toile, 103,5 × 191 cm,
Musée d'Orsay, Paris

pp. 8-9 :

Olympia

**Paul Gauguin
(1848-1903)**

———

c. 1891, Oil on canvas/Huile
sur toile, 89 × 130 cm,
Private collection (copy after/copie)

EDWART VIGNOT

ORIGINAL & COPY
L'ART DE LA COPIE

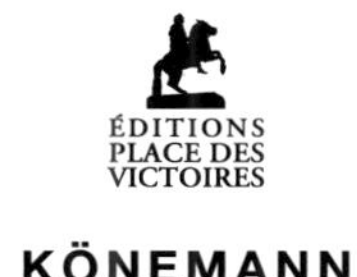

ÉDITIONS
PLACE DES
VICTOIRES

KÖNEMANN

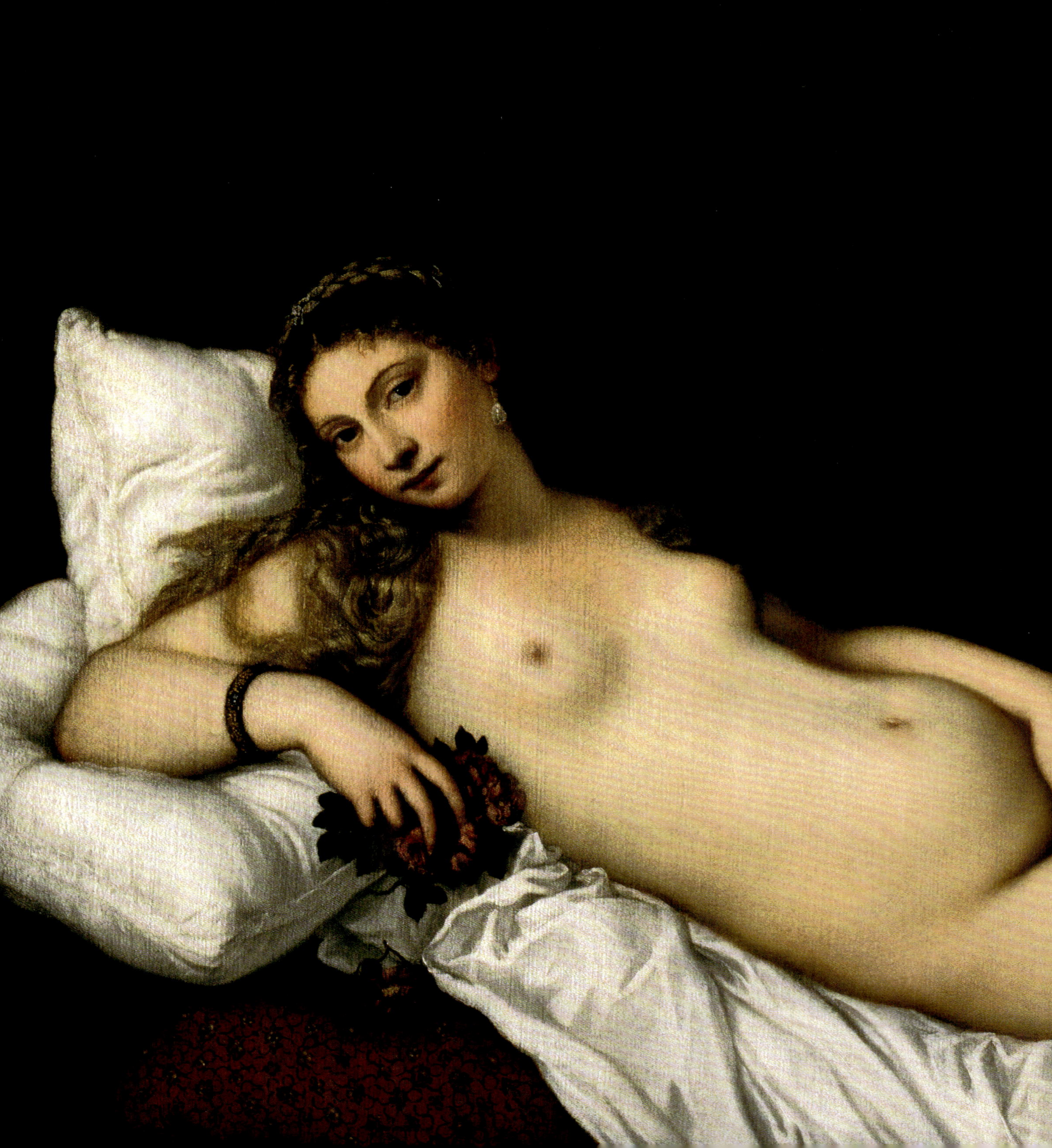

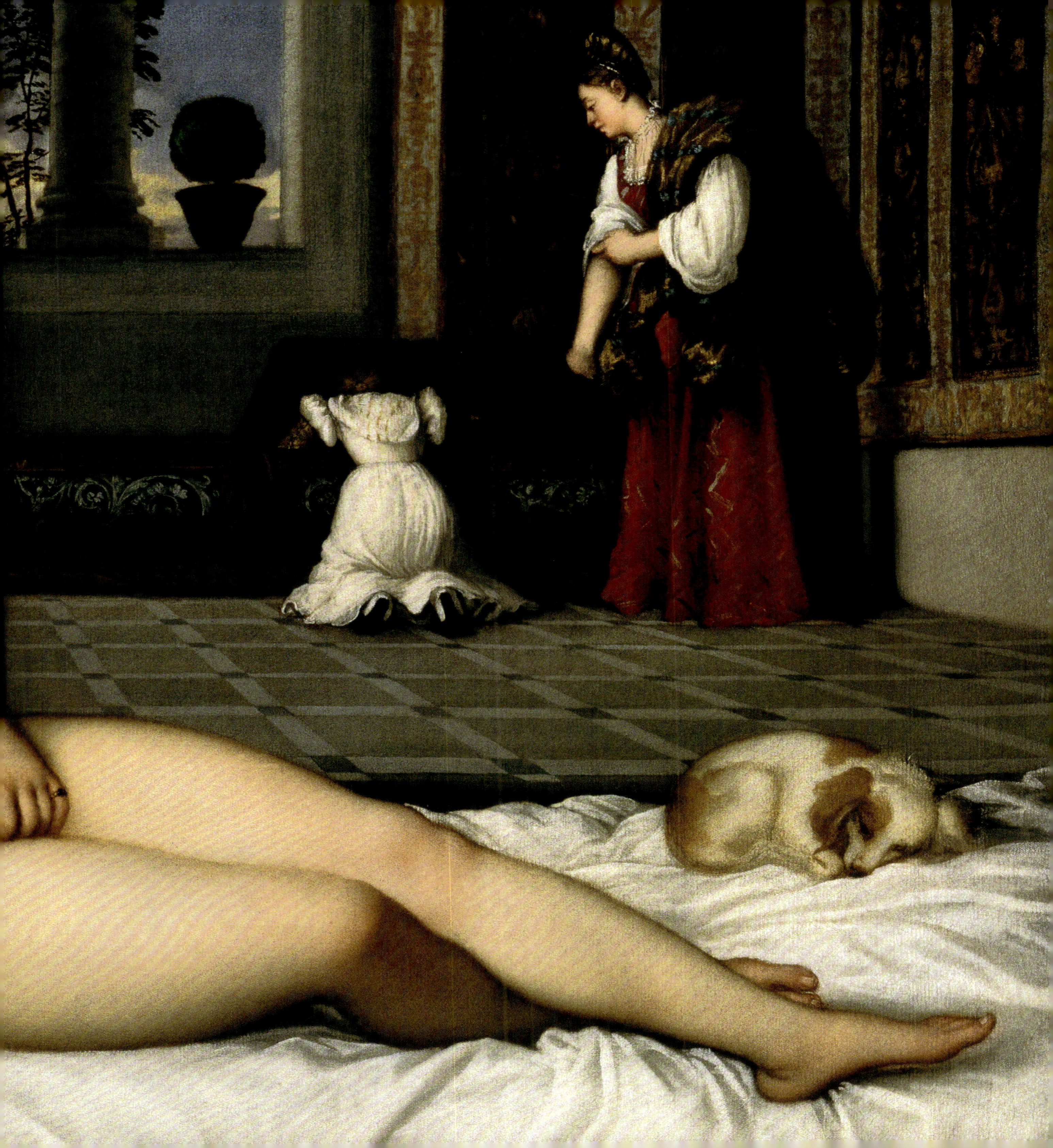

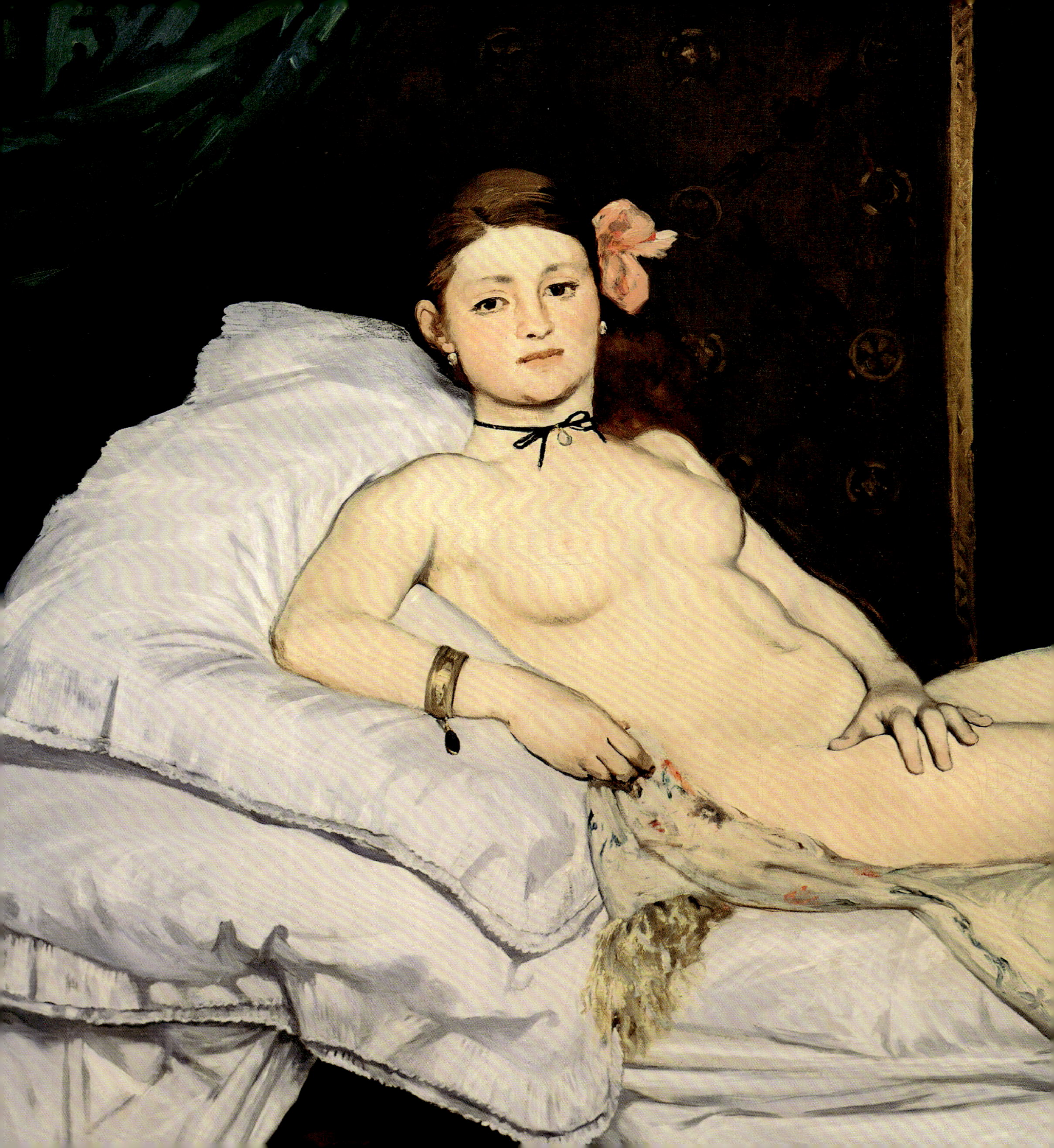

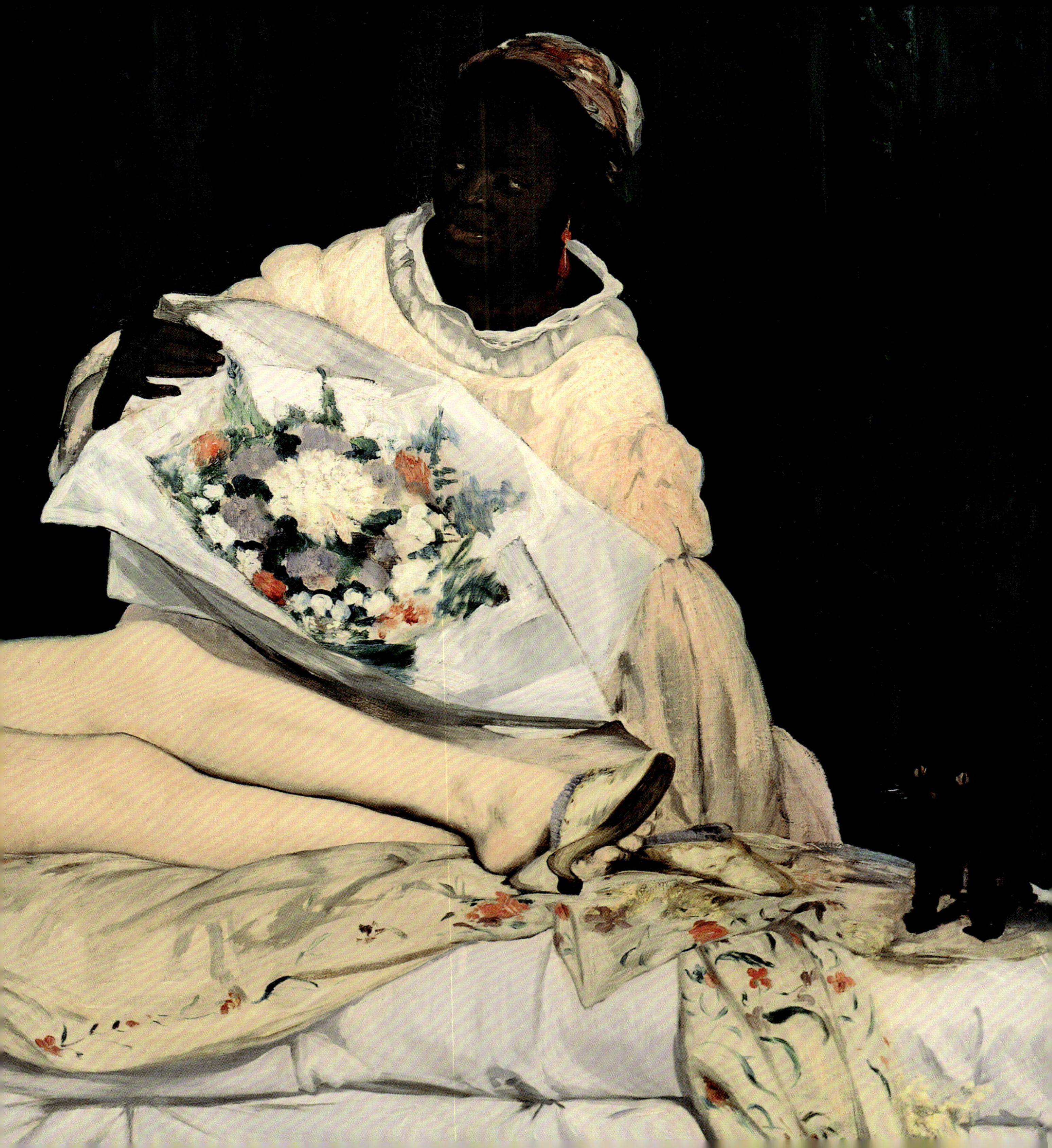

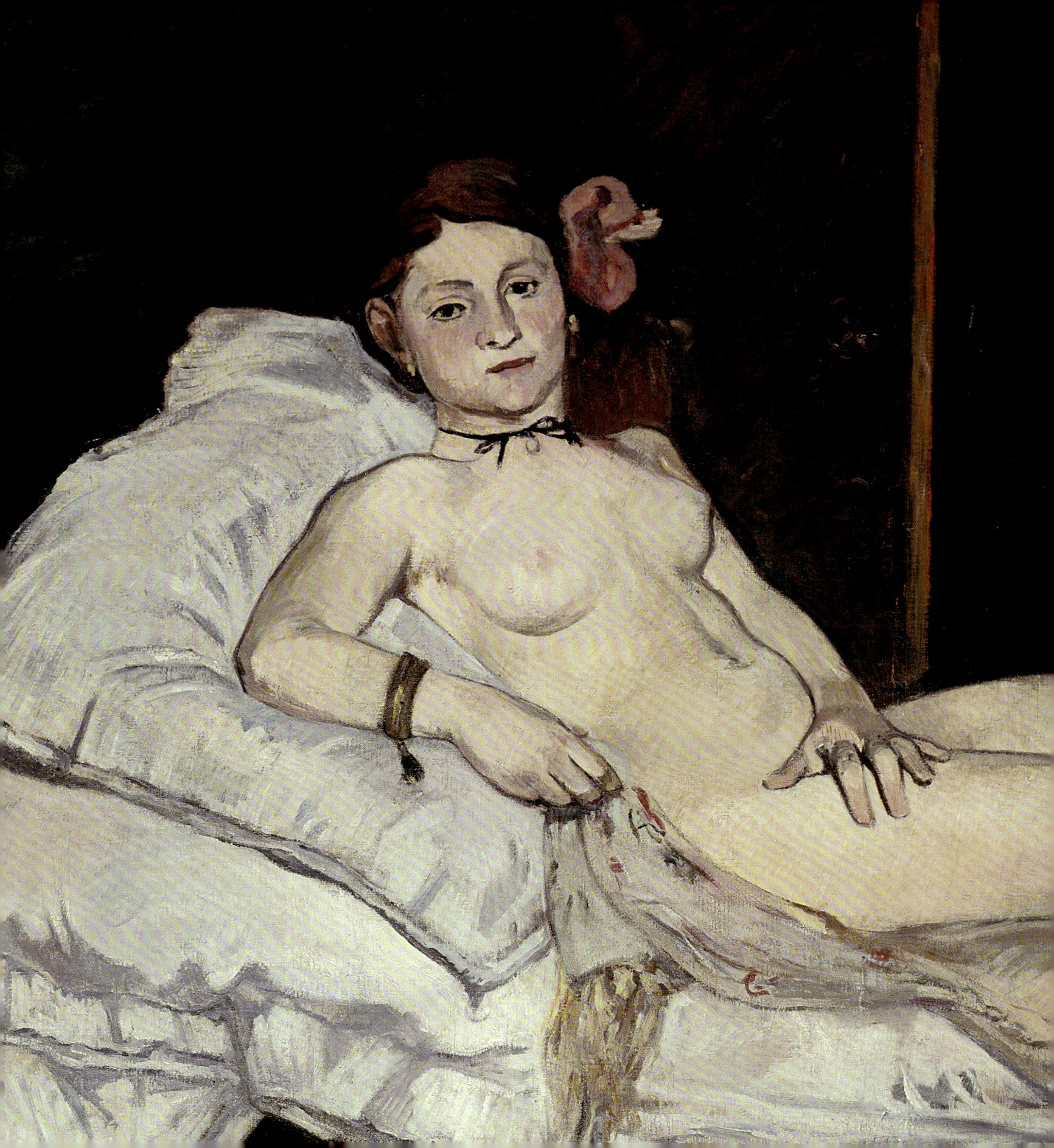

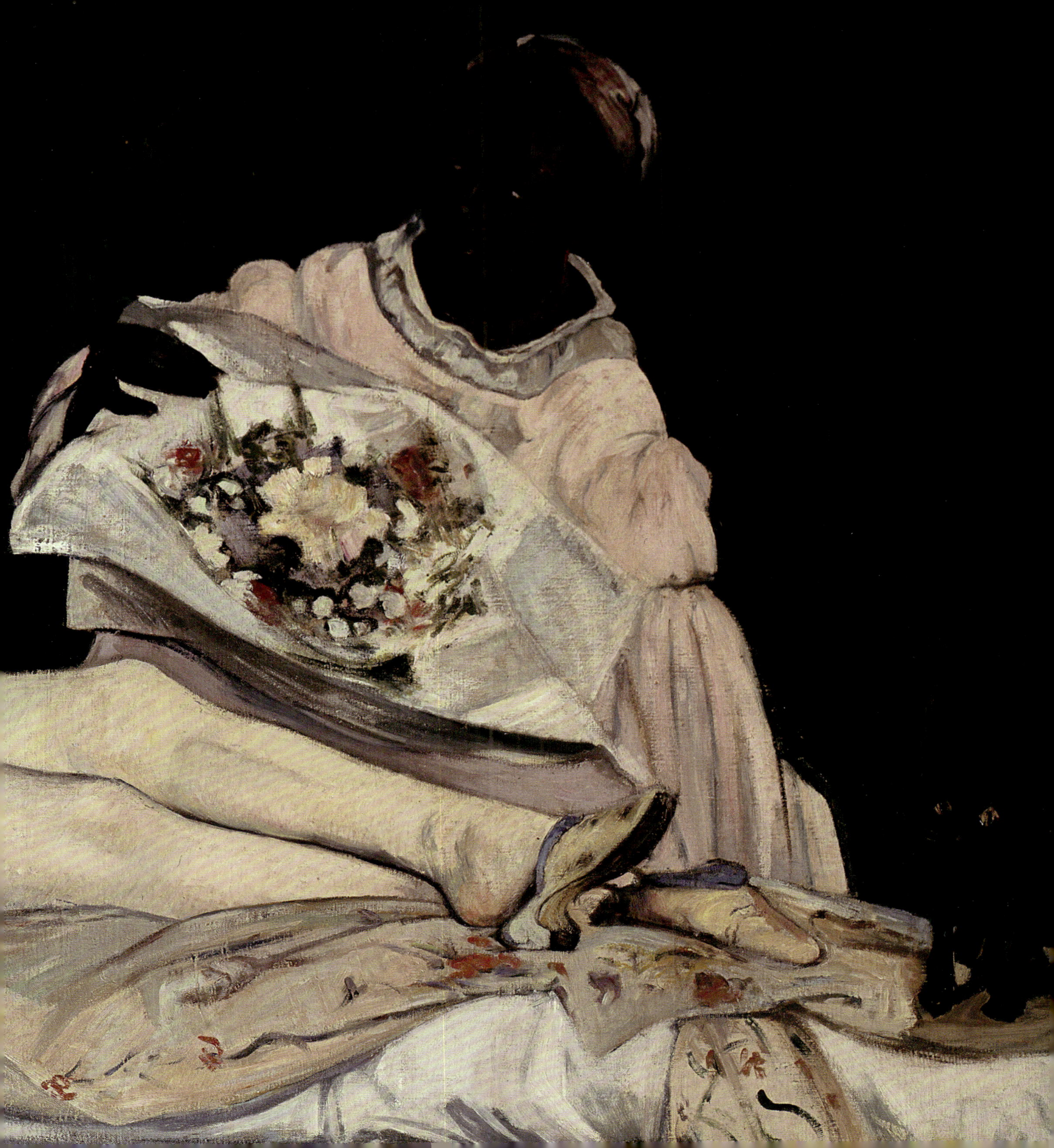

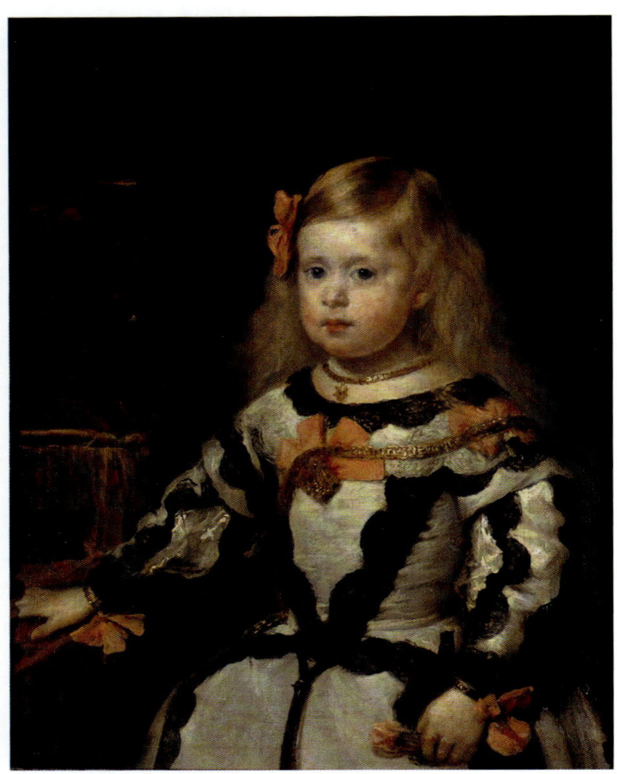

Portrait of the Infanta Maria Margarita of Spain
L'Infante Marie Marguerite, fille de Philippe IV, roi d'Espagne
Porträt der Infantin Maria Margarita, Tochter Philipps IV.
Retrato de la Infanta María Margarita, hija de Felipe IV.
Retrato da Infanta Maria Margarita, filha de Filipe IV.
De infante Maria Margarita, dochter van Filips IV

Diego Velázquez (1599-1660)

———

1653, Oil on canvas/Huile sur toile, 70 × 58 cm,
Musée du Louvre, Paris

Copying is the basis of creation...

Since antiquity, artists have dedicated themselves to copying. Be it in painting, sculpture or architecture - copies are made in all disciplines for different purposes. Among other things, repetition allows the aspiring artist to become a great master himself - in some cases even a genius in his field. The practice therefore also stands for the career of the pupil, who in the end surpasses his master.
Copying is an obligatory part of training. It lays the foundation for a successful future and is taught as early as possible - like aspiring musicians practicing scales. But not

Copier oui, mais créer...

Depuis l'Antiquité, les artistes se sont adonnés à l'art de la copie quelle que soit leur discipline, peinture, sculpture et même architecture. Si la copie peut avoir plusieurs finalités, celle qui nous intéresse dans le présent ouvrage est celle qui permit à des artistes d'apprendre à devenir eux-mêmes de grands artistes – et parfois des génies dans leur domaine –, illustrant ainsi magistralement l'image de l'élève dépassant son maître.
On considère que l'exercice de la copie doit être enseigné le plus tôt possible (comme un jeune pianiste

Kopieren ist die Grundlage des Schaffens ...

Seit der Antike widmen sich Künstler der Kopie. Sei es in der Malerei, der Bildhauerei oder der Architektur – kopiert wird in allen Disziplinen zu unterschiedlichen Zwecken. Unter anderem erlaubt die Wiederholung dem angehenden Künstler, selber zu einem großen Meister zu werden – in manchen Fällen sogar zu einem Genie auf seinem Gebiet. Die Praxis steht daher auch für den Werdegang des Schülers, der am Ende seinen Meister übertrifft.
Das Kopieren ist ein obligatorischer Teil der Ausbildung. Es legt die Basis für eine erfolgreiche Zukunft und

Portrait of the Infanta Maria Margarita
L'Infante Marie Marguerite
Porträt der Infantin Maria Margarita
Retrato de la Infanta María Margarita
Retrato da Infanta Maria Margarita
De infante Maria Margarita

Edgar Degas (1834-1917)

———

1861/62, Etching and dry point/Eau-forte
et pointe sèche, 16,9 × 12,1 cm,
Yale University Art Gallery, New Haven
(copy after/copie)

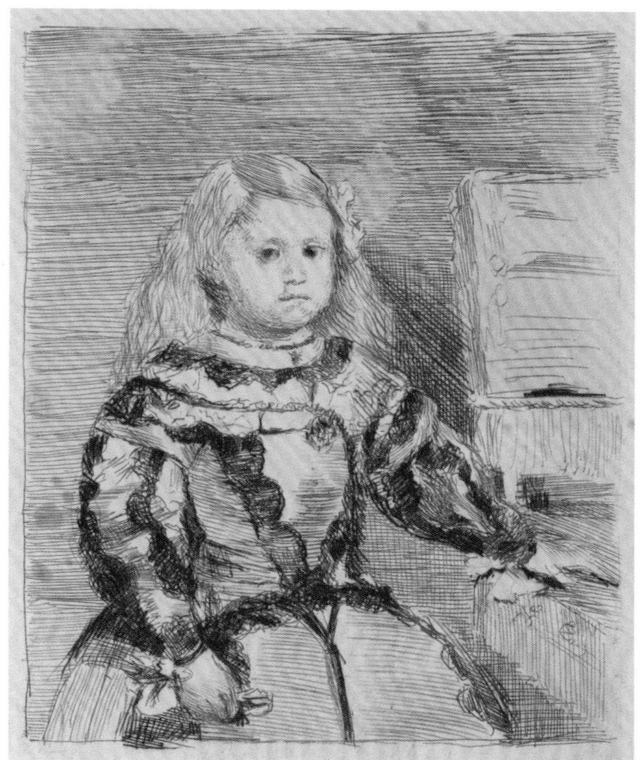

La copia es la base de la creación...

Desde la antigüedad, los artistas se han dedicado arealizar copias. Ya sea en la pintura, la escultura o la arquitectura, las copias se realizan en todas las disciplinas para diferentes propósitos. Entre otras cosas, la repetición permite al aspirante a artista convertirse él mismo en un gran maestro, en algunos casos incluso en un genio en su campo. La práctica, por lo tanto, también representa la carrera del alumno, que al final supera a su maestro.
La copia es una parte obligatoria de la formación. Sienta las bases para un futuro exitoso y se enseña lo

A cópia é a base da criação...

Desde a antiguidade que os artistas se dedicam à cópia. Seja em pintura, escultura ou arquitetura - cópias são feitas em todas as disciplinas para diferentes propósitos. Entre outras coisas, a repetição permite que o aspirante a artista se torne um grande mestre - em alguns casos até mesmo um gênio em seu campo. A prática, portanto, também representa a carreira do aluno, que no final supera seu mestre.
A cópia é uma parte obrigatória do treinamento. Ele estabelece a base para um futuro de sucesso e é ensinado o mais cedo possível - como praticar escalas com

Kopiëren is de basis van het scheppen...

Al sinds de klassieke oudheid houden kunstenaars zich bezig met kopiëren. Of dat nu in de schilderkunst, beeldhouwkunst of architectuur is – in alle disciplines worden voor verschillende doelen kopieën gemaakt. De herhaling stelt de aspirant-kunstenaar onder meer in staat om zelf een meester te worden, en soms zelfs een genie in zijn vakgebied. De praktijk staat dus ook voor het ontwikkelingsproces van de leerling, die uiteindelijk zijn meester overtreft.
Kopiëren is een verplicht onderdeel van de opleiding. Het legt de basis voor een succesvolle toekomst en

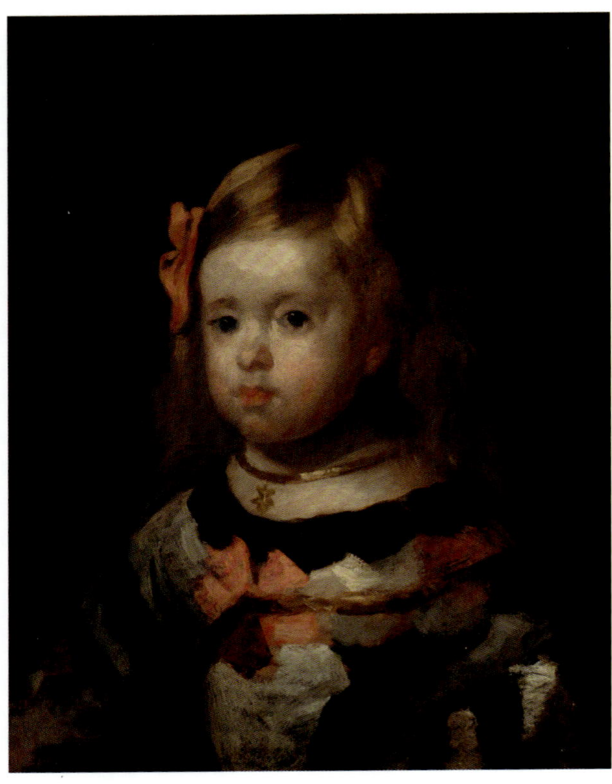

Portrait of the Infanta Maria Margarita
L'Infante Marie Marguerite
Porträt der Infantin Maria Margarita
Retrato de la Infanta María Margarita
Retrato da Infanta Maria Margarita
De infante Maria Margarita

Edgar Degas (1834-1917)

———

c. 1853, Oil on canvas/Huile sur toile, 47 × 39 cm,
Private collection (copy after/copie)

only do most careers begin in this way, as their careers progress many artists also lose the desire to copy - which enables them to find their own style and motifs.

Looking at the careers of great artists, it is striking that copies from their young years already bear the signature of a future genius. That's why they often look like works of art in their own right. Which raises the question: Is the copy of a great master still a copy at all?

fait ses gammes), qu'il est un passage obligé pour forger les bases solides d'un futur et véritable artiste. Ceci est vrai dans la majorité des cas. Mais bien souvent, l'envie de copier perdurera durant toute sa carrière, lui donnant ainsi la possibilité de renouveler son style tout comme ses sujets.

Lorsqu'on étudie la genèse des grands créateurs, ce qui frappe, ce sont souvent les copies de jeunesse dans lesquelles on peut déceler les prémices d'un génie en devenir. Génie qui, transcendant le modèle copié, lui confère un nouveau statut. Alors, une copie faite par grand maître est-elle encore une copie ?

wird so früh wie möglich unterrichtet – wie das Üben der Tonleitern bei angehenden Musikern. Doch beginnen nicht nur die meisten Laufbahnen auf diese Art, mit dem Voranschreiten der Karriere verlieren zahlreiche Künstler auch die Lust an der Kopie – was ihnen ermöglicht, ihren eigenen Stil und ihre eigenen Motive zu finden.

Wenn man den Werdegang großer Künstler betrachtet, fällt auf, dass die Kopien aus ihren jungen Jahren bereits die Handschrift eines zukünftigen Genies tragen. Deshalb wirken diese oft wie eigenständige Kunstwerke. Wodurch sich die Frage stellt: Ist die Kopie eines großen Meisters überhaupt noch eine Kopie?

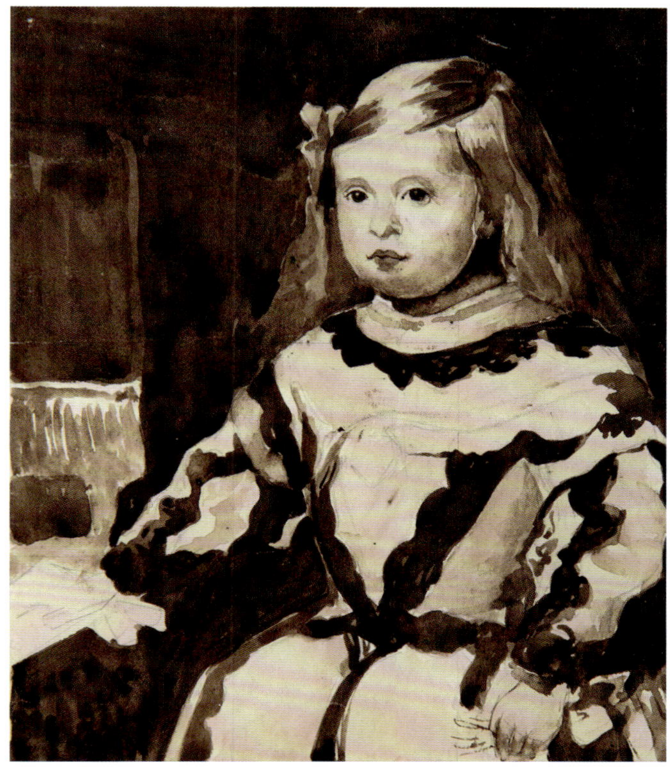

Portrait of the Infanta Maria Margarita
L'Infante Marie Marguerite
Porträt der Infantin Maria Margarita
Retrato de la Infanta María Margarita
Retrato da Infanta Maria Margarita
De infante Maria Margarita

Edgar Degas (1834-1917)

———

c. 1861/62, Sepia ink wash over pencil/Lavis
d'encre sépia sur trait de crayon,
18 × 15 cm, Private collection
(copy after/copie)

antes posible, al igual que la práctica de escalas con los aspirantes a músicos. Pero no sólo la mayoría de las carreras comienzan de esta manera, a medida que sus carreras progresan, muchos artistas también pierden el deseo de copiar, lo que les permite encontrar su propio estilo y motivos.
Mirando las carreras de los grandes artistas, es sorprendente que las copias de sus años jóvenes ya lleven la firma de un futuro genio. Es por eso que a menudo parecen obras de arteindependientes. Lo que plantea la cuestión: ¿Sigue siendo una copia laa copia de un gran maestro?

aspirantes a músicos. Mas não só a maioria das carreiras começa desta forma, como também muitos artistas perdem o desejo de copiar, o que lhes permite encontrar o seu próprio estilo e motivos.
Olhando para as carreiras de grandes artistas, é impressionante que as cópias de seus jovens anos já tenham a assinatura de um futuro gênio. É por isso que muitas vezes se parecem com obras de arte por direito próprio. O que levanta a questão: A cópia de um grande mestre ainda é uma cópia?

wordt zo vroeg mogelijk onderwezen. Zo oefenen aankomende muzikanten de toonladders. Maar niet alleen beginnen de meeste loopbanen op deze manier, in het verdere verloop van hun carrière verliezen veel kunstenaars ook de behoefte om te kopiëren, waardoor ze hun eigen stijl en onderwerpen ontdekken. Als je naar de carrière van grote kunstenaars kijkt, valt op dat de kopieën uit hun jonge jaren al de handtekening dragen van hun toekomstige genialiteit. Daarom zien die er vaak uit als op zichzelf staande kunstwerken. Wat de vraag oproept: is de kopie van een grootmeester eigenlijk wel een kopie?

MANTEGNA ~ BELLINI

Bellini painted numerous variants of this work, based on the original by Mantegna, who became his brother-in-law in 1453. By adding some figures and enlarging the detail, the picture appears less dramatic than the original. According to experts, the artist portrayed his father Jacopo Bellini as Joseph of Nazareth in the center.

Bellini exécute cette copie d'après une composition originale d'Andrea Mantegna, devenu son beau-frère en 1453. En ajoutant deux figures et en ouvrant davantage son cadre, Bellini donne plus de respiration à l'original, le rend plus doux, moins dramatique. Pour l'anecdote, saint Joseph, au centre, selon les spécialistes, serait le portrait de Jacopo Bellini, père de l'artiste.

Bellini malte zahlreiche Varianten dieses Werkes, das auf dem Original von Mantegna basiert, der im Jahr 1453 sein Schwager wurde. Indem er einige Figuren hinzufügt und den Bildausschnitt vergrößert, wirkt das Bild weniger dramatisch, als das Original. Fachleuten zufolge porträtierte der Künstler in der Mitte seinen Vater Jacopo Bellini als Josef von Nazareth.

Bellini pintó numerosas variantes de esta obra, basadas en el original de Mantegna, que se convirtió en su cuñado en 1453. Al omitir algunas de las figuras del original y reducir el tamaño de la imagen, Bellini aumentó la dramaturgia. Según los expertos, el artista retrató a su padre Jacopo Bellini como José de Nazaret en el centro.

Bellini pintou numerosas variantes desta obra, com base no original de Mantegna, que se tornou seu cunhado em 1453. Ao omitir algumas das figuras do original e reduzir o tamanho da imagem, Bellini aumentou a dramaturgia. Segundo especialistas, o artista retratou seu pai Jacopo Bellini como José de Nazaré no meio.

Bellini schilderde talrijke varianten van dit werk naar het origineel van Mantegna, die in 1453 zijn zwager werd. Door enkele figuren toe te voegen en de uitsnede te vergroten, werkt het schilderij minder dramatisch dan het origineel. Volgens deskundigen schilderde de kunstenaar zijn vader Jacopo Bellini als Jozef van Nazareth in het midden.

The Presentation at the Temple
La Présentation du Christ au Temple
Die Darbringung Christi im Tempel
La Presentación de Cristo en el Templo
A Apresentação de Cristo no Templo
De presentatie van Christus in de tempel

Giovanni Bellini (1430-1516)

c. 1470, Oil on wood/Huile sur bois, 80 × 105 cm, Galleria Querini-Stampalia, Venezia (copy after/copie)

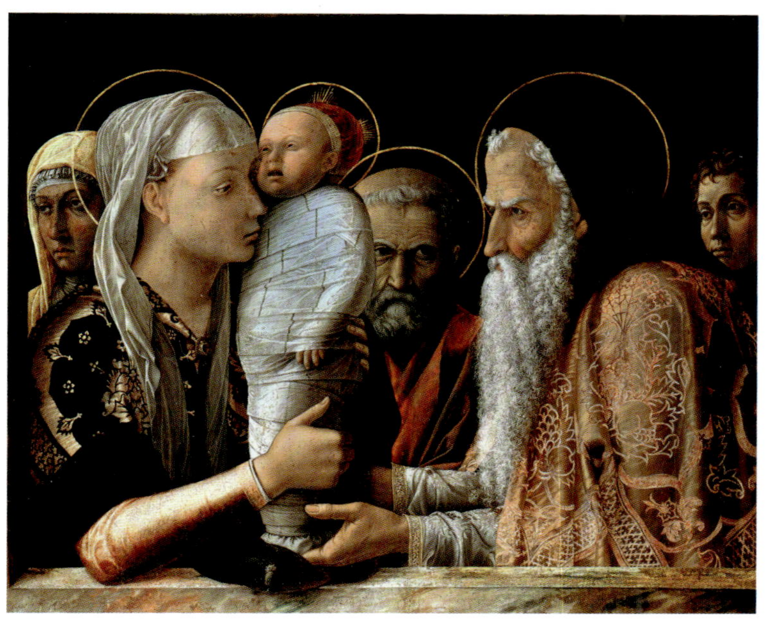

The Presentation at the Temple

La Présentation du Christ au Temple

Die Darbringung Christi im Tempel

La Presentación de Cristo en el Templo

A Apresentação de Cristo no Templo

De presentatie van Christus in de tempel

Andrea Mantegna (1431-1506)

———

c. 1454, Tempera on canvas/Tempera
sur toile, 77,1 × 94,4 cm, Staatliche Museen,
Berlin

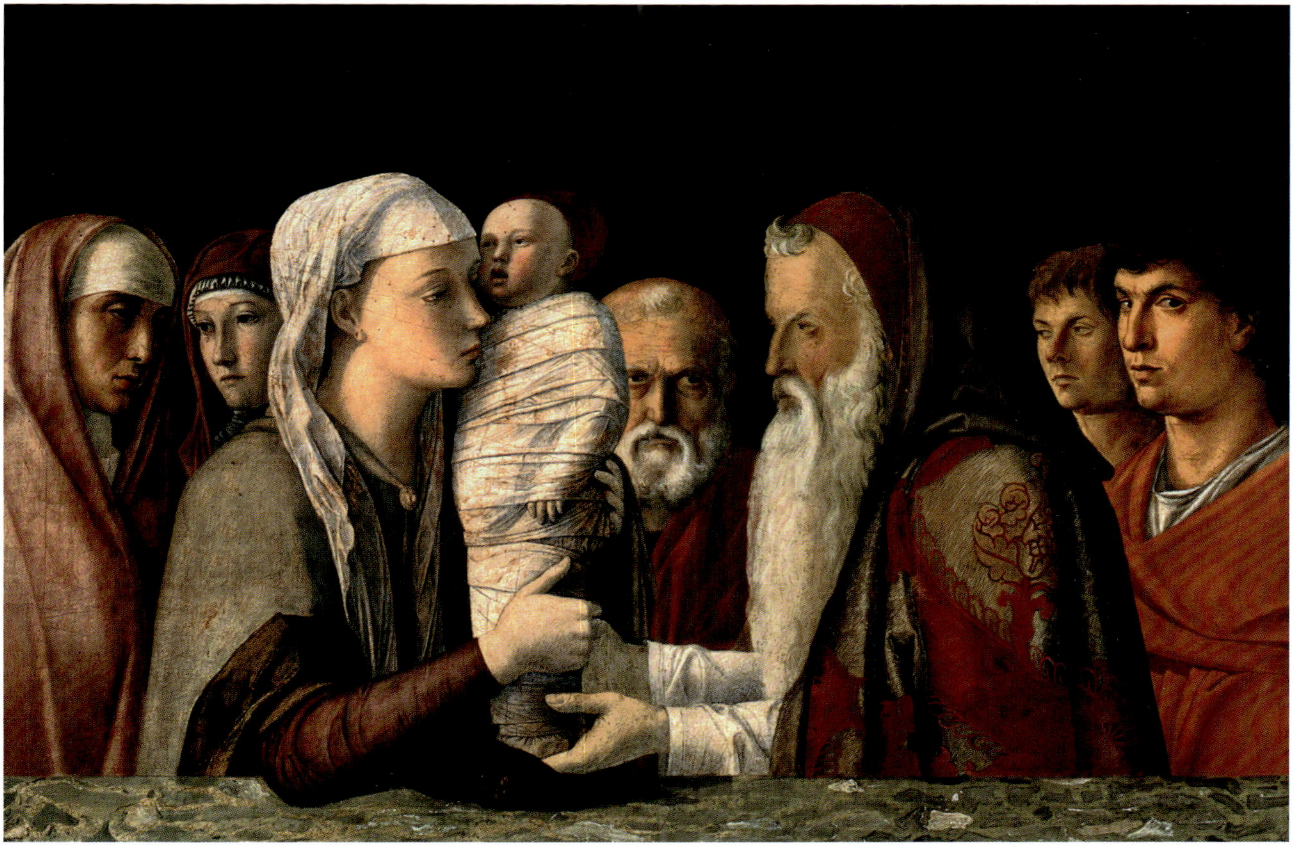

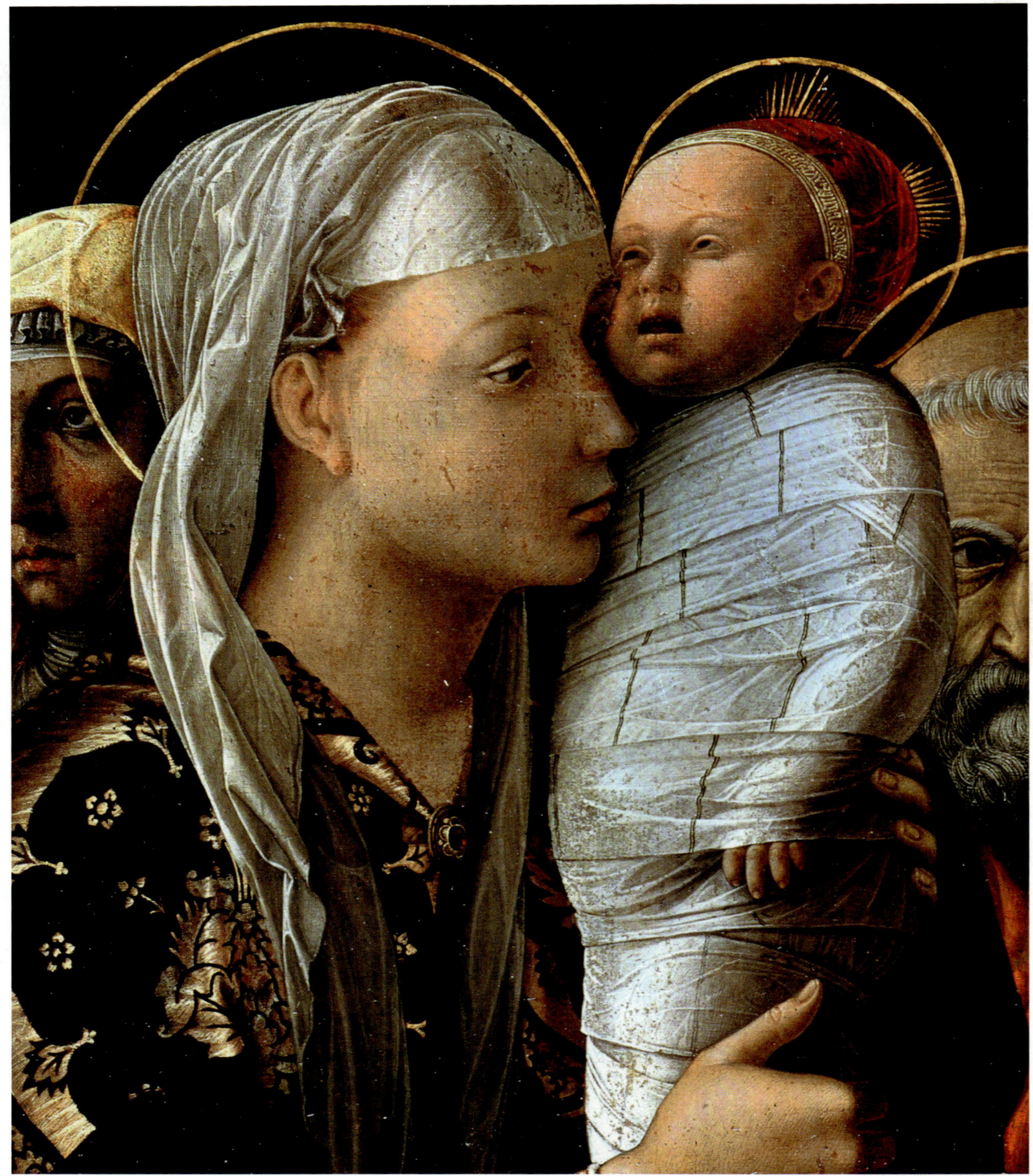

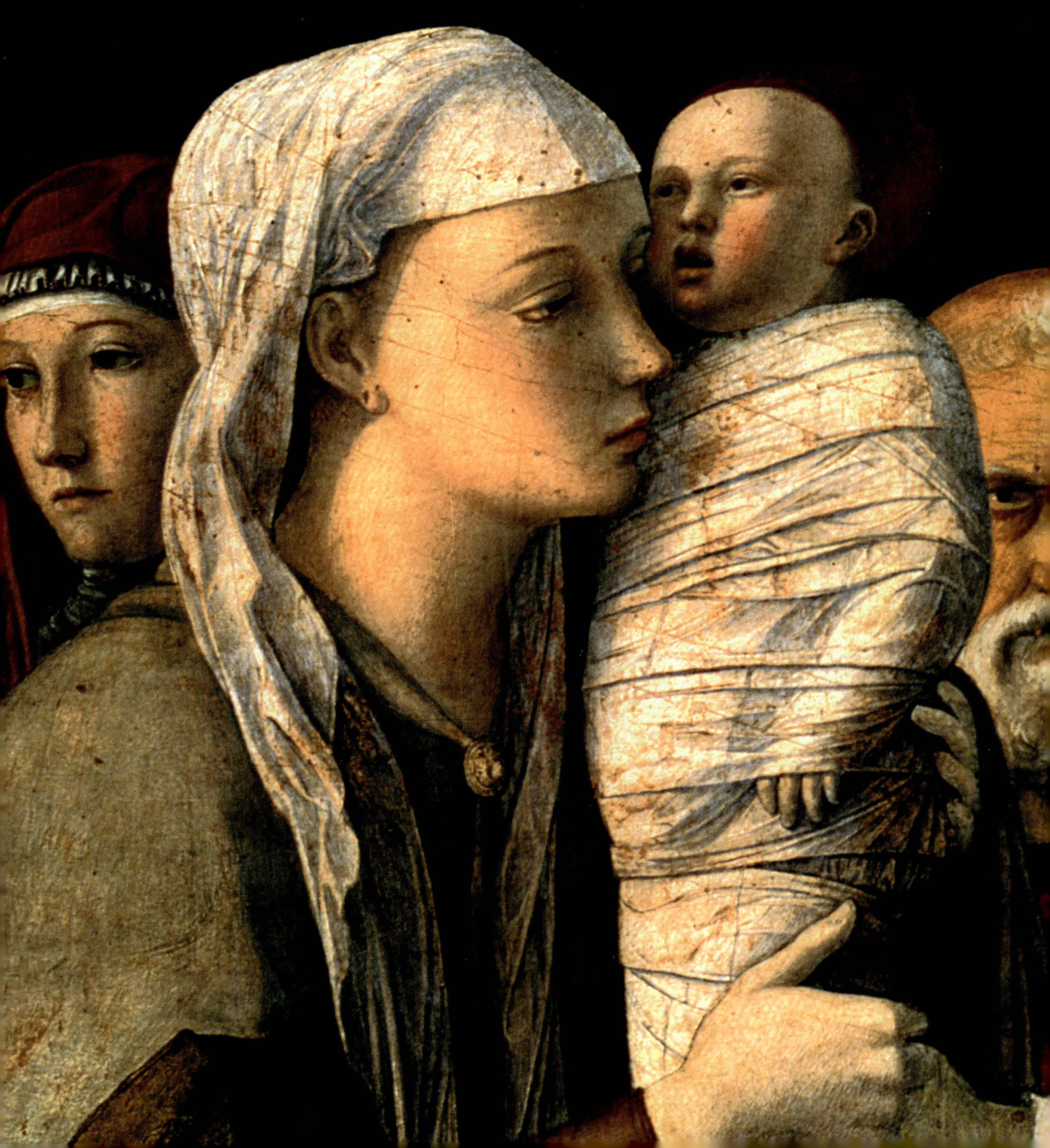

HALS ~ COURBET

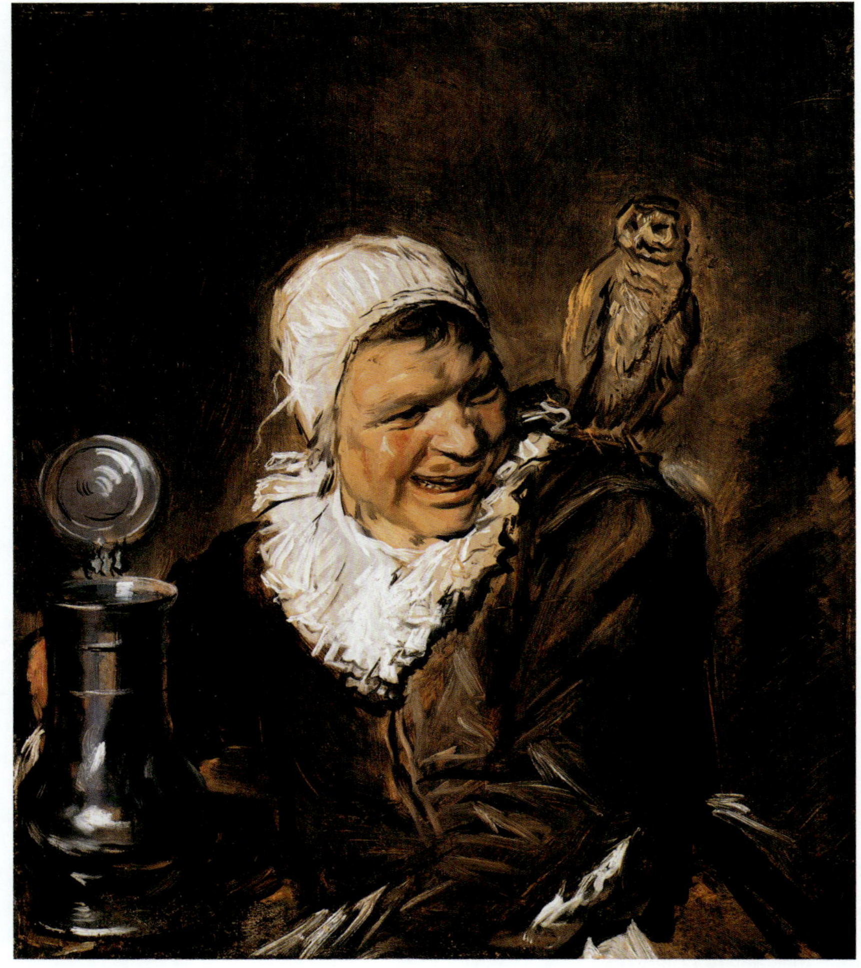

Malle Babbe (Crazy Barbara) or
The Witch of Haarlem

La Malle Babbe (« Barbara la folle »),
dite aussi *La Sorcière de Haarlem*

Die Malle Babbe (Die verrückte Barbara)
oder *Die Hexe von Haarlem*

La Malle Babbe (La loca Bárbara)
o *La Bruja de Haarlem*

A Malle Babbe (A Bárbara Louca)
ou *A Bruxa de Haarlem*

Malle Babbe (Gekke Barbara) of
De heks van Haarlem

Frans Hals (1583-1666)

1633-35, Oil on canvas/Huile sur toile,
78,5 × 66,2 cm, Staatliche Museen, Berlin

Malle Babbe (Crazy Barbara)
or *The Witch of Haarlem*

La Malle Babbe (« Barbara la folle »),
dite aussi *La Sorcière de Haarlem*

Die Malle Babbe (Die verrückte Barbara)
oder *Die Hexe von Haarlem*

La Malle Babbe (La loca Bárbara)
o *La Bruja de Haarlem*

A Malle Babbe (A Bárbara louca)
ou *A Bruxa de Haarlem*

Malle Babbe (Gekke Barbara)
of *De heks van Haarlem*

Gustave Courbet (1819-1877)

c. 1869, Oil on canvas/Huile sur toile,
85 × 71 cm, Hamburger Kunsthalle, Hamburg
(copy after/copie)

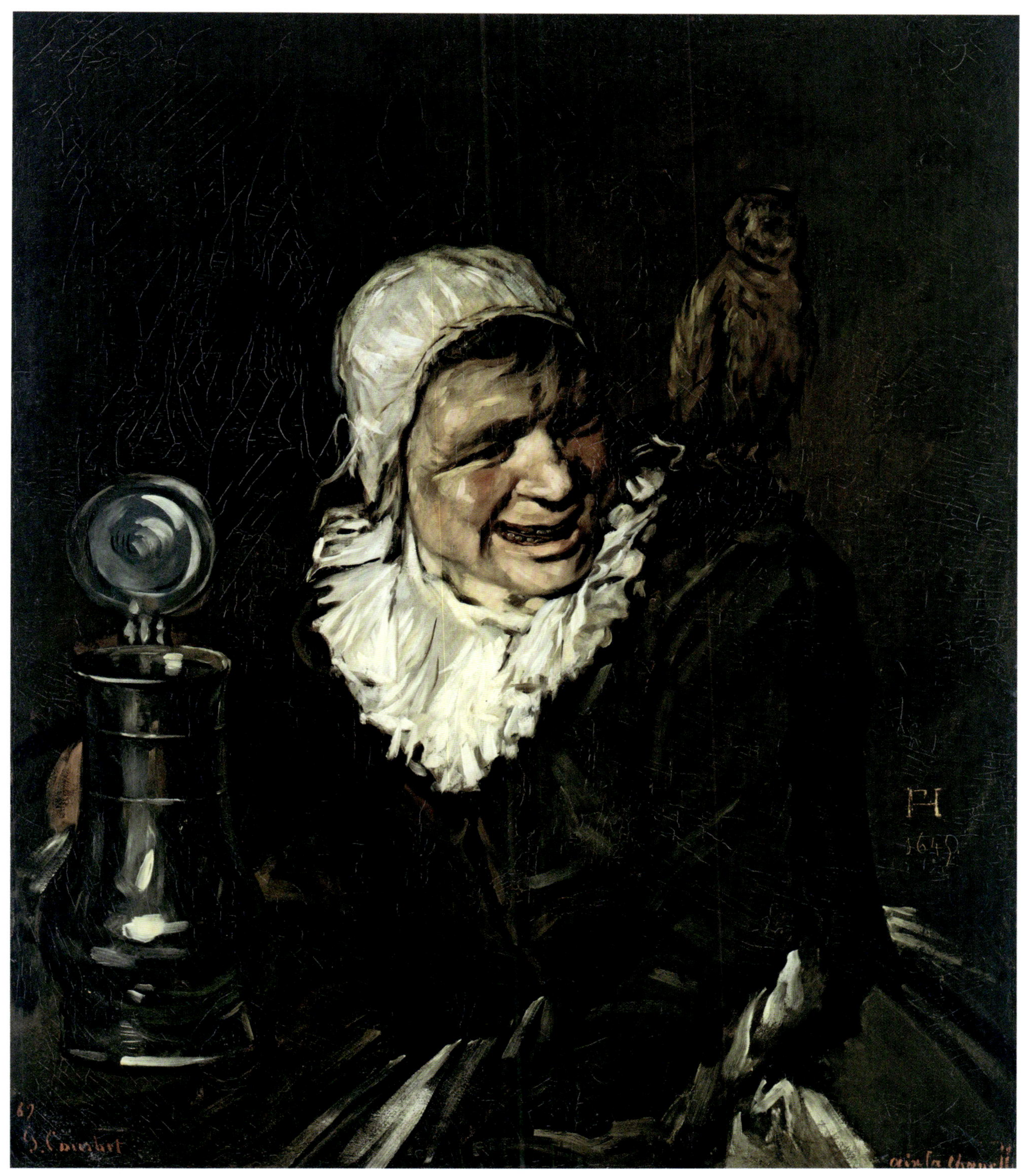

DELACROIX ~ CÉZANNE

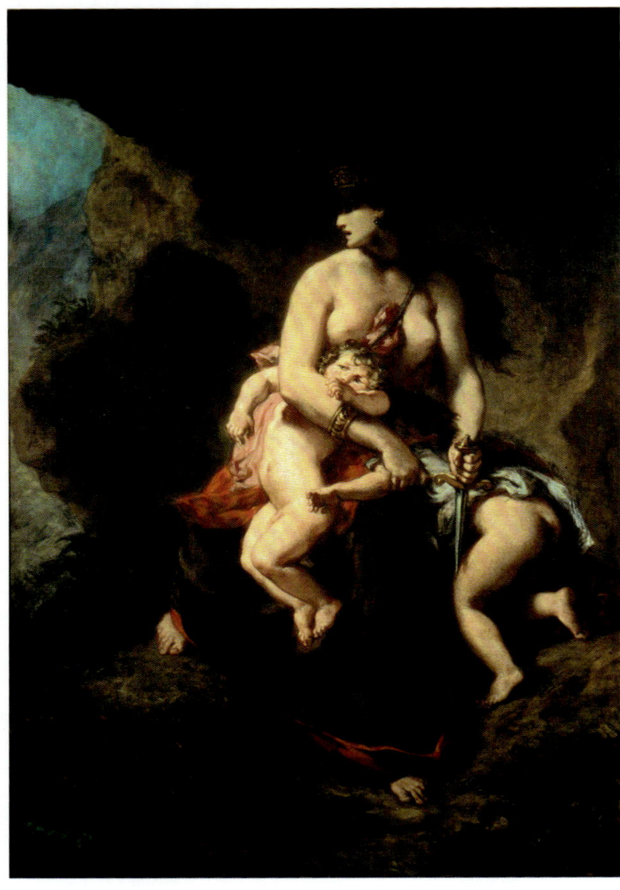

Medea about to kill her children
Médée furieuse
Rasende Medea
Medea furiosa
Medeia Furiosa
Woedende Medea

Eugène Delacroix (1798-1863)

———

c. 1862, Oil on canvas/Huile sur toile,
122 × 84 cm, Musée du Louvre, Paris

Cézanne made countless copies of the works of the great masters, to which dozens of sketches but also watercolors bear witness. This flowing and transparent representation of the *Medea about to kill her children* by Delacroix is one of them. For his copies, Cézanne often used works from his own collection.

Cézanne fit de nombreuses copies d'après les maîtres comme l'attestent ses dizaines de croquis mais également ses aquarelles. Cette version toute en fluidité et transparence de la *Médée* de Delacroix le prouve. Pour la petite histoire, Cézanne prit souvent comme modèles des œuvres appartenant à sa propre collection.

Cézanne fertigte unzählige Kopien von den Werken der großen Meister an, von denen Dutzende Skizzen aber auch Aquarelle zeugen. Diese fließende und transparente Darstellung der *Rasende Medea* von Delacroix ist eine davon. Bei seinen Kopien griff Cézanne oft auf Werke aus seiner eigenen Sammlung zurück.

Paul Cézanne (1839-1906)

———

c. 1880-85, Watercolor, graphite pencil on
paper/Aquarelle, mine graphite sur papier,
39,5 × 26 cm, Kunsthaus, Zürich
(copy after/copie)

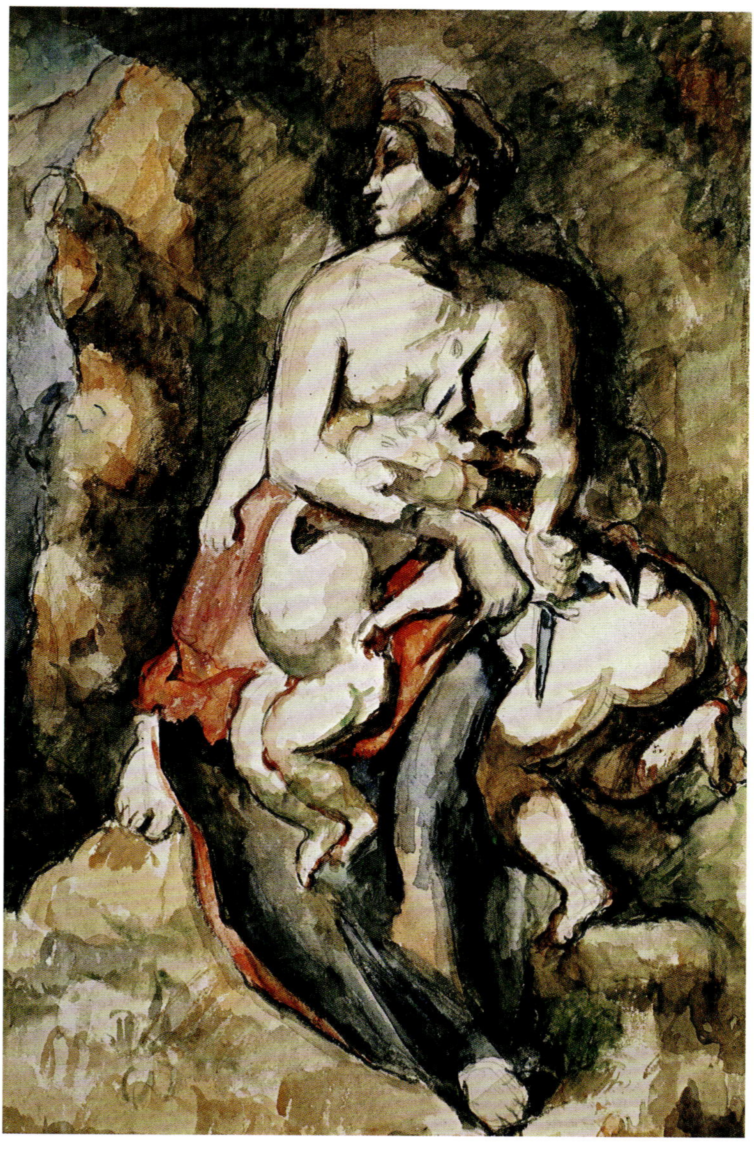

Cézanne hizo innumerables copias
de las obras de los grandes maestros,
de las que son testigos decenas de
bocetos, pero también acuarelas.
Esta representación fluida y
transparente de la *Medea furiosa* de
Delacroix es una de ellas. Para sus
copias, Cézanne utilizaba a menudo
obras de su propia colección.

Cézanne fez inúmeras cópias das
obras dos grandes mestres, das
quais dezenas de esboços, mas
também aguarelas, dão testemunho.
Esta representação fluida e
transparente da *Medeia Furiosa*
de Delacroix é uma delas. Para
suas cópias, Cézanne usava
frequentemente obras de sua
própria coleção.

Cézanne kopieerde talloze werken
van grote meesters, waarvan
tientallen schetsen maar ook
aquarellen getuigen. Deze vloeiende
en transparante weergave van de
Woedende Medea van Delacroix is
daar een van. Voor zijn kopieën
gebruikte Cézanne vaak werken
uit zijn eigen collectie.

REMBRANDT ~ MANET

Édouard Manet's copy of Rembrandt's famous work was probably made during his trip to the Netherlands in 1852. He used small wooden boards that were sturdy and handy to carry his paintings. This allowed Manet to devote himself entirely to copying. He kept the paintings finely sorted in Paris and later used them in his own works.

C'est vraisemblablement lors de son voyage aux Pays-Bas en 1852 qu'Édouard Manet copia cette célèbre toile de Rembrandt. Pratiques, car peu encombrants et peu fragiles, ces petits panneaux de bois permirent à l'artiste de s'adonner à l'art subtil de la copie. De retour à Paris, Manet prit soin de classer ses œuvres inspirées afin de les garder précieusement pour les utiliser lors de la conception de ses œuvres originales futures.

Édouard Manets Kopie des berühmten Werkes von Rembrandt entstand wahrscheinlich während seiner Reise in die Niederlande im Jahr 1852. Als Bildträger nutzte er kleine Holzplatten, die robust und handlich waren. So konnte sich Manet ganz dem Kopieren widmen. Die Gemälde bewahrte er fein sortiert in Paris auf, um sie später bei der Gestaltung seiner eigenen Werke zu verwenden.

Probablemente fue durante su viaje a los Países Bajos en 1852 cuando Édouard Manet copió este famoso cuadro de Rembrandt. Prácticos, ya que no eran muy voluminosos y frágiles, estos pequeños paneles de madera permitieron al artista dedicarse al sutil arte de la copia. De vuelta en París, Manet se encargó de clasificar sus obras inspiradas para conservarlas cuidadosamente y utilizarlas en el diseño de sus futuras obras originales.

Édouard Manet cópia da famosa obra de Rembrandt foi provavelmente feita durante sua viagem à Holanda em 1852. Ele usou pequenas placas de madeira que eram resistentes e úteis para transportar suas pinturas. Isto permitiu ao Manet dedicar-se inteiramente à cópia. Ele manteve as pinturas finamente classificadas em Paris e mais tarde usou-as em suas próprias obras.

Édouard Manet maakte deze kopie van Rembrandts beroemde werk waarschijnlijk tijdens zijn reis naar Nederland in 1852. Als beelddrager gebruikte hij kleine houten paneeltjes, die stevig en handig waren. Hierdoor kon Manet zich volledig wijden aan het kopiëren. Hij bewaarde de schilderijen in Parijs en gebruikte ze later in zijn eigen werk.

The Anatomy Lesson
La Leçon d'anatomie du docteur Tulp
Die Anatomie des Dr. Tulp
La anatomía del Dr. Tulp
A anatomia do Dr. Tulp
De anatomische les van Dr. Nicolaes Tulp

Édouard Manet (1832-1883)

c. 1856, Oil on panel/Huile sur panneau, 24,8 × 39,1 cm, Private collection (copy after/copie)

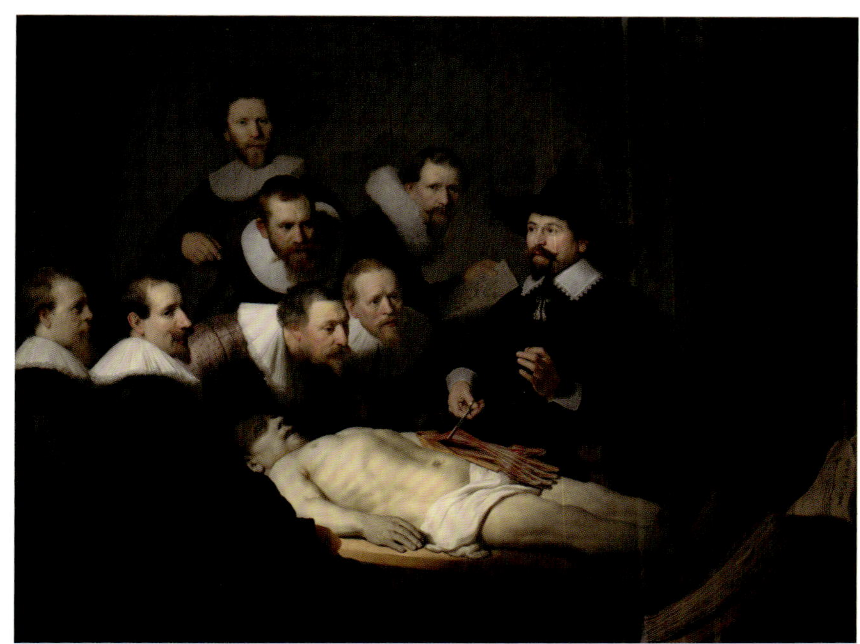

The Anatomy Lesson of Dr. Nicolaes Tulp

La Leçon d'anatomie du docteur Tulp

Die Anatomie des Dr. Tulp

La anatomía del Dr. Tulp

A anatomia do Dr. Tulp

De anatomische les van Dr. Nicolaes Tulp

Rembrandt van Rijn (1606-1669)

1632, Oil on canvas/Huile sur toile,
169,5 × 216 cm, Mauritshuis, Den Haag

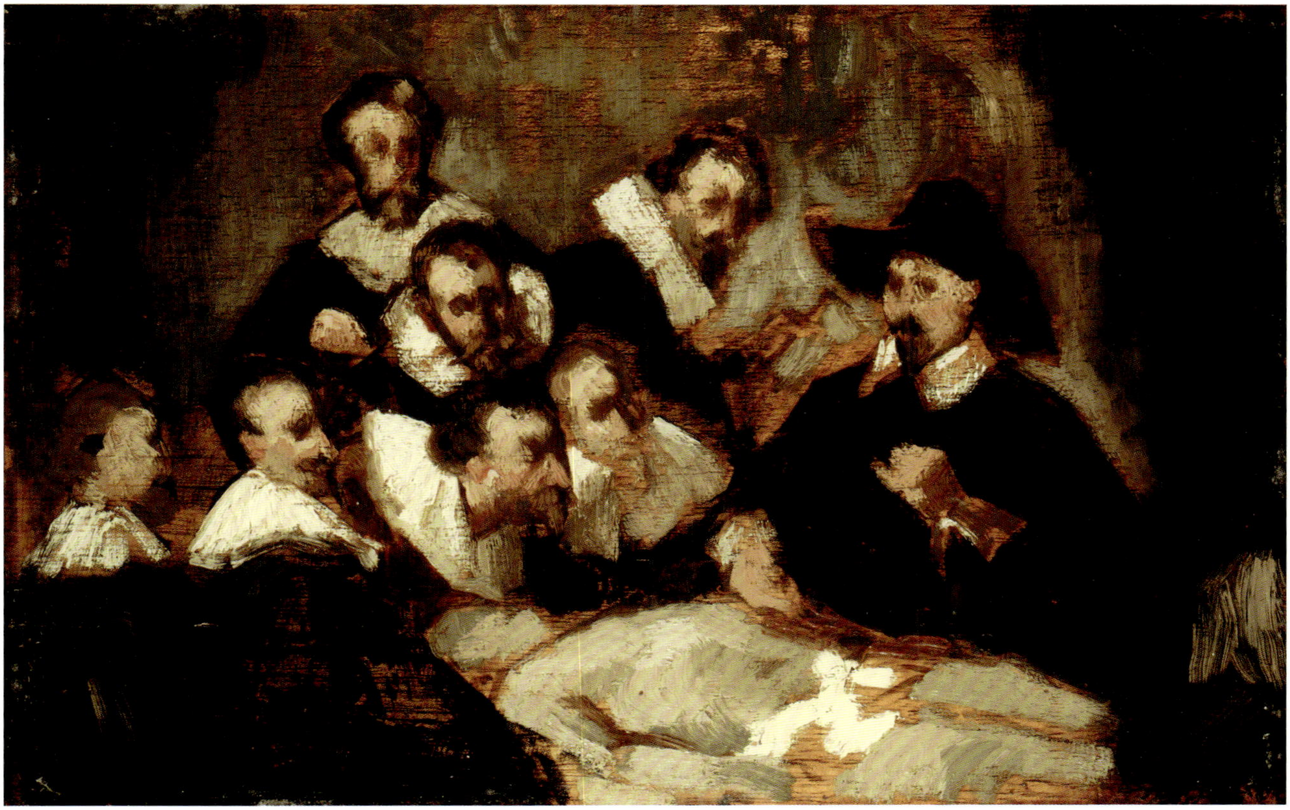

DAVID (WORKSHOP OF/ATELIER DE) ~ ISABEY

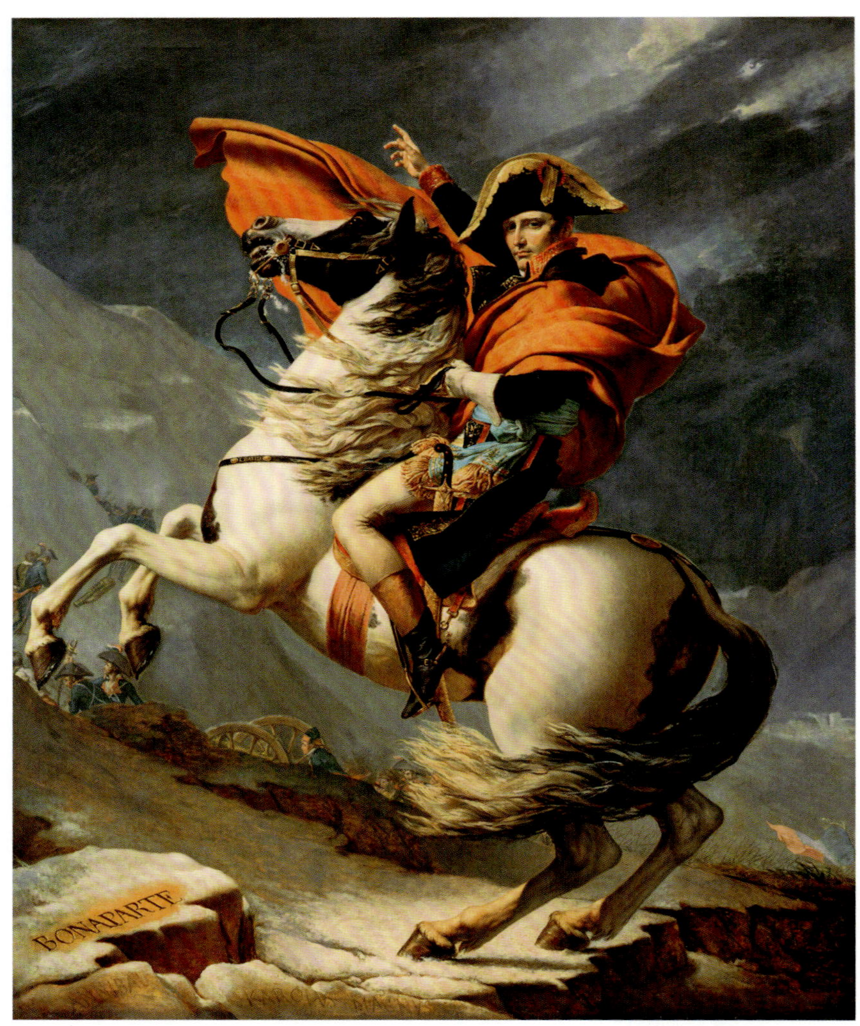

Bonaparte crossing the Alps at Great Saint Bernard Pass, on 20 May 1800

Bonaparte franchissant le mont Saint-Bernard, le 20 mai 1800

Bonaparte beim Überschreiten der Alpen am Großen Sankt Bernhard, am 20. Mai 1800

Bonaparte cruzando los Alpes en el Gran San Bernardo, el 20 de mayo de 1800

Bonaparte cruzando Mont Saint-Bernard, em 20 de maio de 1800

Napoleon steekt de Alpen over bij de Sint-Bernardpas, op 20 mei 1800

Jacques-Louis David (workshop of/ atelier de) (1748-1825)

———

c. 1803, Oil on canvas/Huile sur toile, 268,5 × 224,3 cm, Château de Versailles

Bonaparte crossing the Alps at the Great Saint Bernard Pass

Bonaparte franchissant le mont Saint-Bernard, le 20 mai 1800

Bonaparte beim Überschreiten der Alpen am Großen Sankt Bernhard

Bonaparte cruzando los Alpes en el Gran San Bernardo

Bonaparte cruzando Mont Saint-Bernard, em 20 de maio de 1800

Napoleon steekt de Alpen over bij de Sint-Bernardpas

Jean-Baptiste Isabey (1767-1855)

———

c. 1840, Pencil drawing/Dessin au crayon, 31 × 28 cm, Private collection (copy after/copie)

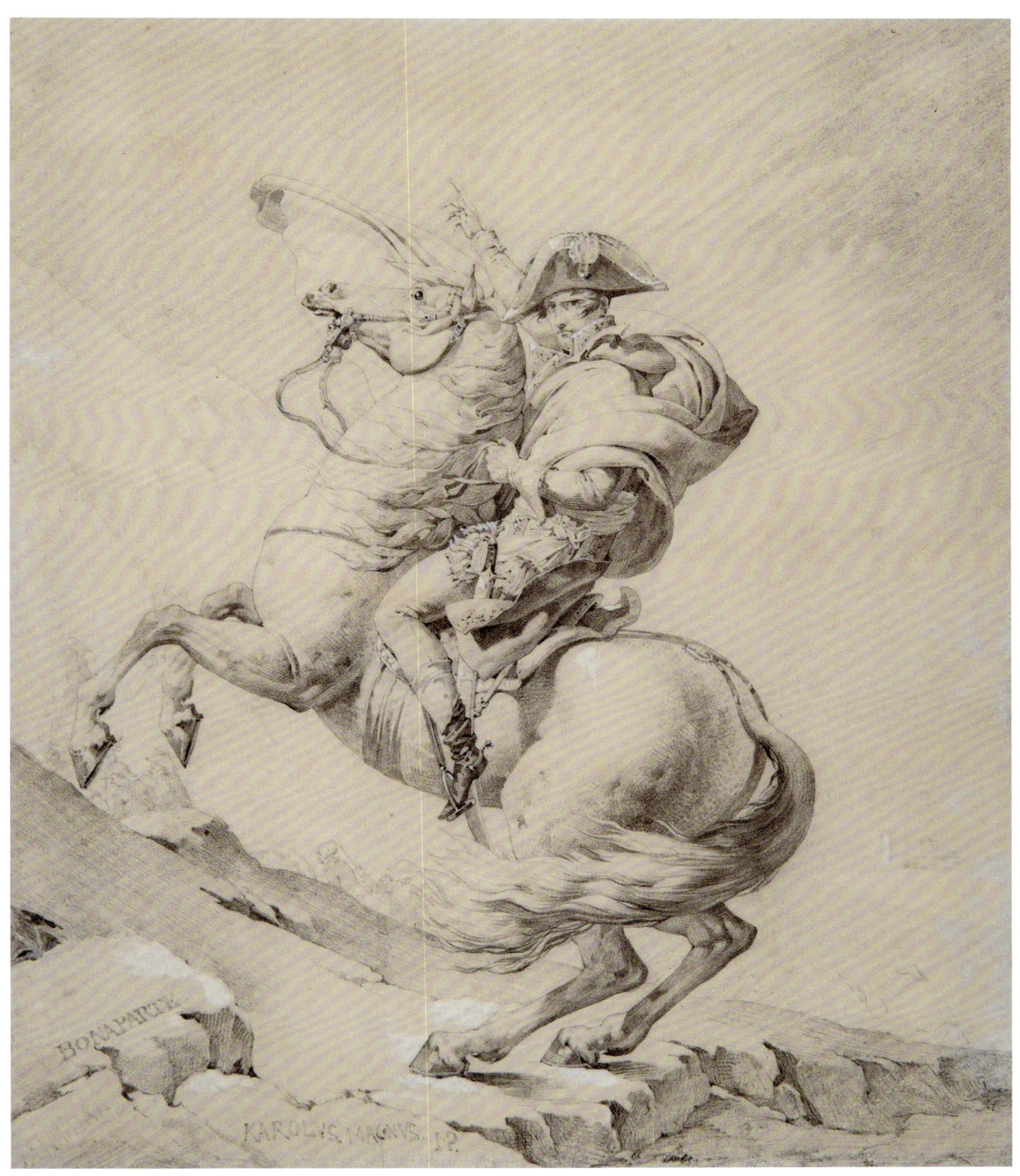
BONAPARTE
KAROLVS MAGNVS IMP

IL VERONESE ~ FANTIN-LATOUR

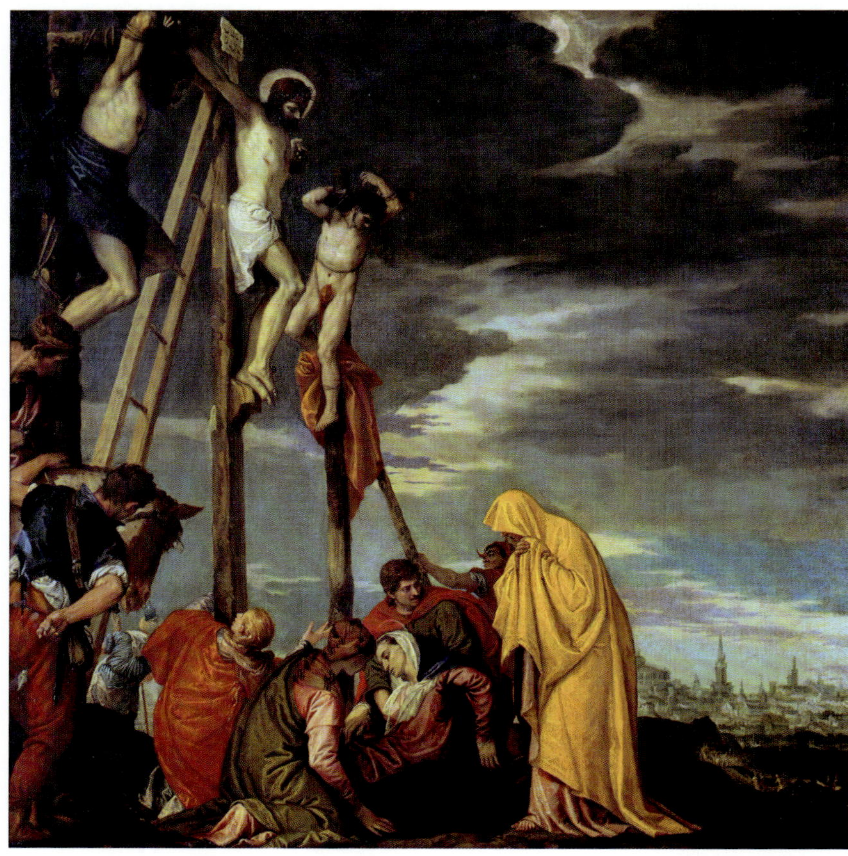

Crucifixion

La Crucifixion

Kreuzigung

Crucifixión

Crucificação

Christus aan het kruis tussen de twee moordenaars

Paolo Caliari (il Veronese) (1528-1588)

c. 1584, Oil on canvas/Huile sur toile, 102 × 102 cm, Musée du Louvre, Paris

Crucifixion

Le Christ entre les larrons

Christus am Kreuz und die beiden Schächer

Cristo en la cruz y los dos ladrones

Cristo entre os ladrões

Christus aan het kruis tussen de twee moordenaars

Henri Fantin-Latour (1836-1904)

c. 1854, Oil on cardboard mounted on wood/Huile sur carton marouflé sur bois, 29,5 × 30 cm, Musée d'Orsay, Paris (copy after/copie)

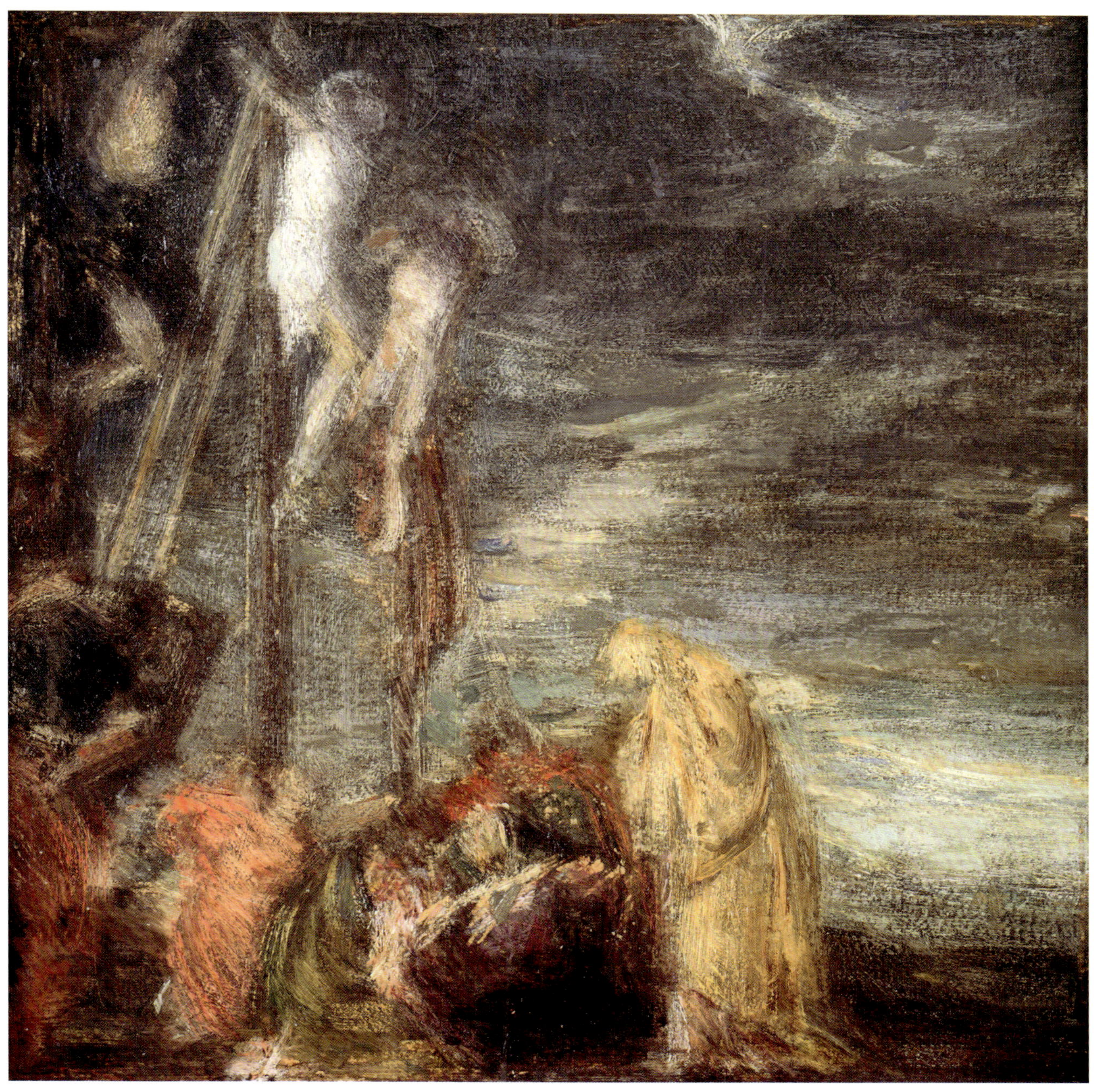

REMBRANDT ~ VAN GOGH

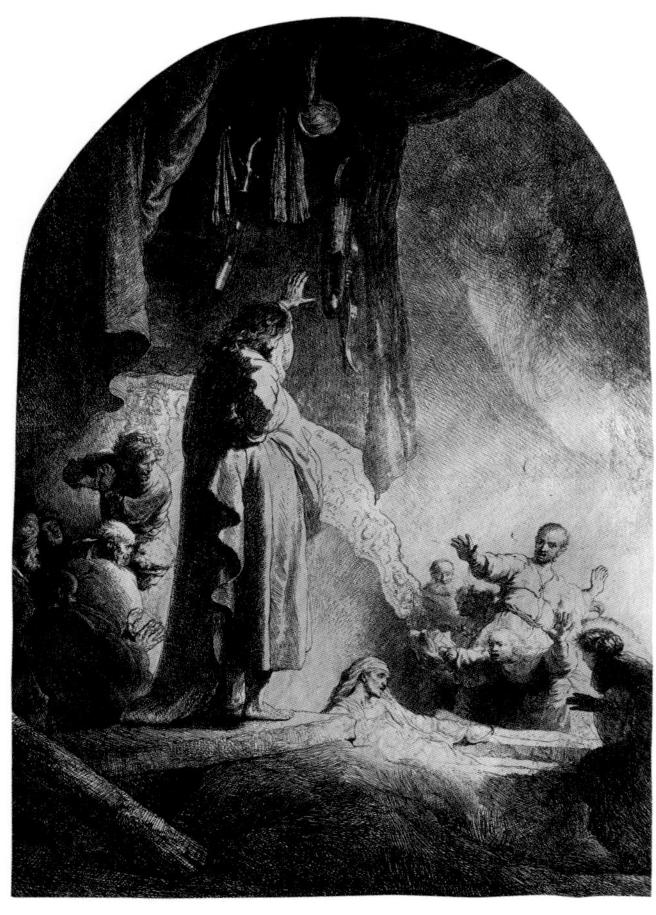

The Raising of Lazarus

La Résurrection de Lazare

Die Auferweckung des Lazarus

La resurrección de Lázaro

A ressurreição de Lázaro

De opwekking van Lazarus

Vincent van Gogh (1853-1890)

—

1890, Oil on paper/Huile sur
papier, 50 × 65,5 cm,
Van Gogh Museum, Amsterdam
(copy after/copie)

The Raising of Lazarus

La Résurrection de Lazare

Die Auferweckung des Lazarus

La resurrección de Lázaro

A ressurreição de Lázaro

De opwekking van Lazarus

Rembrandt van Rijn (1606-1669)

—

c. 1632, Etching/Eau-forte, 36,6 × 25,3 cm,
Petit Palais, Paris

Rembrandt's humanism corresponded exactly to Van Gogh's ideals, who before his career as an artist wanted to become a pastor, like his father. The artist must have greatly appreciated the etching *The Raising of Lazarus* - especially the interaction with the figure to the right of the deceased, which he copied.

L'humanisme de Rembrandt ne pouvait que plaire à Van Gogh qui, avant sa vocation artistique, avait choisi de devenir pasteur comme son père. Il devait apprécier cette gravure représentant la Résurrection de Lazare, et tout particulièrement l'intervention de la figure de droite qu'il retiendra pour sa copie.

Rembrandts Humanismus entsprach genau Van Goghs Idealen, der vor seiner Laufbahn als Künstler Pfarrer werden wollte, wie sein Vater. Die Radierung *Die Auferweckung des Lazarus* muss der Künstler sehr geschätzt haben – vor allem die Interaktion mit der Figur rechts des Toten, die er in seiner Kopie übernahm.

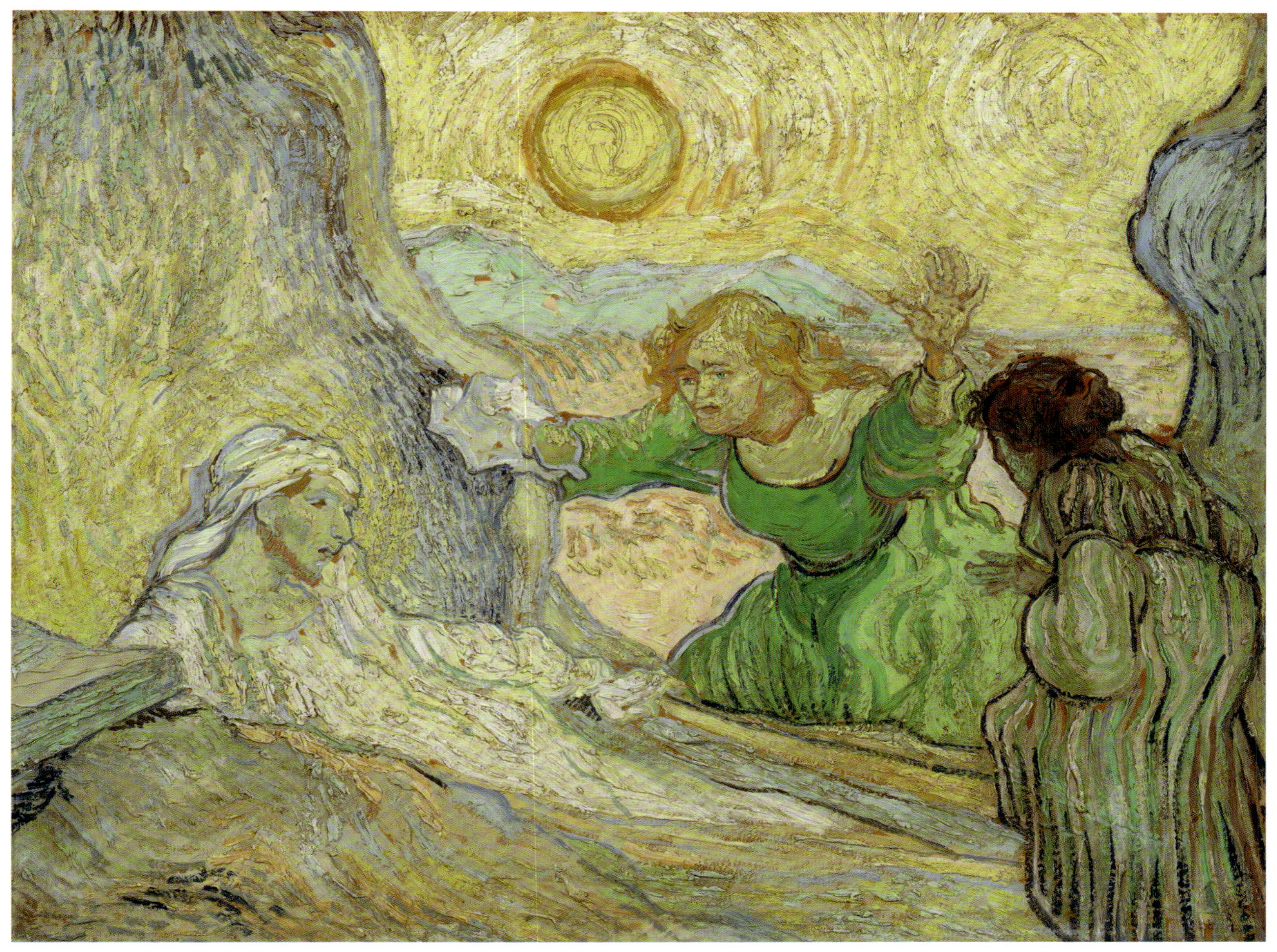

El humanismo de Rembrandt
correspondía a los ideales de Van
Gogh que, antes de su vocación
artística, había elegido ser pastor
como su padre. Debe haber
apreciado este grabado que
representa *La Resurrección de
Lázaro* y, sobre todo, la intervención
de la figura de la mano derecha que
conservaría para su copia.

O humanismo de Rembrandt
correspondia exatamente aos ideais
de Van Gogh, que antes de sua
carreira como artista queria se
tornar um pastor, como seu pai.
O artista deve ter apreciado muito
a gravura *A Ressurreição de Lázaro*
- especialmente a interação com
a figura à direita dos mortos, que
ele copiou.

Rembrandts humanisme kwam
exact overeen met de idealen
van Van Gogh, die voor zijn carrière
als schilder dominee wilde worden,
net als zijn vader. Van Gogh moet
de ets *De opwekking van Lazarus*
zeer gewaardeerd hebben – vooral
de interactie met de figuur rechts
van de doden, die hij overnam in
zijn kopie.

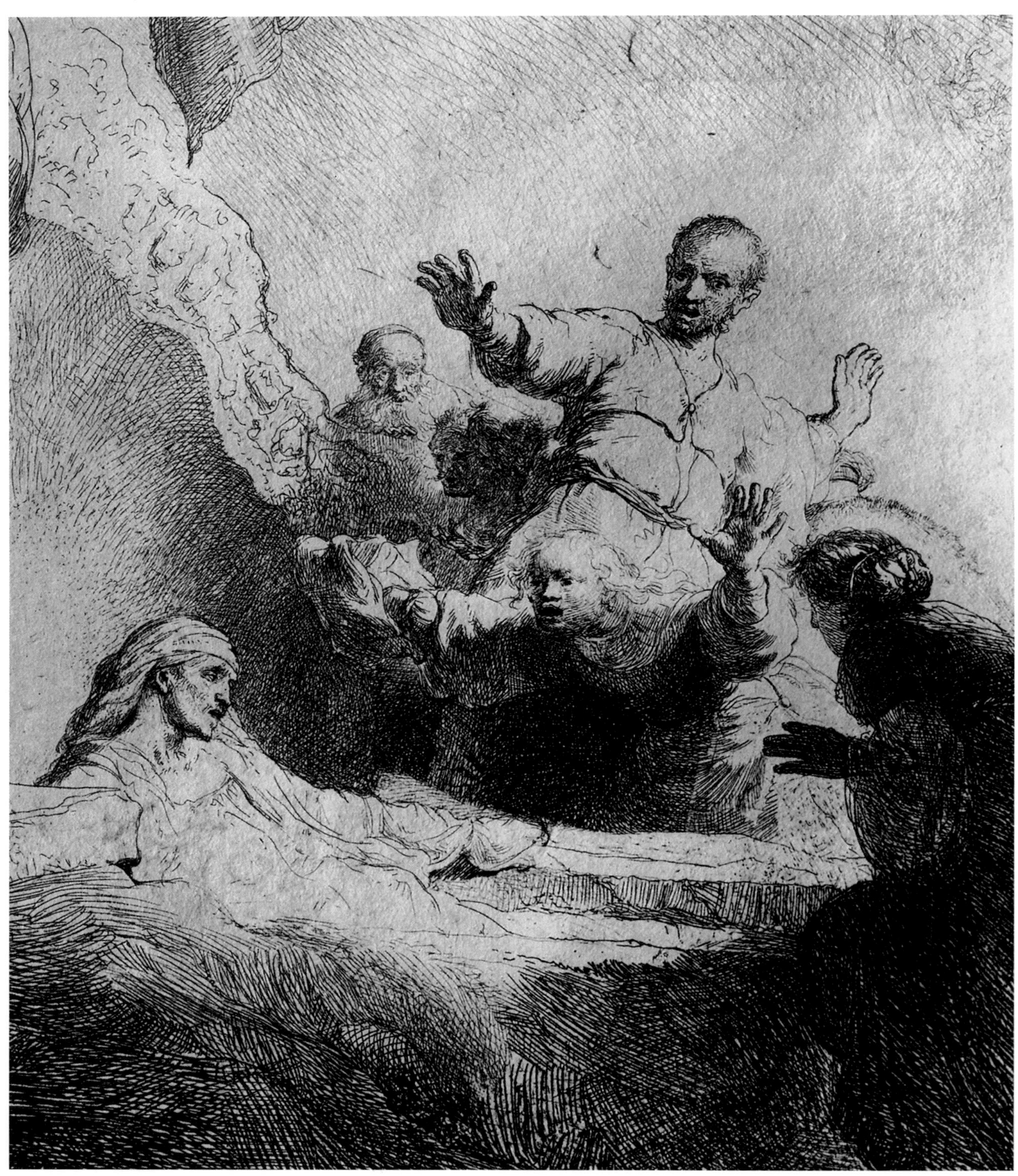

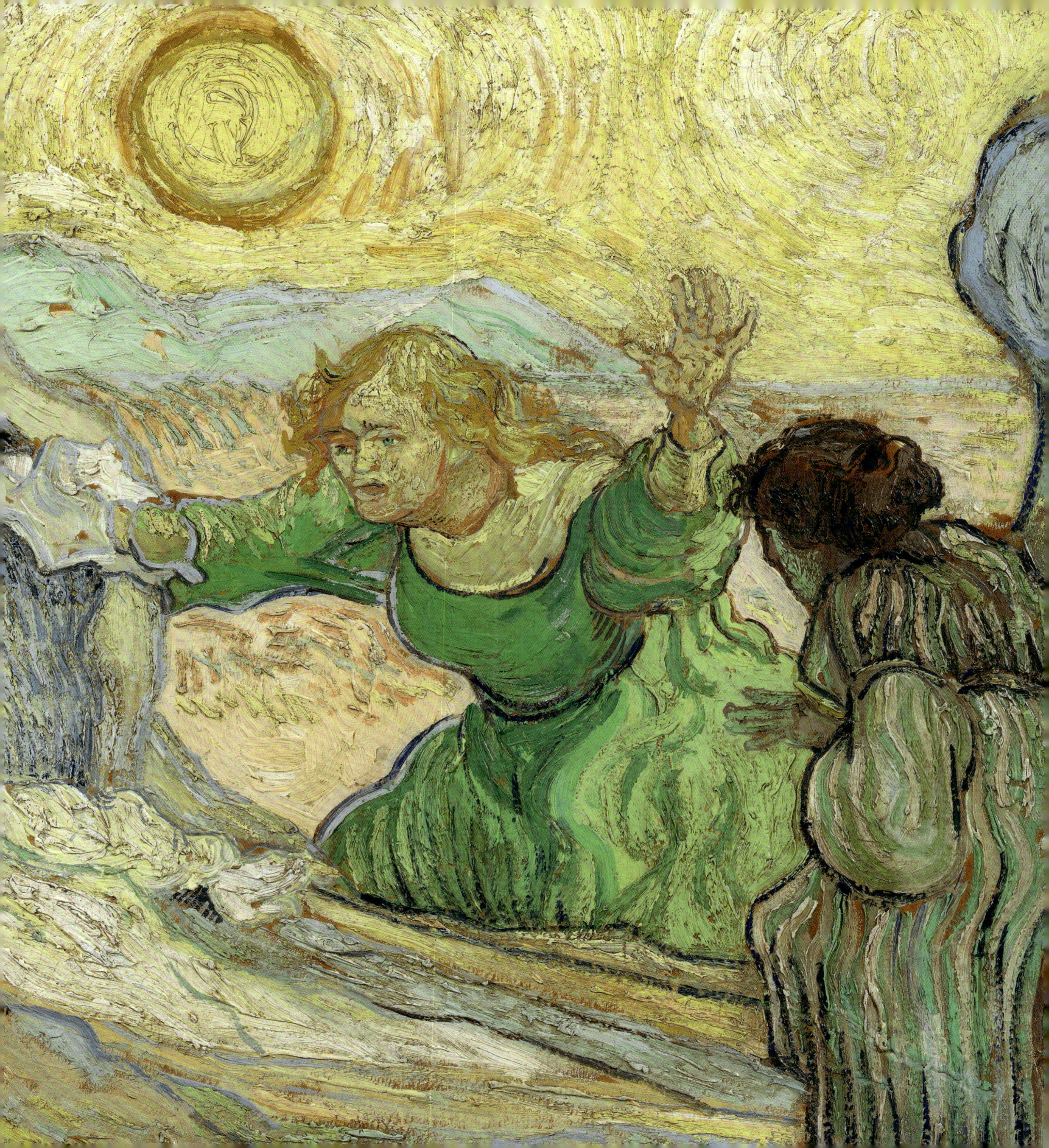

CHARDIN ~ MARQUET ~ SOUTINE

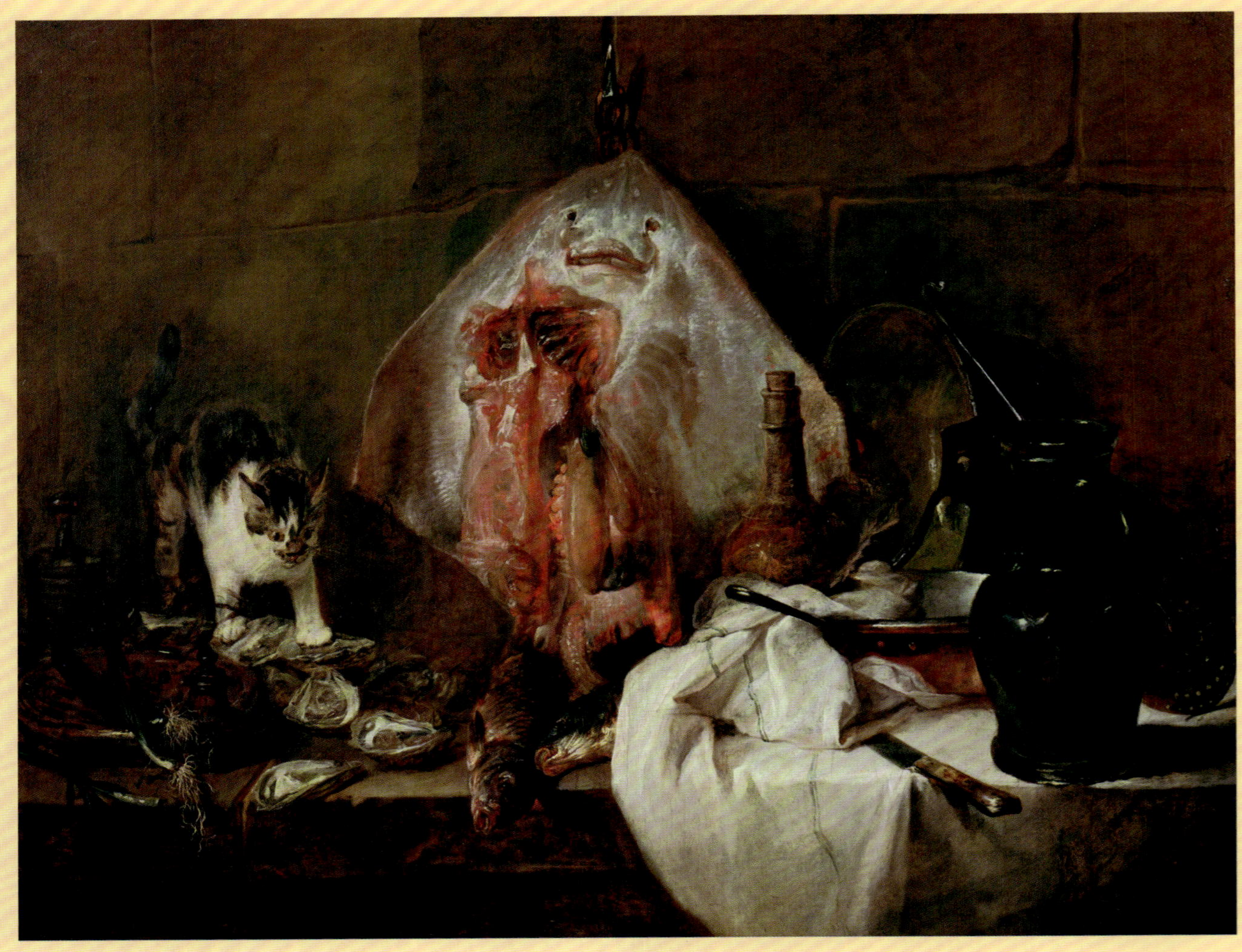

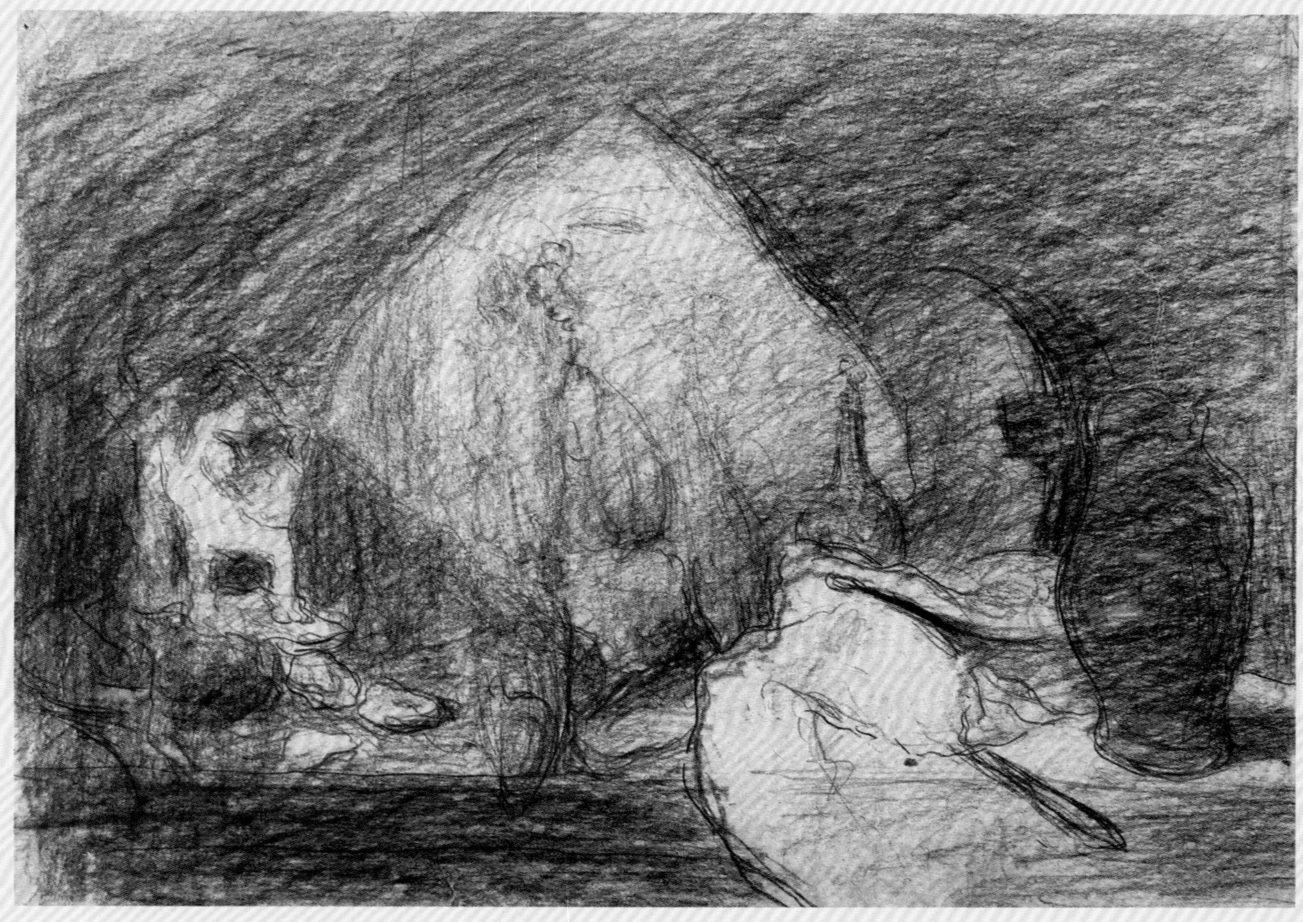

The Ray

La Raie

Der Rochen

La rajada

Arraia

De rog

Albert Marquet (1875-1947)

———

c. 1896, Black pencil drawing/Dessin
au crayon noir, 16,5 × 22,5 cm,
Private collection (copy after/copie)

The Ray

La Raie

Der Rochen

La rajada

Arraia

De rog

Jean-Siméon Chardin (1699-1779)

———

c. 1725/26, Oil on canvas/Huile sur toile,
114 × 146 cm, Musée du Louvre, Paris

CHARDIN ~ MARQUET ~ SOUTINE

Marquet's black-and-white sketch of Chardin's work *The Ray* already shows that light is at the center of his interest. Chaïm Soutine also took up the motif in the early 1920s - 30 years after this drawing was made. Like in his Carcass of Beef, after Rembrandt, he highlighted the disturbing nature of the depiction, among other things through the omnipresence of the red color.

La copie en noir et blanc et toute graphique de l'œuvre de Chardin par Albert Marquet nous démontre que la lumière est bien ici son principal centre d'intérêt. Chaïm Soutine reprendra au début des années 1920, soit près de trente ans après ce dessin, ce fameux sujet et à l'instar de son bœuf écorché d'après Rembrandt, le transcendera pour le rendre puissamment dérangeant, en accentuant, entre autres, l'omniprésence de la couleur rouge.

Marquets Schwarz-Weiß-Skizze von Chardins Werk *Der Rochen* zeigt bereits, dass das Licht im Zentrum seines Interesses steht. Auch Chaïm Soutine greift Anfang der 1920er-Jahre – 30 Jahre nach der Entstehung dieser Zeichnung – das Motiv auf. Wie bei seinem gehäuteten Rind nach Rembrandt treibt er die Darstellung bis ins Verstörende, unter anderem durch die Omnipräsenz der roten Farbe.

El boceto en blanco y negro de Marquet de la obra de Chardin *La rajada* ya muestra que la luz es aquí su principal interés. Chaïm Soutine también retomó el motivo a principios de la década de 1920, 30 años después de que se hiciera este dibujo. Al igual que El buey desollado de Rembrandt, lleva la representación a lo perturbador, entre otras cosas a través de la omnipresencia del color rojo.

O esboço a preto e branco de Marquet da obra *De raios* de Chardin já mostra que a luz está no centro do seu interesse. Chaïm Soutine também retomou o motivo no início da década de 1920 - 30 anos depois deste desenho ter sido feito. Como a vaca esfolada de Rembrandt, ele conduz a descrição para o perturbador, entre outras coisas através da onipresença da cor vermelha.

Marquets zwart-witschets van Chardins werk *De rog* laat al zien dat het licht in het middelpunt van zijn belangstelling stond. Chaïm Soutine pakte het motief begin jaren twintig van de 20e eeuw ook op, dertig jaar na het ontstaan van deze tekening. Net als bij zijn geslachte os naar Rembrandt voert hij de voorstelling door tot in het verontrustende, onder meer door de alomtegenwoordigheid van de kleur rood.

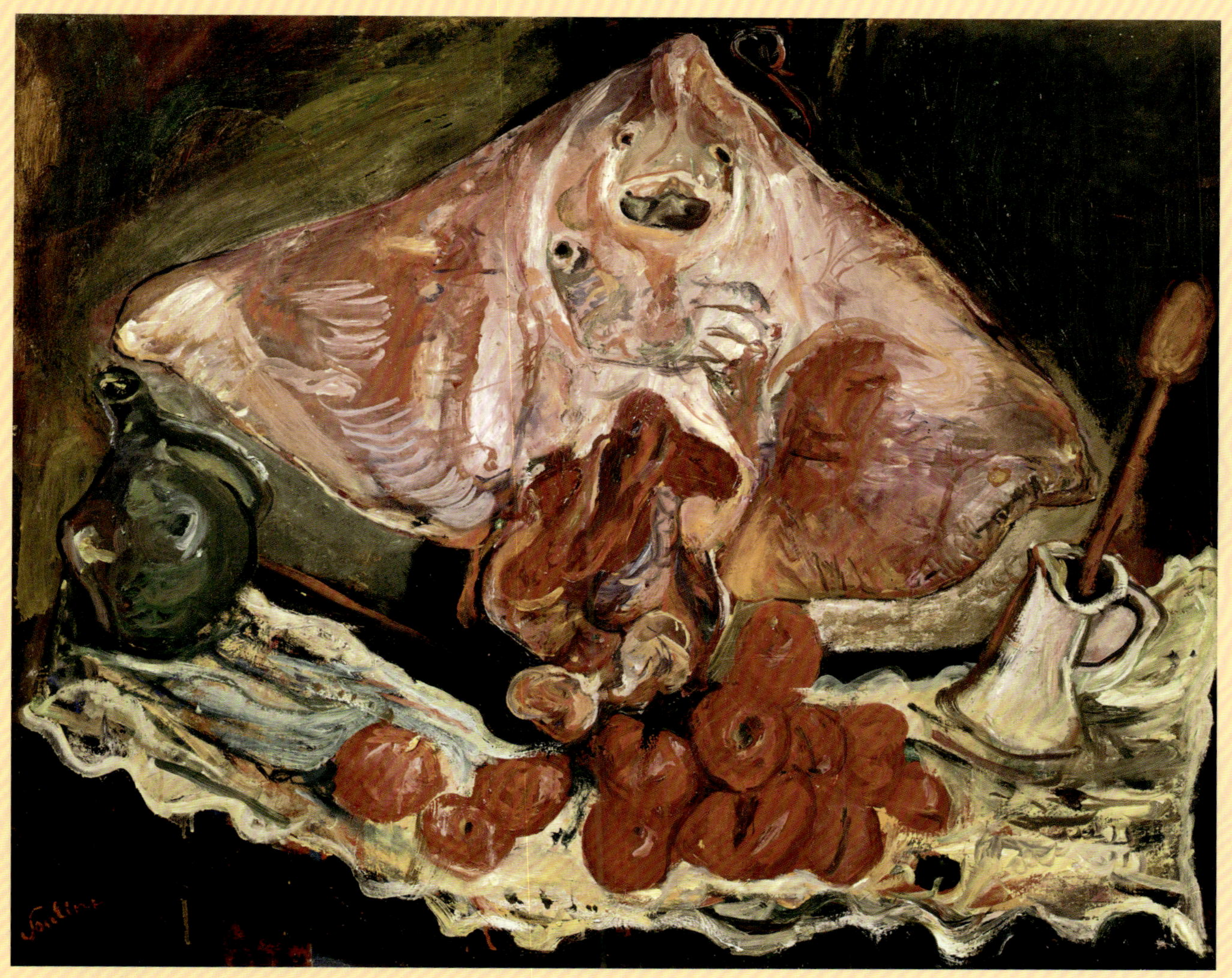

Still life with Rayfish
Nature morte à la raie
Stillleben mit Rochen
Bodegón con rajada
Natureza morta com raios
Stilleven met rog

Chaim Soutine (1894-1943)

———

c. 1924, Oil on canvas/Huile sur toile,
81,3 × 100 cm, Metropolitan
Museum of Art, New-York

WATTEAU ~ DELACROIX

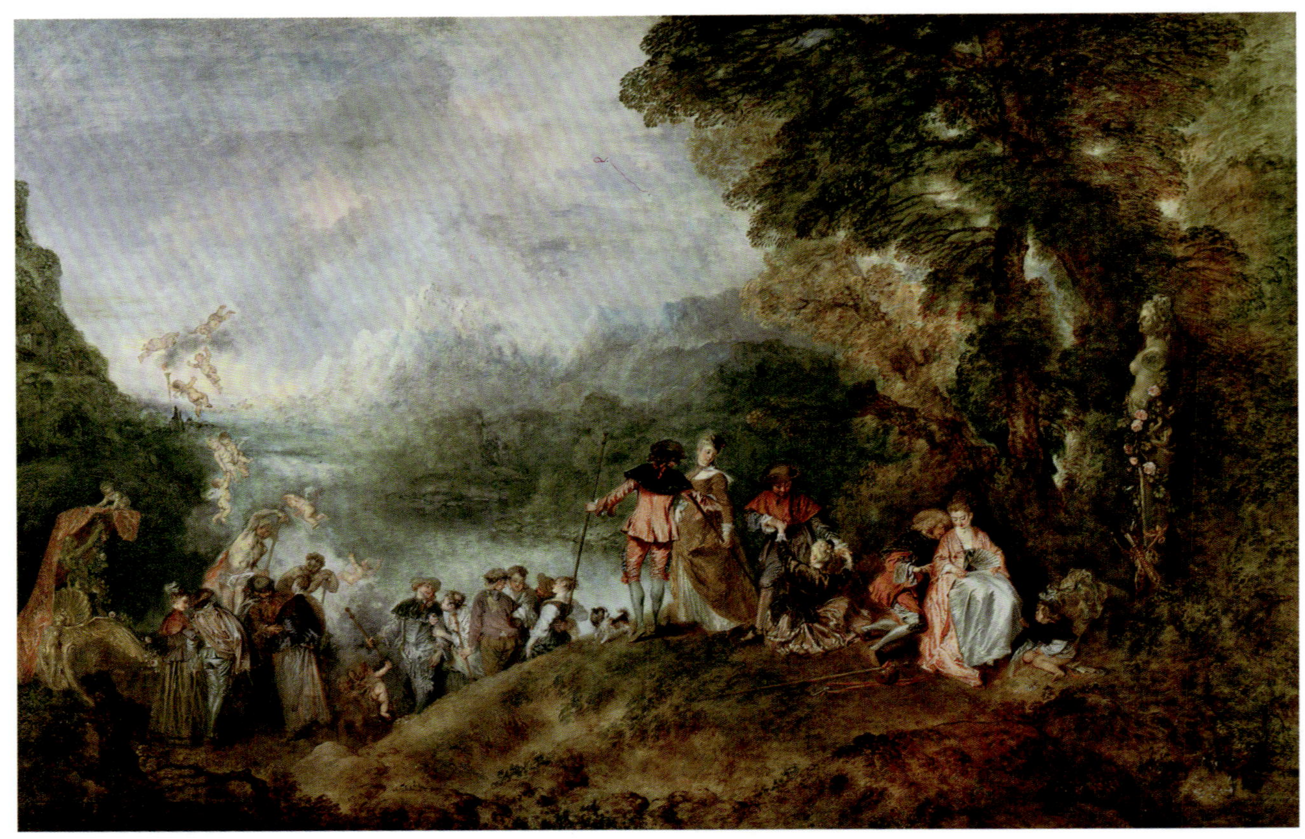

The Embarkation for Kythera

Pèlerinage à l'île de Cythère

Einschiffung nach Kythera

Peregrinación a la isla de Citera

Peregrinação à ilha de Kythera

De inscheping naar Kythera

Jean-Antoine Watteau (1684-1721)

1717, Oil on canvas/Huile sur toile,
129 × 194 cm, Musée du Louvre, Paris

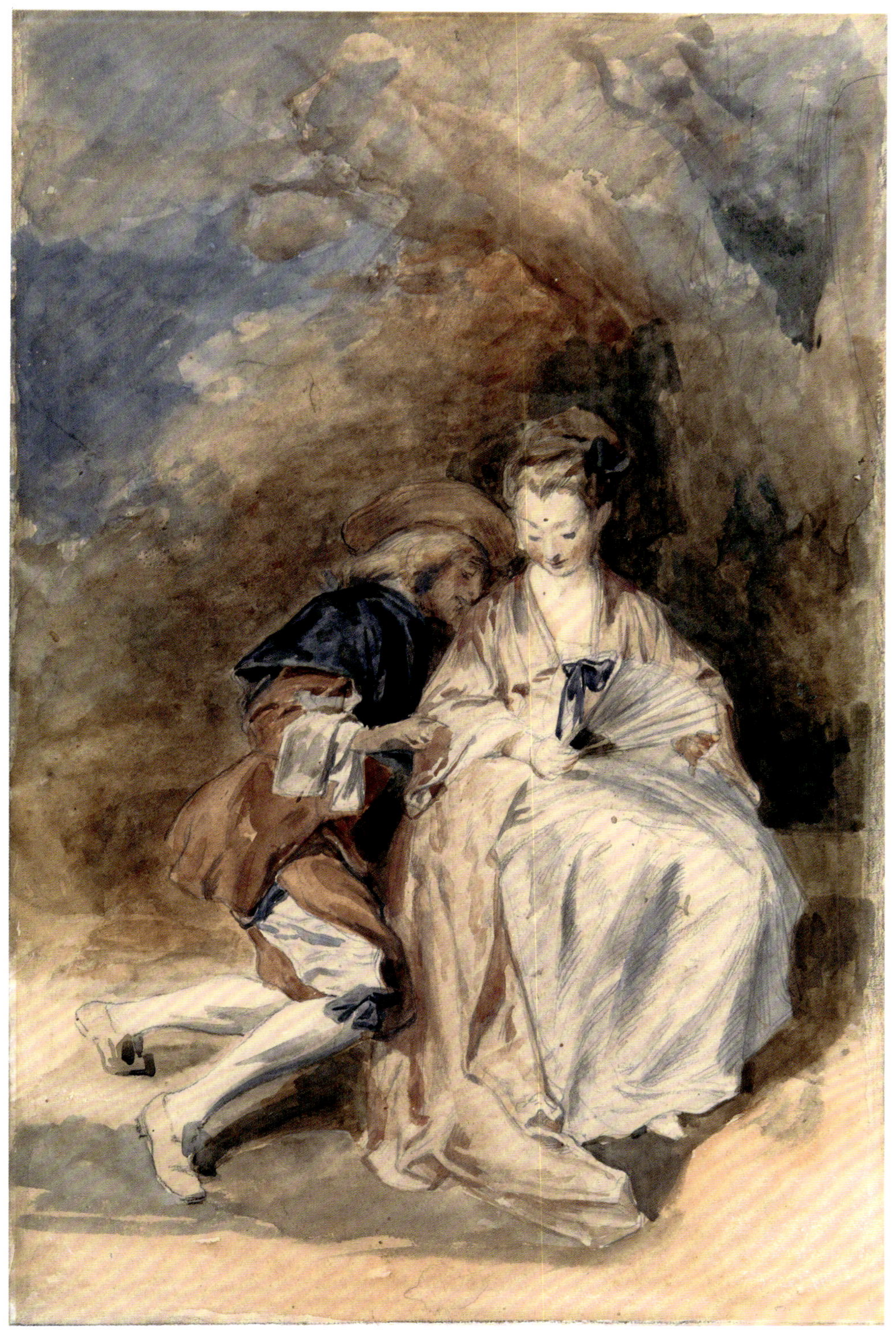

*The lover and the woman
with the fan,* detail of the
group on the right side

*Le Galant et la femme
à l'éventail,* détail du
groupe de droite

*Der Liebhaber und die
Frau mit dem Fächer,*
Detail der Gruppe auf
der rechten Seite

*El amante y la mujer
con el abanico,* detalle
del grupo a la derecha

*O amante e a mulher
com o leque,* detalhe
do grupo do lado direito

*De vrijer en de vrouw
met waaier,* detail van
het groepje rechts

**Eugène Delacroix
(1798-1863)**

———

c. 1816-18, Watercolor
over pencil/Aquarelle sur
traits de crayon, 43 × 28 cm,
Private collection
(copy after/copie)

SCHONGAUER ~ MICHELANGELO

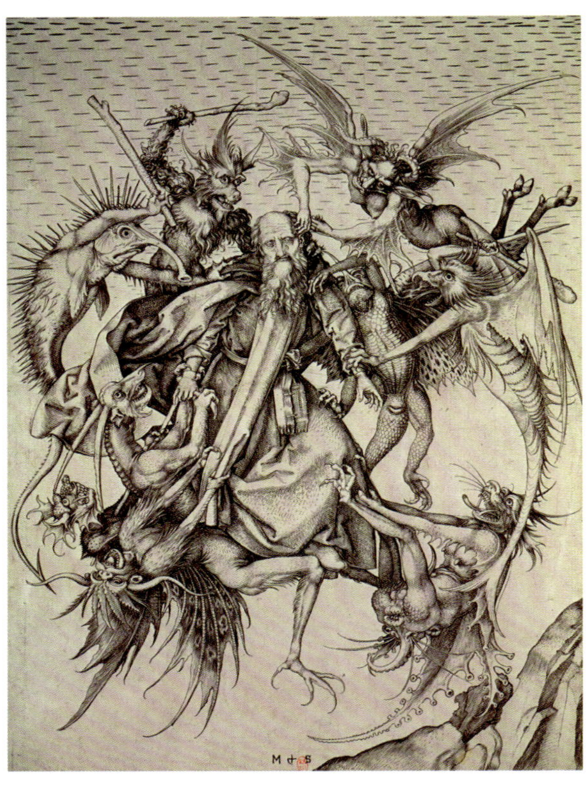

The Temptation of St. Anthony
La Tentation de saint Antoine
Die Peinigung des hl. Antonius
La tentación de San Antonio
O tormento de Santo António
De verzoeking van de heilige Antonius

Martin Schongauer (1440-1491)

———

c. 1470-75, Engraving/Estampe,
31,5 × 23,2 cm, Bibliothèque Nationale,
Paris

Michelangelo's paintings are not just slavish copies of Schongauer's work. The painter, who loved detail, knew how to breathe more life into the depiction of his monsters. In addition, the still young artist added a river in the background that cannot be seen on Schongauer's engraving. It is an emotional and naturalistic depiction of the Arno flowing through Michelangelo's hometown.

Ne vous méprenez pas, ceci n'est pas une copie dite servile ! En effet, Michel-Ange, soucieux du détail, a donné plus de vie dans la représentation des monstres-poissons que celle mise en place par Schongauer. De même, le jeune artiste a ajouté une rivière dans le bas de sa composition – inexistante dans la gravure –, une évocation aussi sensible que naturaliste de l'Arno, fleuve coulant au cœur de sa ville.

Bei Michelangelos Gemälde handelt es sich nicht nur um eine sklavische Kopie von Schongauers Werk. Der detailverliebte Maler verstand es, der Darstellung seiner Monster mehr Leben einzuhauchen. Außerdem fügt der noch junge Künstler einen Fluss im Hintergrund hinzu, der auf Schongauers Stich nicht zu sehen ist. Es ist eine gefühlvolle und naturalistische Darstellung des Arno, der durch die Heimatstadt Michelangelos fließt.

**Michelangelo Buonarroti
(1475-1564)**

1487, Tempera on panel/Tempera sur panneau, 47 × 34,9 cm, Kimbell Art Museum, Fort Worth (copy after/copie)

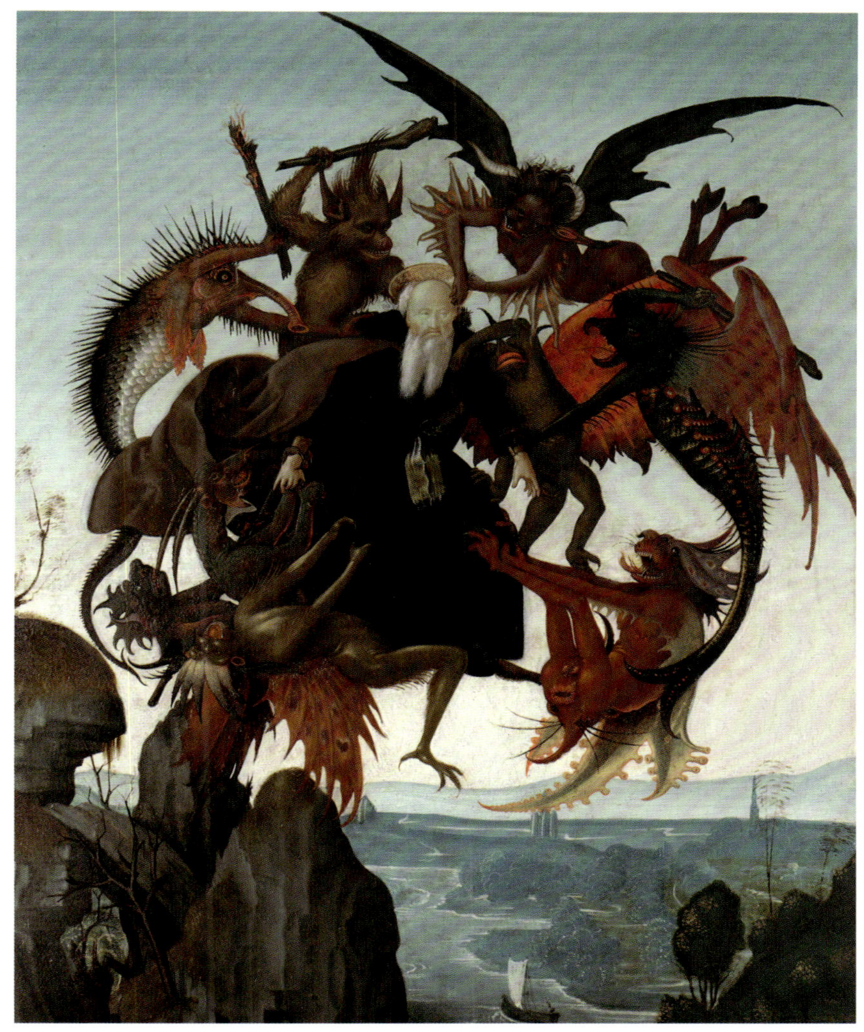

Las pinturas de Miguel Ángel no son sólo copias serviles de la obra de Schongauer. El pintor, amante de los detalles, supo insuflar más vida a la representación de sus monstruos. Además, el joven artista añade un río en el fondo que no se puede ver en el grabado de Schongauer. Es una representación emocional y naturalista del Arno que fluye a través de la ciudad natal de Miguel Ángel.

As pinturas de Michelangelo não são apenas cópias escravas do trabalho de Schongauer. O pintor, que adorava detalhes, sabia como dar mais vida à representação de seus monstros. Além disso, o artista ainda jovem acrescenta um rio no fundo que não pode ser visto na gravura de Schongauer. É uma representação emocional e naturalista do Arno que flui pela cidade natal de Michelangelo.

Bij Michelangelo's schilderij gaat het niet alleen om een slaafse kopie van Schongauers werk. De schilder, die dol was op details, blies zijn voorstelling van monsters meer leven in. Daarnaast voegt de nog jonge kunstenaar op de achtergrond een rivier toe die niet voorkomt op Schongauers gravure. Het is een gevoelige en natuurgetrouwe weergave van de Arno die door Michelangelo's geboorteplaats stroomt.

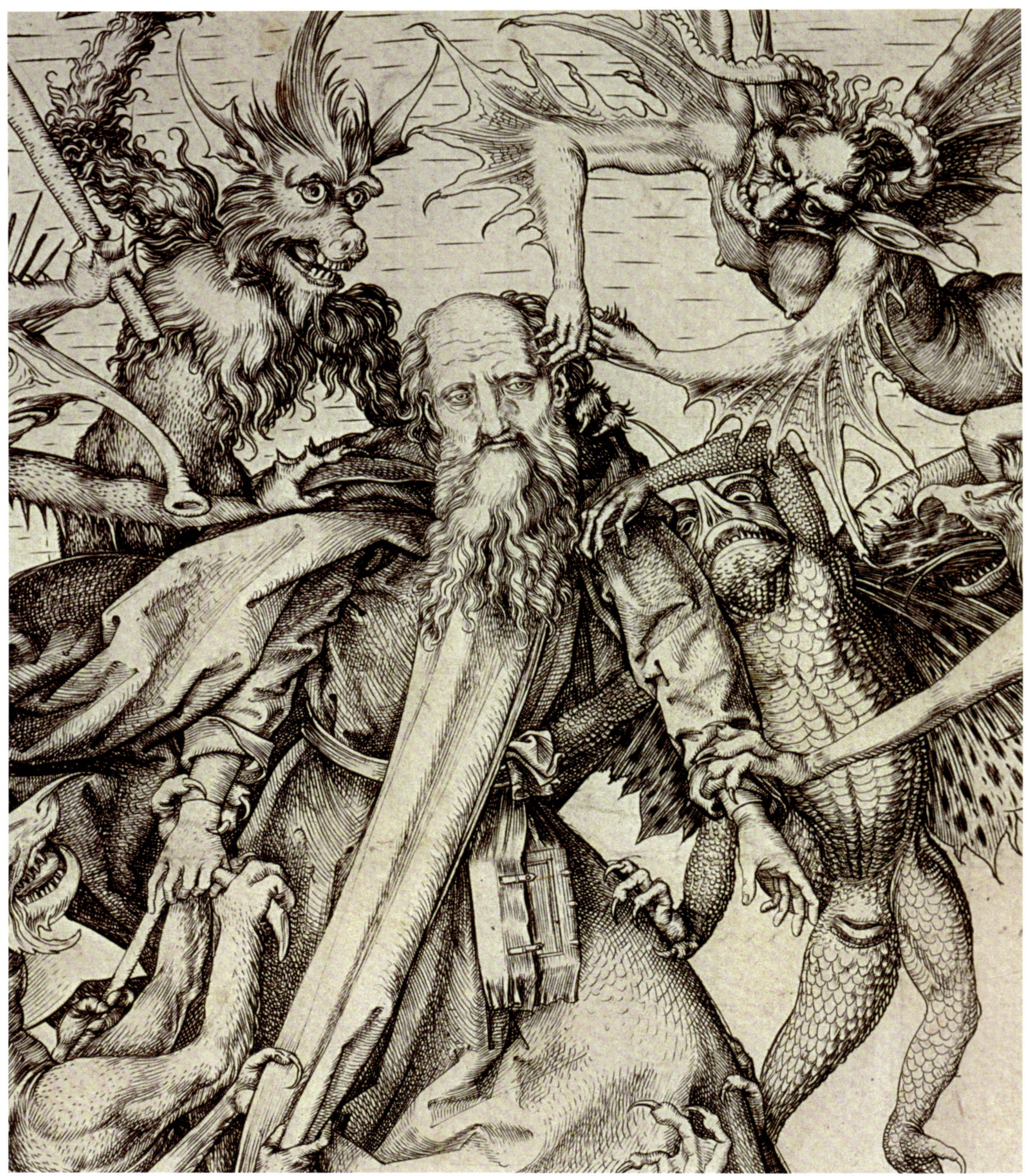

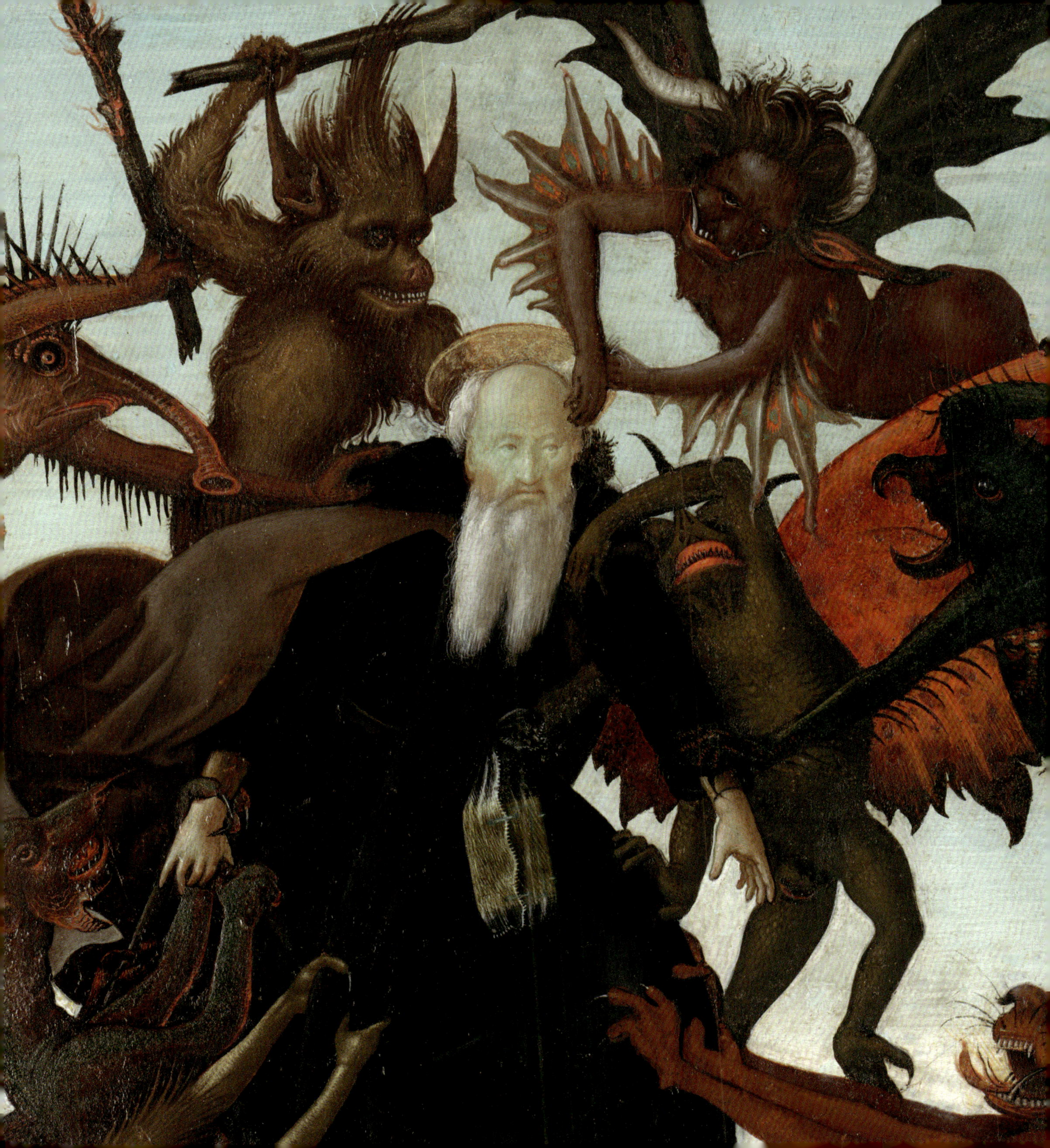

DA VINCI ~ INGRES

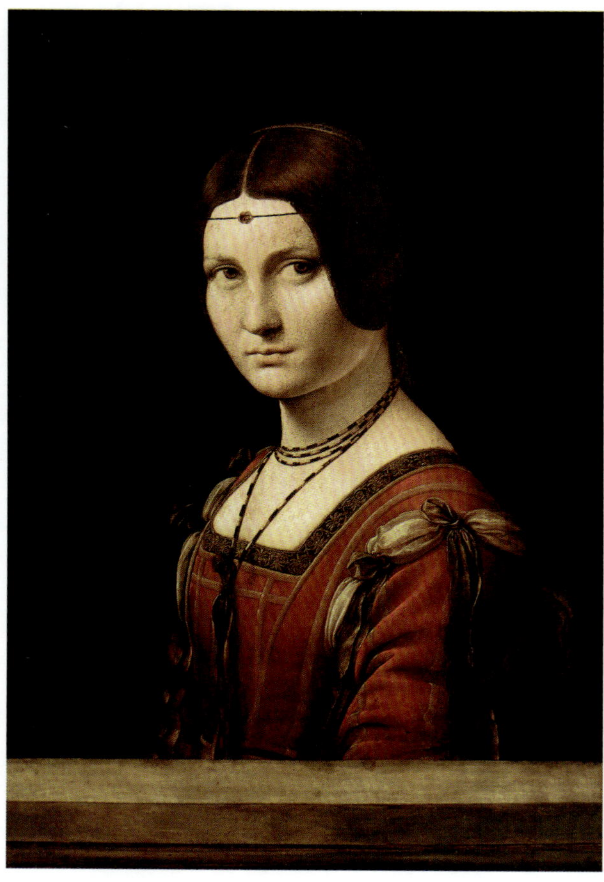

La Belle Ferronnière

Leonardo da Vinci (1452-1519)

———

c. 1495-99, Oil on panel/Huile sur panneau,
63 × 45 cm, Musée du Louvre, Paris

Ingres greatly appreciated Raphael's works. He copied them and was inspired by them. However, examples that were created after da Vinci, such as this meticulous drawing, are rare. The extreme precision with which he executed them confirms that the artist was a true master of line drawing during his lifetime.

Ingres, on le sait, avait une passion pour les œuvres de Raphaël qu'il copia ou dont il s'inspira. Mais rares sont les exemples comme cette spectaculaire reprise au crayon d'après un portrait de Léonard. L'extrême minutie avec laquelle Ingres exécute son dessin confirme bien qu'il est, à son époque, un véritable maître du trait.

Ingres schätzte Raffaels Werke sehr. Er kopierte sie und ließ sich von ihnen inspirieren. Beispiele, die nach da Vinci entstanden, wie diese minutiöse Zeichnung, sind jedoch selten. Die extreme Präzision, mit der er sie ausführte, bestätigt, dass der Künstler zu Lebzeiten ein wahrer Meister der Linienführung war.

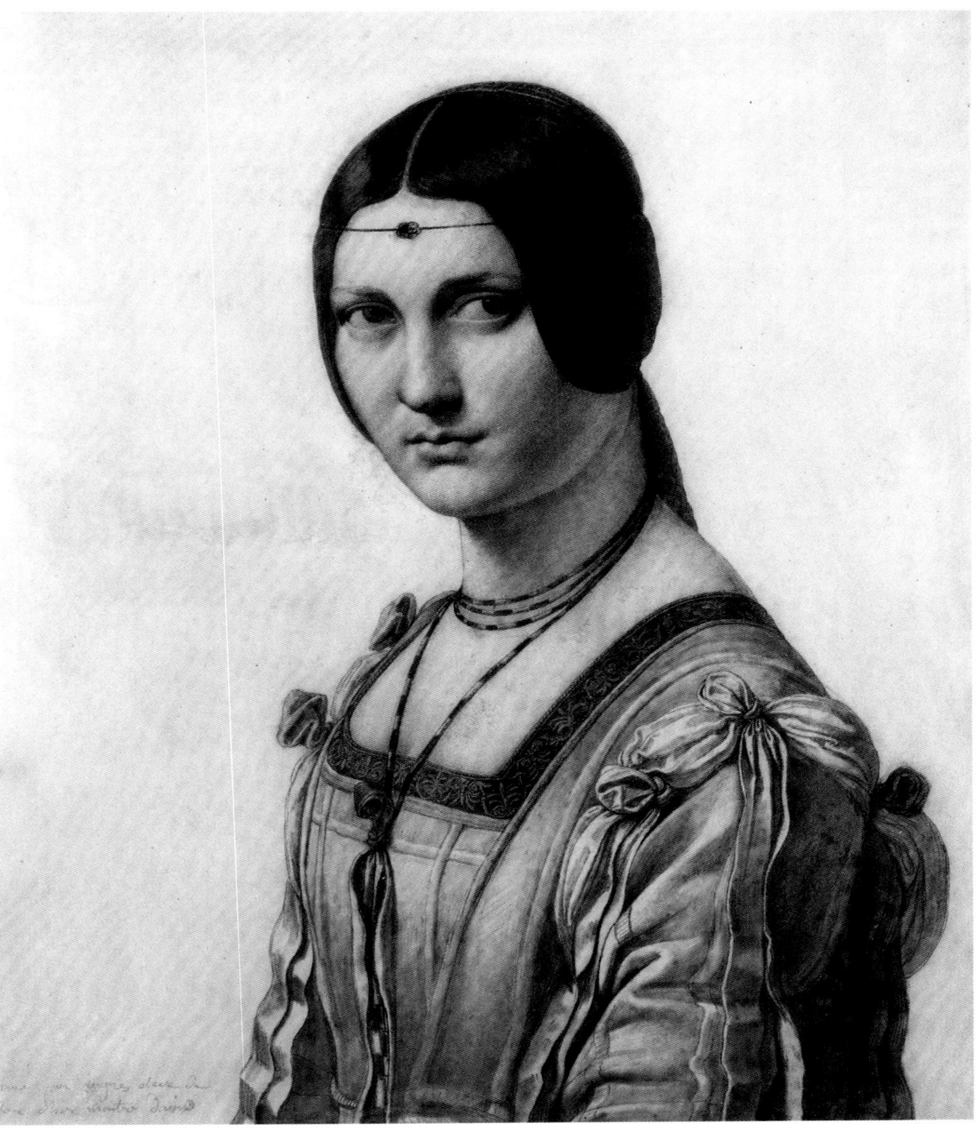

Ingres, como sabemos, tenía pasión por las obras de Rafael, que copió o en las que se inspiró, pero pocos son los ejemplos como esta espectacular portada a lápiz basada en un retrato de Leonardo. La extrema meticulosidad con la que Ingres ejecutó su dibujo confirma que fue, en su momento, un verdadero maestro del dibujo lineal.

Ingres apreciou muito as obras de Rafael. Ele copiou-as e foi inspirado por elas. No entanto, exemplos que foram criados depois de Da Vinci, como este desenho meticuloso, são raros. A precisão extrema com a qual ele executou-los confirma que o artista era um verdadeiro mestre do desenho de linha durante sua vida.

Ingres waardeerde Rafaëls werken zeer. Hij kopieerde ze en werd erdoor geïnspireerd. Voorbeelden die naar Da Vinci zijn gemaakt, zoals deze minutieuze tekening, zijn echter zeldzaam. De extreme precisie waarmee hij haar uitvoerde, bevestigt dat de kunstenaar tijdens zijn leven een meesterlijke tekenaar was.

RUBENS ~ GAINSBOROUGH

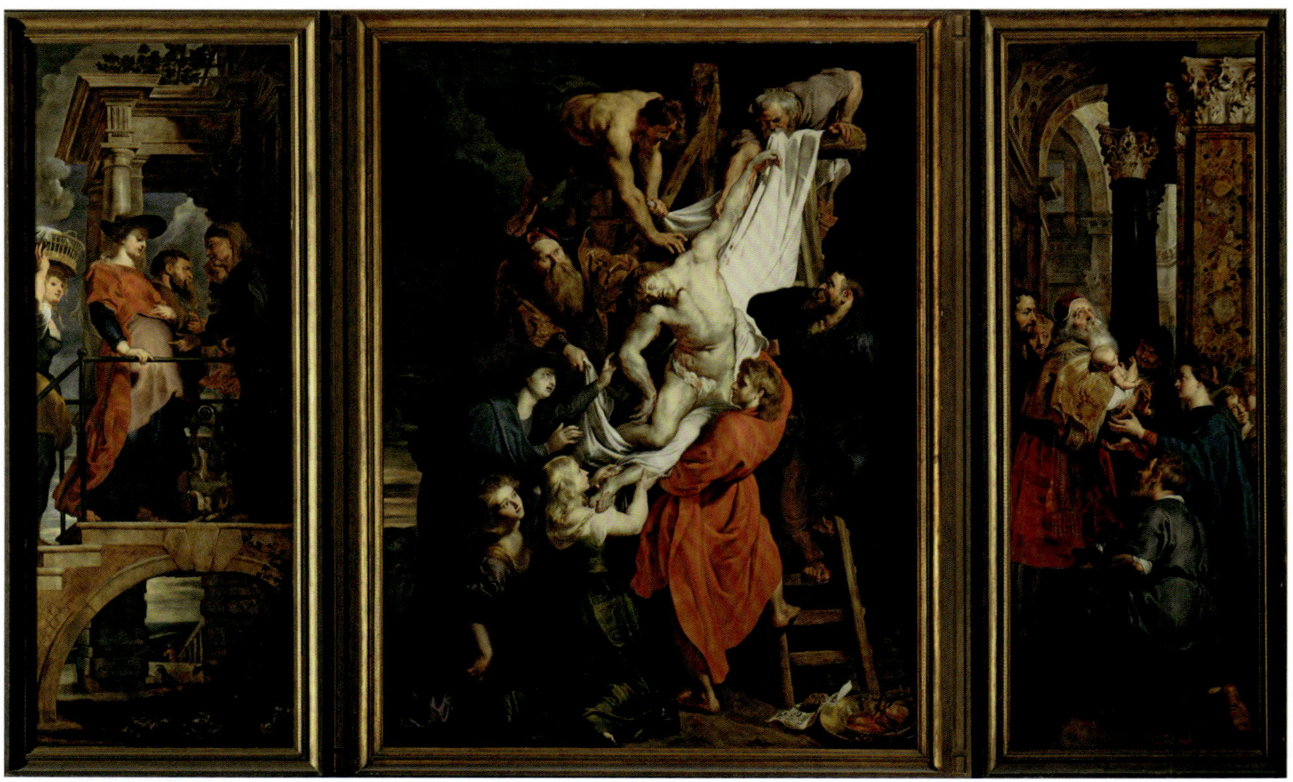

Descent from the Cross
La Descente de Croix
Kreuzabnahme
Descendimiento de Cristo
A Deposição da Cruz
Kruisafneming

Peter Paul Rubens (1577-1640)

———

c. 1612-14, Oil on panel/Huile sur panneau,
420,5 × 320 cm, Onze Lieve Vrouwekerk,
Antwerpen

Descent from the Cross
La Descente de Croix
Kreuzabnahme
Descendimiento de Cristo
A Deposição da Cruz
Kruisafneming

Thomas Gainsborough (1727-1788)

———

1765-70, Oil on canvas/Huile sur toile,
125,5 × 101,5 cm, Gainsborough House,
Sudbury (copy after/copie)

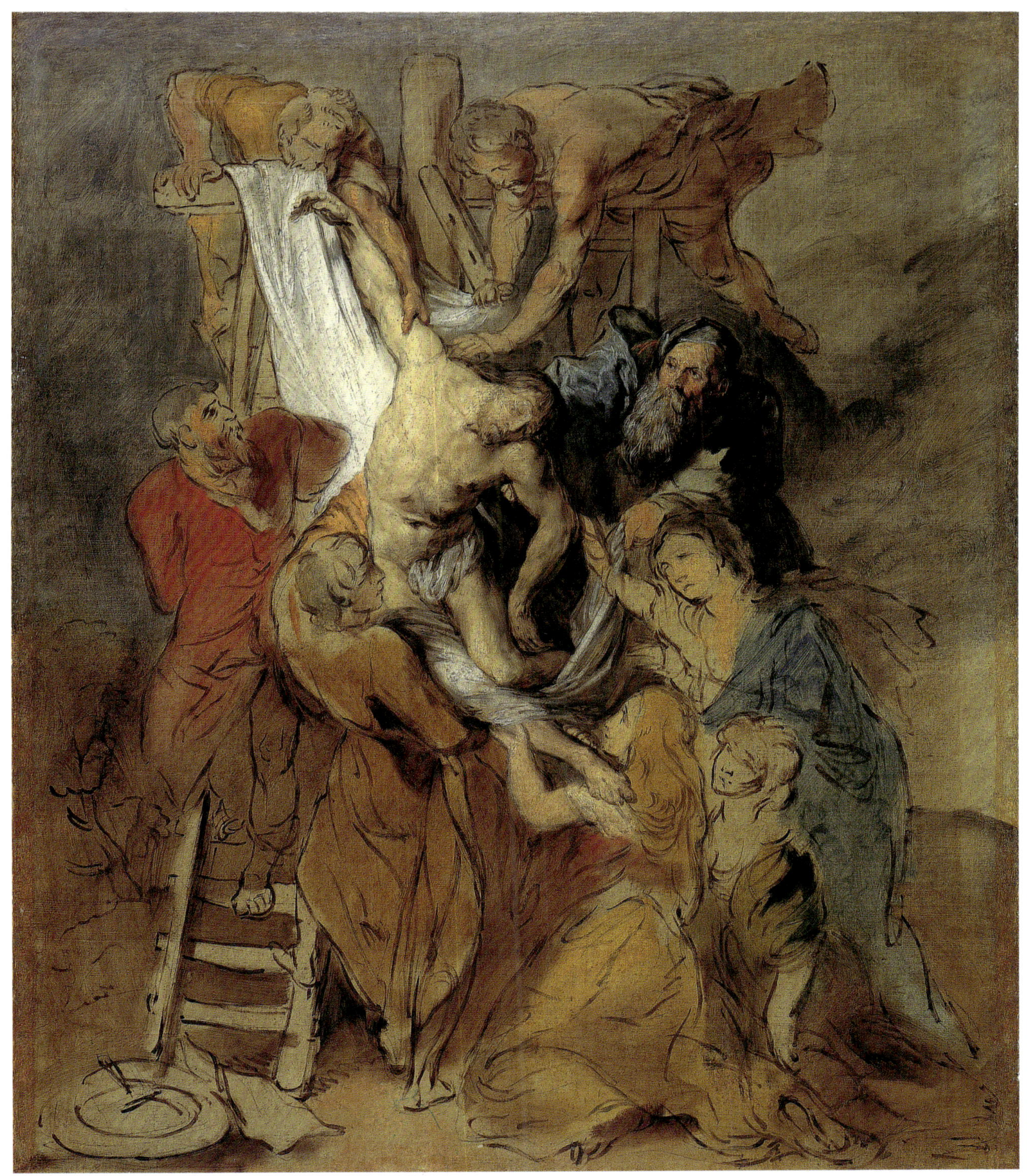

IL TINTORETTO ~ MANET

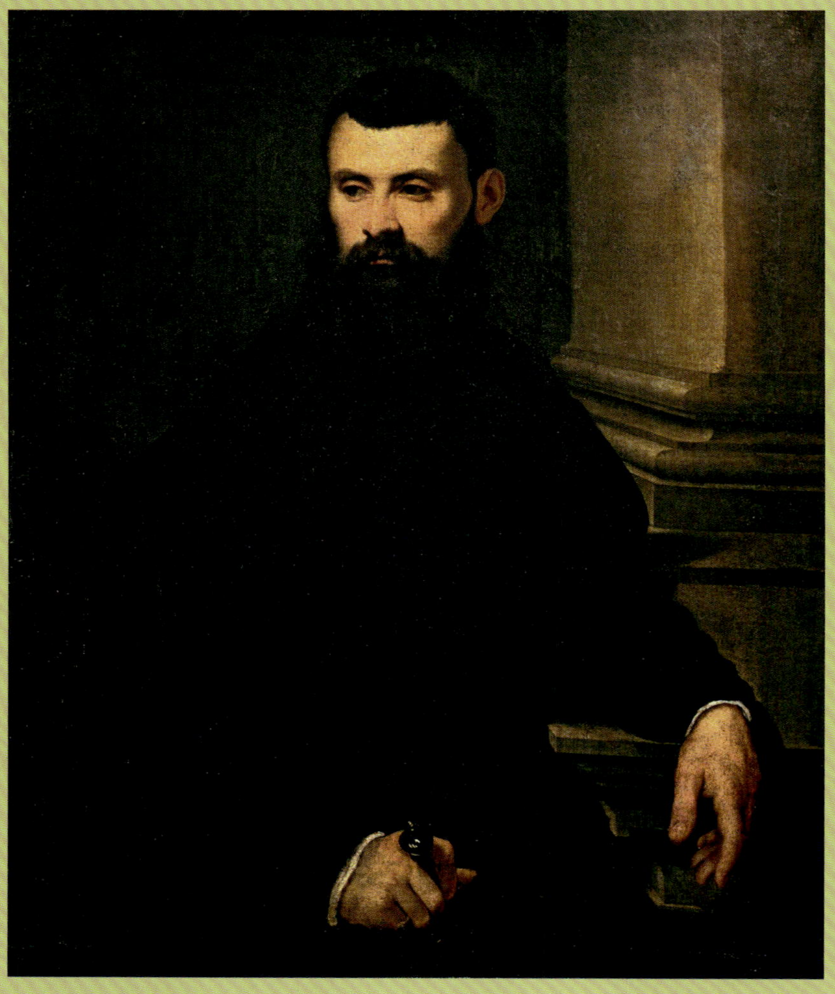

**Jacopo Robusti (Il Tintoretto)
(1518-1594)**

———

c. 1540, Oil on canvas/Huile sur toile,
100 × 83 cm, Musée du Louvre, Paris

Édouard Manet (1832-1883)

———

c. 1850-52, Oil on canvas/Huile sur toile,
32 × 24 cm, Private collection
(copy after/copie)

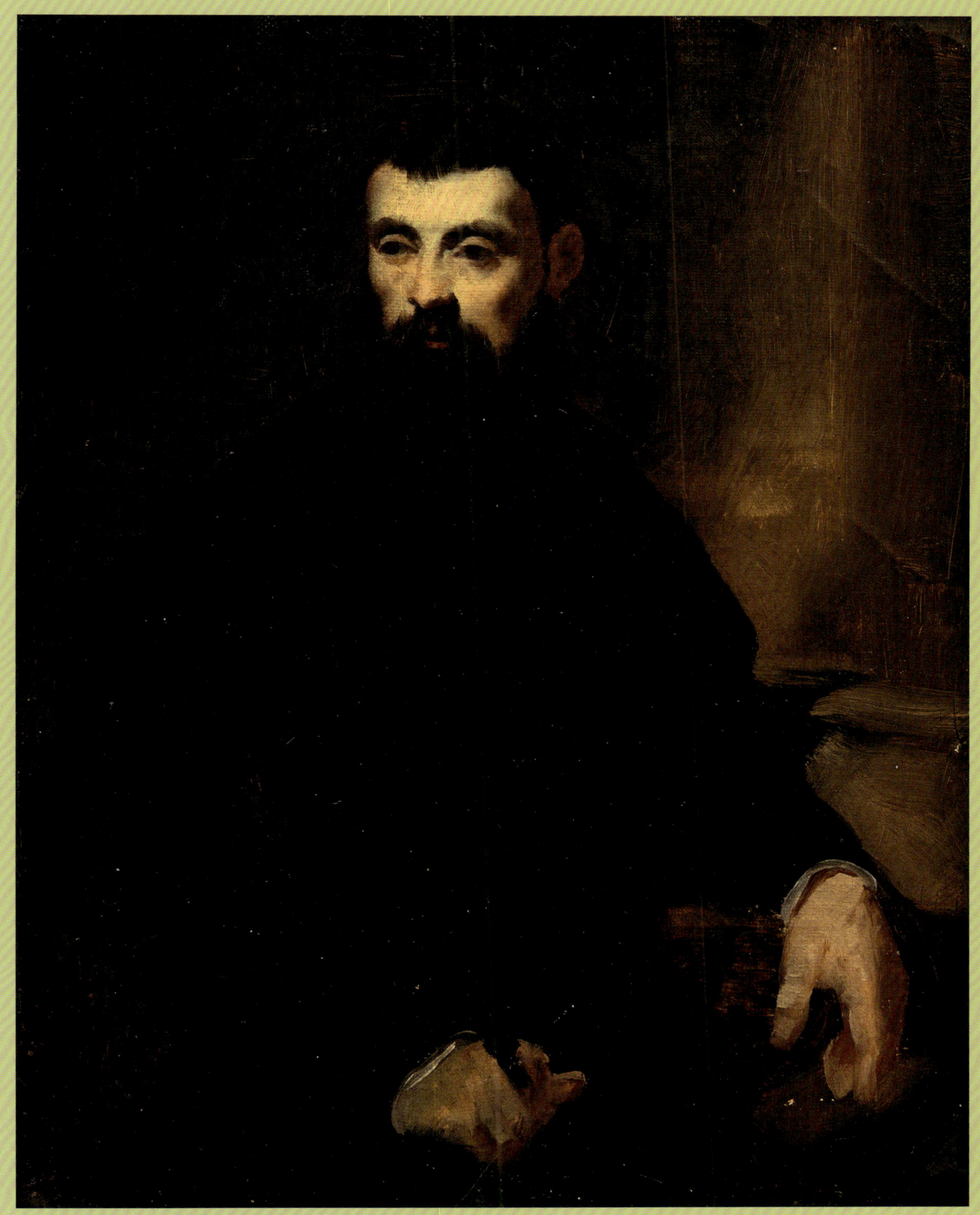

IL TINTORETTO ~ MANET

For Manet, copying was more than a simple exercise - he saw it as a way of opening up new worlds that would be useful to him in creating new works. So the question arises whether he already had the idea for the portrait of his friend Zachari Astruc when he painted the man dressed in black in the Louvre. At least that's what the final painting suggests.

Très souvent chez Manet copier est plus qu'un simple exercice, c'est aussi une manière de s'approprier un univers qui lui permettra dans un temps plus ou moins rapproché de « fabriquer » une de ses nouvelles créations. Quand il reprend la pose du gentilhomme en noir exposé au Louvre, avait-il déjà en tête l'idée de brosser le portrait de son bon ami Zachari Astruc ? À en croire le résultat final visible sur sa toile, la question mérite bien d'être elle aussi posée.

Für Manet war das Kopieren mehr als eine einfache Übung – er sah darin eine Möglichkeit, neue Welten zu erschließen, die ihm bei der Entstehung neuer Werke nützlich sein würden. So stellt sich die Frage, ob er bereits die Idee für das Porträt seines Freundes Zachari Astruc hatte, als er den in schwarz gekleideten Mann im Louvre abmalte. Zumindest deutet das endgültige Gemälde darauf hin.

Para Manet, la copia era más que un simple ejercicio: la veía como una forma de abrir nuevos mundos que le serían útiles para crear nuevas obras. Así que surge la pregunta de si ya tenía la idea del retrato de su amigo Zachari Astruc cuando pintó al hombre vestido de negro en el Louvre. Al menos eso es lo que sugiere la pintura final.

Para Manet, copiar era mais do que um simples exercício - via-o como uma forma de abrir novos mundos que lhe seriam úteis na criação de novos trabalhos. Surge então a questão de saber se ele já tinha a idéia para o retrato de seu amigo Zachari Astruc quando pintou o homem vestido de preto no Louvre. Pelo menos é o que a pintura final sugere.

Voor Manet was kopiëren meer dan een eenvoudige oefening. Hij zag er een manier in om nieuwe werelden te openen die nuttig voor hem konden zijn bij het maken van nieuwe werk. De vraag is dus of hij al het idee had om zijn vriend Zachari Astruc te portretteren toen hij de in het zwart geklede man in het Louvre naschilderde. Daar wijst het uiteindelijke schilderij tenminste wel op.

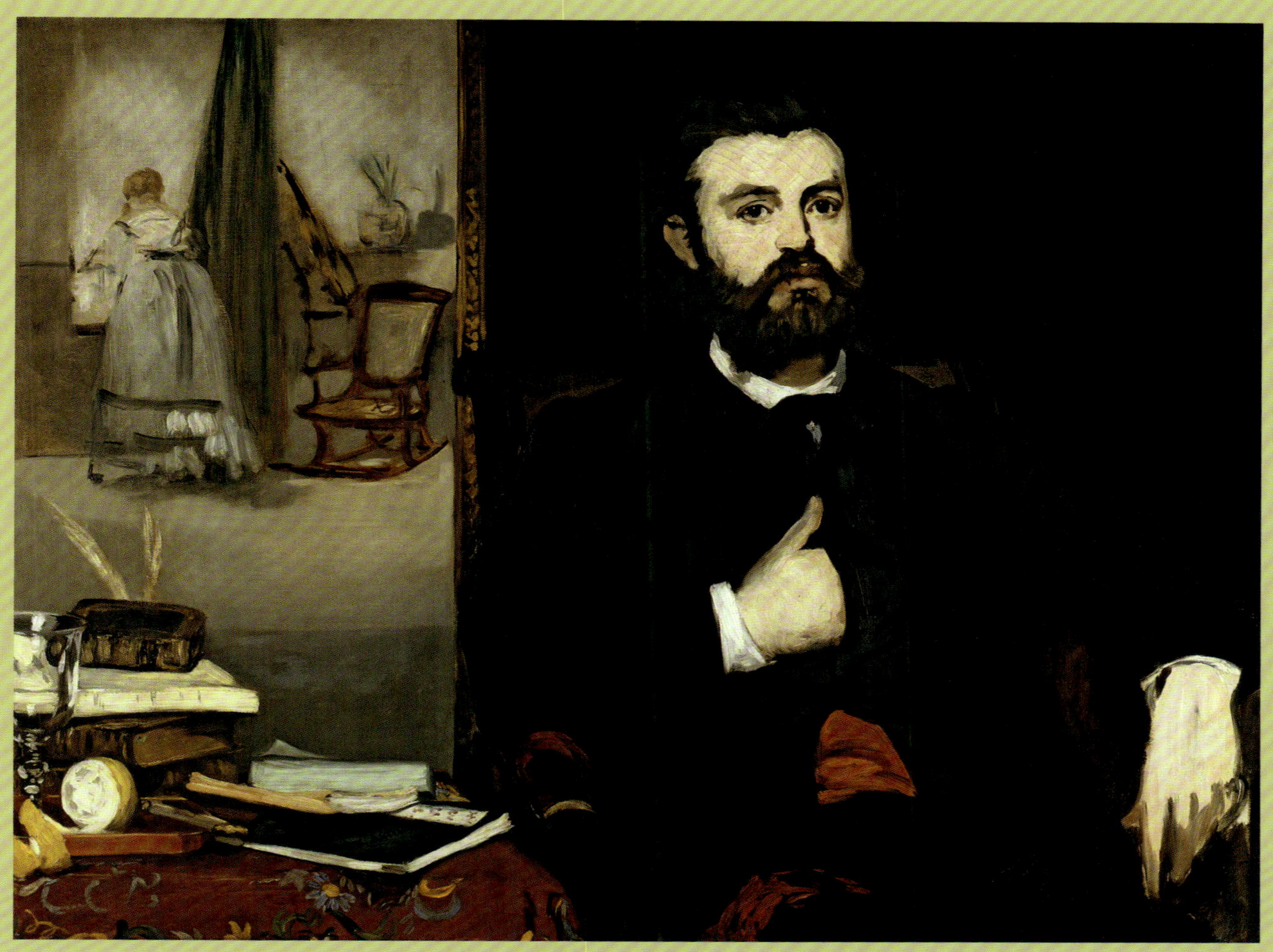

Portrait of the Poet Zacharie Astruc
Portrait du poète Zacharie Astruc
Bildnis des Dichters Zacharie Astruc
Retrato del poeta Zacharie Astruc
Retrato do poeta Zacharie Astruc
Portret van de dichter Zacharie Astruc

Édouard Manet (1832-1883)

———

c. 1866, Oil on canvas/Huile sur toile,
90,5 × 116 cm, Kunsthalle Bremen

HIROSHIGE ~ VAN GOGH

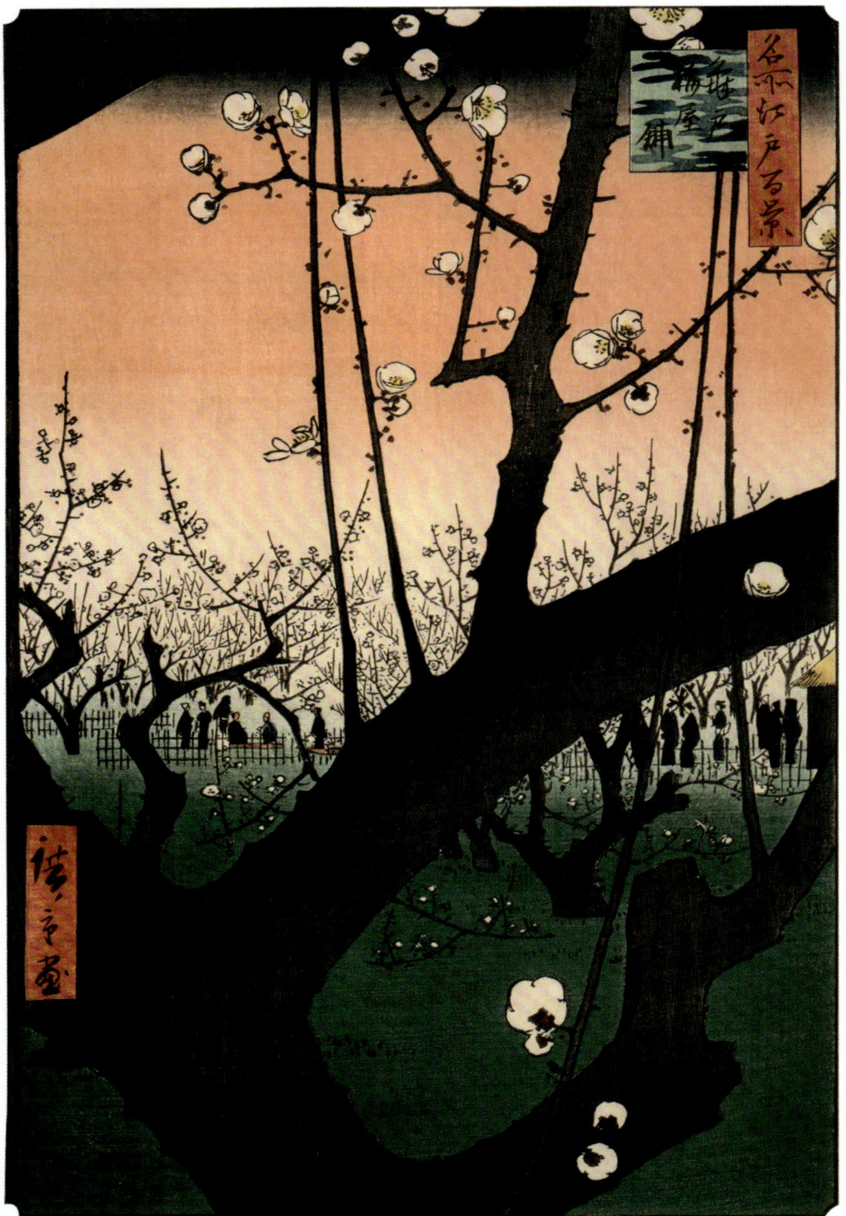

Plum Garden at Kameido
Le Jardin des pruniers à Kameido
Garten der Pflaumenbäume in Kameido
Jardín de ciruelos en Kameido
Jardim de ameixoeiras em Kameido
De residentie met de pruimenbomen in Kameido

Utagawa Hiroshige (1797-1858)

—

c. 1856, Color woodblock/Gravure sur bois colorisée, 36,8 × 25 cm, Tokyo Fuji Art Museum, Tokyo

Japonaiserie: Flowering Plum Orchard
Japonaiserie : Le prunier en fleurs
Japonaiserie: Blühender Pflaumenbaum
Japonaiserie: Ciruelo en flor
Japonaiserie: Ameixoeira em flor
Japonaiserie: De bloeiende pruimenboom

Vincent van Gogh (1853-1890)

—

1887, Oil on canvas/Huile sur toile, 55 × 46 cm, Van Gogh Museum, Amsterdam (copy after/copie)

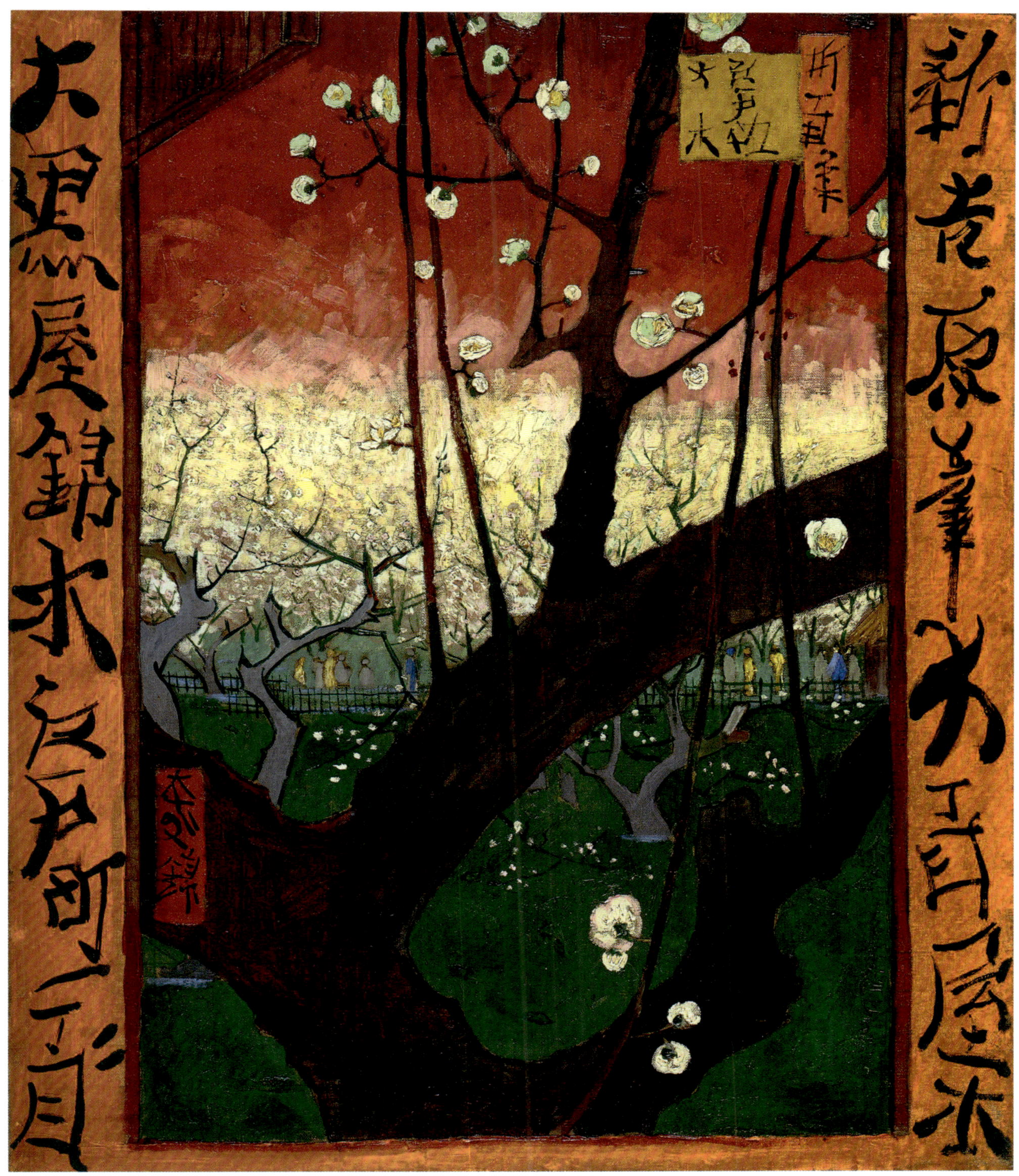

HIROSHIGE ~ VAN GOGH

Japanese woodblock prints became popular in the second half of the 19th century through Claude Monet, among others. Many artists used them as a source of inspiration. Van Gogh copied the colorful prints several times, especially those of his role model Utagawa Hiroshige. His practice taught him how to position monochrome surfaces and how to use new image details.

Rendue populaire par Claude Monet au début de la seconde moitié du XIXe siècle, l'estampe japonaise fut pour de nombreux artistes une source nouvelle et précieuse d'inspiration. Van Gogh copia souvent ces gravures très colorées et plus particulièrement celles signées par un de ses maîtres, Utagawa Hiroshige. À travers ce paysage il apprend à se familiariser avec la pose des aplats de couleurs, mais aussi à cadrer ses sujets différemment.

Japanische Farbholzschnitte wurden in der zweiten Hälfte des 19. Jahrhunderts unter anderem durch Claude Monet populär. Vielen Künstlern dienten sie als Quelle der Inspiration. Van Gogh kopierte mehrfach die bunten Drucke, vor allem die seines Vorbilds Utagawa Hiroshige. Durch die Praktik lernte er das Setzen einfarbiger Flächen sowie die Verwendung von neuen Bildausschnitten.

Los grabados japoneses en madera se hicieron populares en la segunda mitad del siglo XIX a través de Claude Monet, entre otros. Muchos artistas los utilizaron como fuente de inspiración. Van Gogh copió los coloridos grabados varias veces, especialmente los de su modelo Utagawa Hiroshige. Su práctica le enseñó a establecer superficies monocromas y a usar nuevos detalles de imagen.

As gravuras japonesas em blocos de madeira tornaram-se populares na segunda metade do século XIX através de Claude Monet, entre outros. Muitos artistas usaram-nos como fonte de inspiração. Van Gogh copiou as estampas coloridas várias vezes, especialmente as de seu modelo de papel Utagawa Hiroshige. A sua prática ensinou-o a definir superfícies monocromáticas e a utilizar novos detalhes de imagem.

Japanse houtsneden werden in de tweede helft van de 19e eeuw populair, onder andere door Claude Monet. Ze dienden veel kunstenaars als bron van inspiratie. Van Gogh kopieerde de kleurrijke prenten meerdere malen, vooral die van zijn grote voorbeeld Utagawa Hiroshige. Door het kopiëren leerde hij hoe hij effen oppervlakken en nieuwe beelduitsneden kon gebruiken.

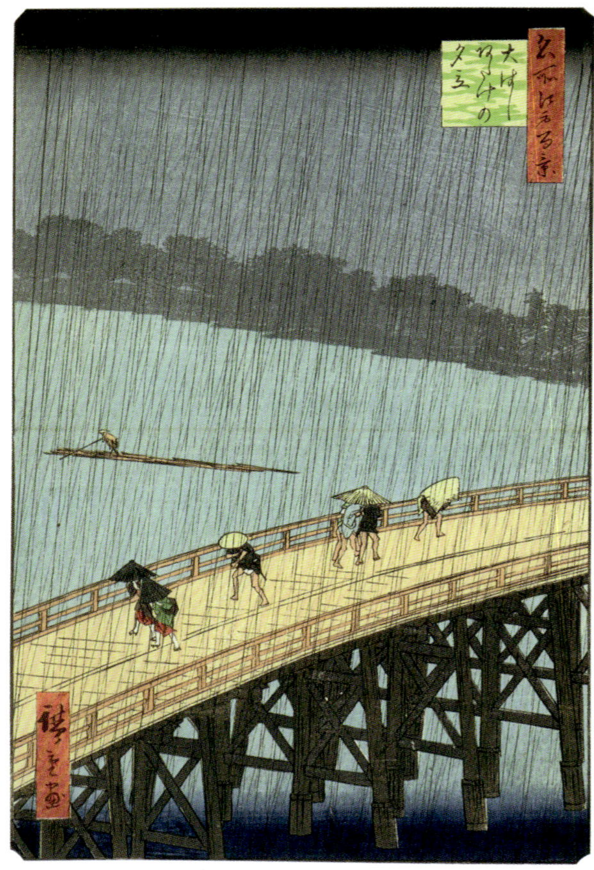

Sudden Shower over Shin-Ōhashi and Atake

Averse sur le pont Shin-Ōhashi à Atake

Regenschauer über der großen Brücke in Atake

El puente Ohashi en Atake bajo una lluvia repentina

Chuva súbito na ponte Ōhashi.

Onverwachte avondbui op de grote brug bij Atake

Utagawa Hiroshige (1797-1858)

1857, Color woodblock/Gravure sur bois colorisée,
35,9 × 24,8 cm, Fitzwilliam Museum, Cambridge

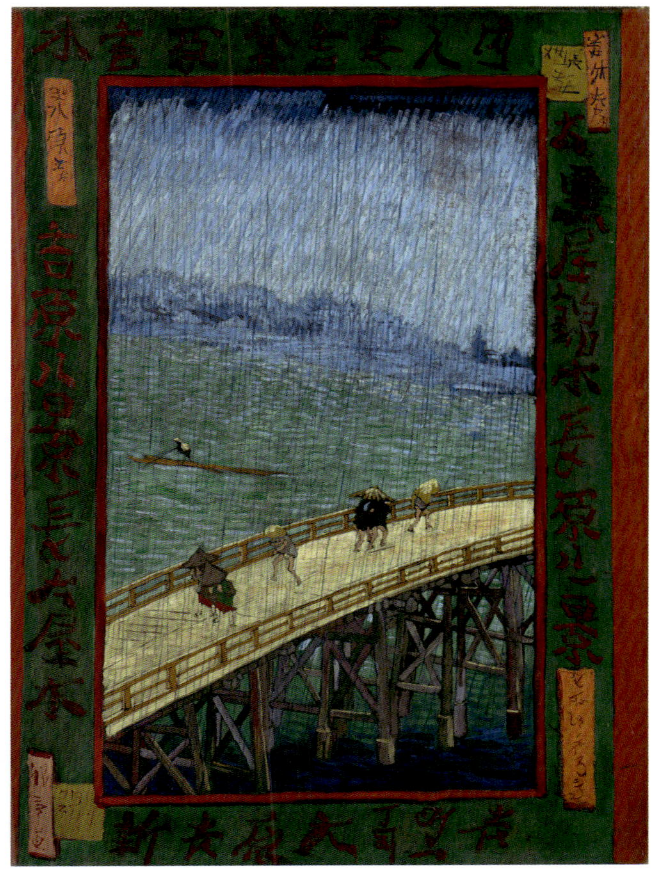

Japonaiserie: Bridge in the Rain

Japonaiserie : Le pont sous la pluie

Japonaiserie: Brücke im Regen

Japonaiserie: Puente bajo la lluvia

Japonaiserie: Ponte na chuva

Japonaiserie: Brug in de regen

Vincent van Gogh (1853-1890)

1887, Oil on canvas/Huile sur toile,
73,3 × 53,8 cm, Van Gogh Museum,
Amsterdam (copy after/copie)

TIZIANO ~ RUBENS

The Rape of Europa

Le Viol d'Europe

Der Raub der Europa

El rapto de Europa

O roubo da Europa

De ontvoering van Europa

Tiziano Vecellio (1489-1576)

———

1562, Oil on canvas/Huile sur toile,
178 × 205 cm, Isabella Stewart Gardner
Museum, Boston

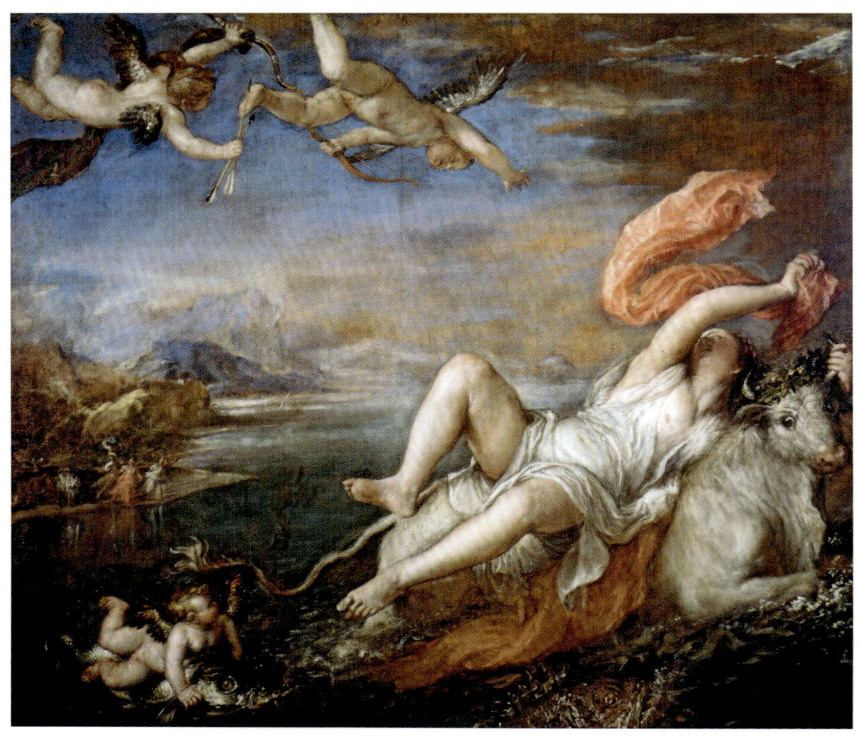

The Rape of Europa

Le Viol d'Europe

Der Raub der Europa

El rapto de Europa

O Roubo da Europa

De ontvoering van Europa

Peter Paul Rubens (1577-1640)

———

c. 1628/29, Oil on canvas/Huile sur toile,
182,5 × 201,5 cm, Museo del Prado,
Madrid (copy after/copie)

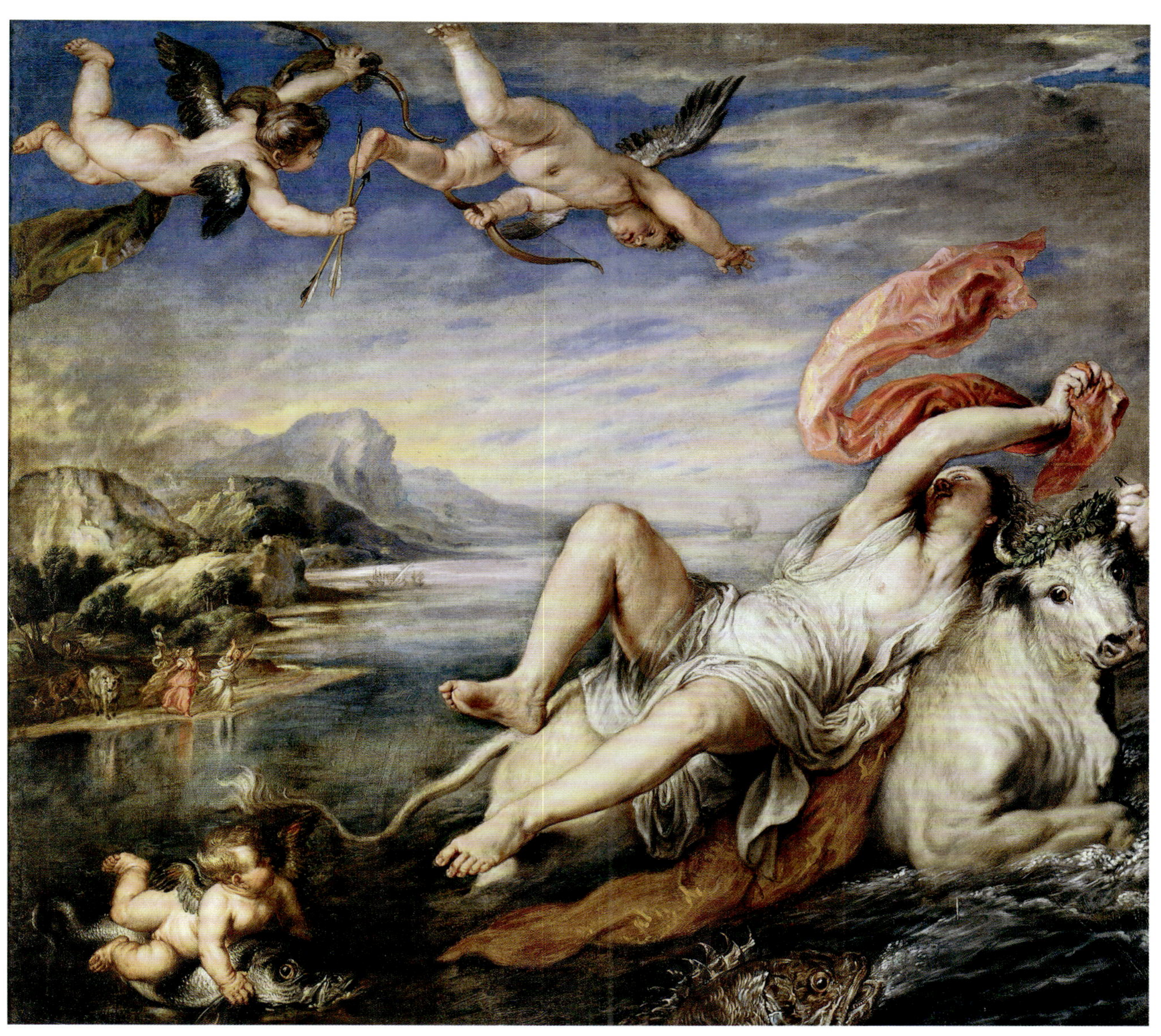

IL PERUGINO ~ DEGAS

When Degas copied the small-format painting in the Louvre around the mid-1850s, it was still attributed to Raphael, as his name can be seen on the back of the wooden board. It was not until 1898 that it was attributed to his teacher Perugino. Apart from this typical problem of provenance, it is particularly surprising that Degas was not interested in the protagonists of the painting, but rather turned his attention to the painterly landscape.

Quand Degas copie cette œuvre de petit format au Louvre au milieu des années 1850, elle est alors considérée comme un tableau de Raphaël (son nom figure au dos du panneau). Ce n'est qu'en 1898 que cette dernière sera rendue à son maître le Pérugin. Au-delà de cette anecdote liée à un problème classique d'attribution, il est amusant de constater que ce ne sont pas les protagonistes de la scène qui intéressent Degas mais plutôt le divin petit paysage qui les entoure.

Als Degas das kleinformatige Gemälde im Louvre gegen Mitte der 1850er-Jahre kopierte, wurde es noch Raffael zugeschrieben, da sein Name auf der Rückseite der Holzplatte zu sehen ist. Erst 1898 wird es seinem Lehrer Perugino zugeordnet. Neben diesem typischen Problem der Provenienz überrascht vor allem, dass Degas sich nicht für die Protagonisten des Gemäldes interessierte, sondern sein Augenmerk auf die malerische Landschaft richtete.

Cuando Degas copió la pintura de pequeño formato en el Louvre a mediados de los años 1850, todavía se le atribuía a Rafael, ya que su nombre se puede ver en la parte posterior del panel. No fue hasta 1898 que se atribuyó a su maestro Perugino. Aparte de este típico problema de procedencia, es particularmente sorprendente que Degas no se interesara por los protagonistas de la pintura, sino que más bien dirigiera su atención al paisaje pictórico.

Quando Degas copiou a pintura em pequeno formato no Louvre, por volta de meados da década de 1850, ainda era atribuída a Rafael, como o seu nome pode ser visto no verso da placa de madeira. Não foi até 1898 que foi atribuído ao seu professor Perugino. Para além deste problema típico da proveniência, é particularmente surpreendente que Degas não estivesse interessado nos protagonistas da pintura, mas tenha voltado a sua atenção para a paisagem pictórica.

Toen Degas dit kleine schilderij omstreeks 1855 kopieerde in het Louvre, werd dat nog toegeschreven aan Rafaël, omdat diens naam op de achterkant van het paneel te zien is. Pas in 1898 werd het toegeschreven aan zijn leraar Perugino. Afgezien van dit herkomstprobleem is het vooral verrassend dat Degas niet geïnteresseerd was in de protagonisten van het schilderij, maar zich richtte op het geschilderde landschap.

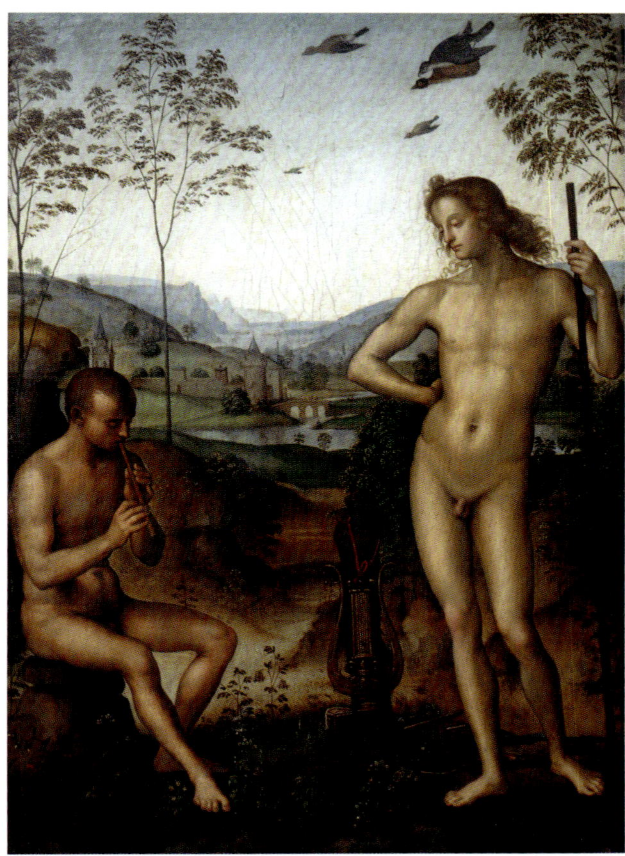

Apollo and Marsyas
Apollon et Marsyas
Apoll und Marsyas
Apolo y Marsyas
Apolo e Marsyas
Apollo en Marsyas

**Pietro Vannucci (Il Perugino)
(1450-1523)**

———

c. 1495-1500, Oil on canvas/Huile sur toile,
39 × 29 cm, Musée du Louvre, Paris

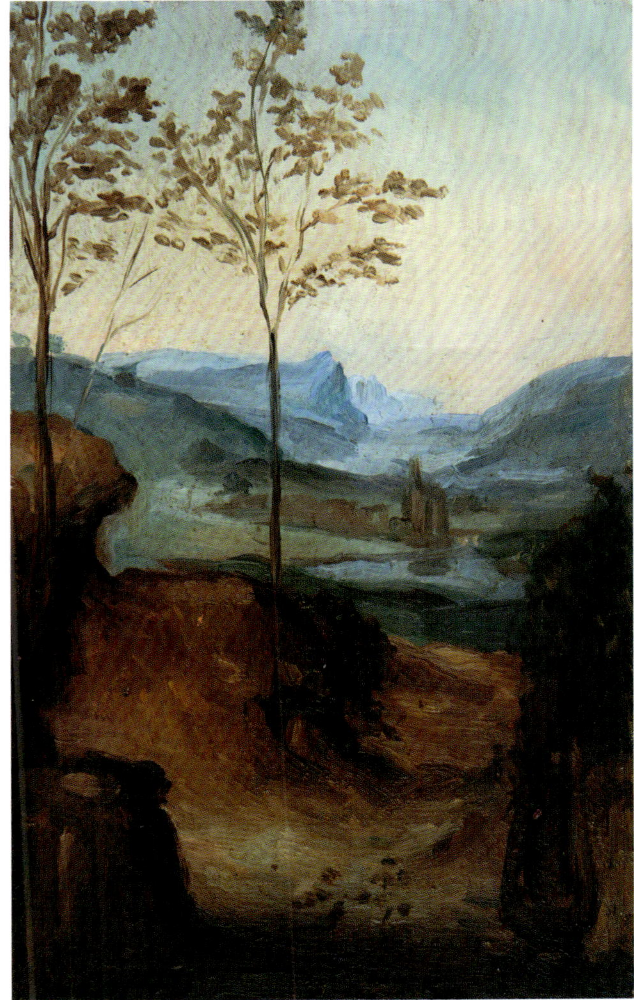

Apollo and Marsyas
Apollon et Marsyas
Apoll und Marsyas
Apolo y Marsyas
Apolo e Marsyas
Apollo en Marsays

Edgar Degas (1834-1917)

c. 1855, Oil on wood/Huile sur bois,
23,4 × 14,4 cm, Private collection
(copy after/copie)

HALS ~ SARGENT

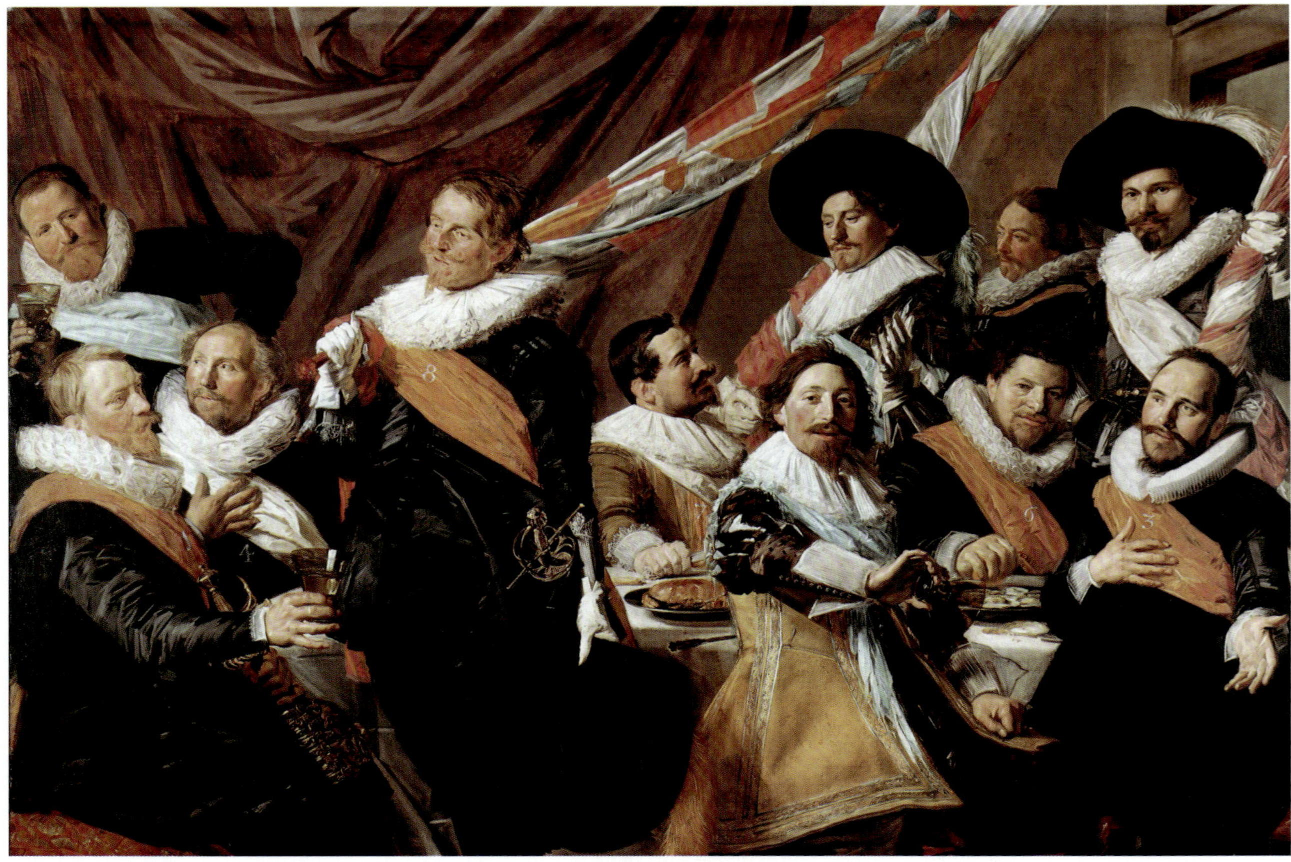

The Banquet of the Officers of the
St. George Civic Guard Company

*Banquet des officiers du corps des
archers de Saint-Georges*

*Festmahl der Offiziere der St.-Georgs-
Schützengilde von Haarlem*

*Fiesta de los oficiales del cuerpo de arqueros
de la iglesia de San Jorge de Haarlem*

*Banquete para os oficiais do Corpo
de Arqueiros de Saint-Georges*

*Feestmaal van de officieren van
de St. Jorisschutterij*

Frans Hals (1580-1666)

———

c. 1627, Oil on canvas/Huile sur toile,
179 × 257,5 cm, Frans Hals Museum,
Haarlem

*The Standard Bearer from the
St. George Civic Guard Company*

*Banquet des officiers du corps des
archers de Saint-Georges,* détail

*Festmahl der Offiziere der St.-Georgs-
Schützengilde von Haarlem,* Detail

*Fiesta de los oficiales del cuerpo
de arqueros de la iglesia de San Jorge
de Haarlem,* detalle

*Banquete para os oficiais do Corpo de
Arqueiros de Saint-Georges,* detalhe

*Feestmaal van de officieren van de
St. Jorisschutterij,* detail

John Singer Sargent (1856-1925)

n. d., Oil on canvas/Huile sur toile,
76,2 × 63,5 cm, Private collection
(copy after/copie)

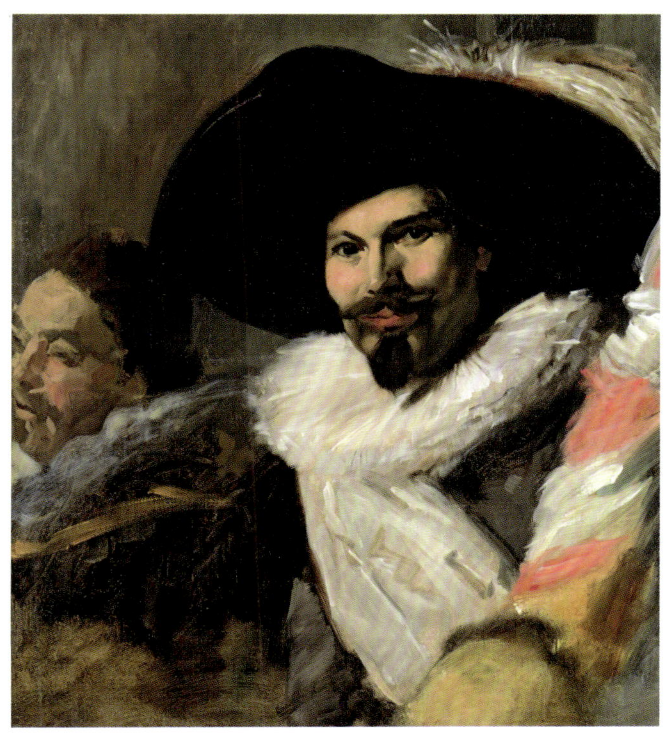

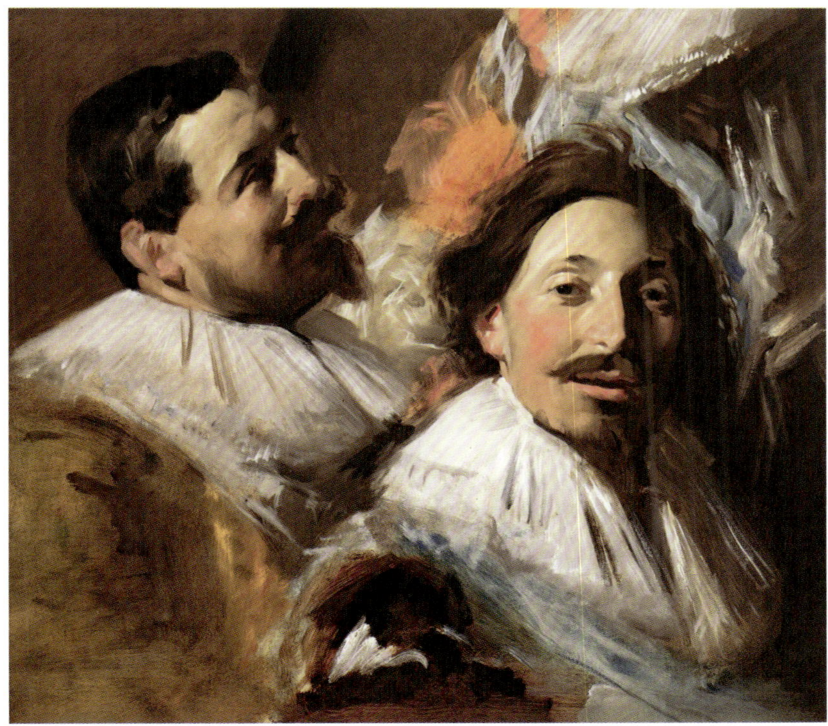

*Two Heads from The Banquet of the
Officers of the St. George Civic Guard
Company*

*Banquet des officiers du corps des
archers de Saint-Georges,* détail

*Festmahl der Offiziere der St.-Georgs-
Schützengilde von Haarlem,* Detail

*Fiesta de los oficiales del cuerpo
de arqueros de la iglesia de San Jorge
de Haarlem,* detalle

*Banquete para os oficiais do Corpo
de Arqueiros de Saint-Georges,* detalhe

*Feestmaal van de officieren van
de St. Jorisschutterij,* detail

John Singer Sargent (1856-1925)

c. 1880, Oil on canvas/Huile sur toile,
58,5 × 63,5 cm, Private collection
(copy after/copie)

UCCELLO ~ DEGAS

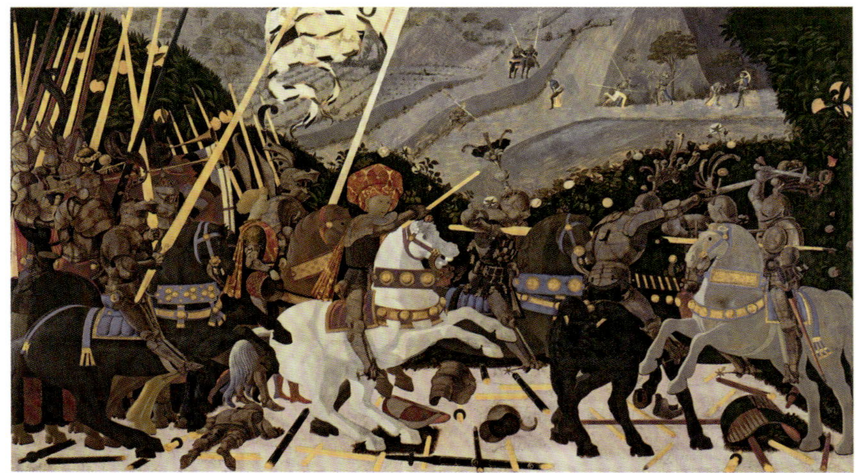

Paolo Uccello (1397-1475)

——

c. 1438-40, Tempera on wood/Tempera sur bois, 182 × 320 cm, The National Gallery, London

Degas' passion for the old Italian masters is already recognizable in his early work. In addition to this watercolor copy of the London version of the painting, he made another of the Uffizi version. Wherever he was, Degas was inspired by the masters of European painting.

La passion de Degas pour les maîtres anciens italiens est vive et ce dès ses premières œuvres. À cette magistrale copie à l'aquarelle du tableau de Londres il faut ajouter celle qu'il fit d'après celui des Offices. Où qu'il se trouve, Degas cherche toujours à se confronter aux maîtres de la peinture européenne.

Degas Passion für die alten italienischen Meister ist bereits in seinem Frühwerk erkennbar. Neben dieser als Aquarell ausgeführten Kopie der Londoner Version des Gemäldes, fertigt er eine weitere der Version in den Uffizien an. Wo auch immer er sich aufhielt – Degas ließ sich von den Meistern der europäischen Malerei inspirieren.

La pasión de Degas por los viejos maestros italianos ya se reconoce en sus primeros trabajos. Además de esta copia en acuarela de la versión londinense del cuadro, realizó otra de la versión Uffizi. Dondequiera que estuviera, Degas se inspiró en los maestros de la pintura europea.

A paixão de Degas pelos antigos mestres italianos já é reconhecida em seus primeiros trabalhos. Além desta cópia em aquarela da versão londrina da pintura, ele fez outra da versão Uffizi. Onde quer que estivesse, Degas foi inspirado pelos mestres da pintura europeia.

Degas' liefde voor de oude Italiaanse meesters is al zichtbaar in zijn vroege werk. Naast deze in aquarel uitgevoerde kopie van de Londense versie van het schilderij maakte hij nog een andere versie van het schilderij in het Uffizi. Waar hij ook was, Degas liet zich inspireren door de meesters van de Europese schilderkunst.

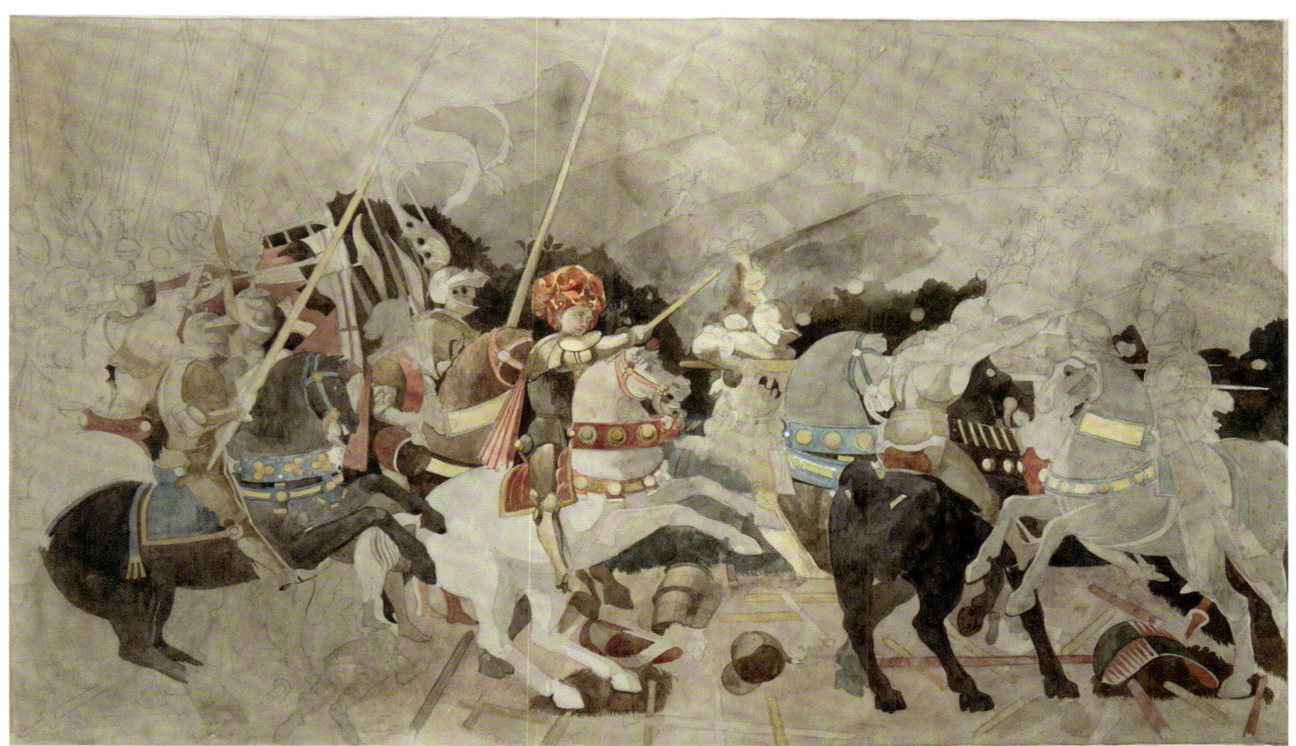

The Battle of San Romano
La Bataille de San Romano
Die Schlacht von San Romano
La batalla de San Romano
A Batalha de San Romano
De slag om San Romano

Edgar Degas (attributed to/attribué à)
(1834-1917)

———

c. 1855, Watercolor over pencil/Aquarelle
sur traits de crayon, 32 × 55 cm,
Private collection (copy after/copie)

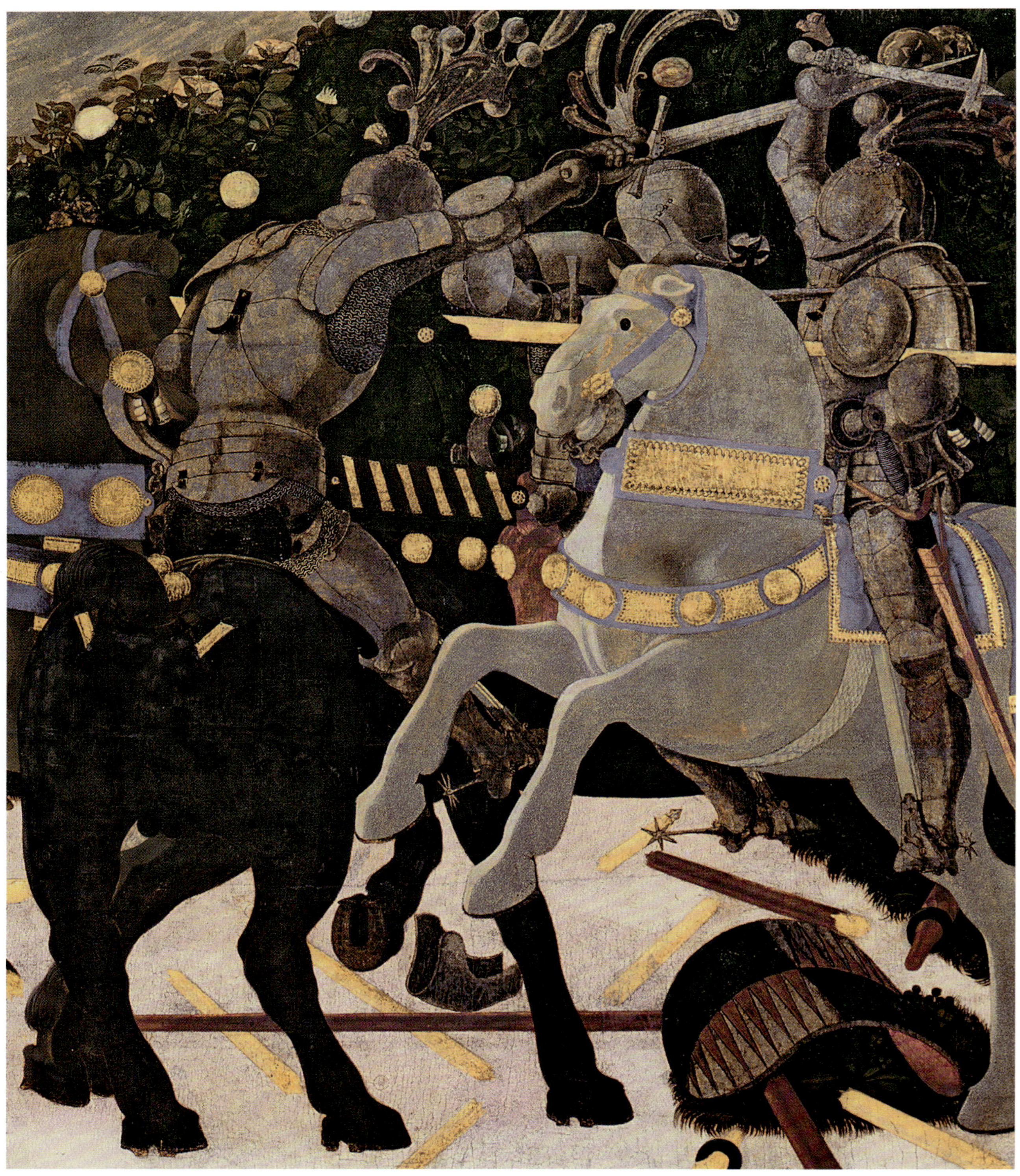

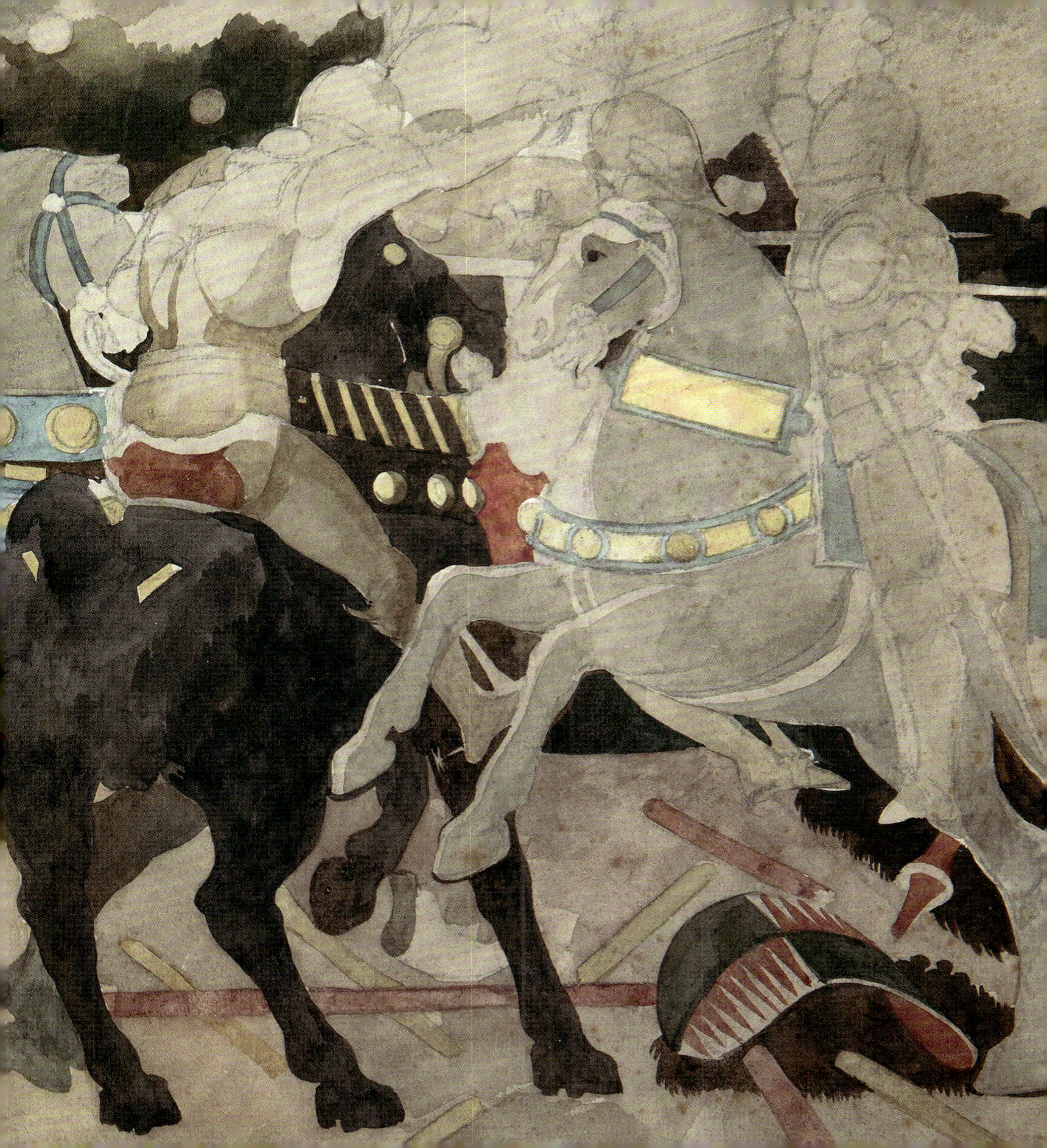

INGRES ~ HEQUET ~ DEGAS

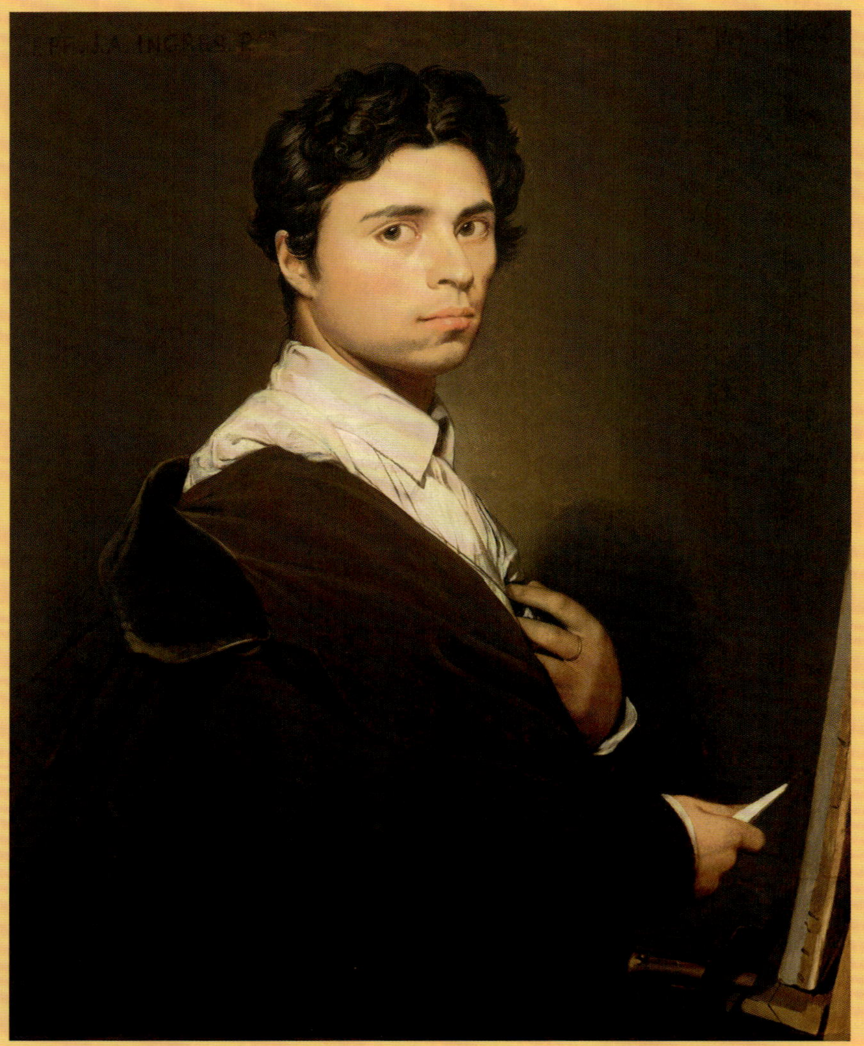

Self-Portrait Aged 24
Autoportrait à 24 ans
Selbstbildnis im Alter von 24 Jahren
Autorretrato a la edad de 24 años
Auto-retrato aos 24 anos de idade
Zelfportret op 24-jarige leeftijd

**Jean-Auguste-Dominique Ingres
(1780-1867)**

———

1804, Oil on canvas/Huile sur toile,
77 × 63 cm, Musée Condé, Chantilly

Portrait as a Young Man
Portrait de Ingres à 24 ans
Porträt des 24-jährigen Ingres
Retrato de Ingres, de 24 años
Retrato de Ingres de 24 anos
Portret van Ingres op 24-jarige leeftijd

Madame Hequet (fl 1845-1865)

———

c. 1850-60, Oil on canvas/Huile sur toile,
86,4 × 69,9 cm, Metropolitan
Museum of Art, New-York
(copy after/copie)

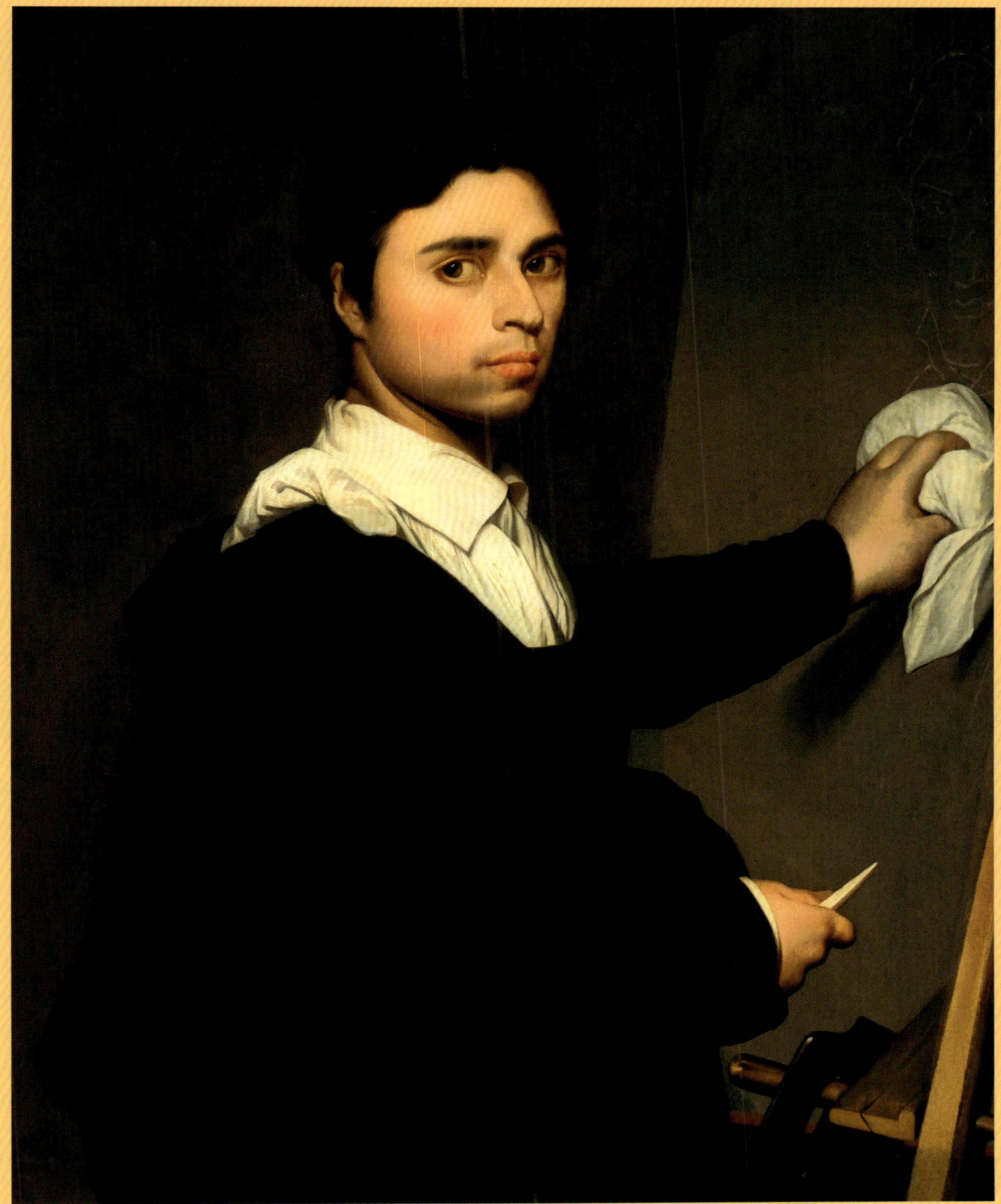

INGRES ~ HEQUET ~ DEGAS

Hequet was a student of Ingres. Her very precise and sensitive version of the self-portrait illustrates the purpose of a copy: learning the painting technique of another artist - a master of his trade. Degas probably also knew of Ingres' painting when he painted his self-portrait. At least he was aware of its appearance through its distribution as a graphic print.

La version très proche mais aussi très sensible que fit une des élèves d'Ingres, madame Hequet, permet de comprendre à quoi doit servir une copie : apprendre à maîtriser la technique picturale d'un autre artiste, d'un maître. Quand Degas décide de peindre ce très élégant autoportrait, il est fort à parier qu'il devait connaître l'original d'Ingres, ou du moins avait-il eu connaissance de cette image à travers sa diffusion gravée.

Hequet war eine Schülerin von Ingres. Ihre sehr genaue und überaus feinfühlige Version des Selbstporträts verdeutlicht den Zweck einer Kopie: das Erlernen der Maltechnik eines anderen Künstlers – eines Meisters seines Faches. Auch Degas kannte wahrscheinlich Ingres Gemälde, als er sein Selbstporträt malte. Zumindest war er sich dessen Aussehen durch die Verbreitung als Druckgrafik bewusst.

Hequet era estudiante de Ingres. Su versión muy precisa y sensible del autorretrato ilustra el propósito de una copia: aprender la técnica pictórica de otro artista, un maestro de su oficio. Degas probablemente también conocía las pinturas de Ingres cuando pintó su autorretrato. Al menos se dio cuenta de su aparición a través de su distribución en forma de impresión gráfica.

Hequet era estudante de Ingres. Sua versão muito precisa e sensível do auto-retrato ilustra o propósito de uma cópia: aprender a técnica de pintura de outro artista - um mestre de seu ofício. Degas provavelmente também conhecia as pinturas de Ingres quando pintou seu auto-retrato. Pelo menos ele estava ciente da sua aparência através da sua distribuição como uma impressão gráfica.

Hequet was een leerlinge van Ingres. Haar zeer precieze en gevoelige versie van diens zelfportret illustreert het doel van een kopie: het leren van de schildertechniek van een andere kunstenaar, een meester in zijn vak. Ook Degas kende Ingres' schilderij waarschijnlijk toen hij zijn zelfportret schilderde. Hij wist door de verspreiding ervan als grafische print in elk geval hoe het portret eruitzag.

Self-Portrait

Portrait de l'artiste

Selbstporträt mit Bleistifthalter

Autorretrato con portalápices

Auto-retrato com suporte para lápis

Portret van de kunstenaar

Edgar Degas (1834-1917)

———

1855, Oil on paper mounted on canvas/
Huile sur papier marouflé sur toile,
81 × 65 cm, Musée d'Orsay, Paris

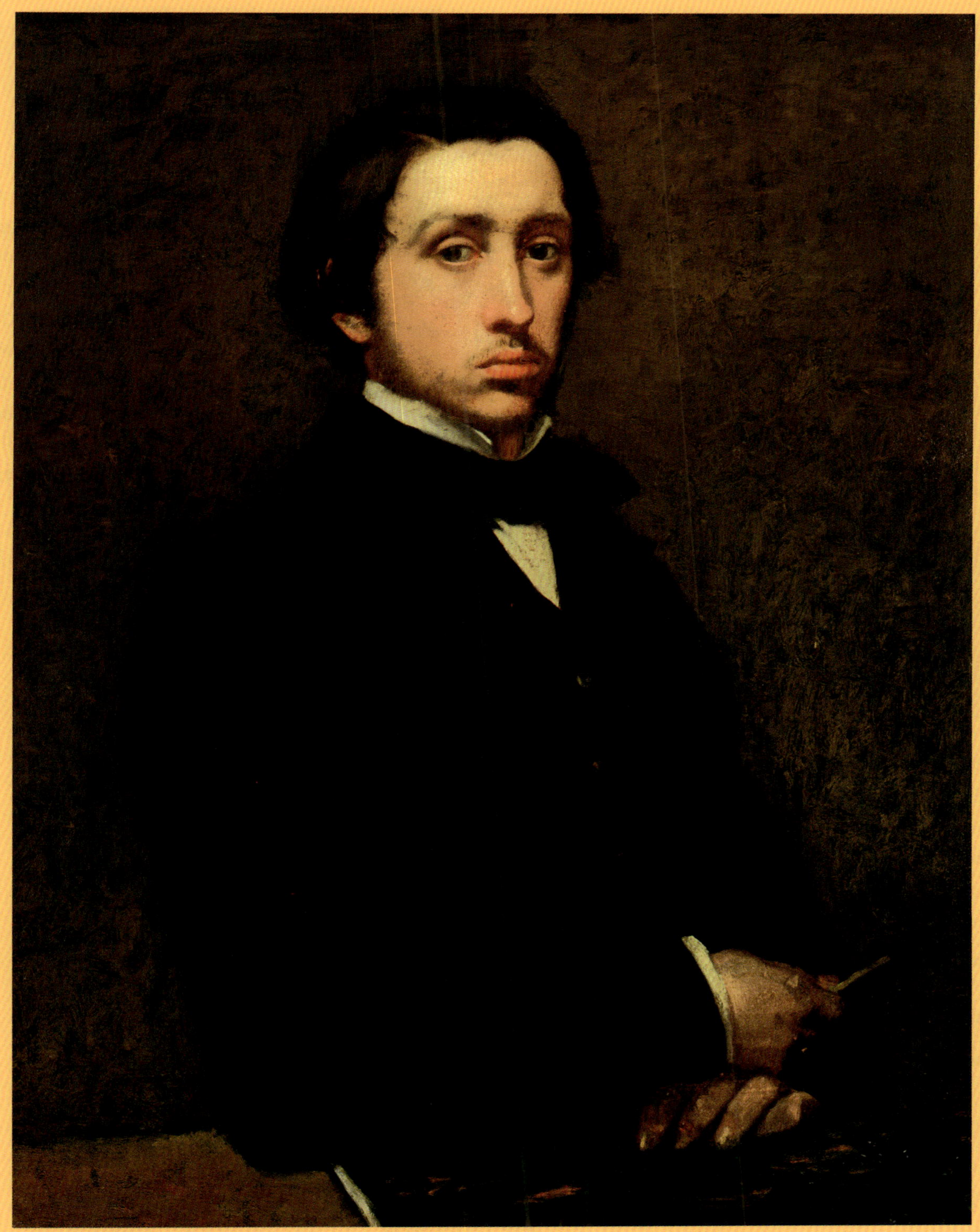

POUSSIN ~ WOODFORDE

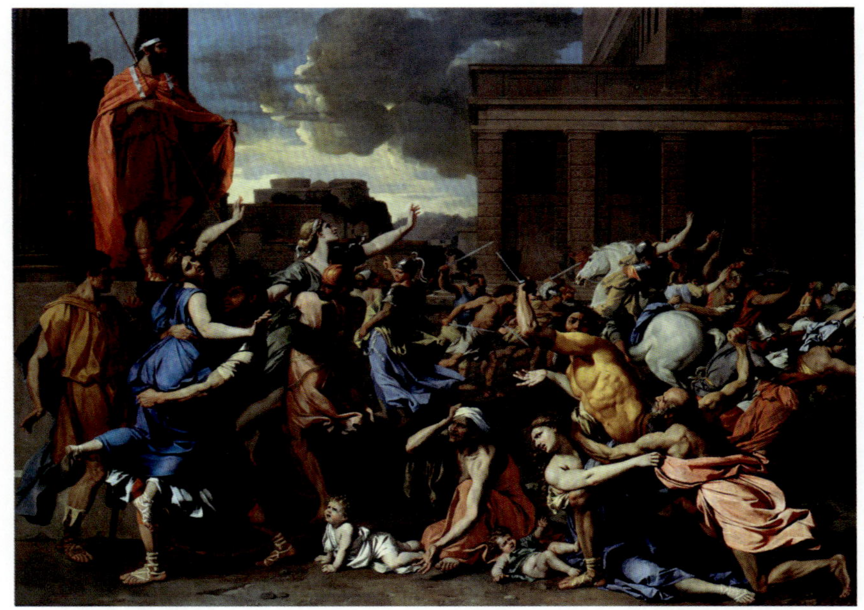

A Group from The Rape of the Sabines,
detail
L'Enlèvement des Sabines, détail
Der Raub der Sabinerinnen, Detail
El rapto de las sabinas, detalle
O Roubo das Sabinianas, detalhe
De ontvoering van de Sabijnse vrouwen,
detail

Samuel Woodforde (1763-1817)

———

n. d., Oil on canvas/Huile sur toile,
113,7 × 109,2 cm, Stourhead, Mere
(copy after/copie)

The Abduction of the Sabine Women

L'Enlèvement des Sabines

Der Raub der Sabinerinnen

El rapto de las sabinas

O Roubo das Sabinianas

De ontvoering van de Sabijnse vrouwen

Nicolas Poussin (1594-1665)

———

c. 1633/34, Oil on canvas/Huile sur toile,
154,6 × 209,9 cm, Metropolitan Museum of
Art, New-York

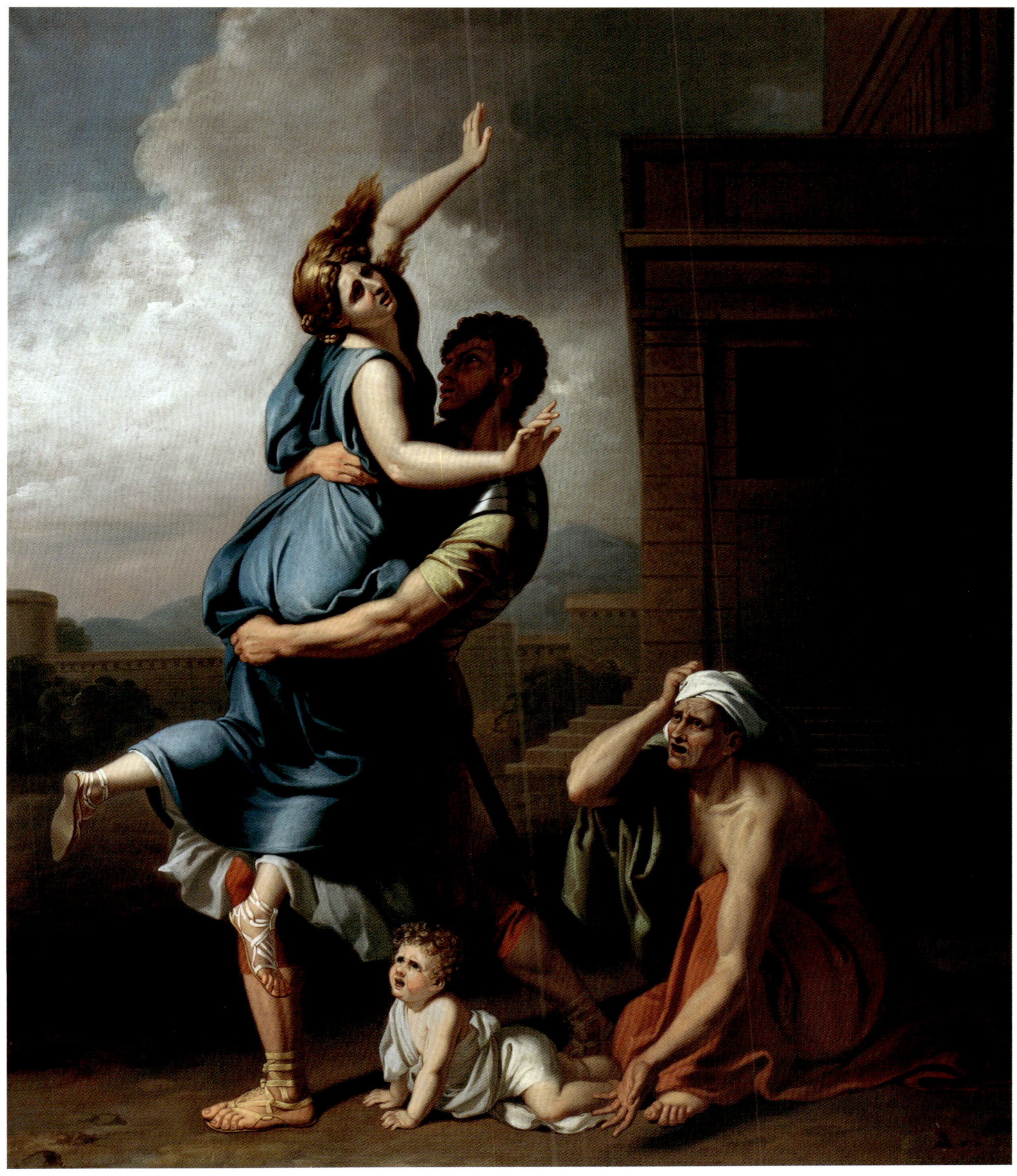

MILLET ~ VAN GOGH

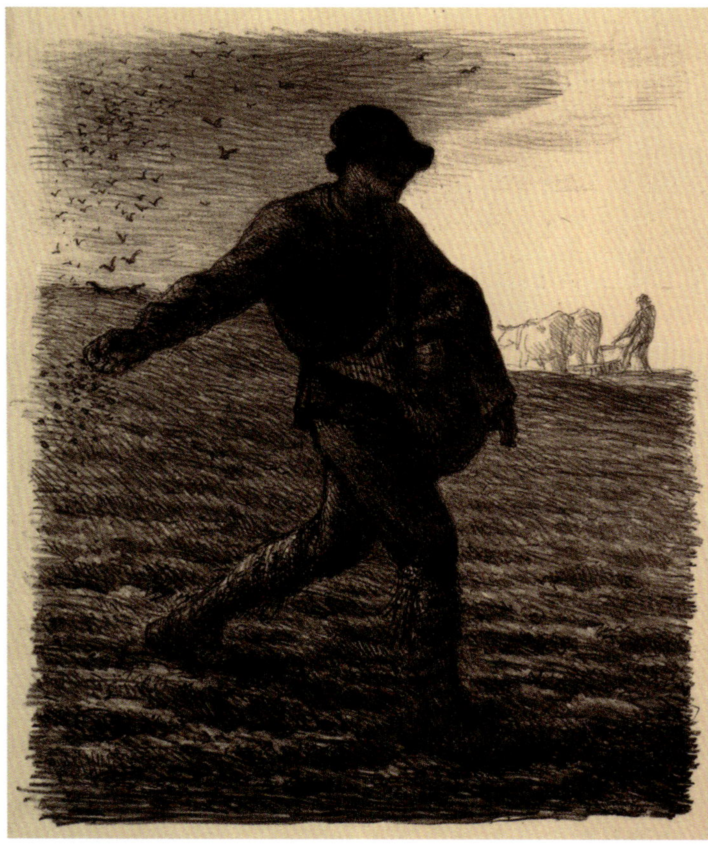

The Sower

Le Semeur

Der Sämann

El sembrador

O semeador

De zaaier

Jean-François Millet (1814-1875)

———

1851, Lithography/Lithographie, 19,4 × 13,3 cm, Metropolitan Museum of Art, New-York

Van Gogh owed his interest in old and contemporary engravings to his brother Theo. In order to train his older brother's curiosity and perception, Theo, who worked as an art dealer, regularly sent him works by other artists. His aim was to inspire Vincent with other styles and new iconographies.

C'est à Théo, son jeune frère, que Van Gogh doit son intérêt pour les gravures anciennes et même contemporaines… En effet, afin d'éveiller sa curiosité et d'exercer son sens du dessin, le cadet, un marchand d'art, avait pris l'habitude de lui faire parvenir des images d'autres artistes afin qu'il puisse s'inspirer, tantôt de leur style, tantôt de leur iconographie.

Seinem Bruder Theo verdankte Van Gogh das Interesse an alten und zeitgenössischen Stichen. Um die Neugier und den Blick seines älteren Bruders zu schulen, ließ ihm Theo, der als Kunsthändler arbeitete, regelmäßig Werke anderer Künstler zukommen. Sein Ziel war es, Vincent durch andere Stile und neue Ikonographien zu inspirieren.

Vincent van Gogh (1853-1890)

———

c. 1890, Oil on canvas/Huile sur toile,
81 × 65 cm, Private collection
(copy after/copie)

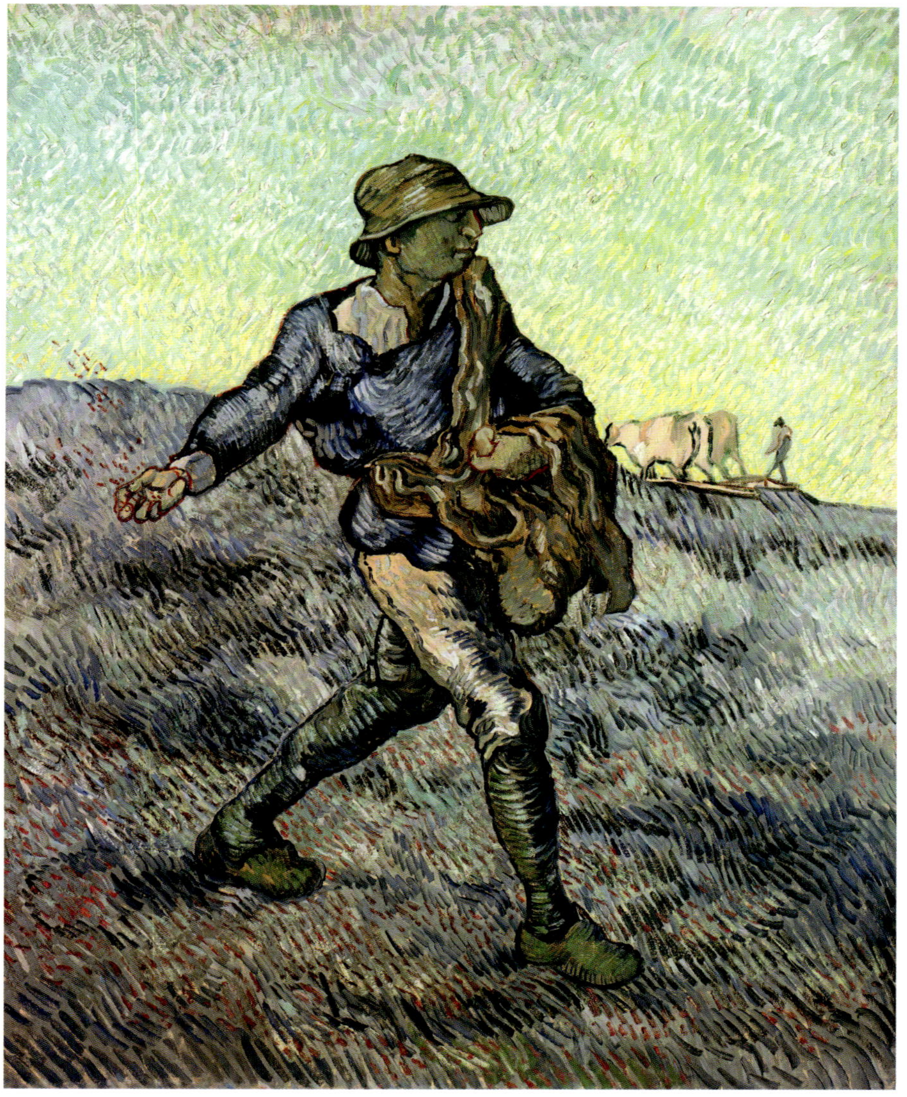

Van Gogh debía su interés por el grabado antiguo y contemporáneo a su hermano Theo. Para entrenar la curiosidad y la mirada de su hermano mayor, Theo, que trabajaba como marchante de arte, le enviaba regularmente obras de otros artistas. Su objetivo era inspirar a Vincent con otros estilos y nuevas iconografías.

Van Gogh devia o seu interesse em gravuras antigas e contemporâneas ao seu irmão Theo. Para treinar a curiosidade e o olhar do irmão mais velho, Theo, que trabalhava como comerciante de arte, enviava-lhe regularmente obras de outros artistas. Seu objetivo era inspirar Vincent com outros estilos e novas iconografias.

Van Gogh dankte zijn interesse in oude en eigentijdse gravures aan zijn broer Theo. Om de nieuwsgierigheid en blik van zijn oudere broer te trainen, stuurde Theo, die als kunsthandelaar werkte, hem regelmatig werken van andere kunstenaars. Zijn doel was om Vincent te inspireren met andere stijlen en nieuwe iconografieën.

FABRITIUS ~ FRAGONARD ~ BOUCHER

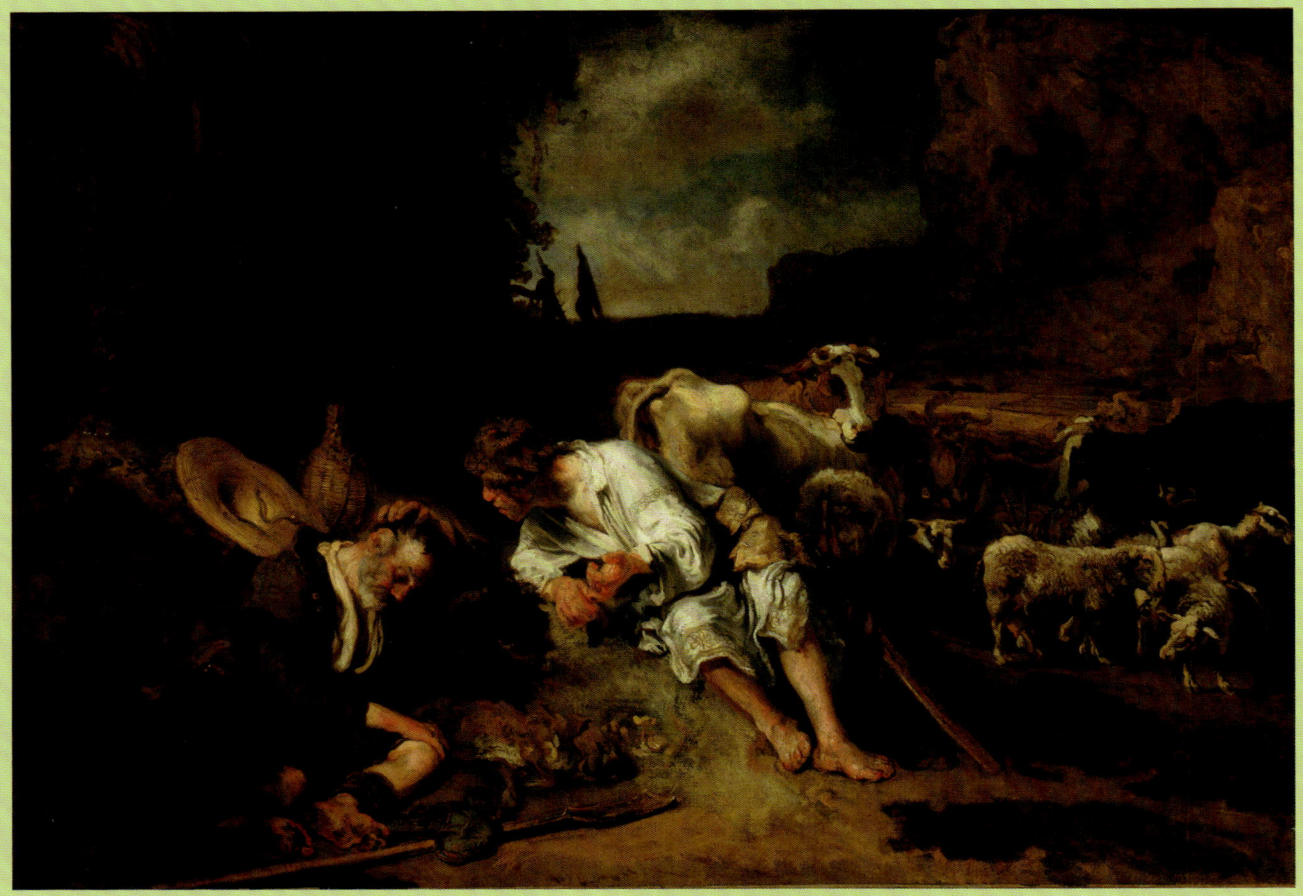

Mercury, Argus and Io

Mercure, Argus et Io

Merkur, Argus und Io

Mercurio, Argus e Io

Mercúrio, Argus e Io

Mercurius, Argus en Io

Carel Fabritius (1622-1654)

———

c. 1645-47, Oil on canvas/Huile sur toile,
73,5 × 104 cm, Los Angeles County
Museum of Art, Los Angeles

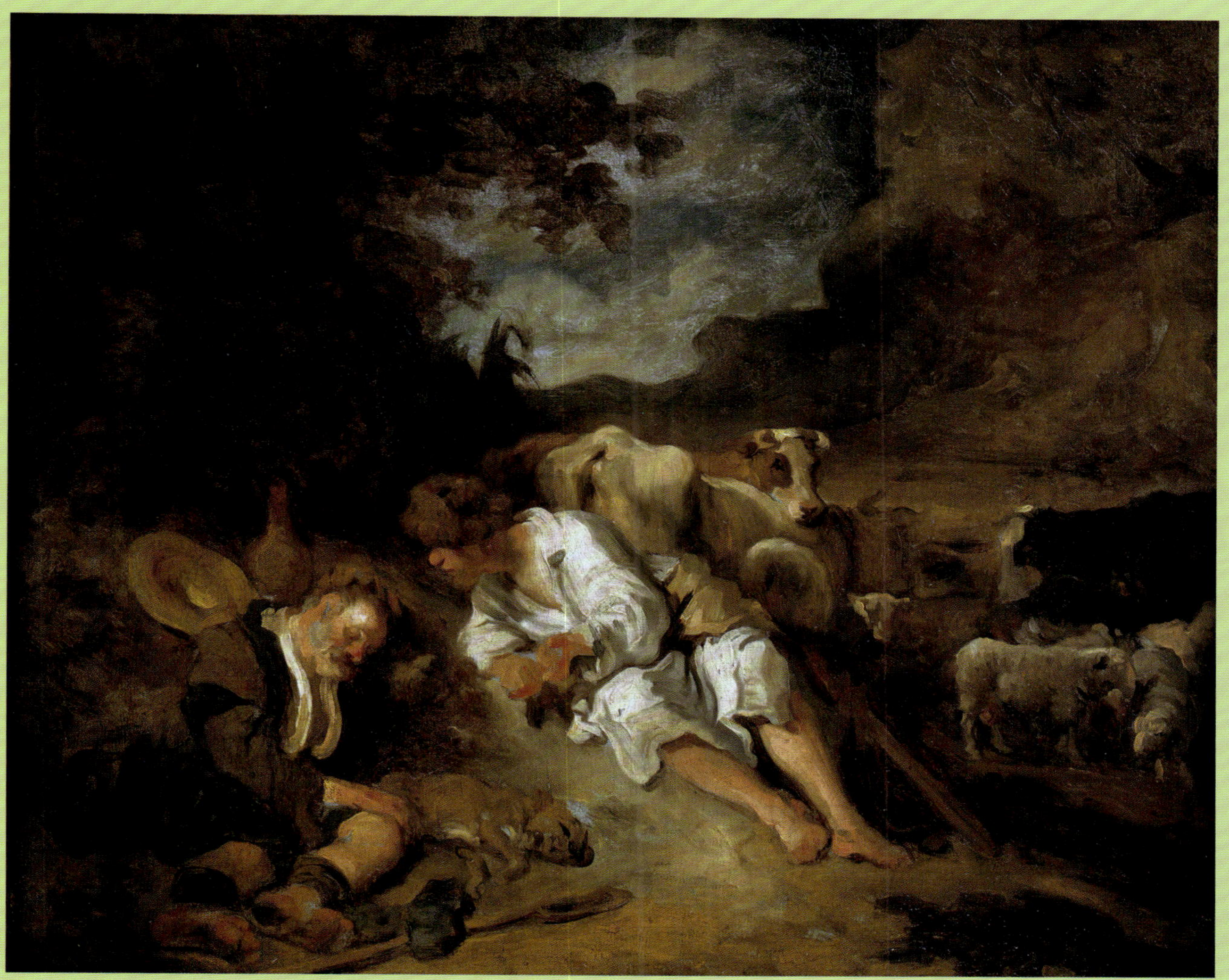

*Mercury and Argus, the guardian
of Io transformed into a cow,
is put to sleep by Mercury*

*Mercure s'apprêtant à tuer le géant
Argus afin de délivrer la nymphe Io,
transformée en vache*

*Merkur und Argus, der Wächter der
in eine Kuh verwandelten Io,
wird von Merkur eingeschläfert*

*Mercurio y Argus, el guardián
de Io, convertido en vaca, se queda
dormido tocada por Mercurio*

*Mercúrio prestes a matar o gigante
Argus para entregar a ninfa Io,
transformada em vaca*

*Mercurius brengt Argus, de bewaker
van de in een koe veranderde Io,
in slaap*

Jean-Honoré Fragonard (1732-1806)

———

c. 1761/62, Oil on canvas/Huile sur toile,
59 × 73 cm, Musée du Louvre, Paris
(copy after/copie)

FABRITIUS ~ FRAGONARD ~ BOUCHER

Boucher first copied the sleeping dog as a drawing before painting it in oil on paper. The result is an independent portrait of the dog that goes beyond a simple copy. When Fragonard, a student of Boucher's, made his version of the original, he retained the composition of the painting formerly attributed to Rembrandt. Today it is attributed to Carel Fabritius.

Quand Boucher isole la figure de cette ravissante chienne en train de dormir, il le fait d'abord au crayon, puis il la peint à l'huile sur papier. Bien plus qu'une simple copie, cette œuvre sensible est un véritable portait de chien. Quand Fragonard qui fut l'élève de Boucher copiera à son tour l'animal, il le fera sans l'extraire du reste de la composition de cette toile, autrefois attribuée à Rembrandt. Aujourd'hui, on en a donné la paternité à Carel Fabritius.

Boucher kopierte den schlafenden Hund zuerst als Zeichnung, bevor er ihn in Öl auf Papier malte. Das Resultat ist ein eigenständiges Porträt des Hundes, das über eine einfache Kopie hinausgeht. Als Fragonard, ein Schüler Bouchers, seine Version des Originals anfertigt, behält er die Komposition des Gemäldes bei, das früher Rembrandt zugeordnet wurde. Heute wird es Carel Fabritius zugeschrieben.

Boucher primero copió el perro durmiente como un dibujo antes de pintarlo al óleo sobre papel. El resultado es un retrato independiente del perro que va más allá de una simple copia. Cuando Fragonard, un estudiante de Boucher, hace su versión del original, conserva la composición de la pintura atribuida anteriormente a Rembrandt. Hoy se atribuye a Carel Fabritius.

Boucher primeiro copiou o cão dorminhoco como um desenho antes de pintá-lo em óleo sobre papel. O resultado é um retrato independente do cão que vai além de uma simples cópia. Quando Fragonard, um estudante de Boucher, faz sua versão do original, ele mantém a composição da pintura anteriormente atribuída a Rembrandt. Hoje é atribuído a Carel Fabritius.

Boucher kopieerde de slapende hond eerst als tekening en schilderde hem daarna met olieverf op papier. Het resultaat is een zelfstandig portret van de hond dat een eenvoudige kopie te boven gaat. Toen Fragonard, een leerling van Boucher, zijn versie van het origineel maakte, pakte hij de compositie van het schilderij erbij, dat vroeger aan Rembrandt werd toegeschreven. Nu wordt het toegeschreven aan Carel Fabritius.

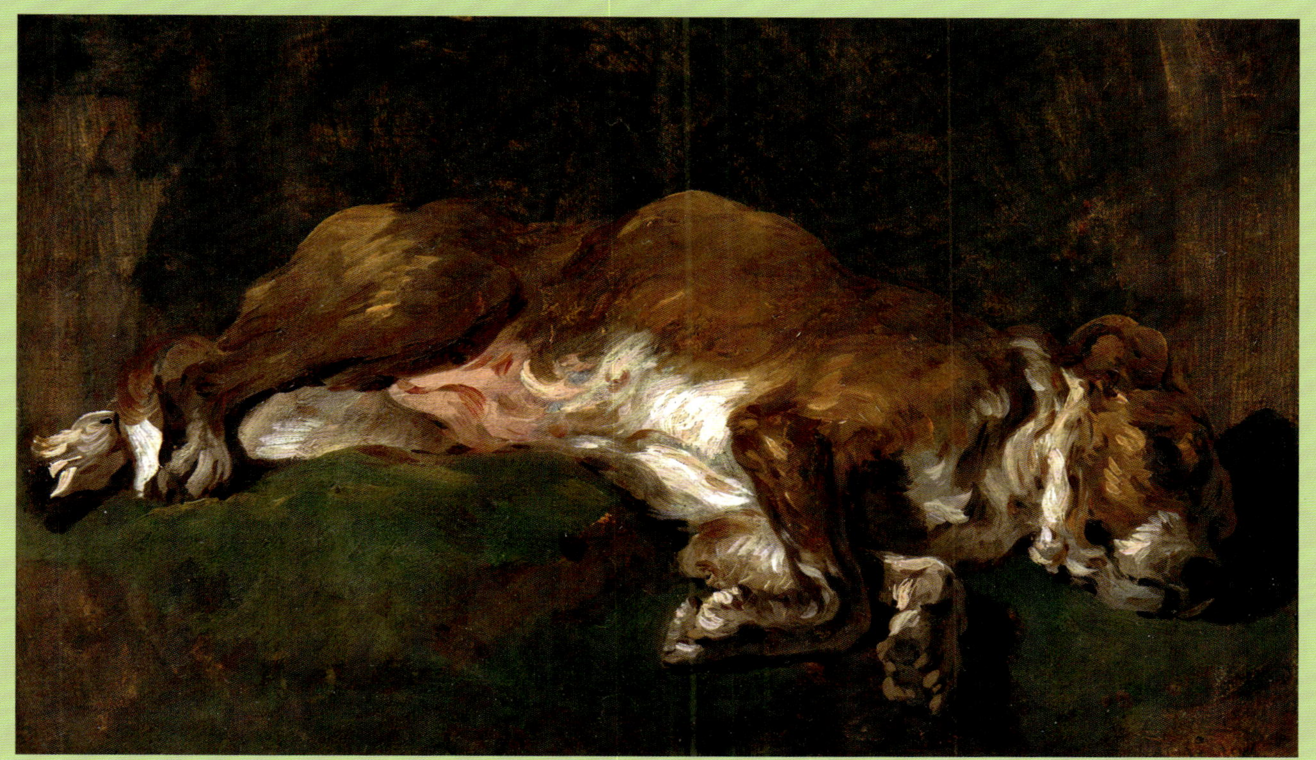

Sleeping Dog
Chienne endormie
Schlafender Hund
Perro durmiendo
Cão dorminhoco
Slapende hond

François Boucher (1703-1770)

———

c. 1750/51, Oil on canvas/Huile sur toile,
22,5 × 37 cm, Private collection
(copy after/copie)

CARAVAGGIO ~ GÉRICAULT

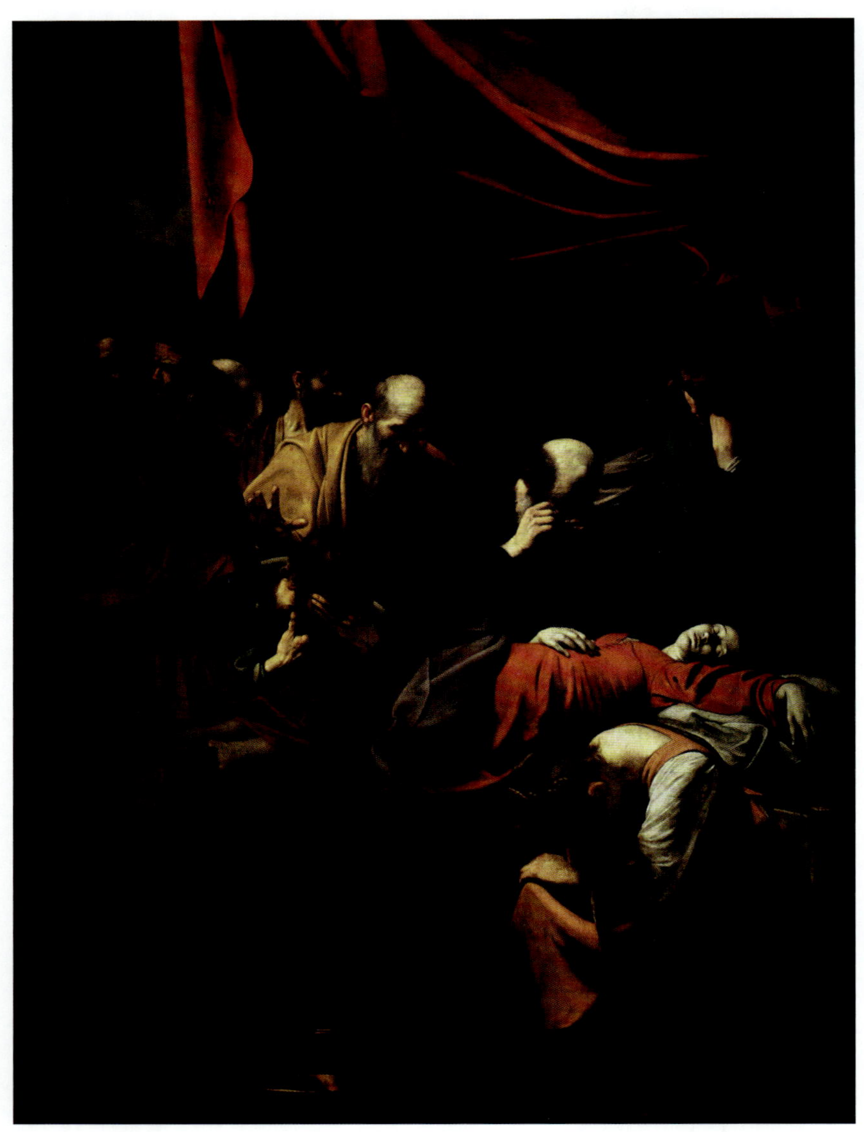

The Death of the Virgin
La Mort de la Vierge
Der Tod der Jungfrau Maria
La muerte de la Virgen María
A morte da Virgem Maria
De dood van Maria

**Michelangelo Merisi da Caravaggio
(1571-1610)**

—

c. 1601-06, Oil on canvas/Huile sur toile,
369 × 245 cm, Musée du Louvre, Paris

The Death of the Virgin
La Mort de la Vierge
Der Tod der Jungfrau Maria
La muerte de la Virgen María
A morte da Virgem Maria
De dood van Maria

Théodore Géricault (1791-1824)

—

c. 1812, Oil on canvas/Huile sur toile,
32,5 × 24,5 cm, Private collection
(copy after/copie)

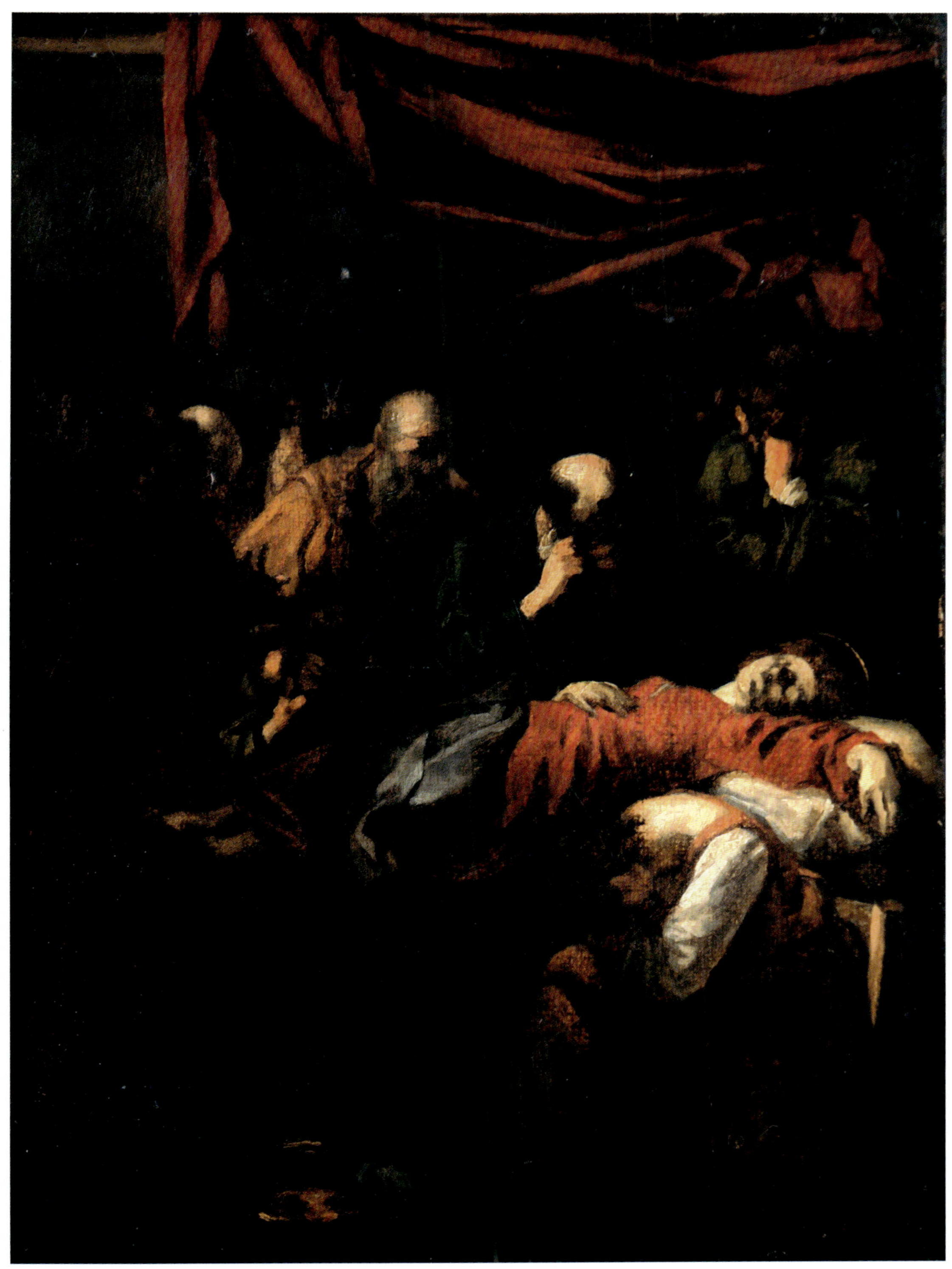

GIOTTO ~ LEIGHTON

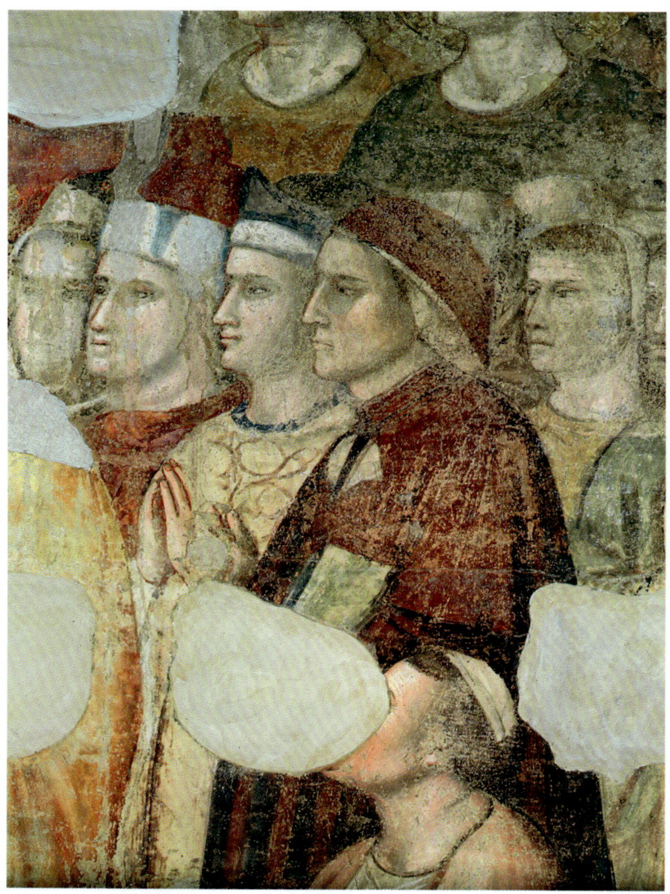

Dante Alighieri, detail of the fresco
in the Chapel of Mary Magdalene

Dante Alighieri, détail de la fresque
dans la chapelle Marie-Madeleine

Dante Alighieri, Detail des Freskos
in der Maria-Magdalena-Kapelle

Dante Alighieri, detalle del fresco
de la Capilla de María Magdalena

Dante Alighieri, detalhe do fresco
na Capela de Maria Madalena

Dante Alighieri, detail van het fresco
in de kapel van Maria Magdalena

Giotto di Bondone (1267-1337)

———

c. 1335, Fresco/Fresque, Museo Nazionale
del Bargello, Firenze

Lord Leighton was fascinated
by Italy all his life, as this pastel
watercolor, depicting a figure
from Giotto's fresco, shows.
The outstanding work demonstrates
once again that copying does not
necessarily have to be a slavish
painting.

Lord Leighton cultiva toute sa vie
son goût pour l'Italie. Pour preuve
cette aquarelle aux couleurs pastel
inspirée par l'une des figures d'une
fresque de Giotto. À travers ce
témoignage graphique d'une grande
délicatesse, Leighton nous prouve
à nouveau que l'art de la copie ne
doit jamais être un exercice servile.

Lord Leighton war sein ganzes
Leben lang von Italien begeistert,
wie dieses Aquarell aus
Pastellfarben beweist, das eine
Figur aus einem Fresko Giottos
zeigt. Die herausragende Arbeit
zeigt einmal mehr, dass das
Kopieren nicht unbedingt ein
sklavisches Abmalen sein muss.

**Frederic Leighton
(1830-1896)**

c. 1852-55, Pencil and watercolor
on paper/Crayon et aquarelle
sur papier, 21 × 13,3 cm,
Leighton House Museum,
London (copy after/copie)

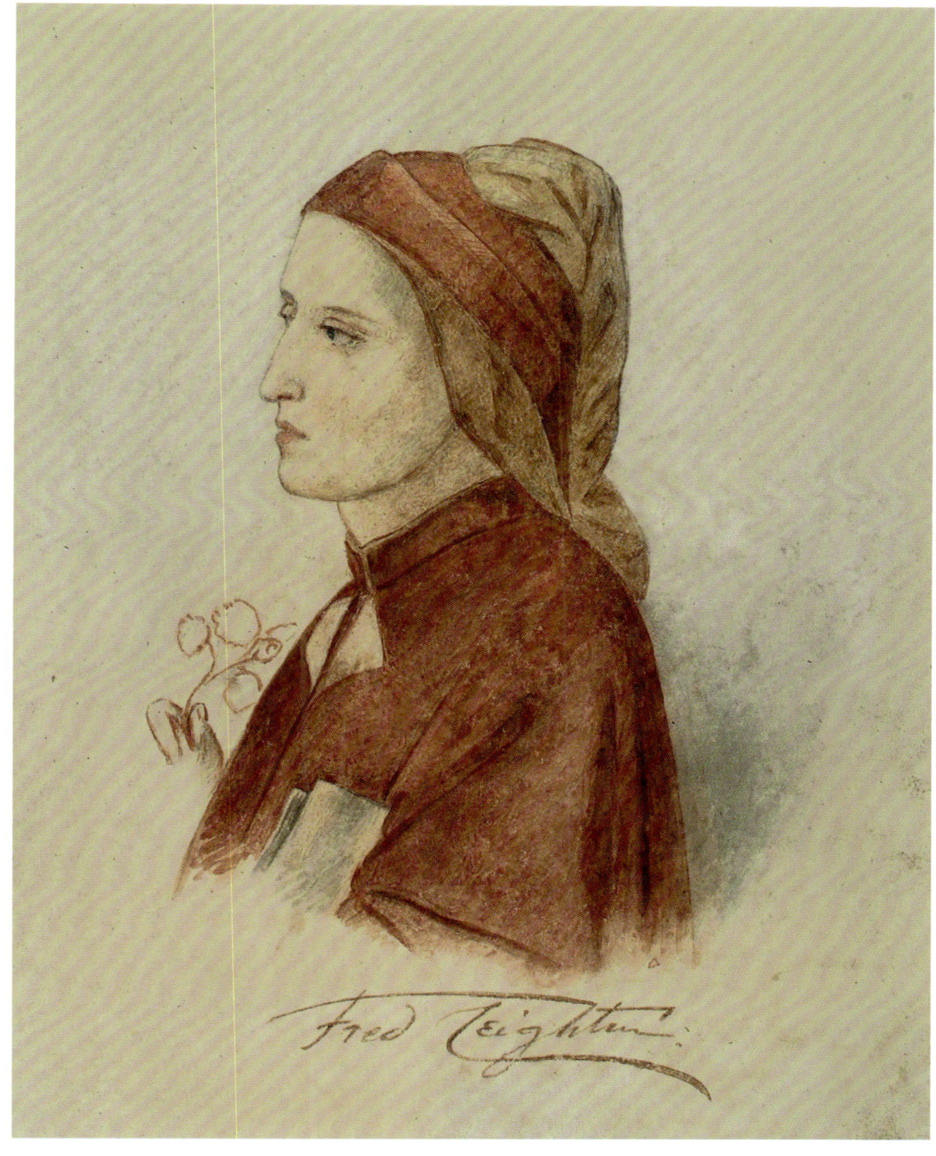

Lord Leighton cultivó su gusto por Italia toda su vida, como lo demuestra esta acuarela en colores pastel inspirada en una de las figuras de un fresco de Giotto.
A través de este testimonio gráfico de gran delicadeza, Leighton demuestra una vez más que el arte de copiar nunca debe ser un ejercicio servil.

Lord Leighton foi fascinado pela Itália durante toda a sua vida, pois esta aquarela pastel mostra uma figura do fresco de Giotto. O excelente trabalho mostra mais uma vez que copiar não tem necessariamente de ser uma pintura servil.

Lord Leighton was zijn hele leven gefascineerd door Italië, zoals deze aquarel in pastelkleuren van een figuur uit Giotto's fresco laat zien. Het opmerkelijke werk toont eens te meer aan dat kopiëren niet noodzakelijkerwijs een slaafs naschilderen is.

IL VERONESE ~ DELACROIX

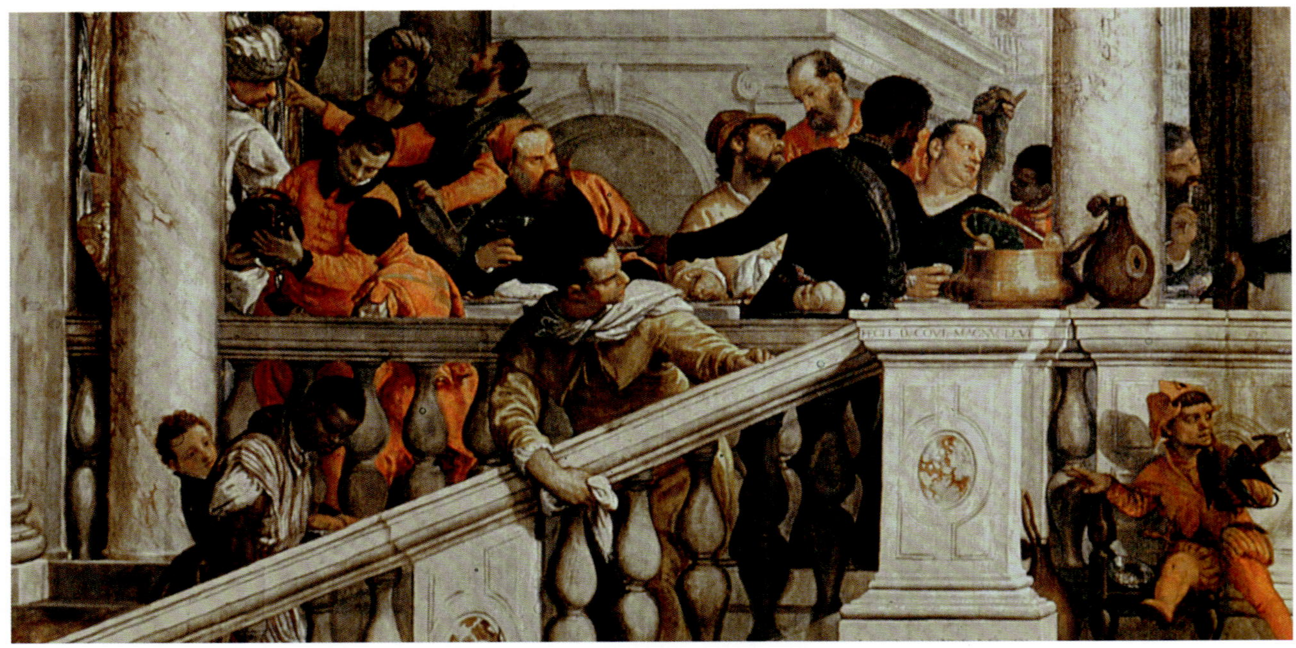

The Feast in the House of Levi, detail

Le Repas chez Levi, détail

Das Gastmahl im Hause des Levi, Detail

El banquete en la casa de los Levitas, detalle

O banquete na casa do Levi, detalhe

Gastmaal in het huis van Levi, detail

Paolo Caliari (il Veronese) (1528-1588)

———

1573, Oil on canvas/Huile sur toile, 560 × 1309 cm, Gallerie dell'Academia, Venezia

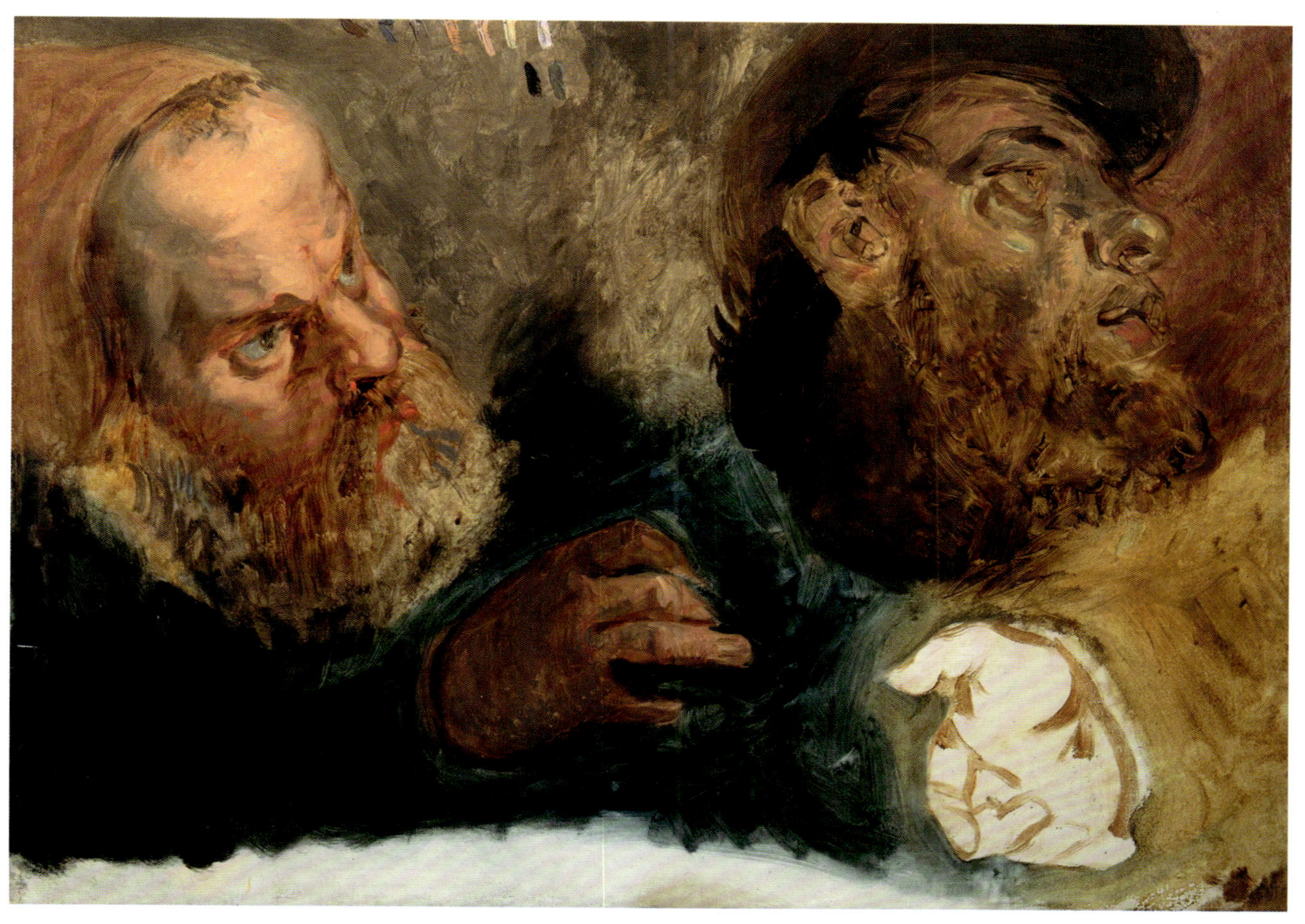

Head and hand study
Études de têtes et d'une main
Kopf- und Handstudie
Estudio de la cabeza y la mano
Estudo da cabeça e da mão
Studie van hoofden en een hand

Eugène Delacroix (1798-1863)

c. 1825, Oil on canvas/Huile sur toile,
32,8 × 24,7 cm, Private collection
(copy after/copie)

RAFFAELLO ~ RUBENS

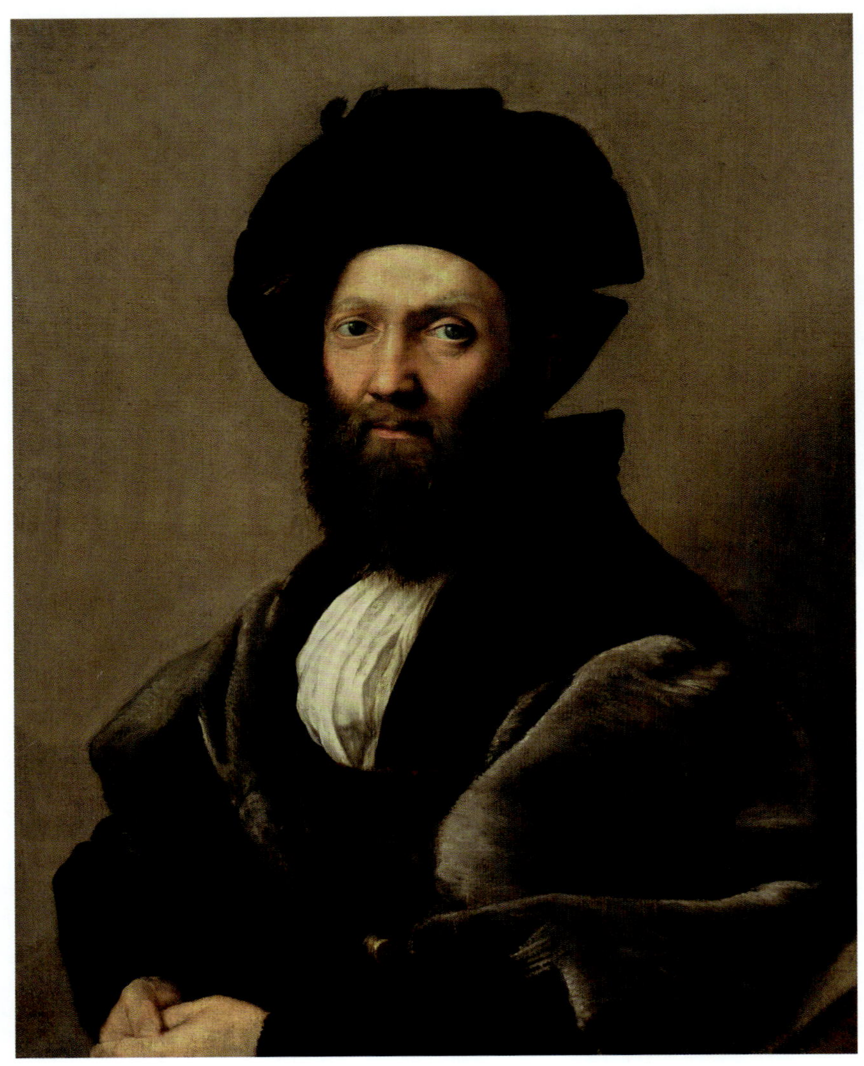

Raffaello Sanzio (1483-1520)

———

c. 1514/15, Oil on canvas/Huile sur toile, 82 × 67 cm, Musée du Louvre, Paris

Peter Paul Rubens (1577-1640)

———

1630, Oil on panel/Huile sur panneau, 90,2 × 67,5 cm, The Courtauld Gallery, London (copy after/copie)

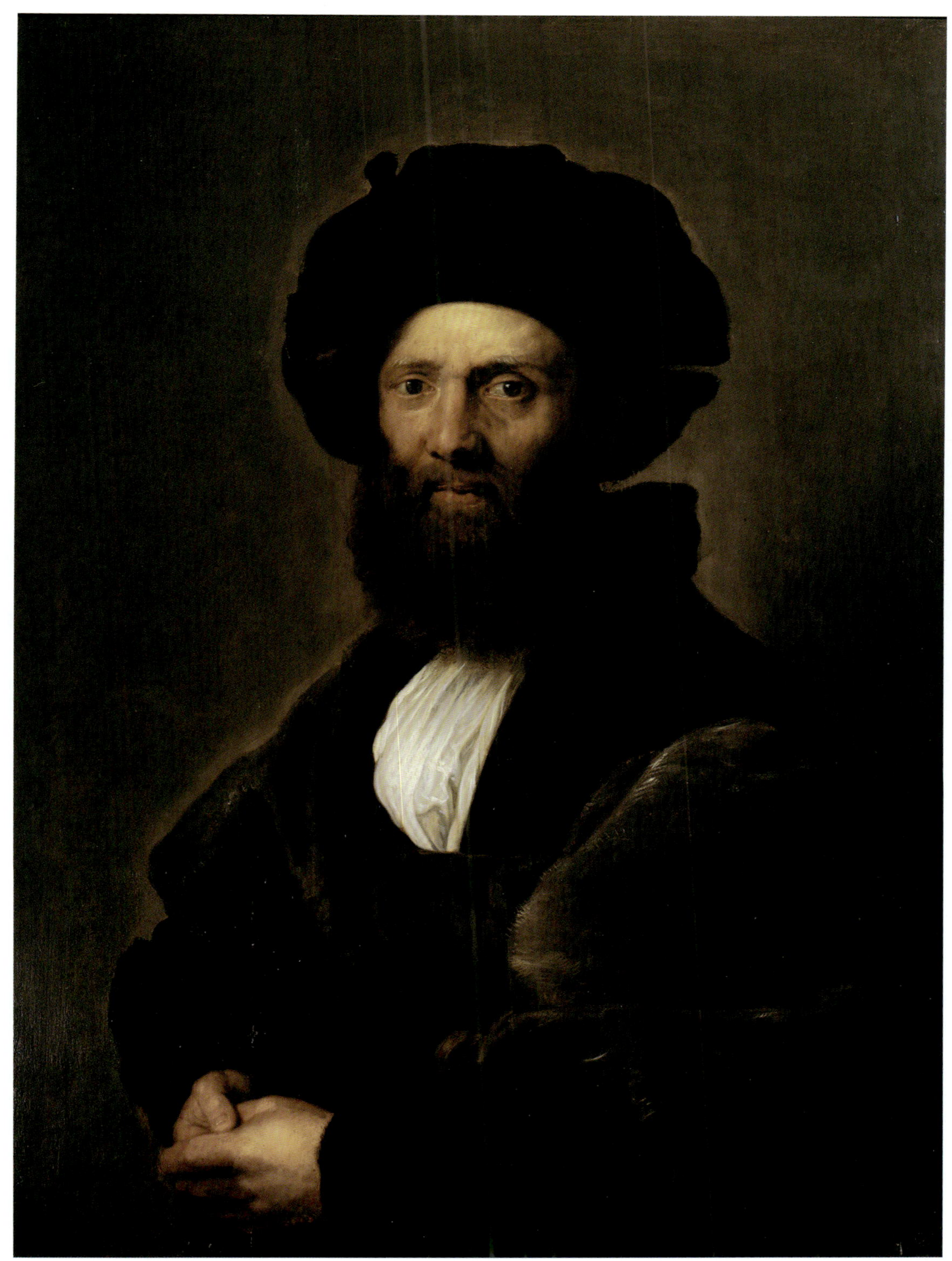

DEL PIOMBO ~ DEGAS

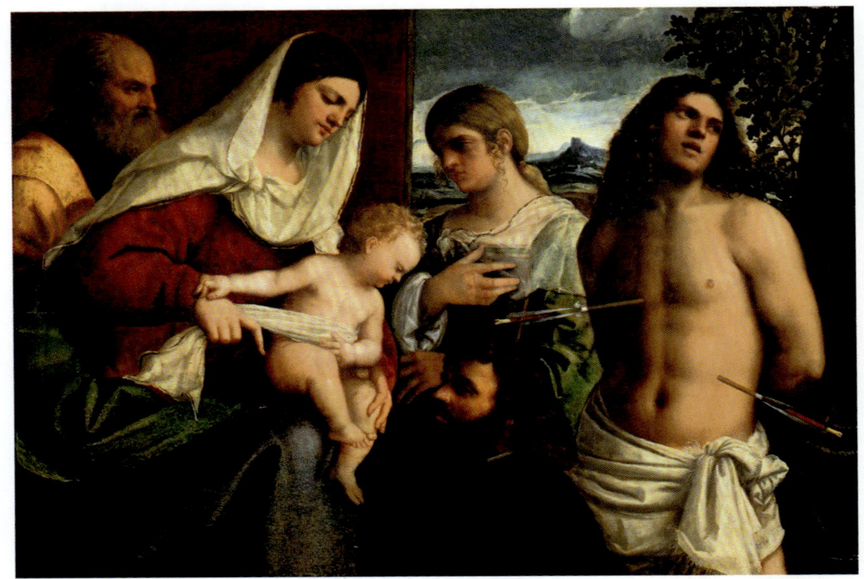

*The Holy Family with St. Catherine,
St. Sebastian and a Donor*

*La Sainte Famille avec sainte Catherine,
saint Sébastien et un donateur*

*Die heilige Jungfrau mit der heiligen
Katharina, dem heiligen Sebastian
und einem Stifter*

*La Santa Virgen con Santa Catalina,
San Sebastián y un benefactor*

*A Virgem Santa com Santa Catarina,
São Sebastião e um benfeitor*

*De heilige familie met Sint-Catharina,
Sint-Sebastiaan en een stichter*

Sebastiano del Piombo (1485-1547)

———

c. 1507/08, Oil on panel/Huile sur panneau,
95 × 136 cm, Musée du Louvre, Paris

The first thing that catches the eye is the detail of the painting, which Degas produced in three versions after Del Piombo. The artist retained fragments of the figures depicted on the original, although he could have left them out for aesthetic reasons. The procedure gives his copy a surrealistic look.

Ce qui est frappant dans cette troisième version connue de Degas d'après Del Piombo c'est son cadrage. En effet, l'artiste « s'entête » à garder des fragments de silhouettes alors qu'il aurait pu, par pur esthétisme, ne pas les faire figurer sur sa toile. Cela donne à ses répliques un caractère pour le moins surréaliste.

Als Erstes fällt der Bildausschnitt des Gemäldes ins Auge, das Degas in drei Versionen nach Del Piombo anfertigt. Der Künstler behält Fragmente der auf dem Original abgebildeten Figuren bei, obwohl er sie aus ästhetischen Gründen hätte aussparen können. Das Vorgehen verleiht seiner Kopie einen surrealistischen Anstrich.

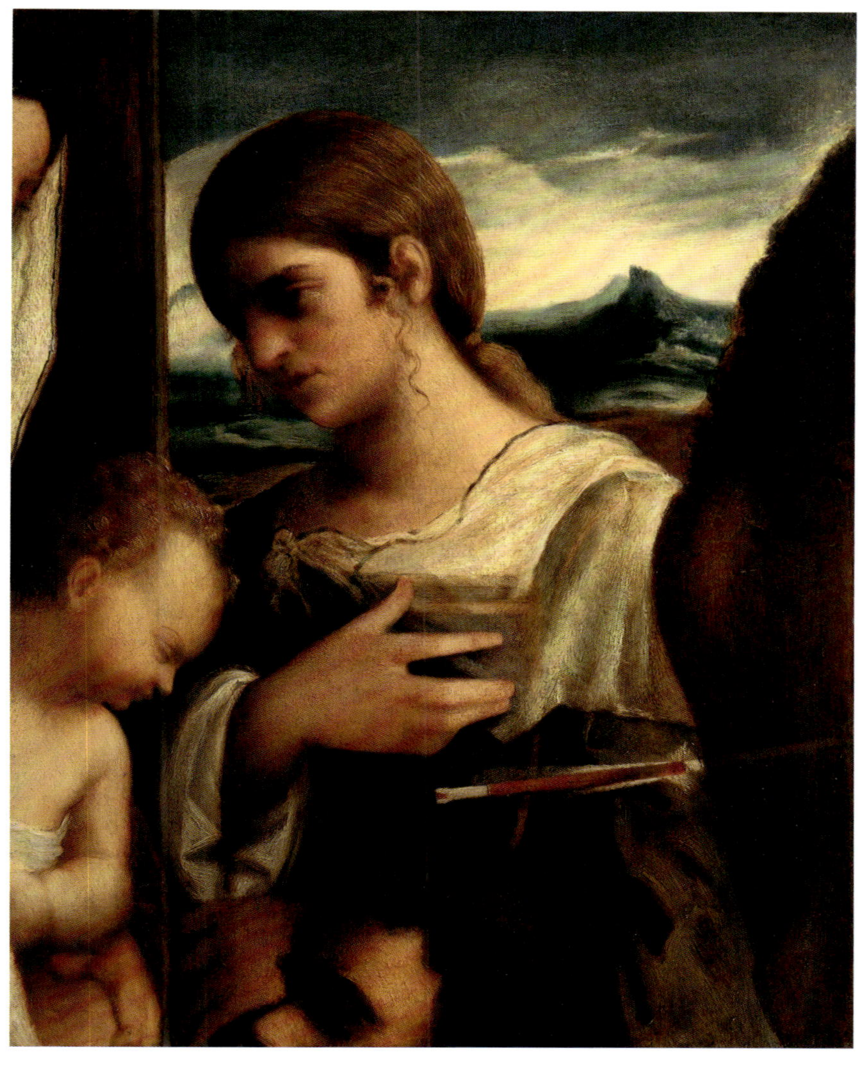

Lo primero que llama la atención es el detalle del cuadro, que Degas realizó en tres versiones según la obra de Del Piombo. El artista conserva fragmentos de las figuras representadas en el original, aunque podría haberlos omitido por razones estéticas. El procedimiento le da a su copia un aspecto surrealista.

A primeira coisa que chama a atenção é o detalhe da pintura, que Degas produziu em três versões depois de Del Piombo. O artista retém fragmentos das figuras retratadas no original, embora pudesse tê-los deixado de fora por razões estéticas. O procedimento dá à sua cópia um olhar surrealista.

Het eerste wat opvalt, is de beelduitsnede van het schilderij naar Del Piombo waarvan Degas drie versies maakte. De kunstenaar houdt fragmenten van de afgebeelde figuren op het origineel, hoewel hij ze om esthetische redenen had kunnen weglaten. Deze aanpak geeft zijn kopie een surrealistisch tintje.

RUBENS ~ DELACROIX

Delacroix began drawing at the age of 14. He was just as good at copying engravings as he was at copying paintings by the great European masters he saw in the Louvre a few years later - many of them booty pieces from Napoleon's campaigns. Delacroix undoubtedly not only copied Rubens, but also adopted some characteristic stylistic elements, such as the clouds painted in ruby red.

Dès l'âge de 14 ans Delacroix dessina. Il copia aussi bien d'après les gravures que, quelques années plus tard au Louvre, d'après les tableaux des grands maîtres européens dont certains étaient le fruit des saisies faites lors des campagnes napoléoniennes. Incontestablement, Delacroix adora non seulement copier Rubens, mais il lui emprunta également certaines caractéristiques stylistiques, comme les fameuses ombres teintées de rouge rubis.

Im Alter von 14 Jahren beginnt Delacroix mit dem Zeichnen. Er ist genauso gut im Kopieren von Stichen, wie von Gemälden der großen europäischen Meister, die er einige Jahre später im Louvre sieht – viele davon Beutestücke aus den Feldzügen Napoleons. Zweifellos kopiert Delacroix Rubens nicht nur, sondern übernimmt auch einige charakteristische Stilelemente, wie die in Rubinrot getünchten Wolken.

Delacroix comenzó a dibujar a los 14 años. Era tan bueno copiando grabados como copiando pinturas de los grandes maestros europeos que vio en el Louvre unos años más tarde, muchos de ellos piezas de botín de las campañas de Napoleón. Sin duda, Delacroix no sólo copia a Rubens, sino que también adopta algunos elementos estilísticos característicos, como las nubes pintadas de rojo rubí.

Delacroix começou a desenhar aos 14 anos. Ele era tão bom em copiar gravuras como em copiar pinturas dos grandes mestres europeus que viu no Louvre alguns anos mais tarde - muitos deles peças de saque das campanhas de Napoleão. Delacroix, sem dúvida, não só copia Rubens, mas também adota alguns elementos estilísticos característicos, como as nuvens pintadas em vermelho rubi.

Delacroix begon op 14-jarige leeftijd met tekenen. Hij kon even goed gravures kopiëren als schilderijen van grote Europese meesters, die hij een paar jaar later in het Louvre zou zien – veel daarvan waren buitgemaakt tijdens de veldtochten van Napoleon. Delacroix kopieerde Rubens ongetwijfeld niet alleen, maar nam ook enkele karakteristieke stijlelementen van hem over, zoals de robijnrood geschilderde wolken.

Eugène Delacroix (1798-1863)

———

Before 1854, Oil on canvas/Huile sur toile, 33 × 41 cm, Musée du Louvre, Paris (copy after/copie)

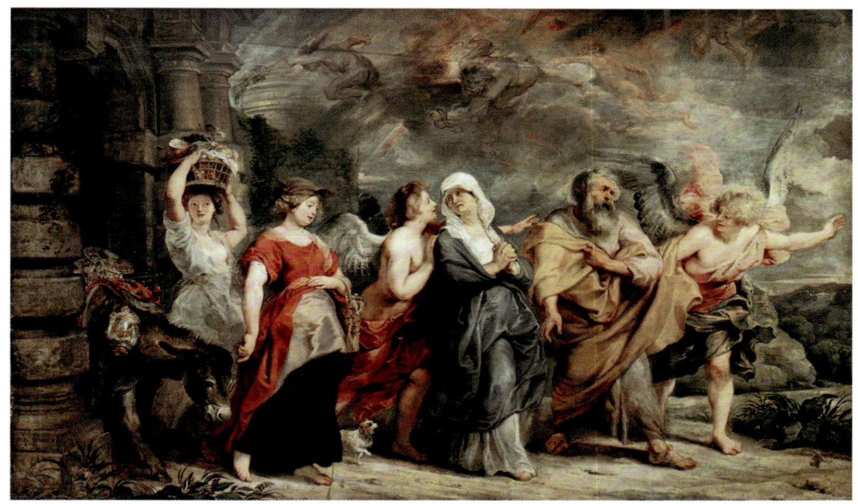

Lot's Family leaving Sodom

Loth et sa famille quittant Sodome

Die Flucht Lots und seiner Familie aus Sodom

La huída de Loth y su familia de Sodoma

A fuga de Lots e sua família de Sodoma

De vlucht van Lot en zijn familie uit Sodom

Peter Paul Rubens (1577-1640)

———

1625, Oil on panel/Huile sur panneau, 74 × 118 cm, Musée du Louvre, Paris

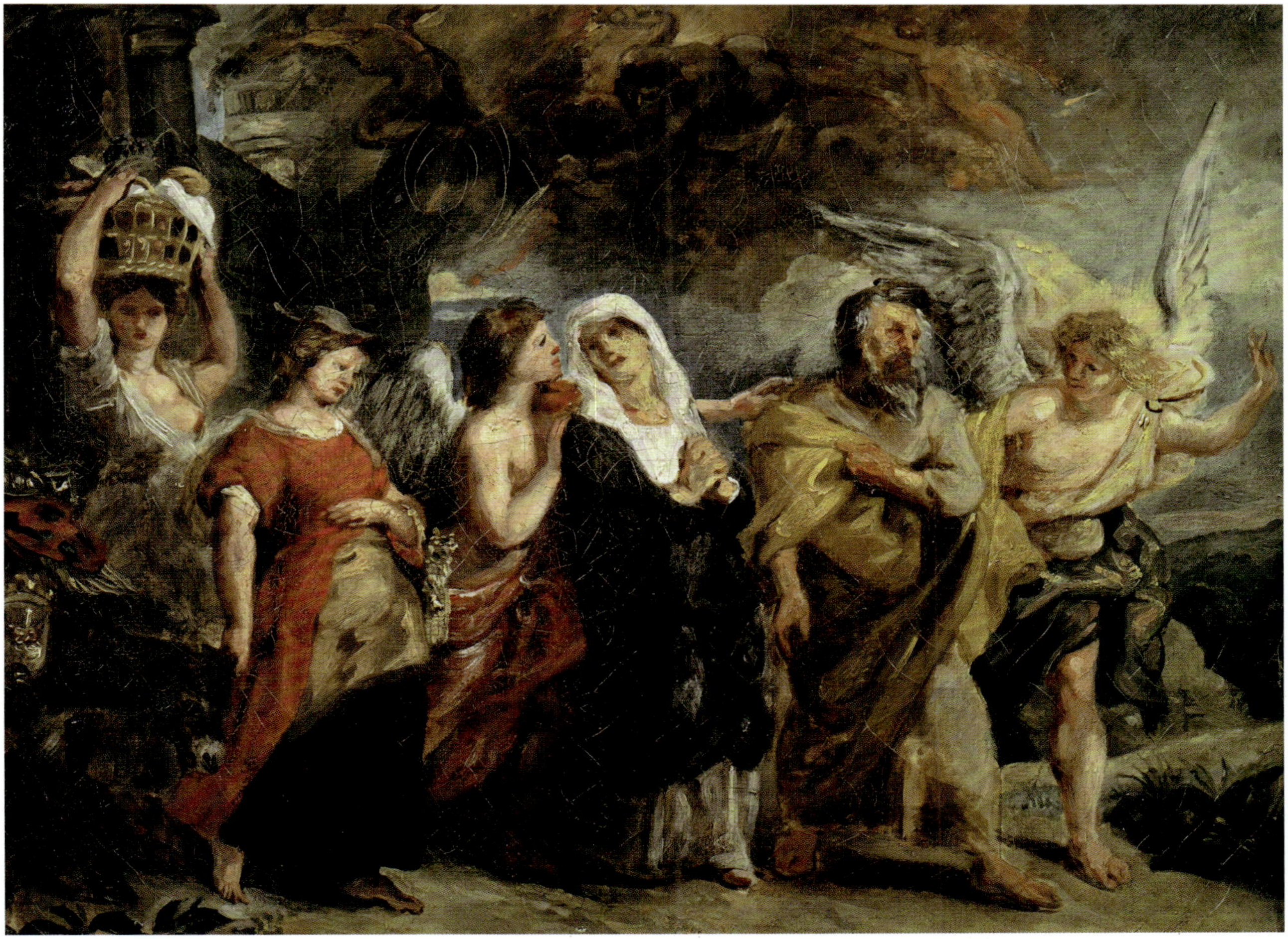

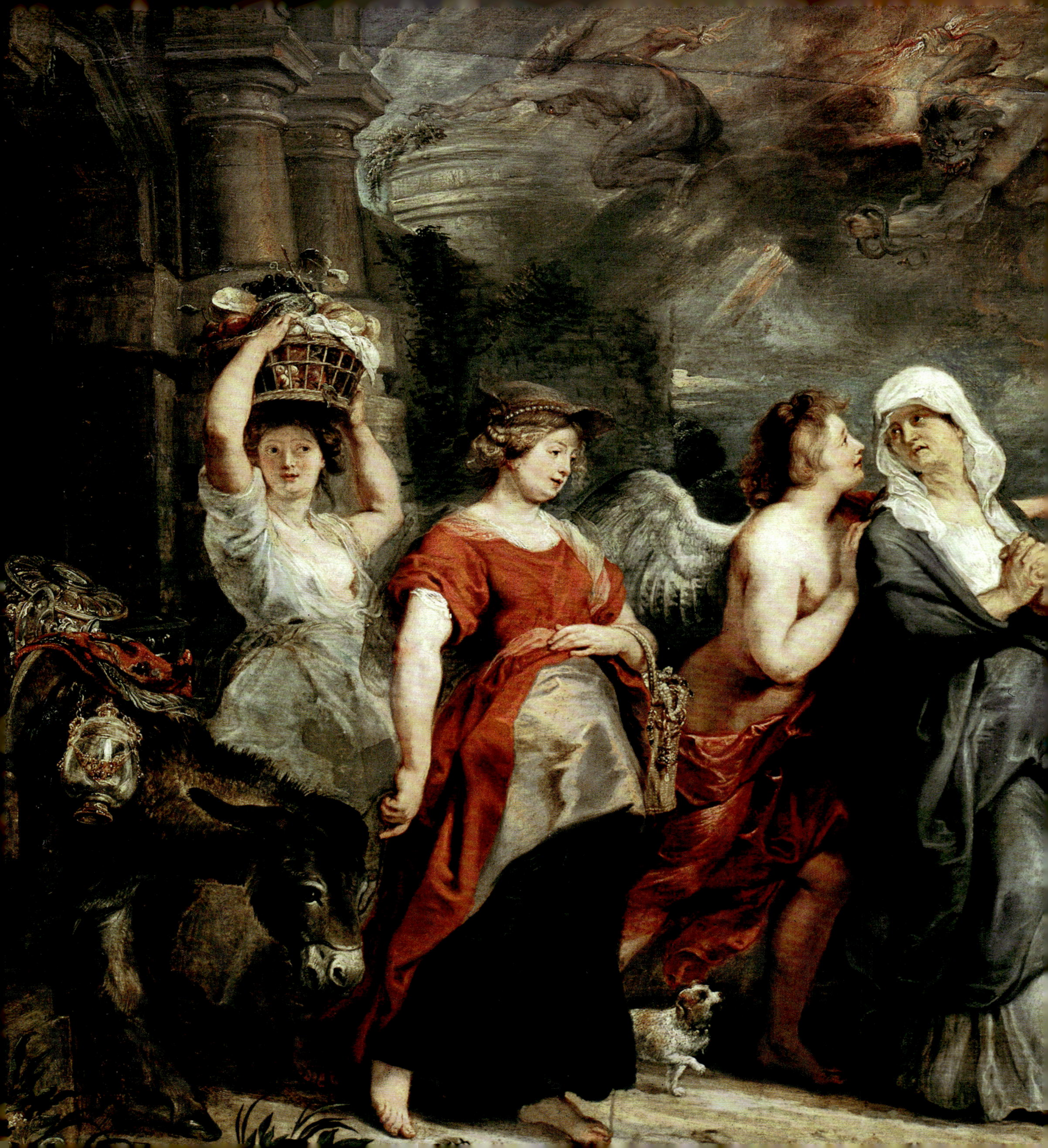

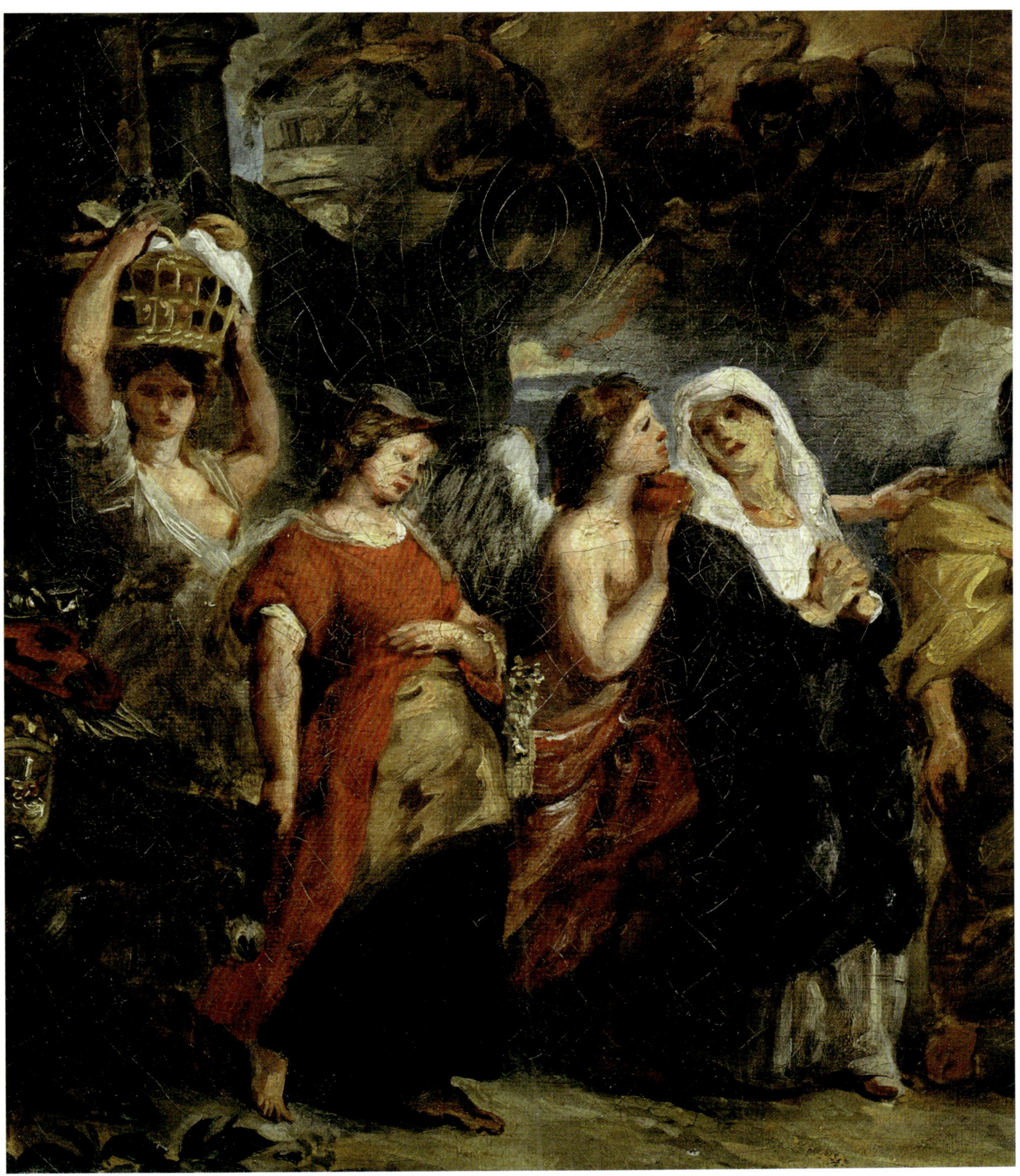

RUBENS ~ DELACROIX

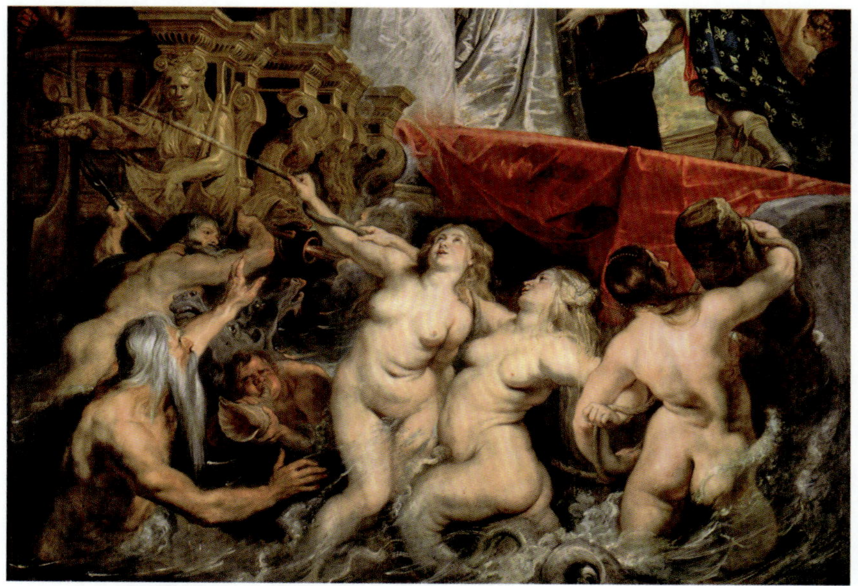

Medici cycle: Arrival (or Disembarkation) of Maria de' Medicis at Marseilles, detail

Cycle de Marie de Médicis : Le Débarquement de Marie de Médicis à Marseille, détail

Medici-Zyklus: Ankunft Maria de' Medicis in Marseille, Detail

Ciclo Medici: Llegada de María de Medicis a Marsella, detalle

Ciclo Médici: Chegada de Maria de' Medicis a Marselha, detalhe

Medicicyclus: De aankomst van Maria de' Medici in Marseille, detail

Peter Paul Rubens (1577-1640)

———

c. 1623-25, Oil on canvas/Huile sur toile, 394 × 295 cm, Musée du Louvre, Paris

Nereid

Néréide

Nereide

Nereida

Nereide

Nereïde

Eugène Delacroix (1798-1863)

———

c. 1822, Oil on canvas/Huile sur toile, 45,7 × 37,5 cm, Kunstmuseum, Basel (copy after/copie)

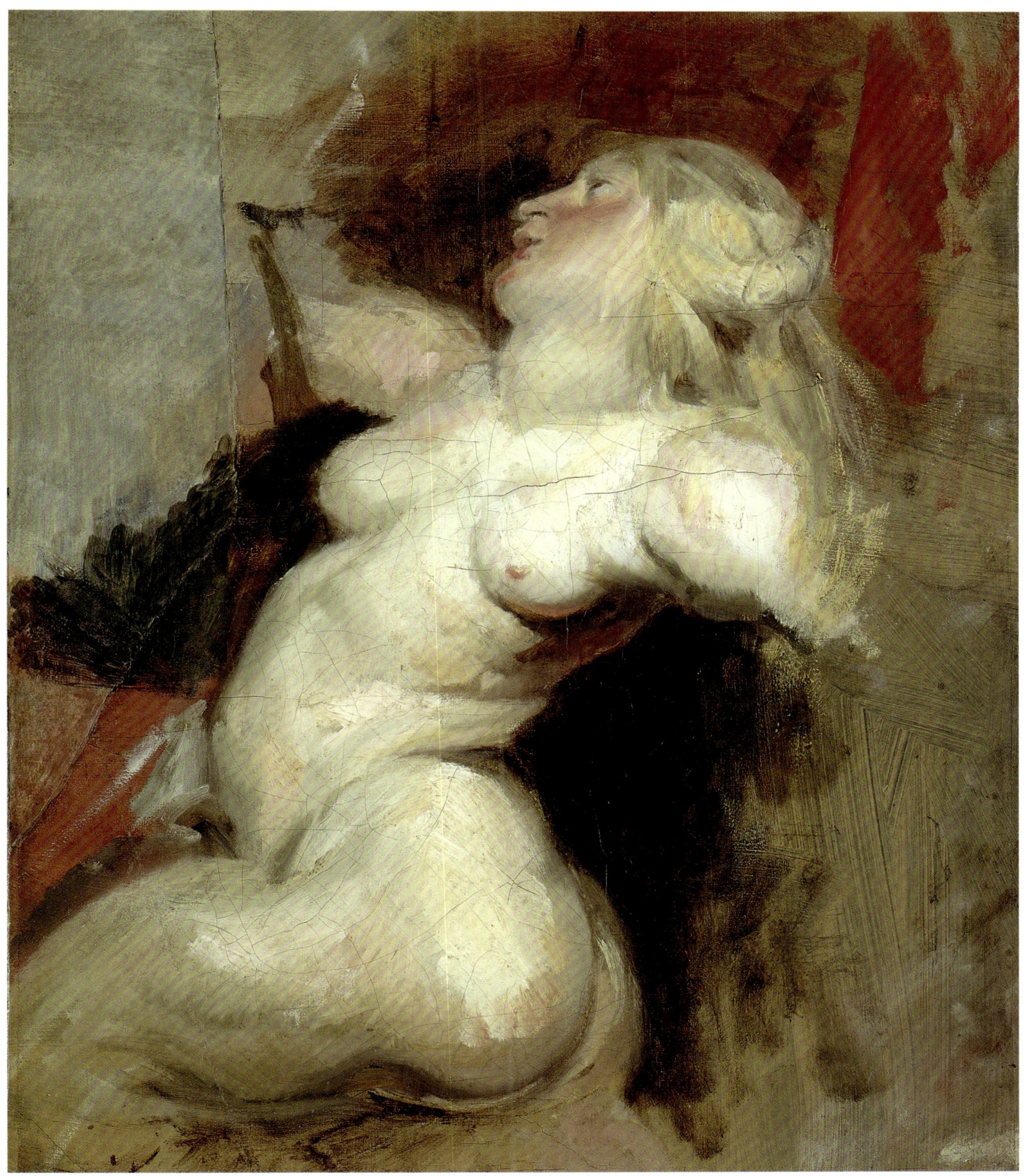

JORDAENS ~ VAN GOGH

The mere fact that Van Gogh pays respect to his compatriot, who worked two centuries before him, gives the work a certain humor. In his virtuoso copy full of brilliant colours, he used wider brushstrokes than in the original, which almost brings the painting into the realm of a caricature. Perhaps the author of the famous sunflowers even wanted to refer to Honoré Daumier, the French master of the trade.

Lorsqu'un Hollandais rend hommage à l'un de ses compatriotes qui a œuvré deux siècles auparavant, cela donne ce tableau plein de vie et surtout d'humour. Par sa copie enlevée et haute en couleur Vincent van Gogh grossit volontairement les traits de son sujet, l'emmenant même aux limites de la caricature. À tel point que l'on est en droit de se demander si l'auteur des *Tournesols* ne rend pas aussi un hommage au génial maître du genre, Honoré Daumier.

Allein der Aspekt, dass Van Gogh seinem Landsmann Respekt zollt, der zwei Jahrhunderte vor ihm wirkte, verleiht dem Werk einen gewissen Humor. Bei seiner virtuosen Kopie voller leuchtender Farben greift er auf breitere Pinselstriche als im Original zurück, was das Gemälde fast schon in den Bereich einer Karikatur rückt. Vielleicht wollte der Urheber der berühmten Sonnenblumen damit sogar auf Honoré Daumier, den französischen Meister des Faches, verweisen.

El hecho de que un holandés rinda homenaje a uno de sus compatriotas que trabajó dos siglos antes, le da vida y sobre todo humor a este cuadro. Vincent van Gogh amplía deliberadamente los rasgos de su tema, incluso llevándolo a los límites de la caricatura, hasta el punto de que uno se pregunta si el autor de *Los girasoles* no rinde también homenaje al genio maestro del género, Honoré Daumier.

O simples fato de Van Gogh respeitar seu compatriota, que trabalhou dois séculos antes dele, dá ao trabalho um certo humor. Em sua cópia virtuosa cheia de cores brilhantes, ele desenha em pinceladas mais largas do que no original, o que quase traz a pintura para o reino de uma caricatura. Talvez o autor dos famosos girassóis quisesse mesmo referir-se a Honoré Daumier, o mestre francês do comércio.

Alleen al het feit dat Van Gogh zijn landgenoot die twee eeuwen voor hem werkte respect betoonde, geeft het werk iets grappigs. In zijn virtuoze kopie vol stralende kleuren werkte hij met bredere penseelstreken dan in het origineel, waardoor het schilderij bijna een karikatuur wordt. Misschien wilde de schilder van de beroemde zonnebloemen daarmee verwijzen naar Honoré Daumier, de Franse meester van het genre.

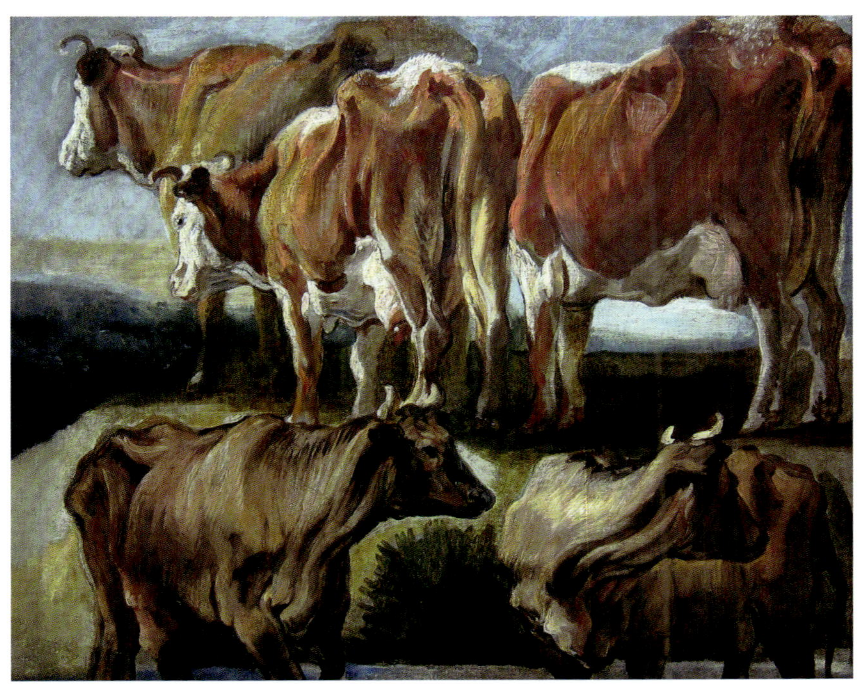

Study of Five Cows
Étude de cinq vaches
Studie mit fünf Kühen
Estudio con cinco vacas
Estudo com cinco vacas
Studie van vijf koeien

Jacobus Jordaens (1593-1678)

———

c. 1620, Oil on canvas/Huile sur toile,
65 × 81 cm, Musée des Beaux-Arts, Lille

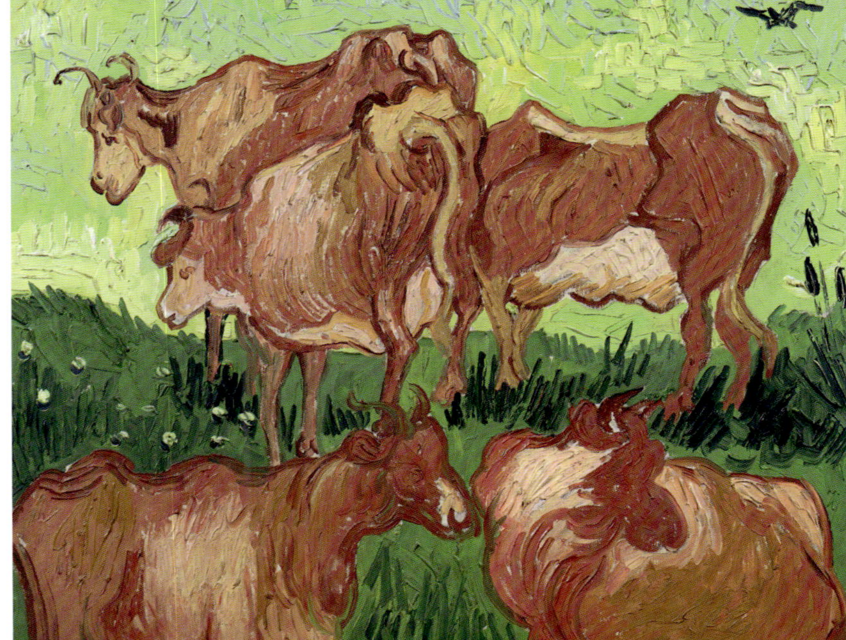

Study of Five Cows
Étude de cinq vaches
Studie mit fünf Kühen
Estudio con cinco vacas
Estudo com cinco vacas
Studie van vijf koeien

Vincent van Gogh (1853-1890)

———

c. 1890, Oil on canvas/Huile sur toile,
55 × 65 cm, Musée des Beaux-Arts, Lille
(copy after/copie)

TIZIANO ~ FANTIN-LATOUR

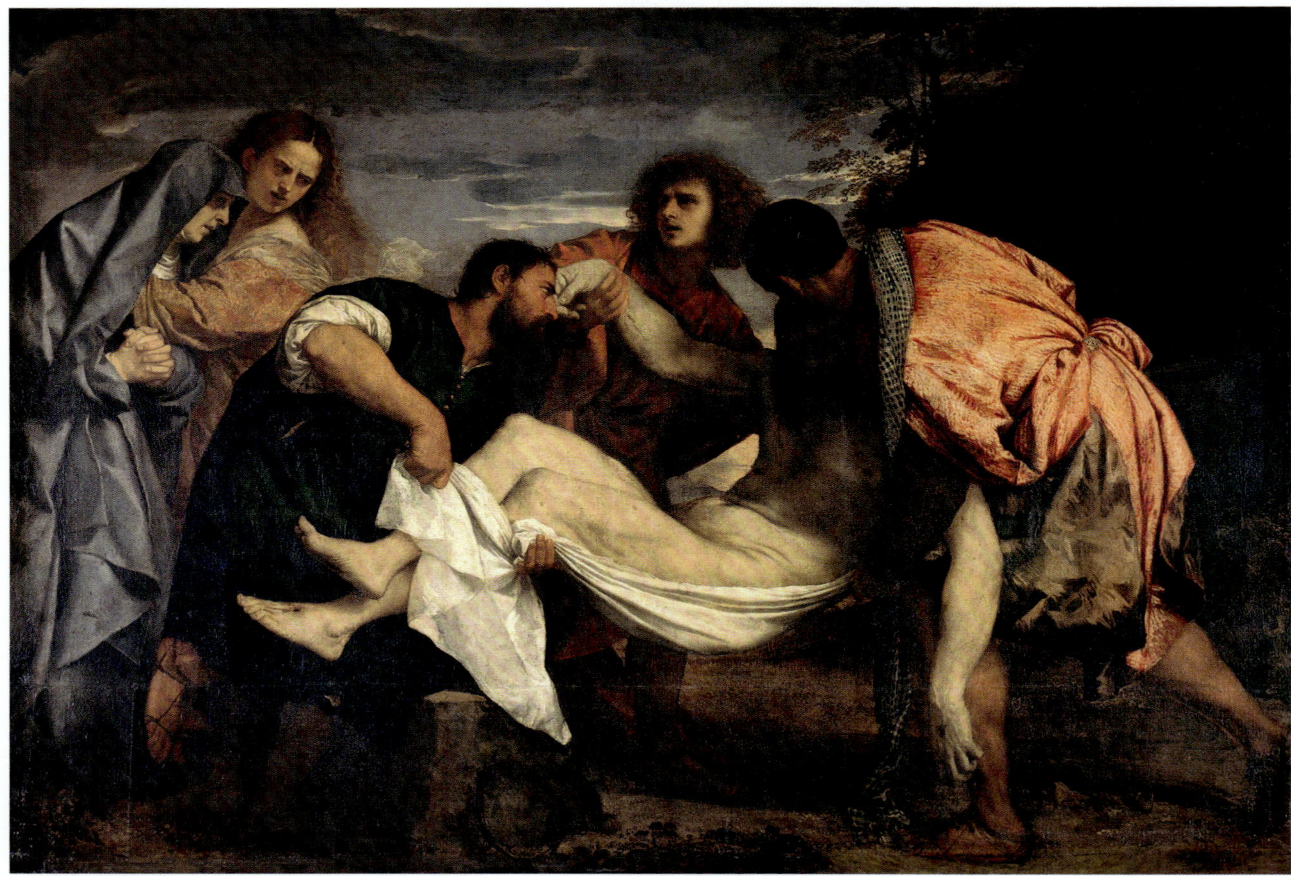

The Entombment of Christ
Le Transport du Christ au tombeau

Grablegung Christi
Entierro de Cristo

O sepultamento de Cristo
De graflegging van Christus

Tiziano Vecellio (1489-1576)

———

c. 1520, Oil on canvas/Huile sur toile,
148 × 212 cm, Musée du Louvre, Paris

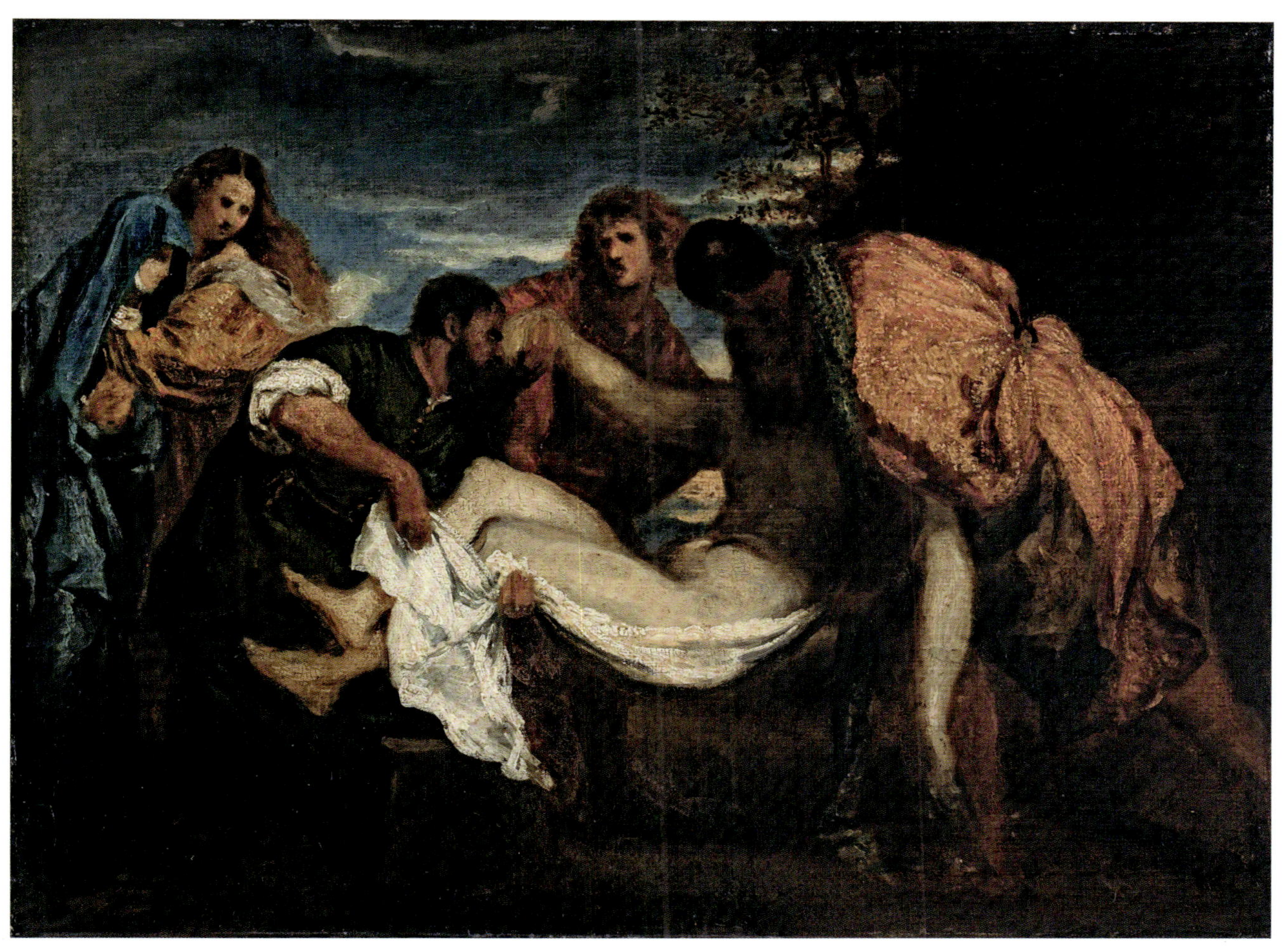

The Entombment
Le Transport du Christ au tombeau
Grablegung Christi
Entierro de Cristo
O sepultamento de Cristo
De graflegging van Christus

Henri Fantin-Latour (1836-1904)

n. d., Oil on canvas glued on millboard/
Huile sur toile collée sur un carton,
44 × 57,3 cm, Fitzwilliam Museum,
Cambridge (copy after/copie)

ANONYMOUS ~ RUBENS

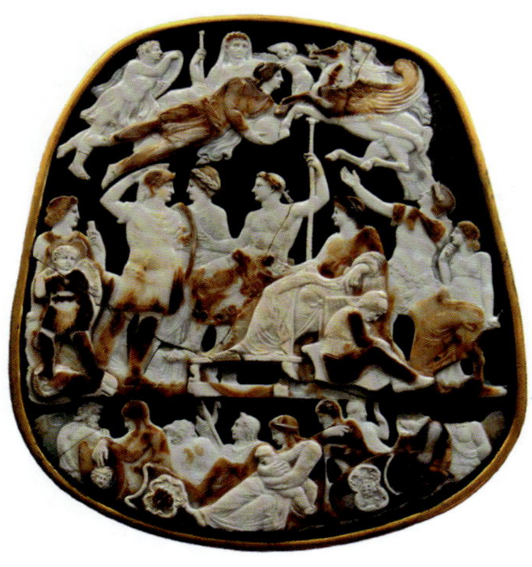

The Great Cameo of France
also *The Apotheosis of Germanicus*

Le Grand Camée de France
dit *L'Apothéose de Germanicus*

Die große Kamee von Frankreich
auch *Die Apotheose des Germanicus*

El Gran Camafeo de Francia también
La Apoteosis de Germánico

O Grande Camafeu da França
também *A Apoteose do Germânico*

De grote camee van Frankrijk of
De Apotheose van Germanicus

Anonymous

———

c. 1st century AD, Sardonyx and
copper/Sardonyx et cuivre, 31 × 26,5 cm,
Cabinet des Médailles, Paris

The Great Cameo of France also
The Apotheosis of Germanicus

Le Grand Camée de France
dit *L'Apothéose de Germanicus*

Die große Kamee von Frankreich
auch *Die Apotheose des Germanicus*

El Gran Camafeo de Francia
también *La Apoteosis de Germánico*

O Grande Caméo da França também
conhecido como A Apoteose Germânico

De grote camee van Frankrijk of
De Apotheose van Germanicus

Peter Paul Rubens (1577-1640)

———

1626, Oil on canvas/Huile sur toile,
100,7 × 78 cm, Ashmolean Museum,
Oxford (copy after/copie)

As a collector of antique objects,
Rubens also owned intaglios and
cameos. In addition, the artist from
Antwerp drew further works or was
inspired by them. This magnificent
masterpiece offered him the
opportunity to try his hand at a
large number of forms.

Immense collectionneur, Rubens,
le plus italien des peintres du Nord,
possédait des antiques mais aussi
des intailles et des camées.
L'Anversois avait pour habitude
de les copier ou de s'en inspirer.
Ce chef-d'œuvre offrit à Rubens
la possibilité de se constituer un
somptueux répertoire de formes.

Rubens besaß als Sammler antiker
Objekte auch Intaglien und
Kameen. Zusätzlich zeichnete der
Künstler aus Antwerpen weitere
Arbeiten ab oder ließ sich von ihnen
inspirieren. Dieses prächtige
Meisterwerk bot ihm die
Gelegenheit, sich an einer großen
Anzahl Formen zu versuchen.

Como coleccionista de objetos
antiguos, Rubens también poseía
intaglios y camafeos. Además, el
artista de Amberes dibujó otras
obras o se inspiró en ellas. Esta
magnífica obra maestra le brindó la
oportunidad de probar suerte en un
gran número de formas.

Como colecionador de objetos
antigos, Rubens também possuía
intaglios e camafeus. Além disso, o
artista de Antuérpia desenhou
outros trabalhos ou foi inspirado
por eles. Esta magnífica obra-prima
ofereceu-lhe a oportunidade de
experimentar a sua mão num
grande número de formas.

Als verzamelaar van antieke
voorwerpen was Rubens ook
eigenaar van intaglio's en cameeën.
Daarnaast tekende de Antwerpse
kunstenaar nog meer werken na of
liet zich daardoor inspireren. Dit
prachtige meesterwerk gaf hem de
kans een groot aantal vormen uit te
proberen.

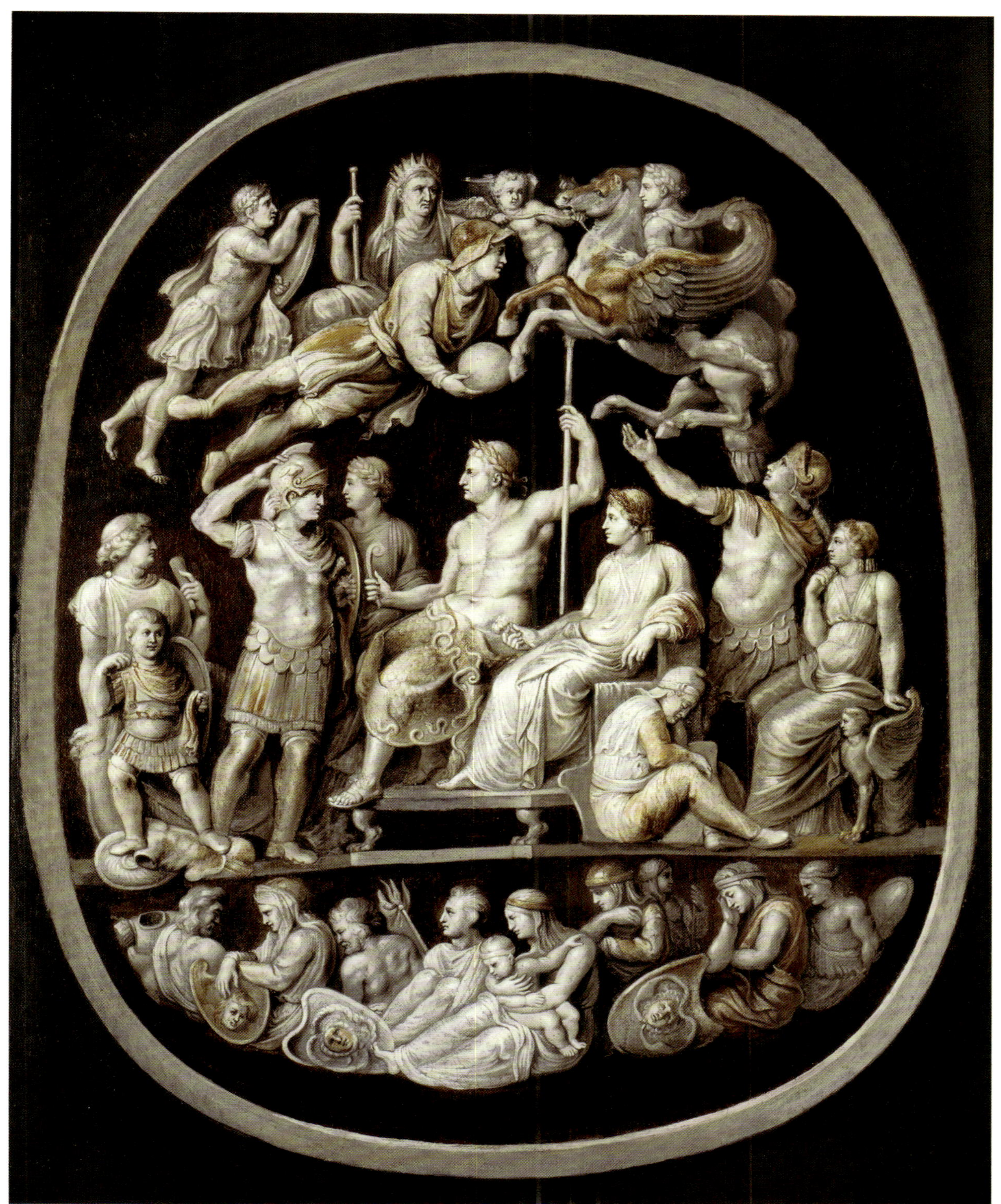

DELACROIX ~ VAN GOGH

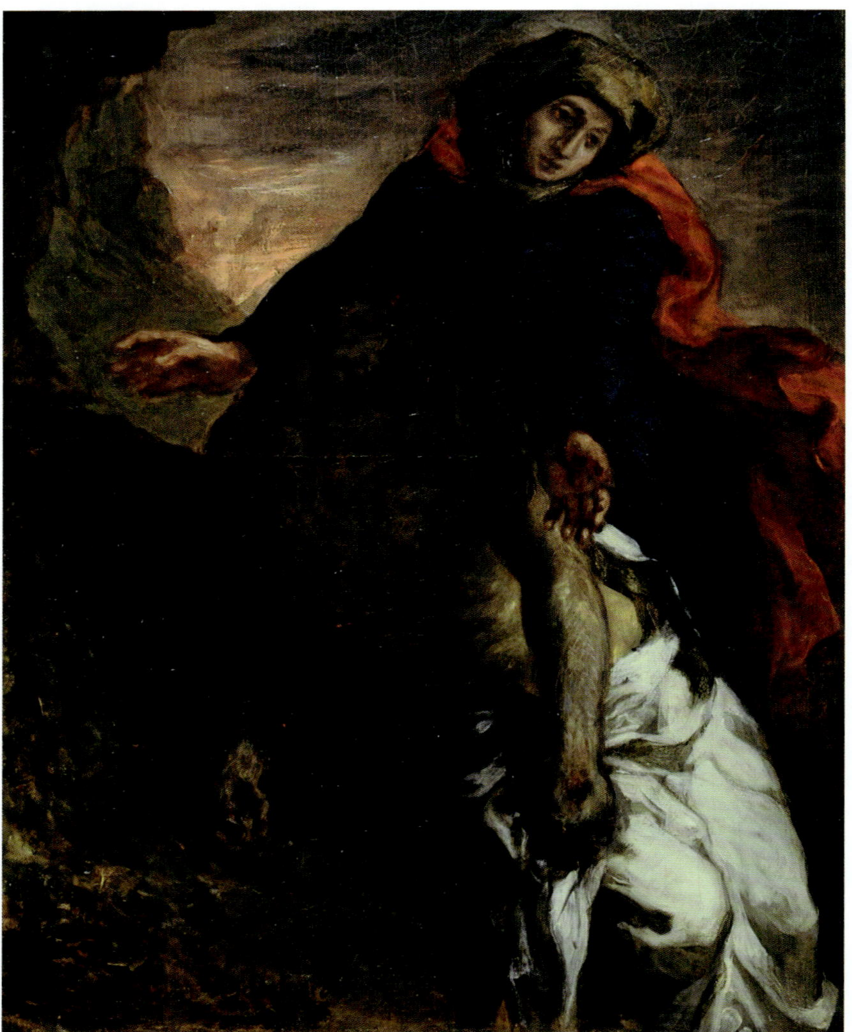

Pietà

Eugène Delacroix (1798-1863)

1850, Oil on canvas/Huile sur toile,
35,6 × 27 cm, Nasjonalmuseet, Oslo

Pietà

Vincent van Gogh (1853-1890)

1889, Oil on canvas/Huile sur toile,
73 × 60,5 cm, Van Gogh Museum,
Amsterdam (copy after/copie)

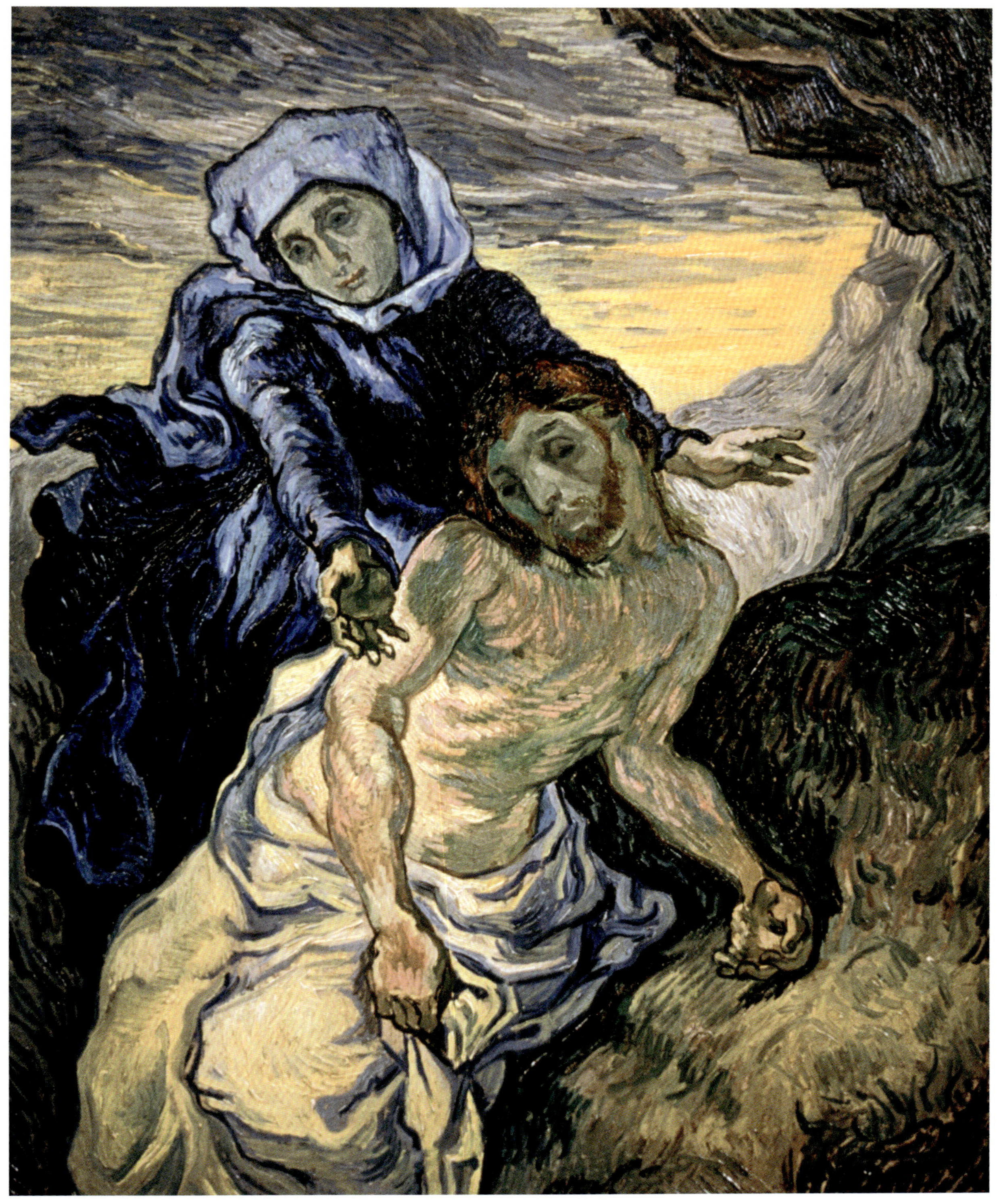

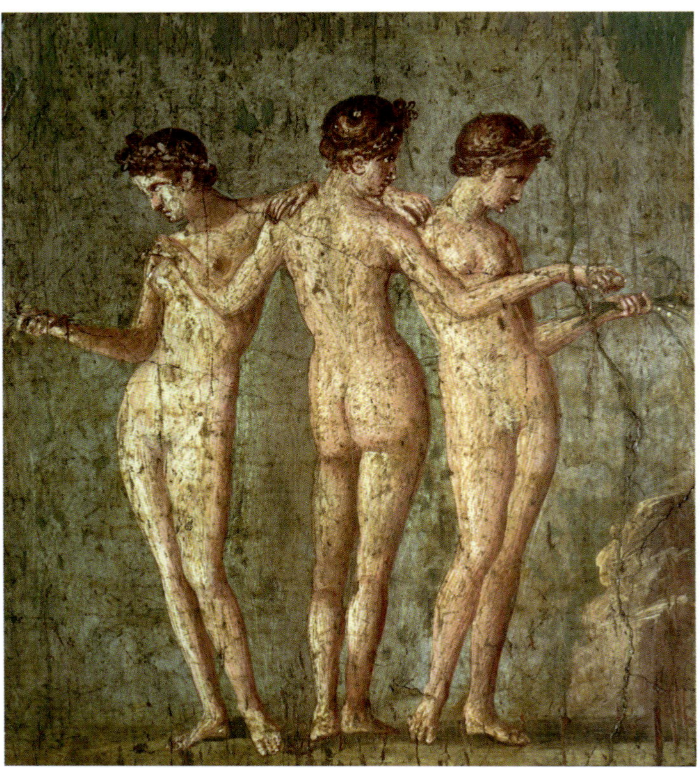

The Three Graces (Fresco from Pompeii)

Les Trois Grâces (fresque, Pompéi)

Die drei Grazien (Fresko aus Pompeji)

Las tres Gracias (fresco de Pompeya)

As Três Graças (Fresco de Pompeia)

De drie Gratiën (fresco uit Pompeji)

Anonymous

———

c. 1st century AD, Fresco/Fresque, Museo
Archeologico Nazionale, Napoli

The copy is one thing - the inspiration another

After practice on the copy, many artists begin to find their own compositions. They often continue to be inspired by their teachers - sometimes to the end of their lives. This influence manifests itself not only in the motifs, but also in the style, the way in which they are implemented. Towards the end of his life, Van Gogh changed his brushstrokes after discovering the works of Monticelli. It also happens, however, that an artist consciously or unconsciously blurs the traces of his inspiration. For example, it is impossible to tell whether Lovis Corinth used Raphael's *Three Graces*

La copie est une chose, l'inspiration, une autre

Il est entendu qu'après s'être exercés à l'art de la copie, les artistes s'émancipent et commencent à créer leurs propres compositions. Il arrive bien souvent que ces mêmes artistes continuent à être inspirés par leurs maîtres et ce, jusqu'à la fin de leur vie. L'influence s'exprime aussi bien par les sujets abordés que par le style – la manière de faire. Ainsi, Van Gogh, à la fin de sa vie, modifiera sa touche après avoir découvert les œuvres de Monticelli. Si cet exemple est manifeste, il arrive aussi que l'artiste volontairement ou involontairement brouille les pistes.

Die Kopie ist eine Sache – die Inspiration eine andere

Nach der Übung an der Kopie beginnen viele Künstler damit, ihre eigenen Kompositionen zu finden. Dabei lassen sie sich oft weiterhin von ihren Lehrern inspirieren – manchmal bis an ihr Lebensende. Dieser Einfluss manifestiert sich nicht nur in den Motiven, sondern auch im Stil, der Art der Umsetzung. So änderte Van Gogh gegen Ende seines Lebens die Pinselführung, nachdem er die Werke von Monticelli für sich entdeckte. Es kommt jedoch auch vor, dass ein Künstler bewusst oder unbewusst die Spuren seiner Inspiration verwischt. Zum Beispiel lässt sich

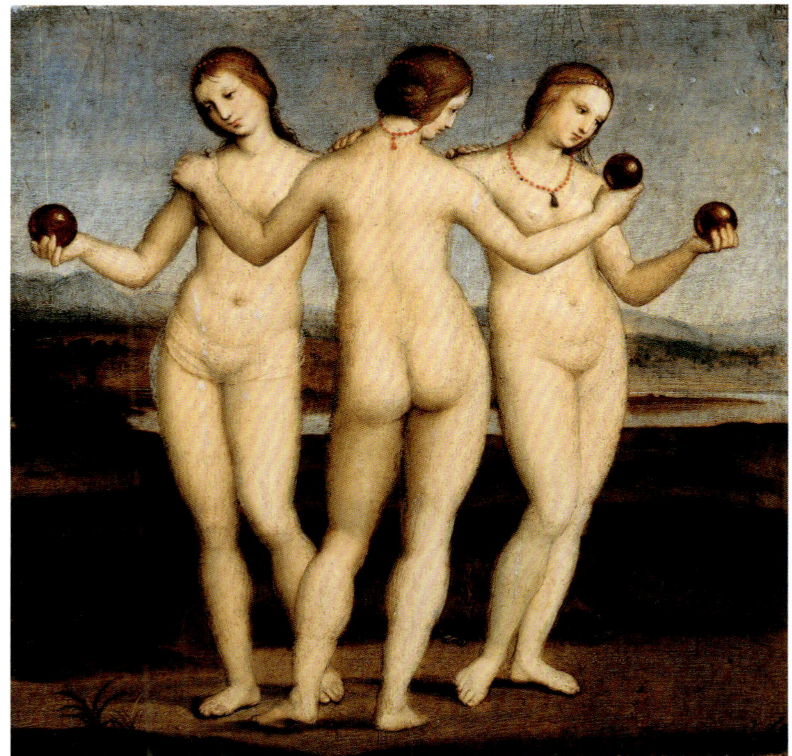

The Three Graces

Les Trois Grâces

Die drei Grazien

Las tres Gracias

As Três Graças

De drie Gratiën

Raffaello Sanzio (1483-1520)

———

1504/05, Oil on panel/Huile sur panneau,
17,8 × 17,6 cm, Musée Condé, Chantilly

La copia es una cosa
- la inspiración otra

Después de practicar realizando
copias, muchos artistas comienzan
a encontrar sus propias
composiciones. A menudo siguen
siendo inspirados por sus maestros,
a veces hasta el final de sus vidas.
Esta influencia se manifiesta no sólo
en los motivos, sino también en el
estilo, en la forma en que se aplican.
Hacia el final de su vida, Van Gogh
cambió sus pinceladas después de
descubrir las obras de Monticelli.
Pero también ocurre que un artista,
consciente o inconscientemente,
desdibuja las huellas de su
inspiración. Por ejemplo, es
imposible saber si Lovis Corinto

A cópia é uma coisa
- a inspiração é outra

Após a prática na cópia, muitos
artistas começam a encontrar suas
próprias composições. Muitas vezes
continuam a ser inspirados pelos
seus professores - por vezes até ao
fim das suas vidas.
Esta influência manifesta-se não só
nos motivos, mas também no estilo,
na forma como são implementados.
No final de sua vida, Van Gogh
mudou suas pinceladas depois de
descobrir as obras de Monticelli. No
entanto, acontece também que um
artista, consciente ou
inconscientemente, desfoca os
traços da sua inspiração. Por
exemplo, é impossível dizer se Lovis

De kopie is één ding,
de inspiratie een ander

Na het oefenen op de kopie vinden
veel kunstenaars gaandeweg hun
eigen composities. Daarbij laten ze
zich vaak inspireren door hun
leermeesters – soms tot het eind
van hun leven.
Deze invloed manifesteert zich niet
alleen in de onderwerpen, maar ook
in de stijl en de uitvoering. Tegen
het eind van zijn leven veranderde
Van Gogh zijn penseelvoering nadat
hij het werk van Monticelli had
ontdekt. Het komt echter ook voor
dat een kunstenaar bewust of
onbewust de sporen van zijn
inspiratie uitwist. Zo is het
bijvoorbeeld onmogelijk te zeggen

Foreign influences in an artist's work are subtle homages to the teacher.

L'influence est un hommage subtil rendu aux maîtres

Fremde Einflüsse im Werk eines Künstlers sind subtile Huldigungen an den Lehrer.

Las influencias extranjeras en la obra de un artista son sutiles homenajes al maestro.

Influências estrangeiras no trabalho de um artista são homenagens sutis ao professor.

Vreemde invloeden in het werk van een kunstenaar zijn subtiele hommages aan de leermeester.

or a Pompeian fresco for his work. Both would be possible. Sometimes influences only become visible in the eye of the beholder, who discovers an obvious connection or a beautiful coincidence.
Whether contemporary artists, art historians or art lovers, whether with or without historical or biographical background knowledge - we all have the right to address the question of who was influenced by whom. However, the search for truth should never interfere with the pleasure of viewing

À l'instar des *Trois Grâces* de Lovis Corinth. En effet, ce dernier emprunte-t-il à Raphaël ou à la fresque de Pompéi ? Le spectateur amateur, lui, peut affirmer les deux, car l'influence peut également être révélée par le regard de celui qui admire une œuvre reconnaissant en elle une évidente correspondance ou une belle coïncidence.
Les artistes contemporains, les historiens d'art tout comme les amateurs, ne connaissant aucun élément historique et biographique, seront en droit de se poser la question de qui a été influencé et par qui. Cette quête de vérité ne devant en rien gâter le plaisir des yeux !

nicht erkennen, ob sich Lovis Corinth für sein Werk *Drei Grazien* bei Raffael oder einem pompejischen Fresko bediente. Beides wäre möglich. Manchmal werden Einflüsse auch erst im Blick des Betrachters sichtbar, der einen offensichtlichen Zusammenhang oder einen schönen Zufall entdeckt. Egal ob zeitgenössische Künstler, Kunsthistoriker oder Kunstliebhaber, ob mit oder ohne geschichtliches oder biografisches Hintergrundwissen – wir alle haben das Recht, uns mit der Frage zu befassen, wer von wem beeinflusst wurde. Allerdings sollte die Suche nach der Wahrheit niemals das Vergnügen der Betrachtung beeinträchtigen.

Lovis Corinth (1858-1925)

1904, Oil on canvas/Huile sur toile,
164,5 × 150 cm, Neue Pinakothek,
München

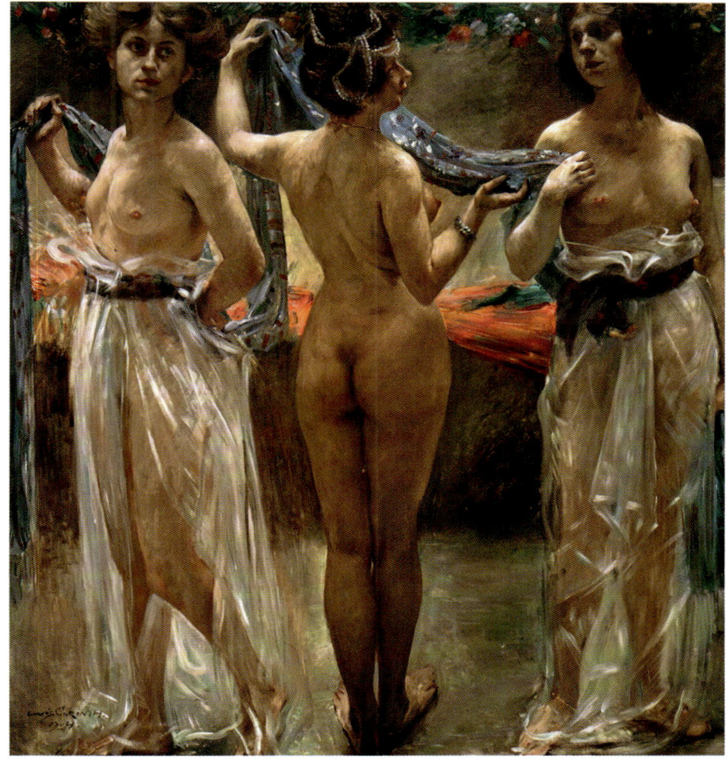

utilizó *Las Tres Gracias* de Rafael o un fresco pompeyano para su obra. Ambos serían posibles. A veces las influencias sólo se hacen visibles en el ojo del observador, que descubre una conexión obvia o una bella coincidencia.
Ya se trate de artistas contemporáneos, historiadores de arte o amantes del arte, con o sin conocimientos históricos o biográficos, todos tenemos derecho a abordar la cuestión de quién ha sido influenciado por quién. Sin embargo, la búsqueda de la verdad nunca debe interferir con el placer de contemplar la obra.

Corinto usou as Três Graças de Rafael ou um afresco pompeu para sua obra. Ambos seriam possíveis. Às vezes, as influências só se tornam visíveis no olho do observador, que descobre uma conexão óbvia ou uma bela coincidência.
Quer se trate de artistas contemporâneos, historiadores de arte ou amantes de arte, com ou sem conhecimento histórico ou biográfico - todos temos o direito de abordar a questão de quem foi influenciado por quem. No entanto, a busca da verdade nunca deve interferir com o prazer de ver.

of Lovis Corinth voor zijn *Drie Gratiën* een werk van Rafaël of een Pompejaans fresco tot voorbeeld nam. Beide zouden kunnen. Soms worden invloeden pas zichtbaar in het oog van de toeschouwer die een duidelijk verband of een mooi toeval ontdekt.
Of het nu gaat om hedendaagse kunstenaars, kunsthistorici of kunstliefhebbers, met of zonder historische of biografische achtergrondkennis, we hebben allemaal het recht om ons te buigen over de vraag wie door wie is beïnvloed. Het zoeken naar de waarheid mag echter nooit het plezier van het kijken in de weg staan.

IL PERUGINO ~ RAFFAELLO

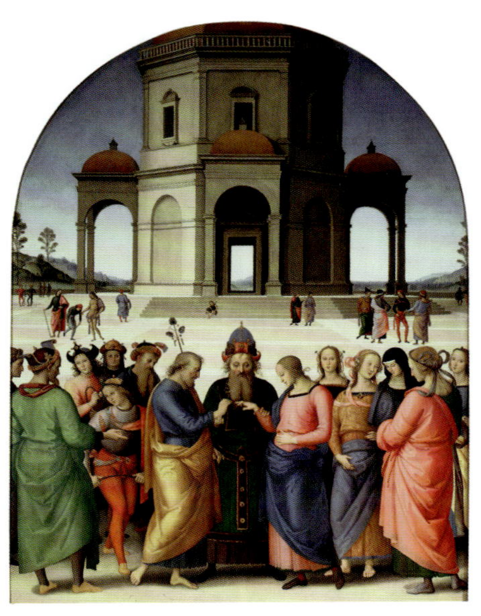

Marriage of the Virgin
Le Mariage de la Vierge
Vermählung der Jungfrau
Matrimonio de la Virgen María
Casamento da Virgem Maria
Het huwelijk van de Maagd Maria

Pietro Vannucci (dit Il Perugino)
(1450-1523)

———

1500-04, Tempera and oil on wood/
Tempera et huile sur bois, 236 × 186 cm,
Musée des Beaux-Arts, Caen

Marriage of the Virgin
Le Mariage de la Vierge
Vermählung Mariä
Matrimonio de la Virgen María
Casamento da Virgem Maria
Het huwelijk van de Maagd Maria

Raffaello Sanzio
(1483-1520)

———

1504, Oil on wood/Huile sur bois,
170 × 118 cm, Pinacoteca di Brera,
Milano

The two paintings are very similar in their execution, since Raphael was a pupil of Perugino. But also the composition shows a remarkable similarity. Both are due to the fact that students often take on design elements from their teachers and thus pay respect to them.

Si la facture est sensiblement la même, puisque Pérugin fut le maître de Raphaël, la composition elle aussi affiche de notables ressemblances entre les deux œuvres. Quoi de plus normal pour un élève – qui deviendra à son tour un maître –, d'emprunter ou de rendre hommage au professeur qui lui inculqua les rudiments de son futur métier, de sa future passion.

Die Ausführungen der beiden Gemälde ähneln sich deutlich, schließlich war Raffael ein Schüler Peruginos. Aber auch die Komposition weisst eine beachtliche Übereinstimmung auf. Beides ist dem Aspekt geschuldet, dass Schüler oft Gestaltungselemente ihrer Lehrer übernehmen und ihnen dadurch Respekt zollen.

Las dos pinturas son muy similares en su ejecución, ya que Rafael fue alumno de Perugino. Pero también la composición muestra una similitud notable. Ambos se deben al hecho de que los estudiantes a menudo asumen elementos de diseño de sus profesores y, por lo tanto, los respetan.

As duas pinturas são muito semelhantes em sua execução, já que Raphael era um aluno de Perugino. Mas também a composição mostra uma semelhança notável. Ambos se devem ao facto de que os alunos muitas vezes assumem elementos de design dos seus professores e, portanto, pagam-lhes respeito.

De twee schilderijen lijken qua uitvoering sterk op elkaar – Rafaël was tenslotte een leerling van Perugino. Maar ook de compositie vertoont een opmerkelijke gelijkenis. Dat is te wijten aan het feit dat studenten vaak compositie-elementen van hun leermeesters overnamen en hen zo respect betuigden.

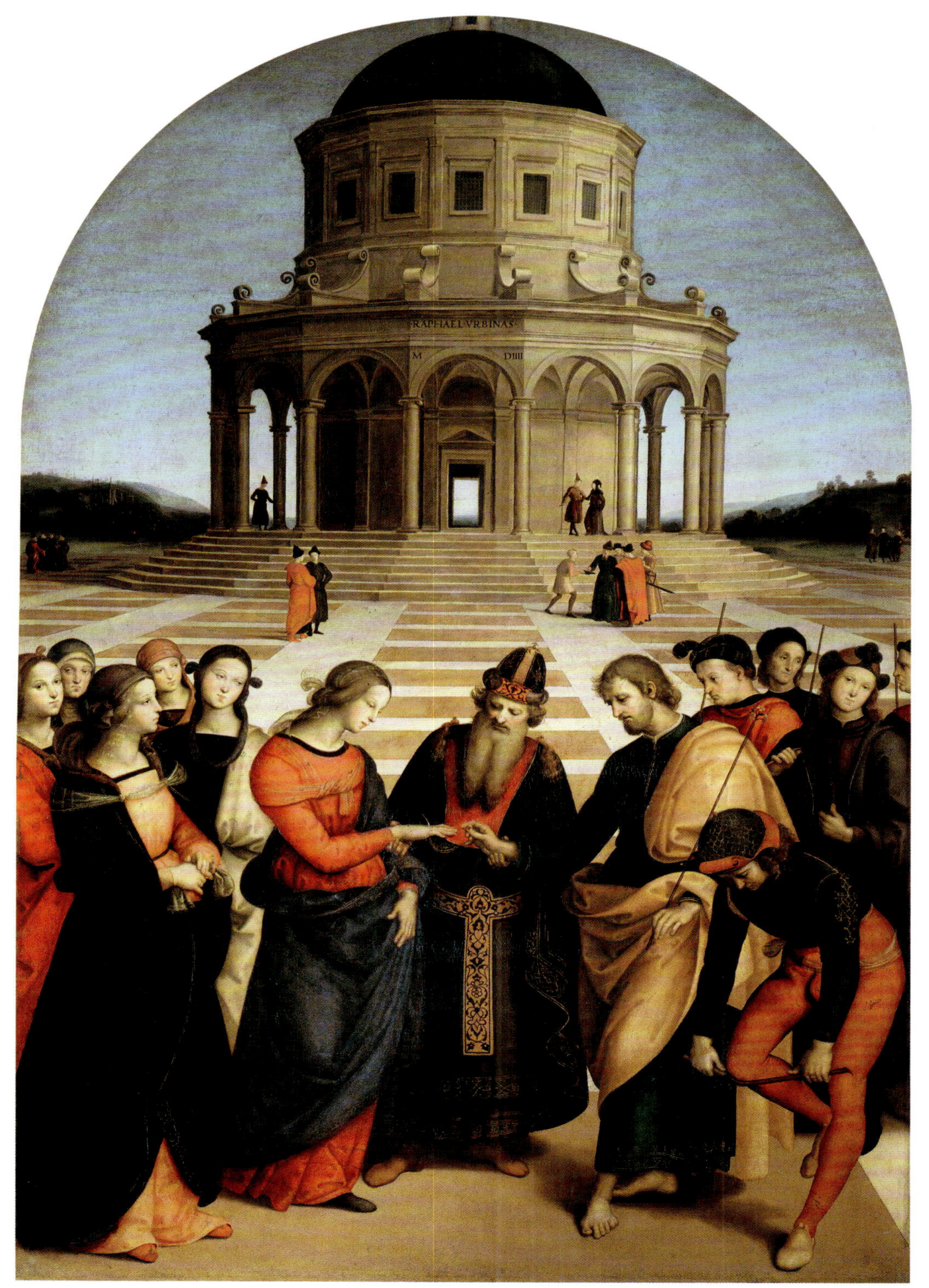

RAPHAEL·VRBINAS·
M   DIIII

TURNER ~ DELACROIX

In 1824 a large exhibition was held in Paris dedicated to British painters such as Bonington, Constable and Turner. Many Romantic painters were concerned with depicting the sky. Delacroix was so fascinated that in the summer of 1825 he travelled by ship to Brittany to study the new British style of painting. All his life he paid respect to it with his watercolors.

En 1824, à Paris, une importante exposition fut consacrée aux peintres anglais comme Bonington, Constable ou Turner. Une grande partie des artistes romantiques furent marqués par la subtilité des rendus atmosphériques. Delacroix sera tellement séduit par cette manière de faire qu'il prendra même le bateau l'année suivante, à l'été 1825, pour aller étudier *in situ* cet art britannique si novateur. Toute sa production à l'aquarelle, et durant sa vie entière, en sera à jamais reconnaissante.

Im Jahr 1824 fand in Paris eine große Ausstellung statt, die britischen Malern wie Bonington, Constable oder Turner gewidmet war. Viele Maler der Romantik beschäftigten sich mit der Darstellung des Himmels. Delacroix war derart fasziniert davon, dass er im Sommer 1825 mit dem Schiff in die Bretagne reiste, um die neue britische Malkunst zu studieren. Sein ganzes Leben lang sollte er ihr mit seinen Aquarellen Respekt zollen.

En 1824, en París, se dedicó una importante exposición a pintores ingleses como Bonington, Constable o Turner. Muchos de los artistas románticos estaban marcados por la sutileza de la representación atmosférica. Delacroix se sintió tan seducido por esta forma de hacer las cosas que incluso tomó el barco al año siguiente, en el verano de 1825, para estudiar este innovador arte británico in situ. Toda su producción de acuarelas, y a lo largo de toda su vida, se lo agradecerá eternamente.

Em 1824 foi realizada uma grande exposição em Paris dedicada a pintores britânicos como Bonington, Constable e Turner. Muitos pintores românticos estavam preocupados em representar o céu. Delacroix ficou tão fascinado que no verão de 1825 ele viajou de navio para a Bretanha para estudar a nova arte britânica da pintura. Toda a sua vida ele devia respeitá-la com as suas aguarelas.

In 1824 werd in Parijs een grote tentoonstelling gehouden die gewijd was aan Britse schilders als Bonington, Constable en Turner. Veel romantische schilders hielden zich bezig met de weergave van de lucht. Delacroix was daar zo door gefascineerd dat hij in de zomer van 1825 per schip naar Bretagne reisde om de nieuwe Britse schilderkunst te bestuderen. Zijn hele leven zou hij die respect betonen met zijn aquarellen.

Eugène Delacroix (1798-1863)

c. 1852-55, Watercolor on paper/Aquarelle sur papier, 20 × 31 cm, Musée Marmottan Monet, Paris

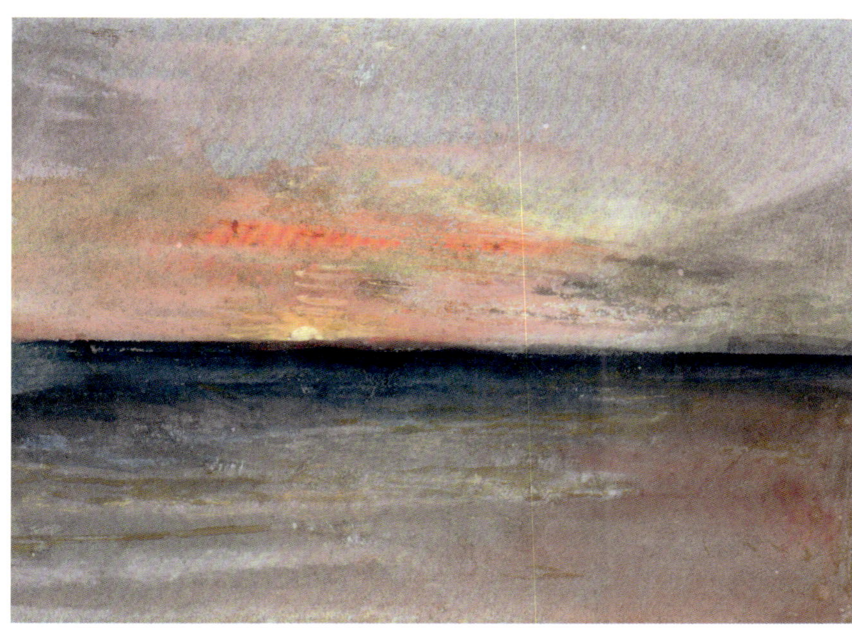

Sunset

Couché du soleil

Sonnenuntergang

Puesta de sol

Pôr-do-sol

Zonsondergang

**Joseph Mallord William Turner
(1775-1851)**

———

c. 1830, Oil on canvas/Huile sur toile,
Private collection

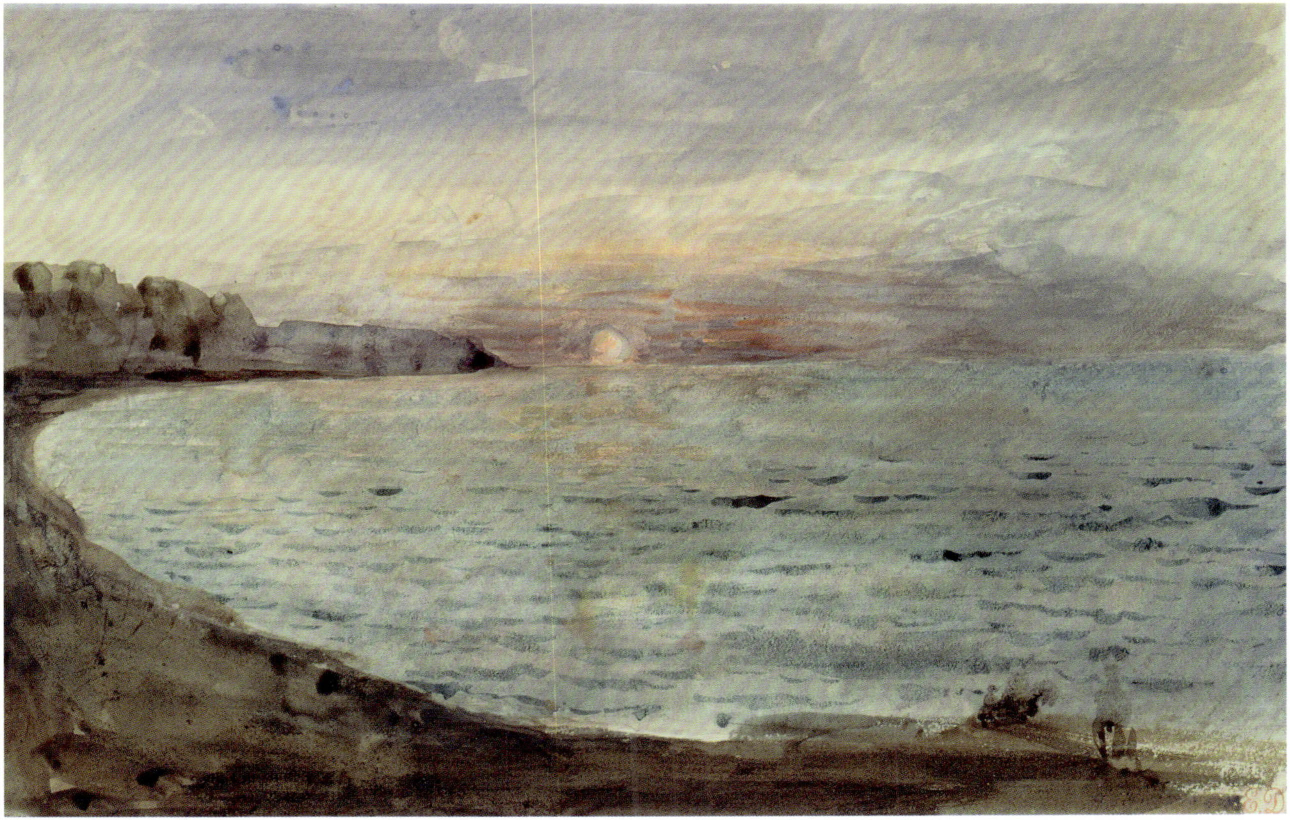

MANET ~ MORISOT

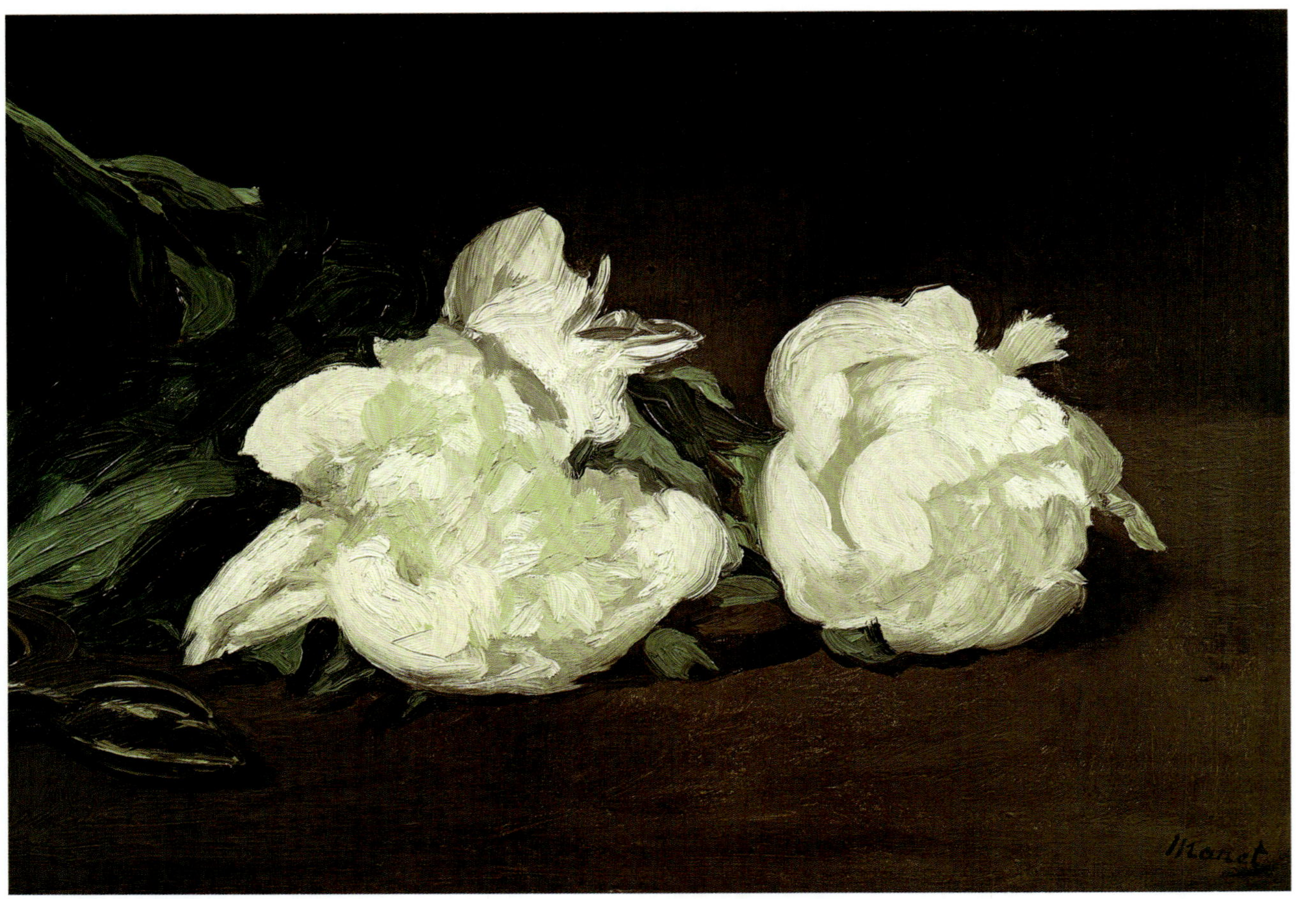

The coarse and powerful execution contrasts with the delicate motif. Manet's advice and, above all, his works shaped the work of Berthe Morisot - not just her copies. Even though the painter was never a student of Manet's, his influence is clearly recognizable.

Si le sujet est extrêmement délicat, sa facture en revanche est large et puissante. Sans doute, les conseils de Manet et surtout ses œuvres furent suivis à la lettre par Berthe Morisot lorsqu'elle s'exerça au pinceau. Bien qu'elle ne fût jamais l'élève de Manet, son style s'en ressent fortement.

Die grobe und kraftvolle Ausführung steht im Kontrast zu dem feingliedrigen Motiv. Manets Ratschläge und vor allem seine Werke prägten das Schaffen von Berthe Morisot – nicht nur ihre Kopien. Auch wenn die Malerin nie eine Schülerin Manets war, ist sein Einfluss deutlich erkennbar.

**Berthe Morisot
(1841-1895)**

———

c. 1869, Oil on canvas/Huile
sur toile, 40,8 × 33 cm,
National Gallery of Art,
Washington

*Branch of White Peonies
and Secateurs*

*Branche de pivoines blanches
et sécateur*

Weiße Pfingstrosen

Ramo de peonías blancas

Peónias brancas

Witte pioenrozen

**Édouard Manet
(1832-1883)**

———

1864, Oil on canvas/Huile
sur toile, 30,5 × 46,5 cm,
Musée d'Orsay, Paris

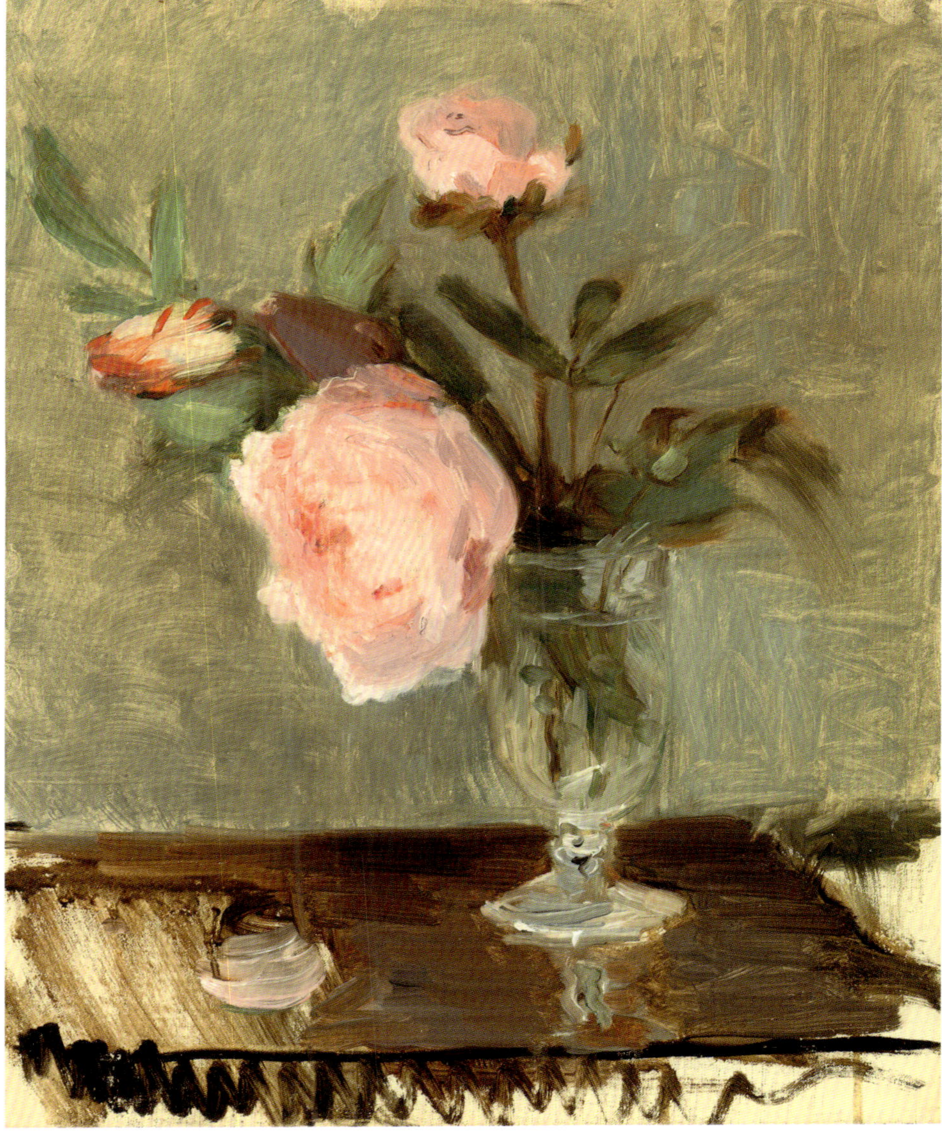

Si bien el tema es extremadamente delicado, su construcción es amplia y poderosa. Sin duda, los consejos de Manet y sobre todo sus obras fueron seguidos al pie de la letra por Berthe Morisot cuando practicaba con un pincel. Aunque nunca fue la estudiante de Manet, su estilo se vio fuertemente afectado.

A execução grosseira e poderosa contrasta com o motivo delicado. Os conselhos de Manet e, sobretudo, as suas obras moldaram a obra de Berthe Morisot - não apenas as suas cópias. Embora o pintor nunca tenha sido aluno de Manet, sua influência é claramente reconhecível.

De grove en krachtige uitvoering contrasteert met het delicate motief. Manets adviezen en vooral zijn werken hebben het oeuvre van Berthe Morisot gevormd – niet alleen haar kopieën. Hoewel de schilderes nooit een leerling van Manet is geweest, is zijn invloed duidelijk herkenbaar.

FRIEDRICH ~ COURBET

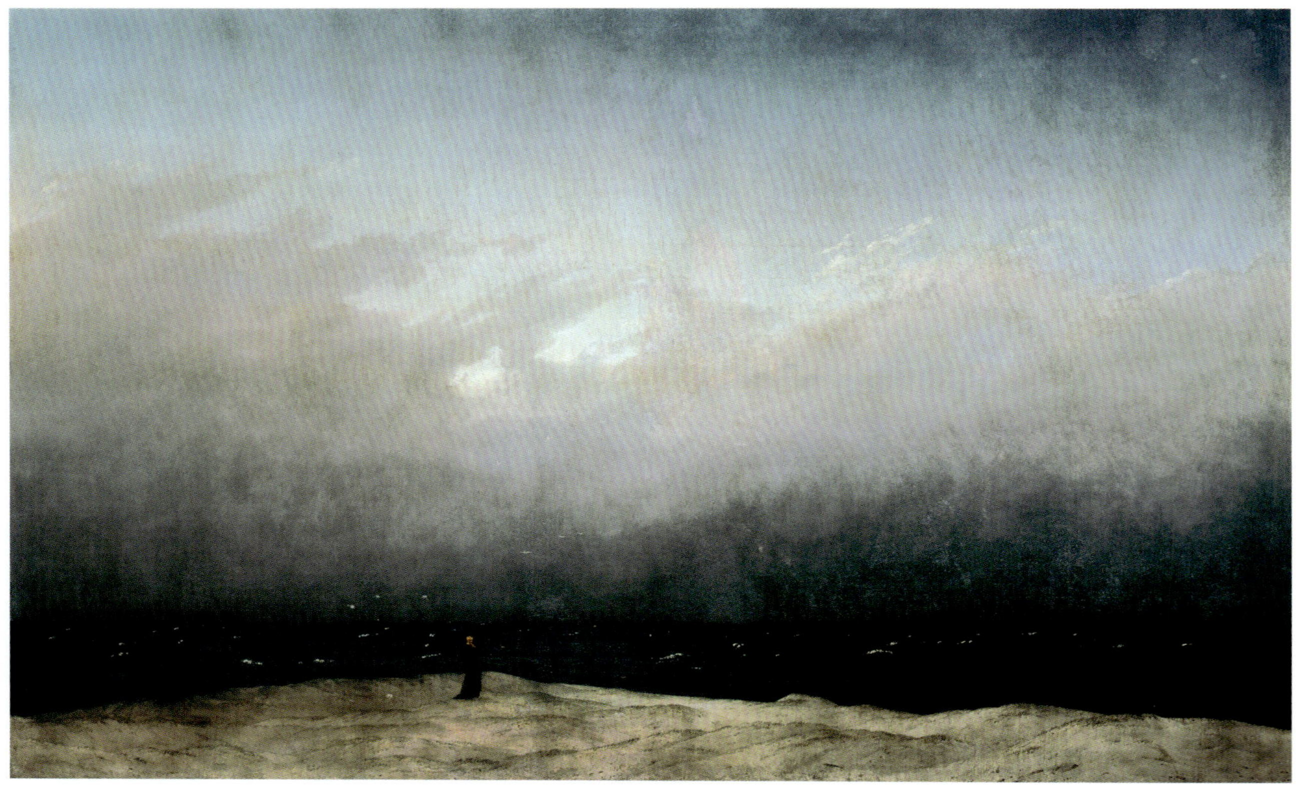

The Monk by the Sea

Le Moine au bord de la mer

Der Mönch am Meer

El monje junto al mar

O monge à beira-mar

Monnik aan zee

Caspar David Friedrich (1774-1840)

———

c. 1808-10, Oil on canvas/Huile sur toile,
110 × 171,5 cm, Alte Nationalgalerie, Berlin

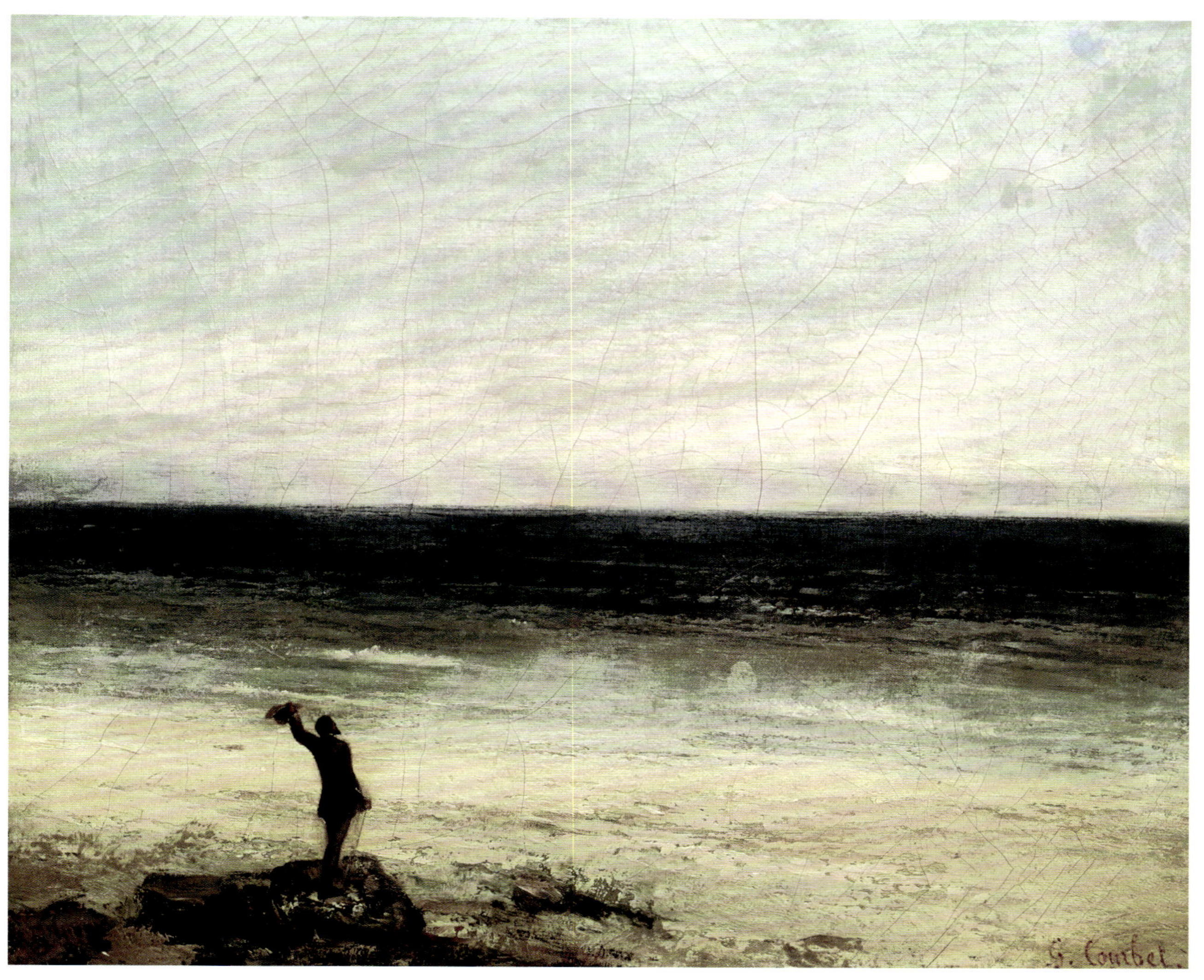

Seaside at Palavas
Le Bord de mer à Palavas
Die Küste bei Palavas
La costa de Palavas
A costa em Palavas
De zee bij Palavas

Gustave Courbet (1819-1877)

———

c. 1854, Oil on canvas/Huile sur toile,
37 × 40 cm, Musée Fabre, Montpellier

VELÁZQUEZ ~ GOYA

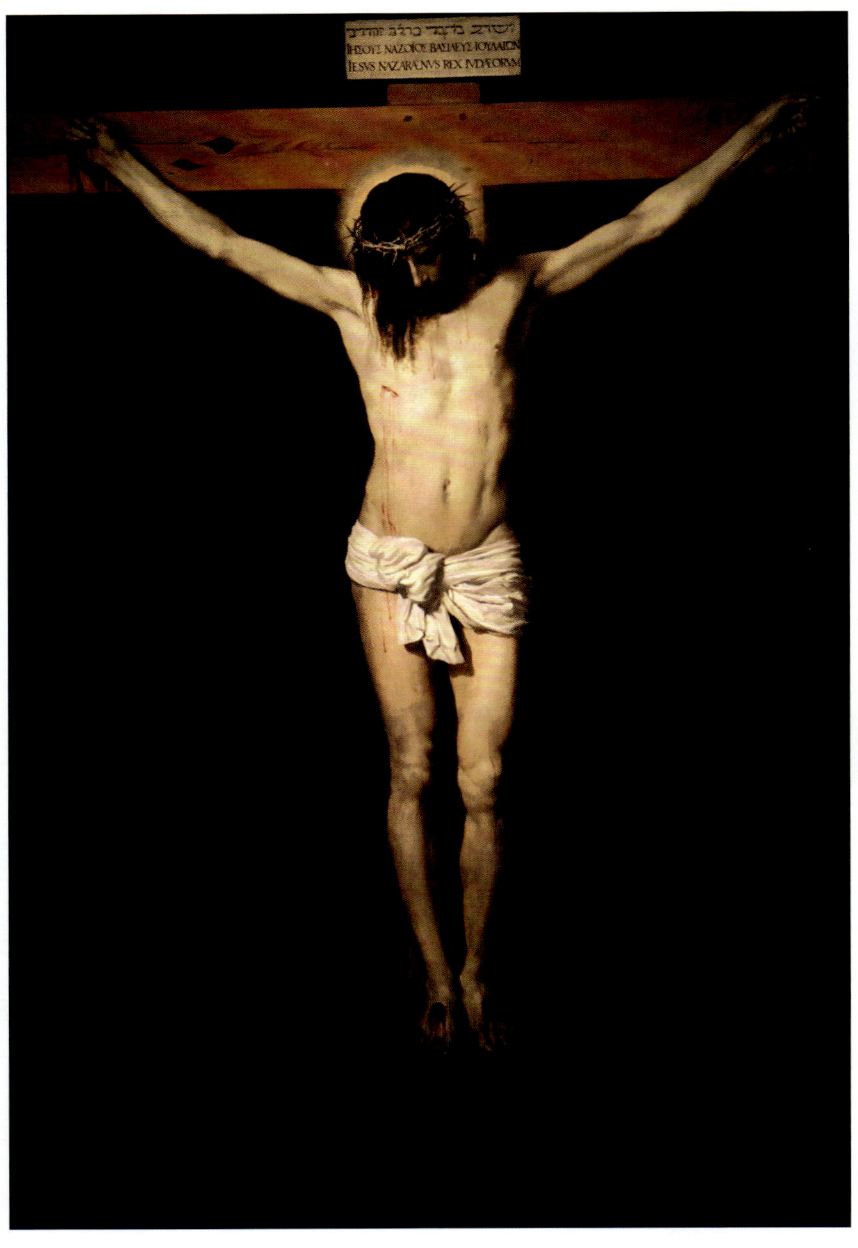

The Crucified Christ
Crucifixion
Christus am Kreuz
Cristo en la cruz
Cristo na cruz
Christus aan het kruis

Diego Velázquez (1599-1660)

———

c. 1632, Oil on canvas/Huile sur toile,
248 × 169 cm, Museo del Prado, Madrid

Christ Crucified
Le Christ en Croix
Christus am Kreuz
Cristo en la cruz
Cristo na cruz
Christus aan het kruis

Francisco de Goya (1746-1828)

1780, Oil on canvas/Huile sur toile,
255 × 154 cm, Museo del Prado, Madrid

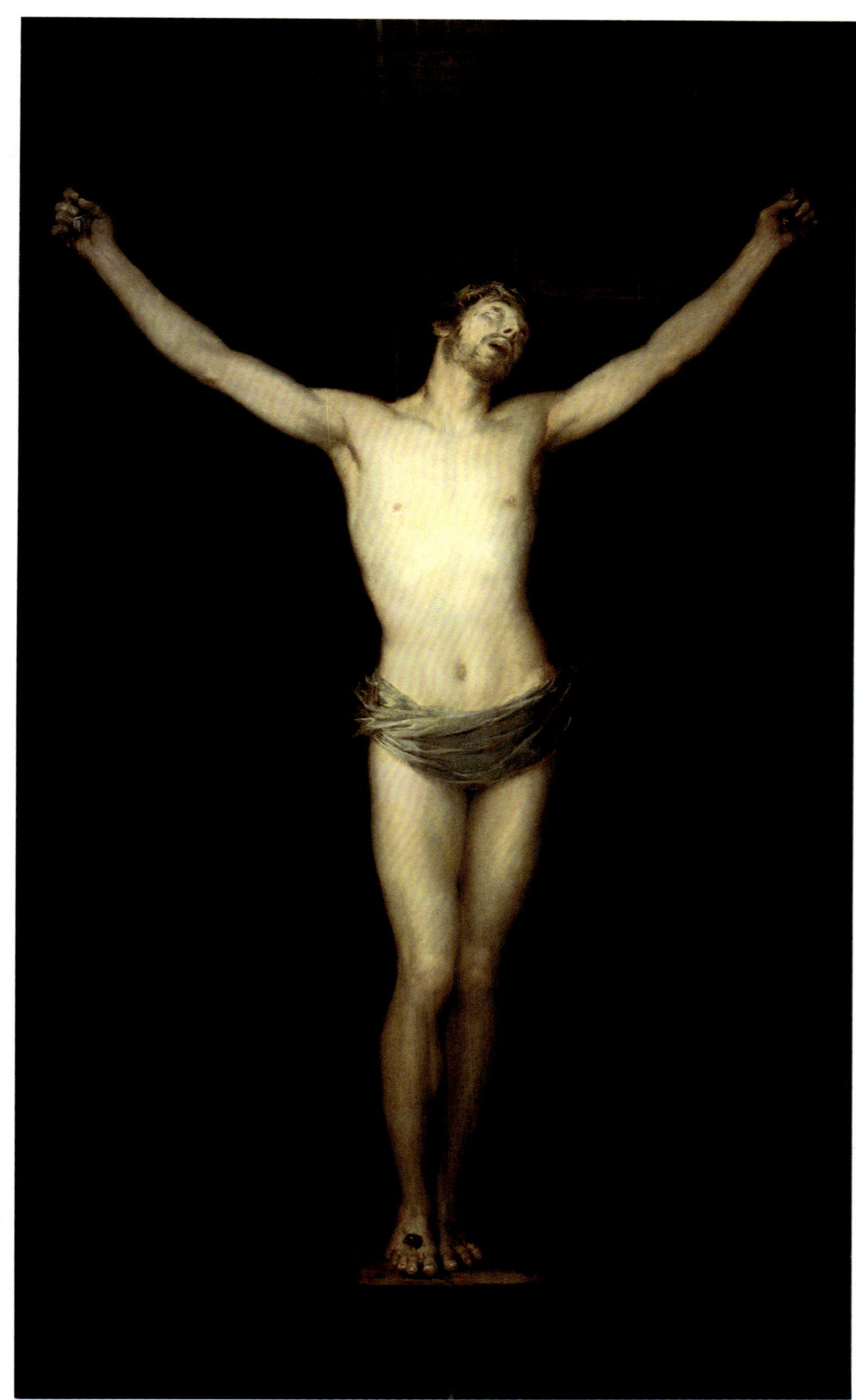

DA VINCI ~ REDON

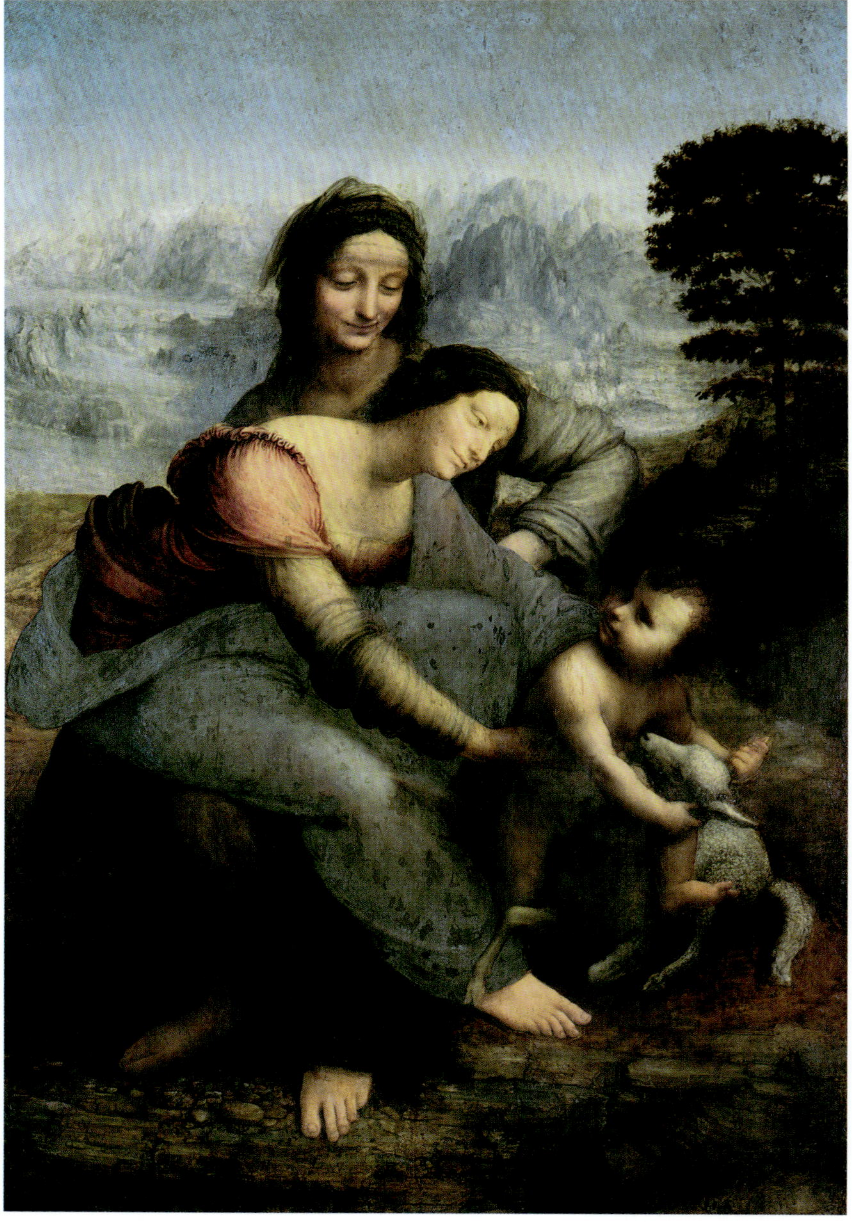

Virgin and Child with St. Anne
La Vierge à l'Enfant avec sainte Anne
Anna selbdritt
Santa Ana, con la Virgen y el Niño
A Virgem e o Menino com Santa Ana
Maria met kind en Sint-Anna
Leonardo da Vinci (1452-1519)

———

c. 1503-19, Oil on wood/Huile sur bois,
168 × 130 cm, Musée du Louvre, Paris

Homage to Leonardo da Vinci
Hommage à Léonard de Vinci
Hommage an Leonardo da Vinci
Homenaje a Leonardo da Vinci
Homenagem a Leonardo da Vinci
Hommage aan Leonardo da Vinci

Odilon Redon (1840-1916)

———

1914, Pastel on paper on cardboard/Pastel
sur papier et carton, 145 × 63 cm, Stedelijk
Museum, Amsterdam

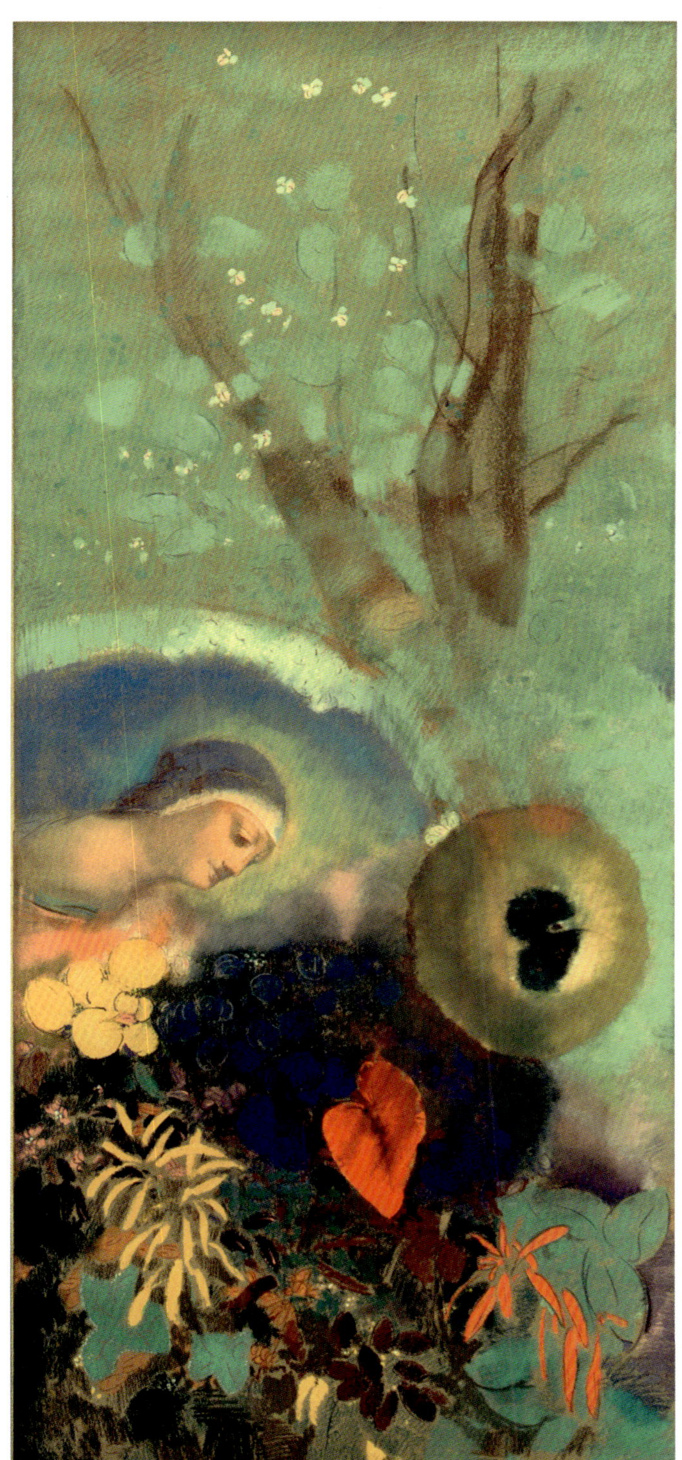

DA VINCI ～ REDON

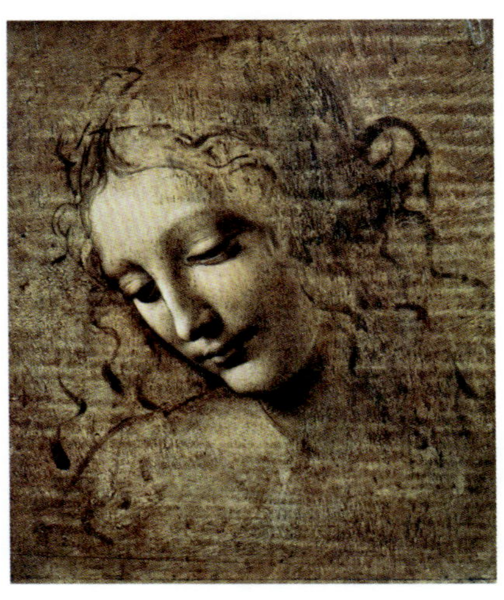

The Scapigliata or *Head of a Young Woman*
La Scapigliata (« L'Ébouriffée ») dite *Tête de jeune fille*
Die Scapigliata oder *Kopf eines Mädchens*
La Scapigliata o *Cabeza de una chica*
La Scapigliata ou *Cabeça de umamenina*
La Scapigliata of *Hoofd van een meisje*

Leonardo da Vinci (1452-1519)

———

c. 1508, Oil with a base of terra ombra, green amber and ceruse on wood/Grisaille à base de terra ombra, ambre verdie et céruse sur bois, 24,7 × 21 cm, Galleria Nazionale, Palazzo della Pilotta, Parma

The Prayer, Face and Flowers
La Prière, visage et fleurs
Das Gebet, Gesicht und Blumen
La oración, el rostro y las flores
A oração, o rosto e as flores
Het gebed, gezicht en bloemen

Odilon Redon (1840-1916)

———

c. 1893, Oil on canvas/Huile sur toile, 32 × 24 cm, Musée des Beaux-Arts, Bordeaux

Sometimes graceful faces or enigmatic profiles can be seen in Redon's works. He was often inspired by Renaissance artists. The painter often referred back to Leonardo da Vinci - his works are recognizable as exact reproductions or sensitive variations.

On peut parfois déceler dans l'œuvre de Redon la présence de gracieux visages ou d'énigmatiques profils. Le plus souvent ils sont inspirés par des artistes de la Renaissance. Léonard de Vinci fut ainsi à plusieurs reprises « sollicité » à l'identique ou avec de délicates variantes.

Manchmal lassen sich auf Redons Werken grazile Gesichter oder rätselhafte Profile erkennen. Oft ließ er sich dabei von den Künstlern der Renaissance inspirieren. Auf Leonardo da Vinci griff der Maler öfter zurück – seine Werke sind als exaktes Abbild oder als feinfühlige Variation erkennbar.

A veces se pueden ver rostros elegantes o perfiles enigmáticos en las obras de Redon. A menudo se inspiraba en los artistas del Renacimiento. El pintor recurrió a menudo a Leonardo da Vinci - sus obras son reconocibles como reproducciones exactas o variaciones sensibles. A Scapigliata ou cabeça de uma menina

Às vezes, rostos graciosos ou perfis enigmáticos podem ser vistos nos trabalhos de Redon. Ele era muitas vezes inspirado por artistas renascentistas. O pintor recorreu frequentemente a Leonardo da Vinci - as suas obras são reconhecíveis como reproduções exactas ou variações sensíveis.

Soms zijn broze gezichten of raadselachtige profielen te zien in Redons werk. Hij liet zich daarbij vaak inspireren door kunstenaars uit de renaissance. De schilder greep geregeld terug op Leonardo da Vinci – diens werken zijn herkenbaar als exacte reproducties of fijngevoelige variaties.

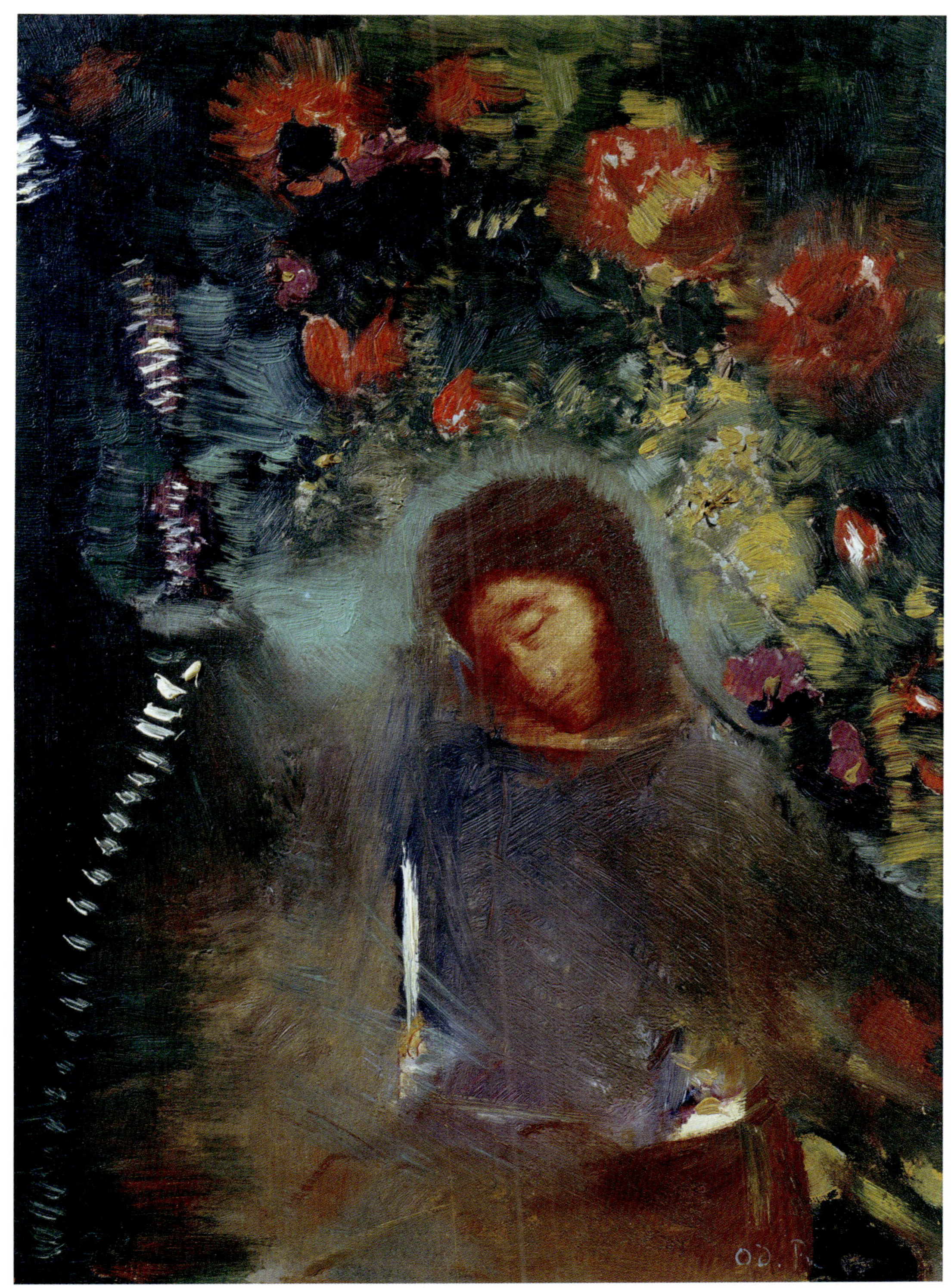

CÉZANNE ~ MACKE

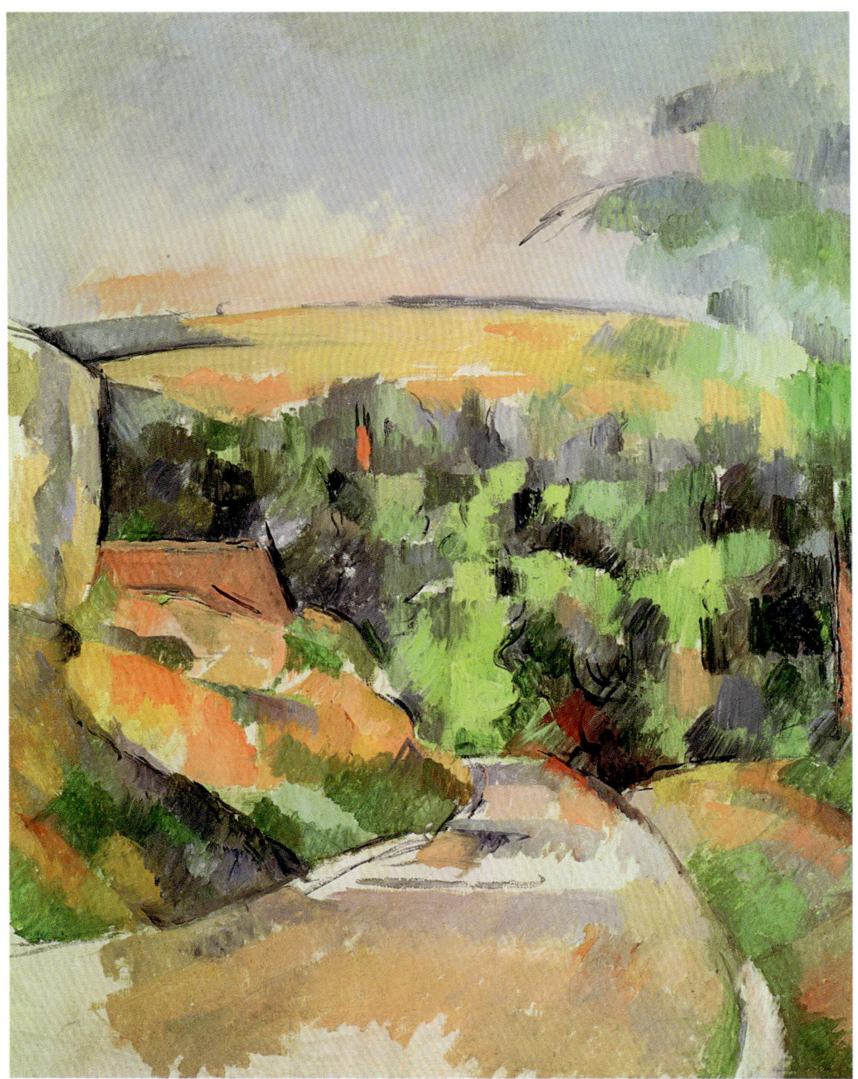

The Bend in the Road

Un virage sur la route

Straßenbiegung

Curva en la carretera

Curva da estrada

Bocht in de weg

Paul Cézanne (1839-1906)

———

1900-06, Oil on canvas/Huile sur toile, 82,1 × 66 cm, National Gallery of Art, Washington

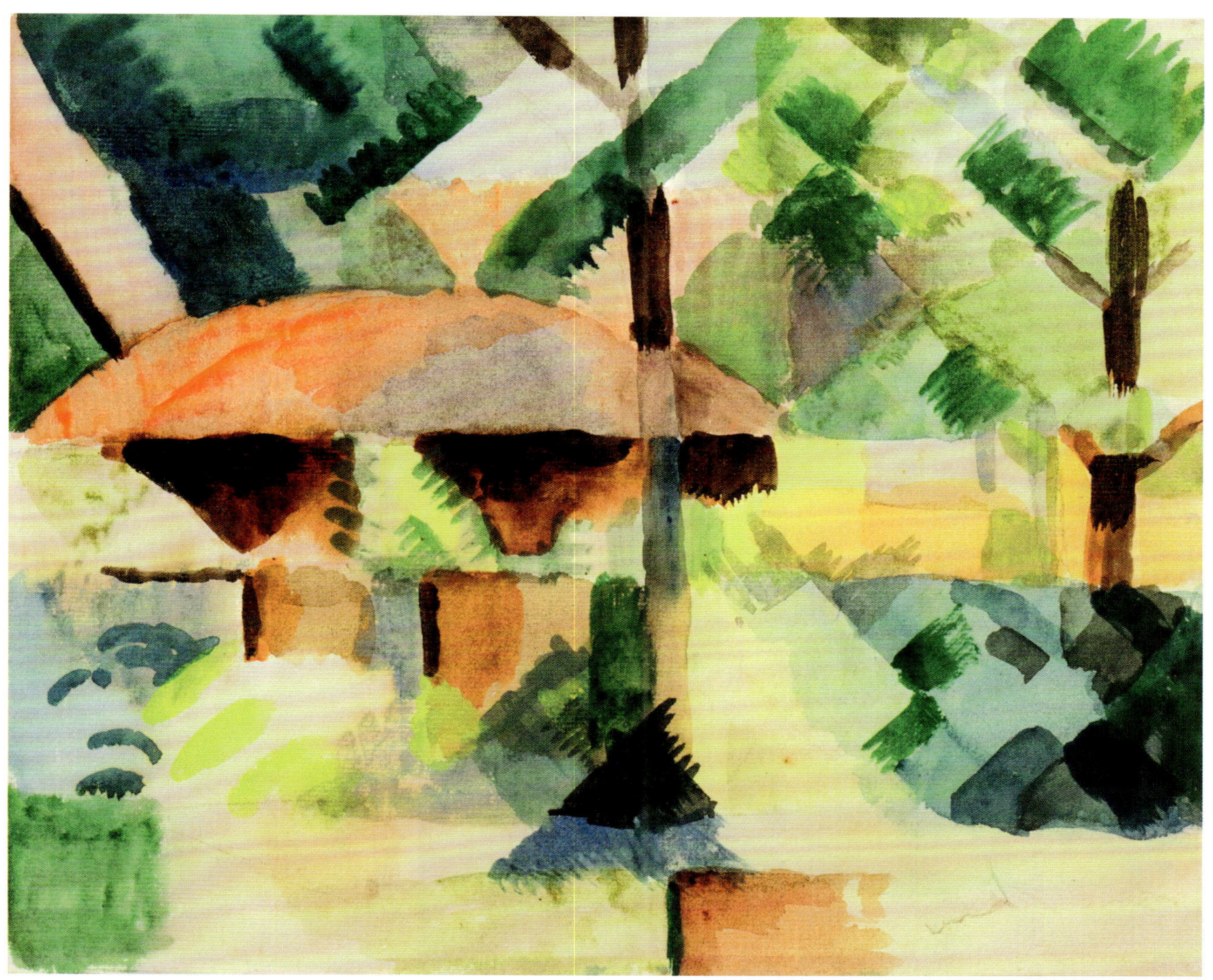

Garden Entrance
Entrée de jardin
Garteneingang
Entrada al jardín
Entrada do jardim
Ingang van de tuin

August Macke (1887-1914)

c. 1914, Oil on canvas/Huile sur toile,
23 × 28,5 cm, Kunstmuseum Moritzburg
Halle, Halle (Saale)

FABRITIUS ~ KERSTING

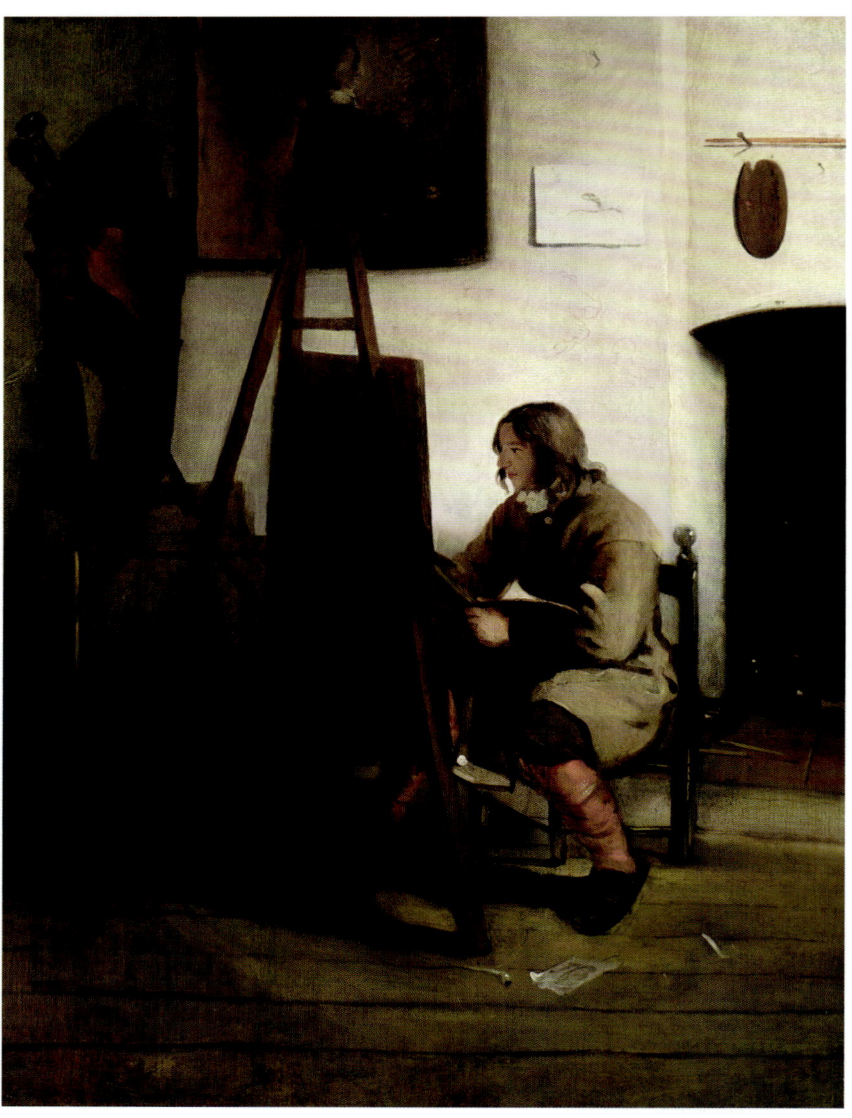

Young Painter in his Studio
Jeune peintre dans son atelier
Junger Maler in seinem Atelier
Joven pintor en su estudio
Jovem pintor no seu estúdio
Jonge schilder in een atelier

Barent Fabritius (1624-1673)

1655-60, Oil on canvas/Huile sur toile,
72 × 54 cm, Musée du Louvre, Paris

Caspar David Friedrich in his Studio
Caspar David Friedrich dans son atelier
Caspar David Friedrich in seinem Atelier
Caspar David Friedrich en su estudio
Caspar David Friedrich em seu estúdio
Caspar David Friedrich in zijn atelier

**Georg Friedrich Kersting
(1785-1847)**

1814-19, Oil on canvas/Huile sur toile,
51,5 × 40,5 cm, Städtische Kunsthalle,
Mannheim

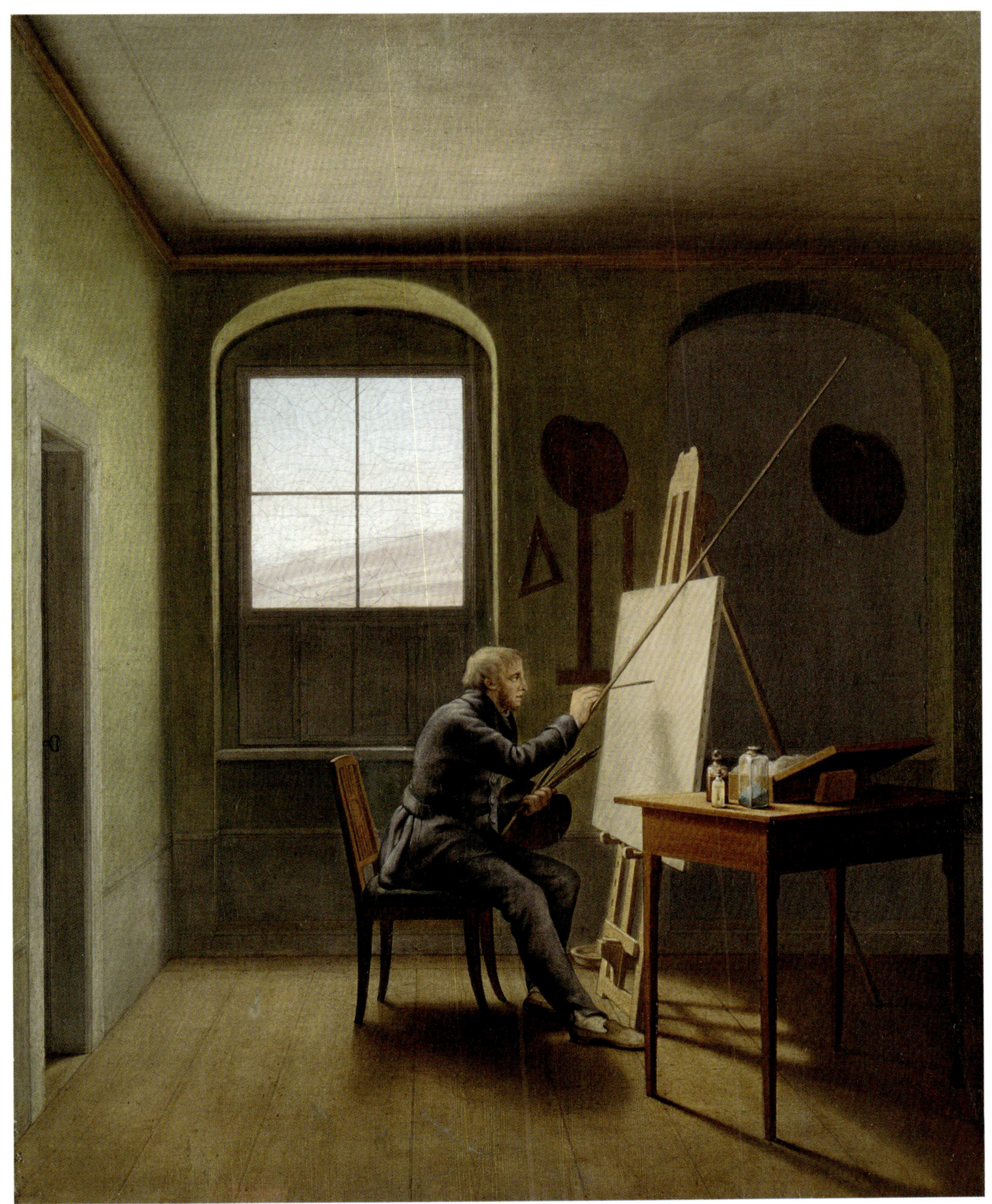

VUILLARD ~ KLIMT

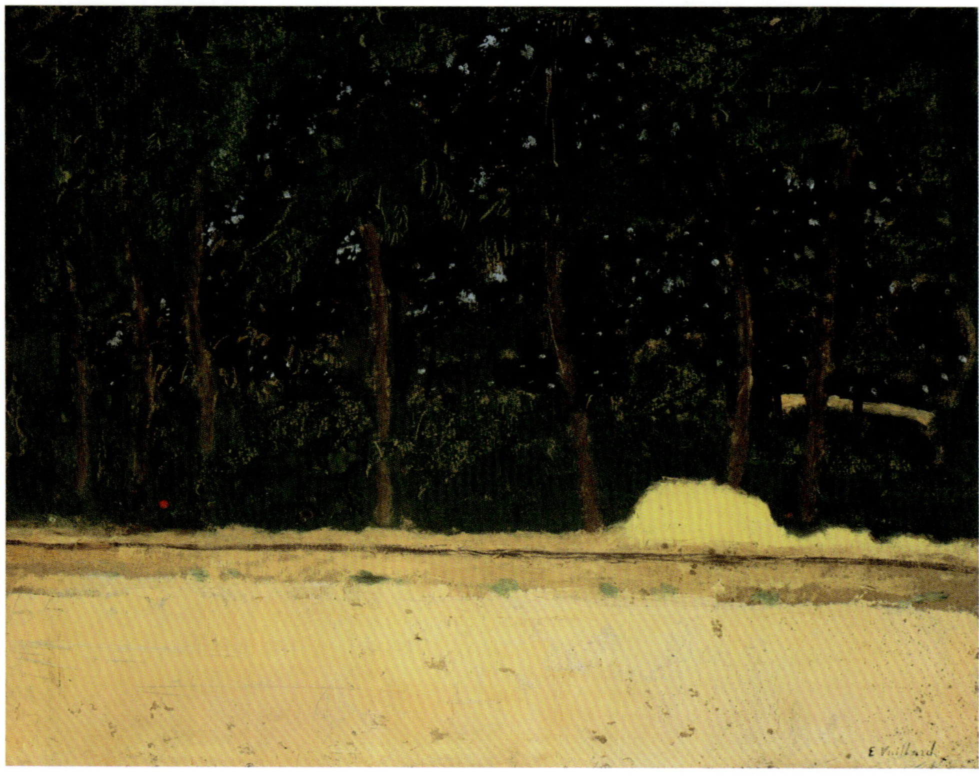

Road at the Edge of the Forest
Route à l'orée de la forêt
Straße am Waldrand
Camino al borde del bosque
Estrada à beira da floresta
Weg langs de rand van het bos

Édouard Vuillard (1868-1940)

———

c. 1904, Oil on cardboard on wood/Huile
sur carton sur bois, 40 × 49 cm,
Private collection

The Apple Tree II
Le Pommier II
Apfelbaum II
Manzano II
Macieira II
Appelboom II

Gustav Klimt (1862-1918)

———

c. 1916, Oil on canvas/Huile sur toile,
80 × 80 cm, Private collection

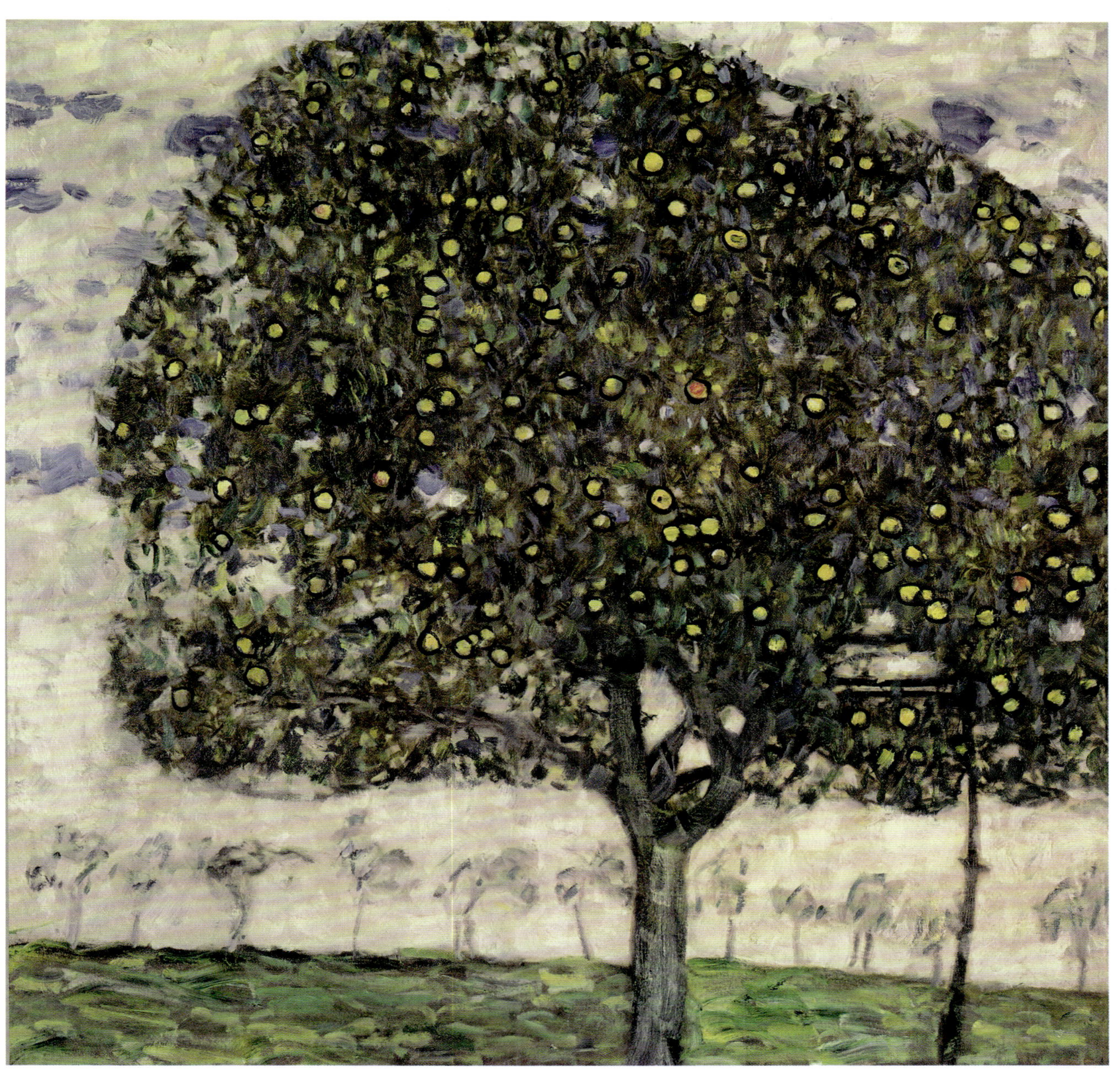

CARAVAGGIO ~ RIBERA

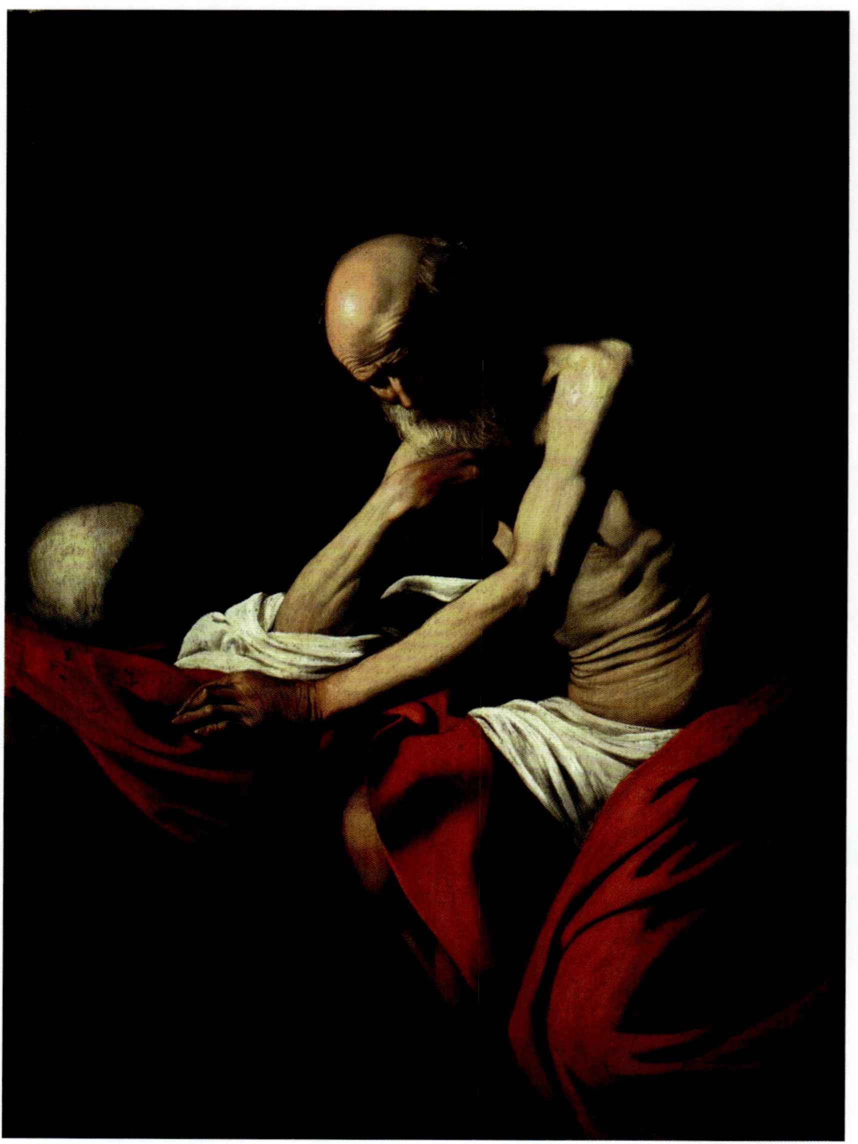

Penitent Saint Jerome
Saint Jérôme pénitent
Der Heilige Hieronymus als Büßer
San Jerónimo como penitente
São Jerônimo como penitente
De mediterende Hiëronymus

**Michelangelo Merisi da Caravaggio
(1571-1610)**

———

1605/06, Oil on canvas/Huile sur toile,
118 × 81 cm, Museu de Montserrat

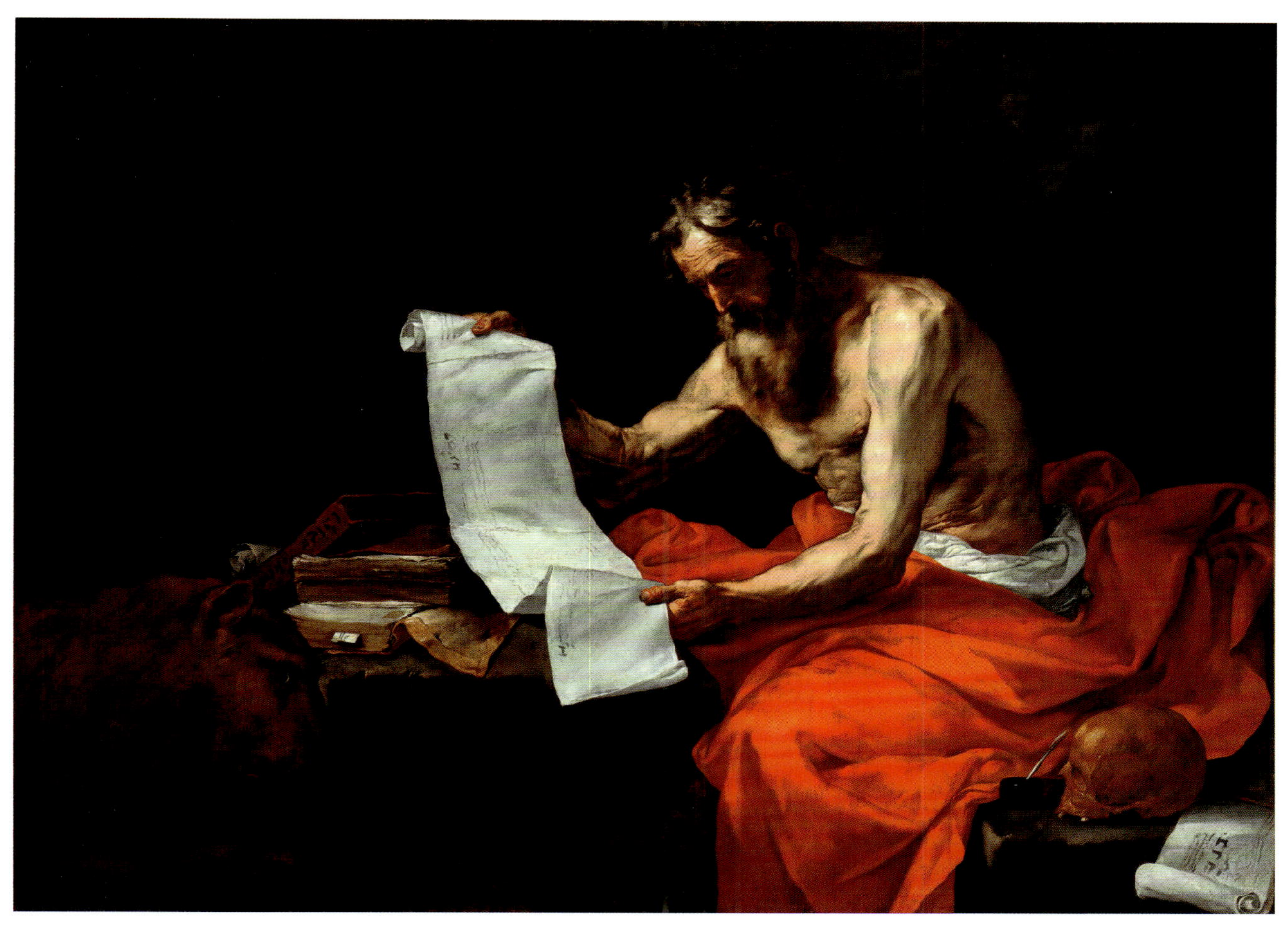

Jusepe de Ribera (1591-1652)

1646, Oil on canvas/Huile sur toile,
146 × 198 cm, Národní Galerie, Praha

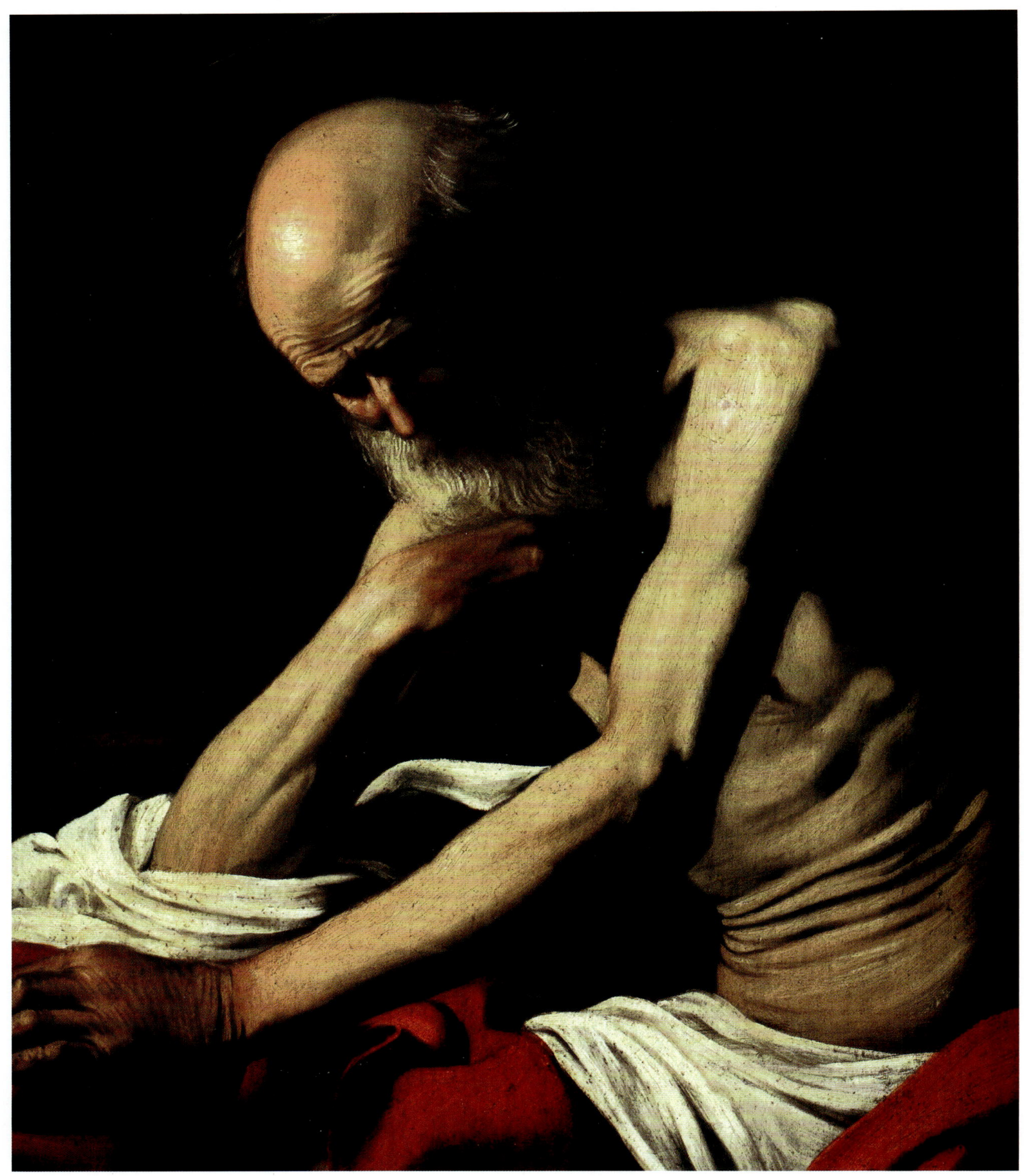

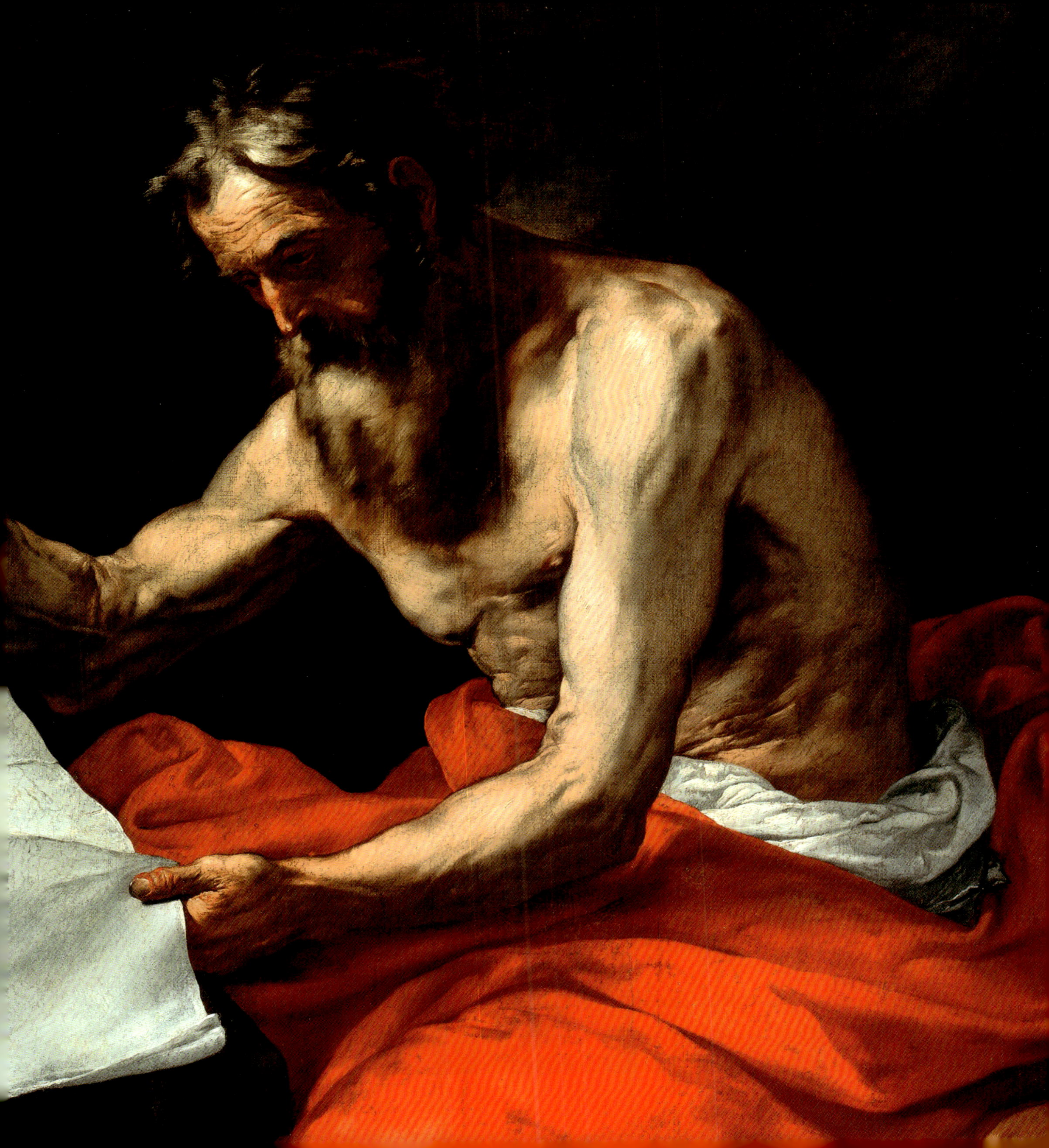

RAFFAELLO ~ MODIGLIANI

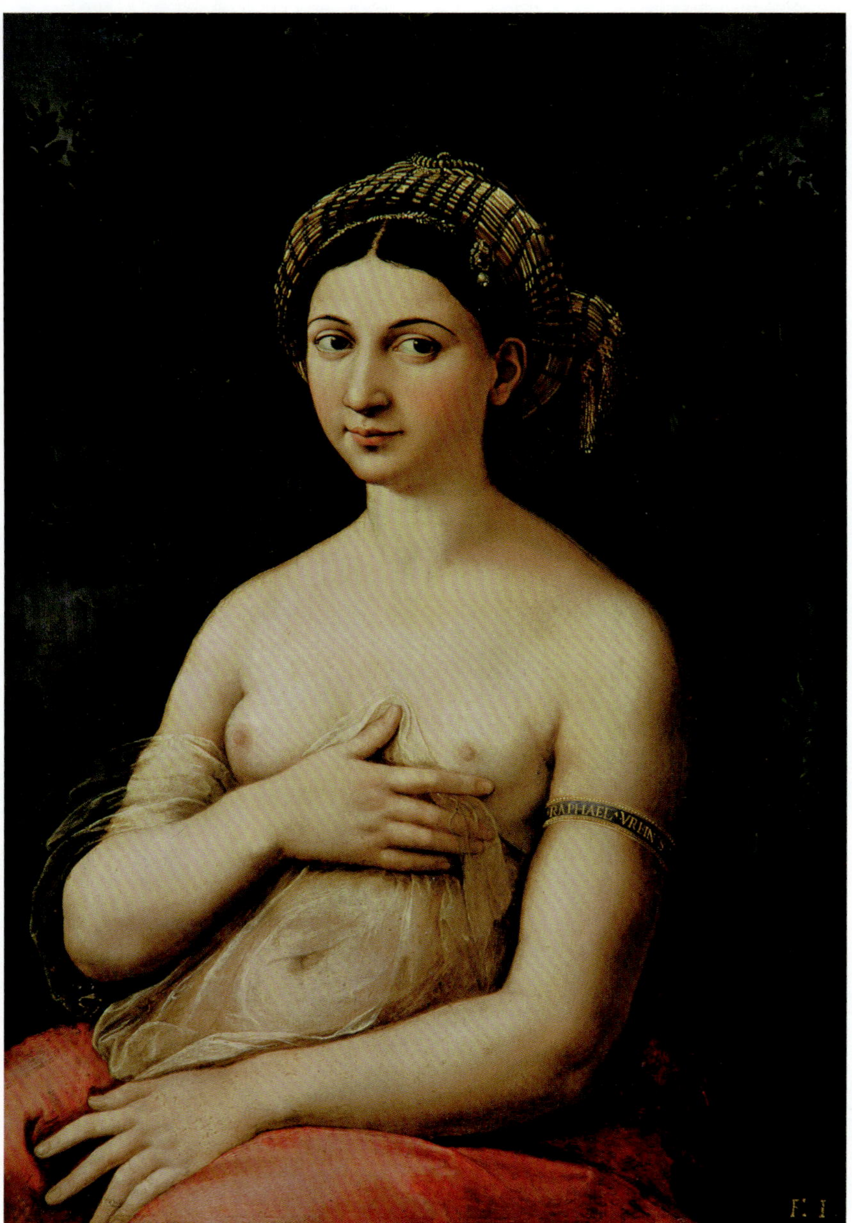

La Fornarina

Raffaello Sanzio (1483-1520)

1518/19, Oil on wood/Huile sur bois,
85 × 60 cm, Gallerie Nazionali Barberini
Corsini, Roma

Portrait of a Young Woman
Portrait d'une jeune femme
Porträt einer jungen Frau
Retrato de una mujer joven
Retrato de uma jovem mulher
Portret van een jonge vrouw

Amedeo Modigliani (1884-1920)

1916-19, Oil on canvas/Huile sur toile,
65,7 × 50,2 cm,
Dallas Museum of Art, Dallas

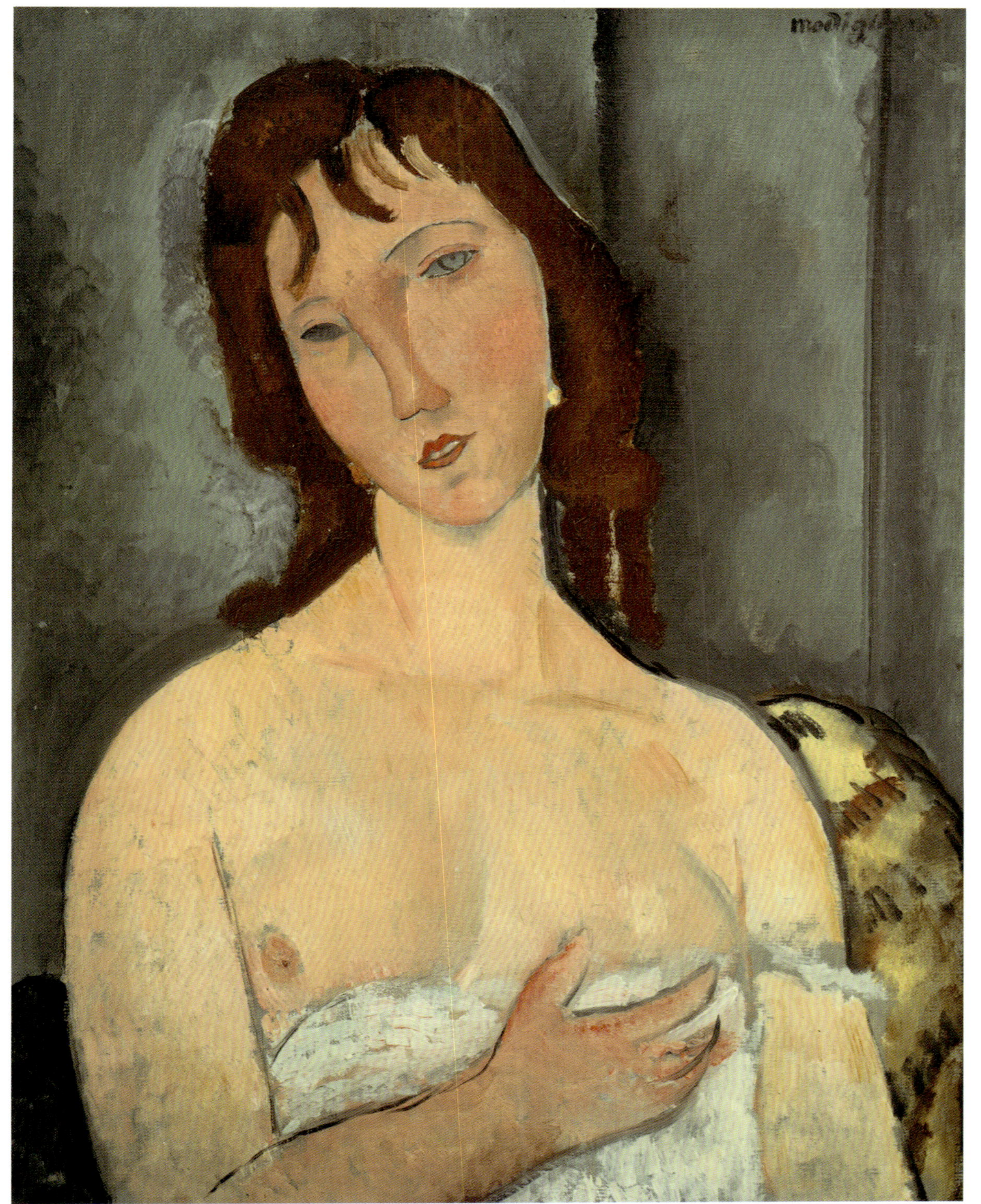

modigliani

LORRAIN ~ GAINSBOROUGH ~ CONSTABLE

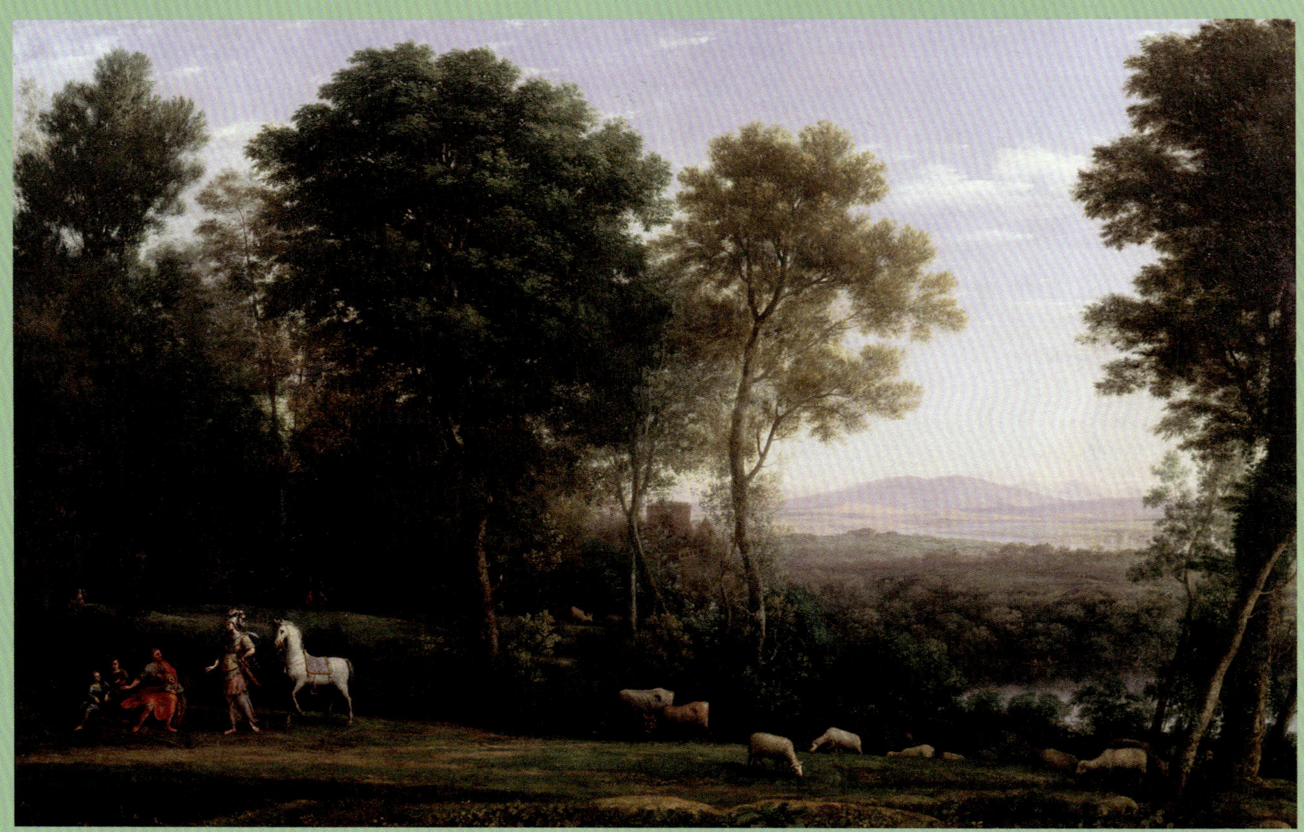

Landscape with Erminia and the Shepherds

Paysage avec Erminia et les bergers

Landschaft mit Erminia und den Schäfern

Paisaje con Erminia y los pastores

Paisagem com Erminia e os pastores

Erminia en de herders

Claude Lorrain (1600-1682)

‾‾‾‾

c. 1666, Oil on canvas/Huile sur toile,
92,5 × 137 cm, Holkham Hall, Wells-next-the-Sea

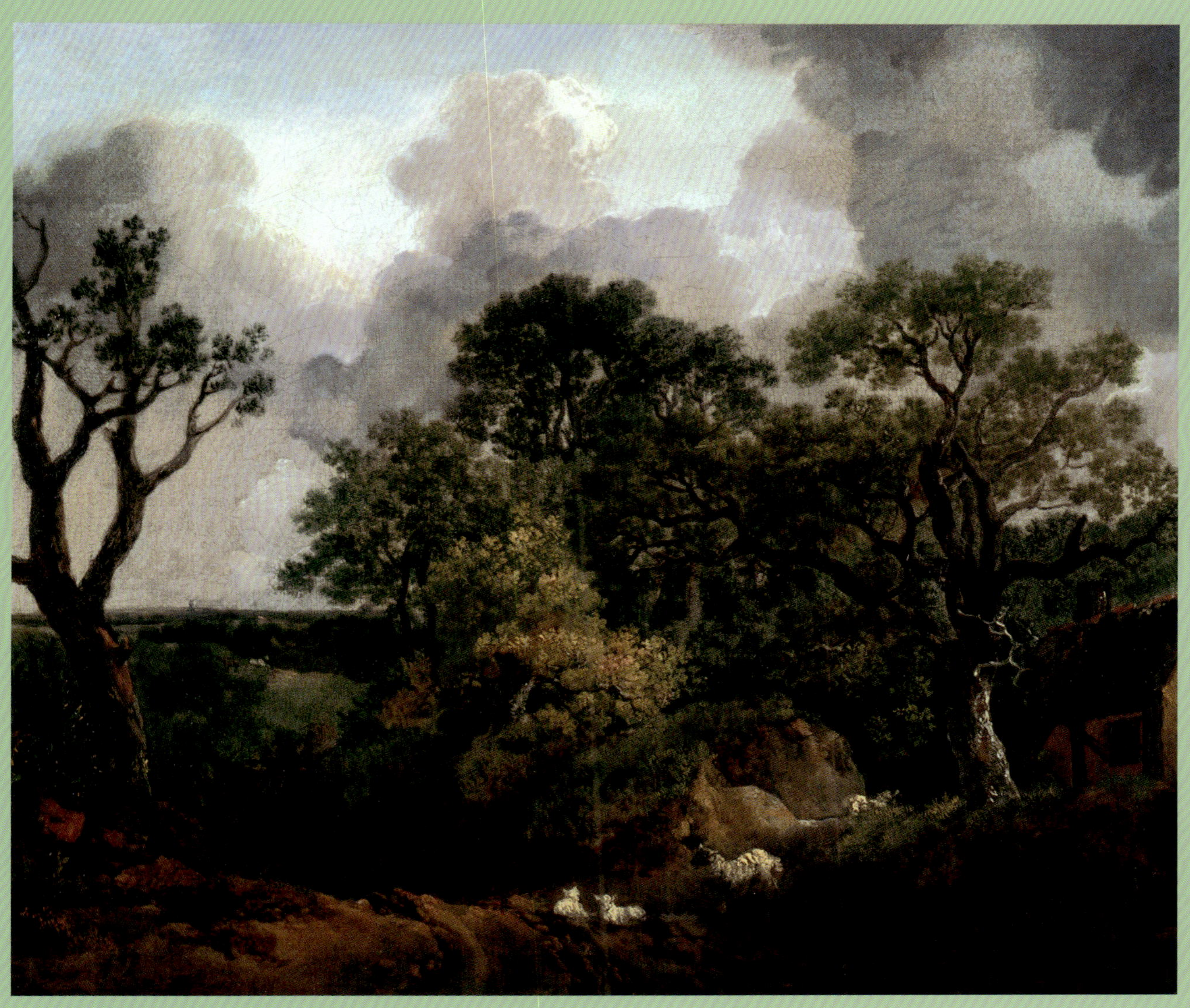

Wooded Landscape
Paysage boisé
Landschaft mit Bäumen
Paisaje con árboles
Paisagem com árvores
Boomachtig landschap

Thomas Gainsborough (1727-1788)

———

n. d., Oil on canvas/Huile sur toile,
Private collection

LORRAIN ~ GAINSBOROUGH ~ CONSTABLE

Lorrain's peaceful landscape with shepherds had everything that fascinated the artist Thomas Gainsborough. His version even surpasses the original and underlines the influence of the French master from the 17th century on the English school of the 18th century. At the beginning of the 19th century, Constable was inspired by Claude Lorrain. His small picture already shows the painter's early impressionist genius.

Baigné d'une douce poésie pastorale, ce paysage du Lorrain avait tout pour séduire l'élégant artiste Thomas Gainsborough. À en juger par le résultat, le subtil pari semble avoir été gagné mettant ainsi en avant l'influence du maître français du XVIIe siècle sur l'école anglaise du XVIIIe. Le XIXe siècle naissant ne sera pas en reste puisqu'à travers cette petite huile sur carton, due au génie impressionniste avant l'heure de Constable, sa nature doit encore beaucoup à Claude Gellée dit le Lorrain.

Lorrains friedliches Landschaftsbild mit Schäfern hatte alles, was den Künstler Thomas Gainsborough faszinierte. Seine Version übertrifft sogar das Original und unterstreicht den Einfluss des französischen Meisters aus dem 17. Jahrhundert auf die englische Schule des 18. Jahrhunderts. Zu Beginn des 19. Jahrhunderts lässt sich Constable von Claude Lorrain inspirieren. In seinem kleinen Bild zeigt sich bereits das frühe impressionistische Genie des Malers.

El tranquilo paisaje de Lorrain con sus pastores tenía todo lo que fascinaba al artista Thomas Gainsborough. Su versión supera incluso la original y subraya la influencia del maestro francés del siglo XVII en la escuela inglesa del siglo XVIII. A principios del siglo XIX, Constable se inspiró en Claude Lorrain. Su pequeño cuadro ya muestra el genio impresionista del pintor.

A paisagem pacífica de Lorrain com pastores tinha tudo o que fascinava o artista Thomas Gainsborough. Sua versão até supera a original e sublinha a influência do mestre francês do século XVII sobre a escola inglesa do século XVIII. No início do século XIX, Constable foi inspirado por Claude Lorrain. O seu pequeno quadro já mostra o génio impressionista precoce do pintor.

Lorrains vredige landschap met herders had alles wat de kunstenaar Thomas Gainsborough fascineerde. Zijn versie overtreft zelfs het origineel en onderstreept de invloed van de Franse meester uit de 17e eeuw op de 18e-eeuwse Engelse school. Aan het begin van de 19e eeuw werd Constable geïnspireerd door Claude Lorrain. Dit kleine werk toont al het vroege impressionistische talent van de schilder.

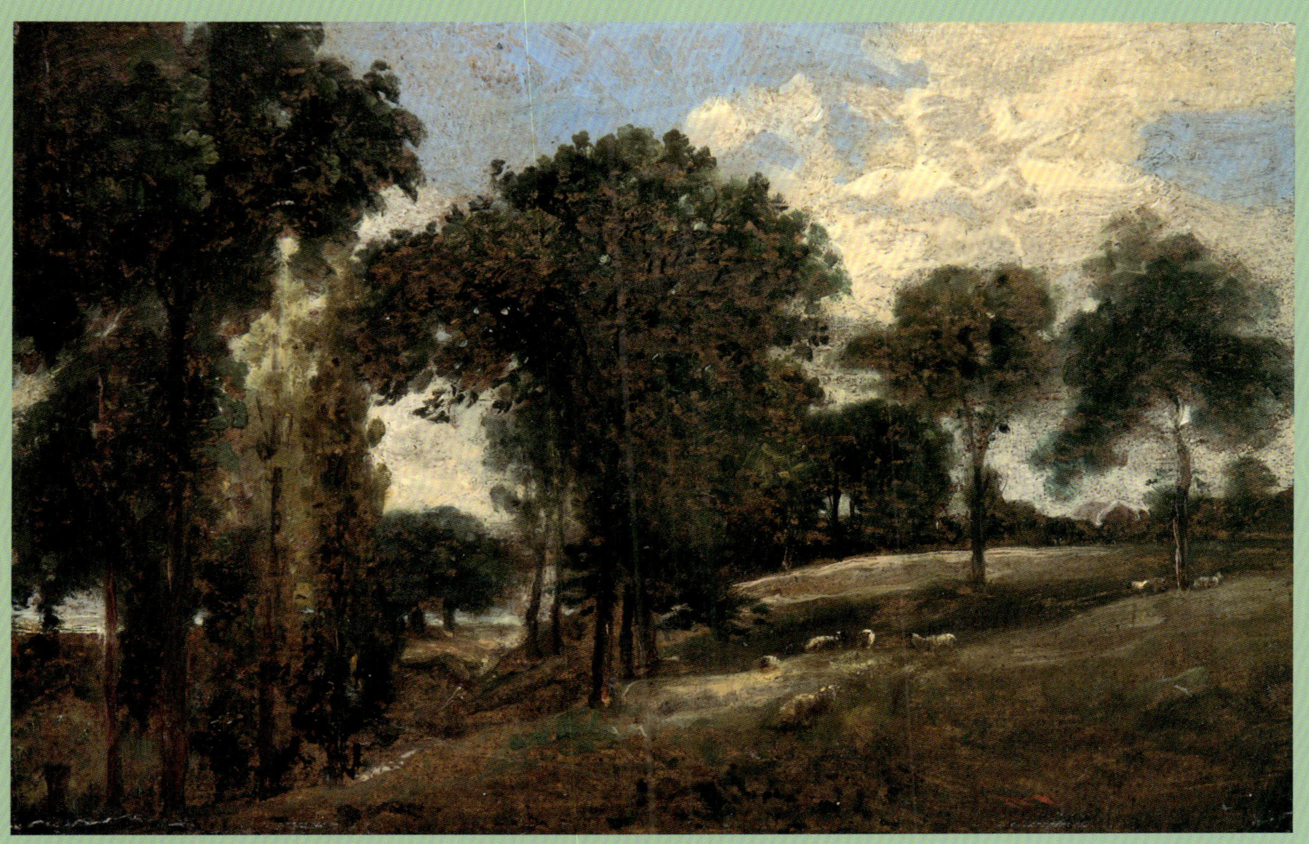

English Landscape
Paysage anglais
Englische Landschaft
Paisaje inglés
Paisagem Inglesa
Engels landschap

John Constable (1776-1837)

———

c. 1820, Oil on cardboard/Huile sur carton,
21,5 × 34,5 cm, Private collection

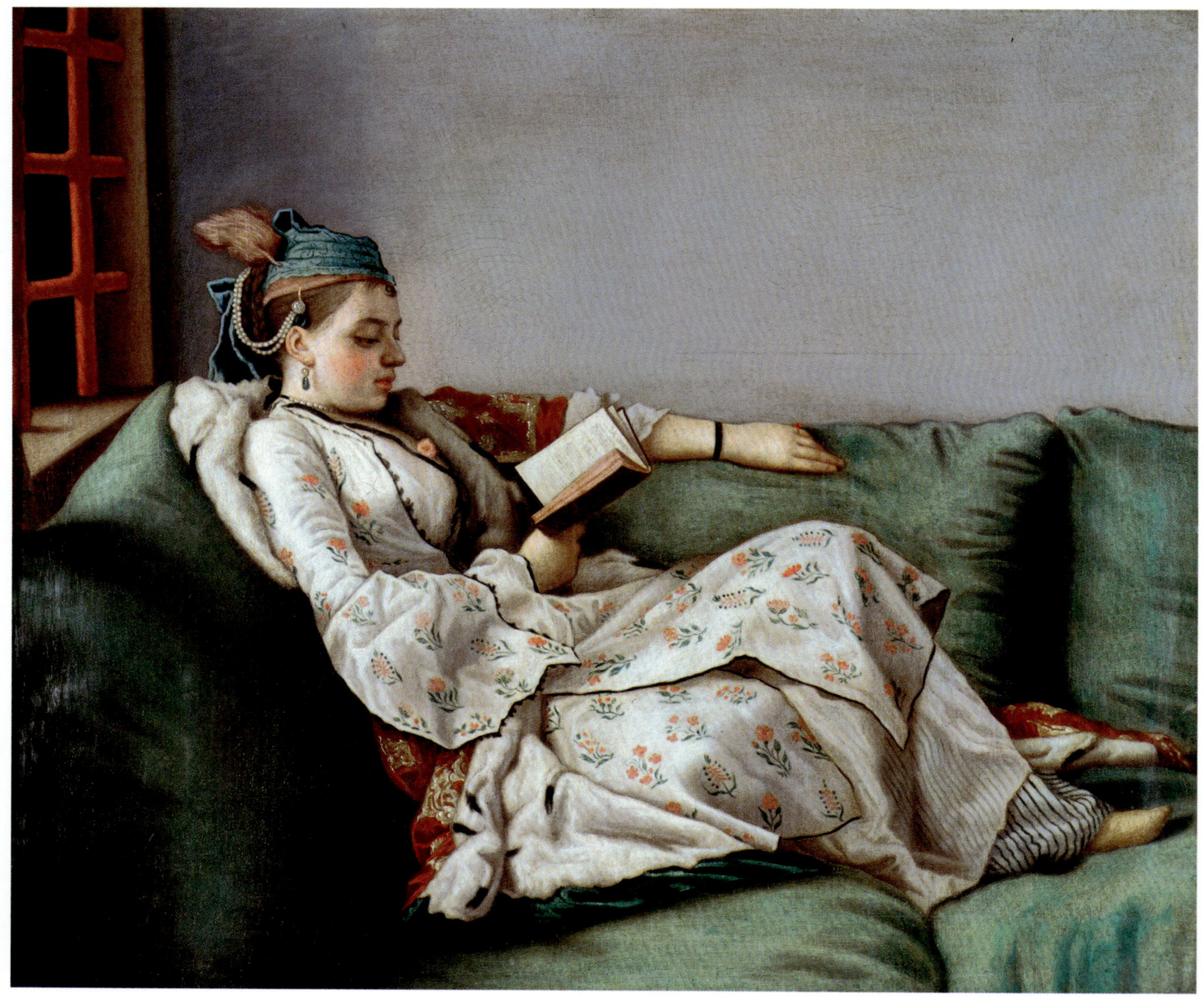

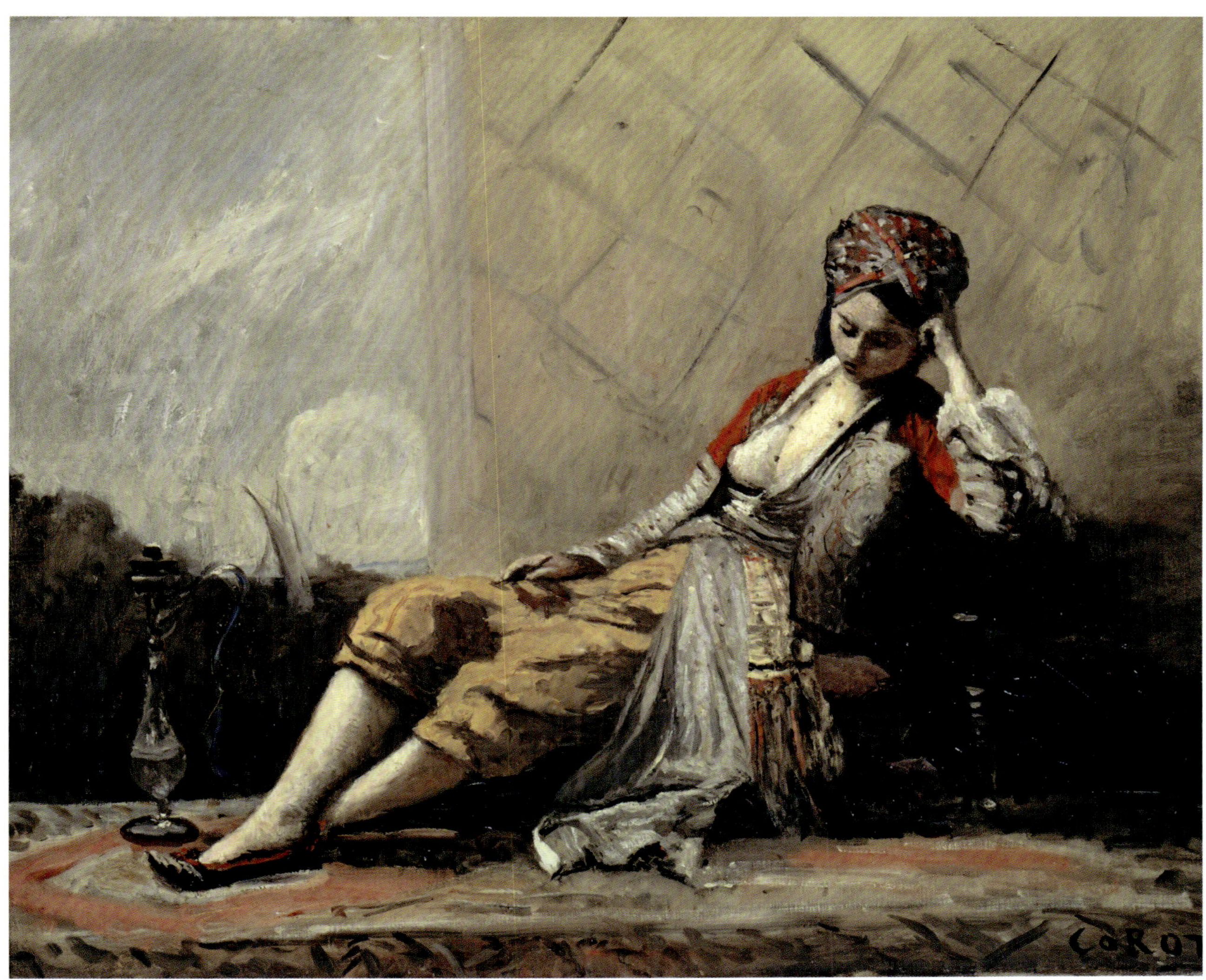

Marie Adelaide of France

Marie-Adélaïde de France

Marie Adelaide von Frankreich

Marie Adelaide de Francia

Marie Adelaide da França

Marie Adelaide van Frankrijk

Jean-Étienne Liotard
(1702-1789)

———

1753, Oil on canvas/Huile sur toile,
50 × 56 cm, Galleria degli Uffizi, Firenze

Odalisque

L'Odalisque

Odaliske

La odalisca

Odalisca

Odalisk

Jean-Baptiste Camille Corot
(1796-1875)

———

1871-73, Oil on canvas/Huile sur toile,
50,7 × 61,2 cm, Kunstmuseum Basel

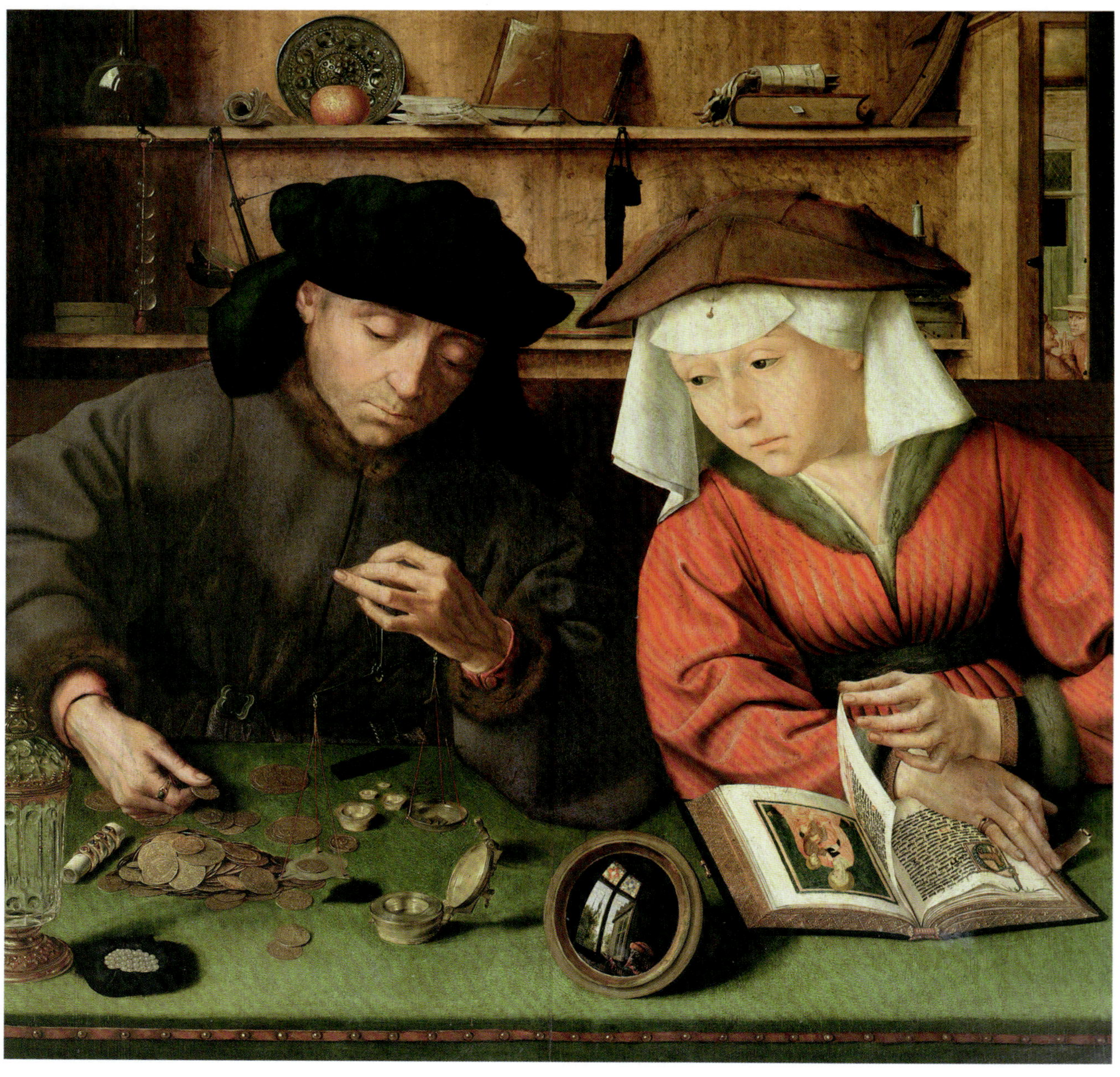

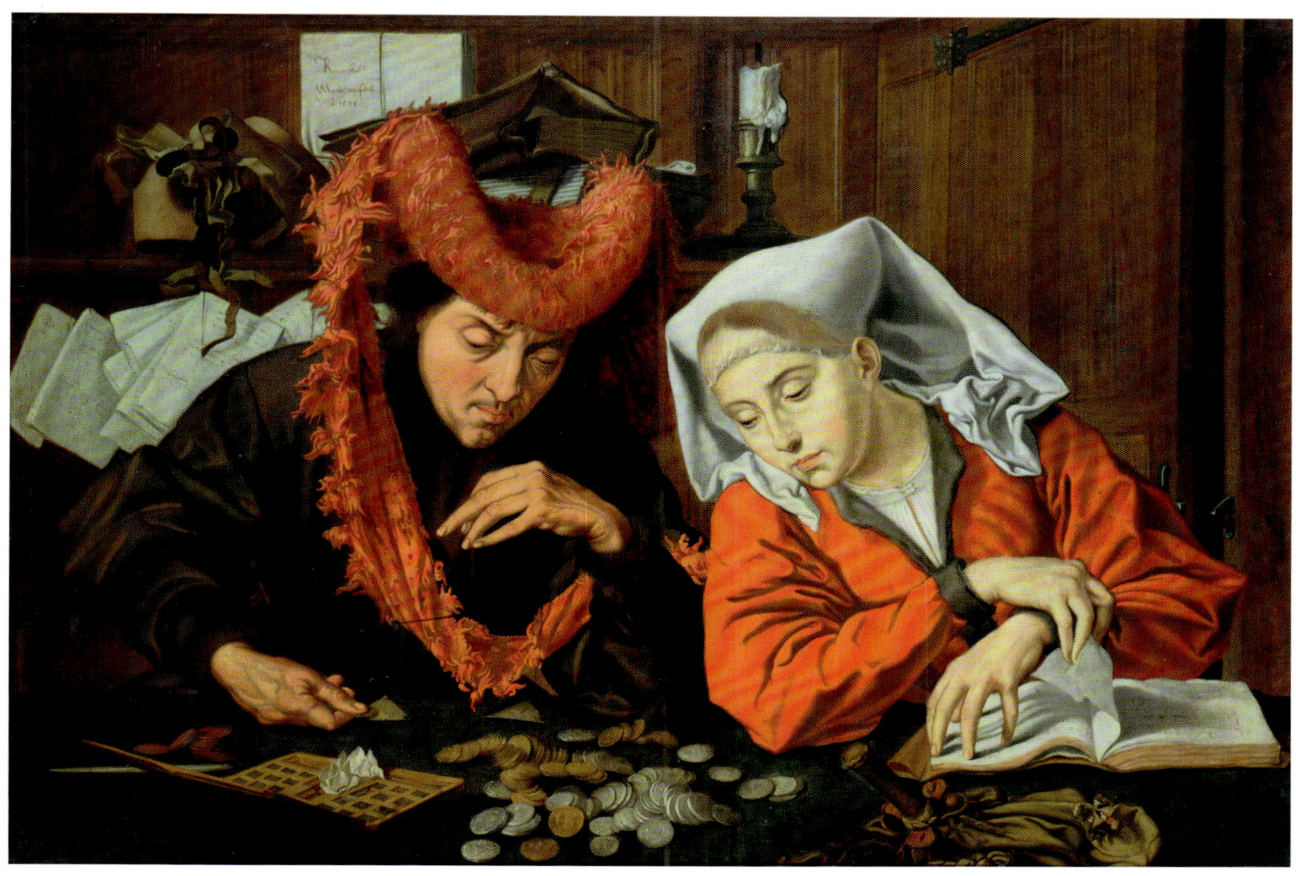

The Moneychanger and his Wife
Un collecteur d'impôt et sa femme
Der Geldwechsler und seine Frau
El cambista y su mujer
O cambista e sua esposa
De geldwisselaar en zijn vrouw

**Marinus van Reymerswaele
(1490-1567)**

c. 1538, Oil on canvas/Huile sur toile,
79 × 112,5 cm, Musée des Beaux-Arts,
Nantes

The Money Lender and his Wife
Le Prêteur et sa femme
Der Geldwechsler und seine Frau
El cambista y su mujer
O cambista e sua esposa
De geldwisselaar en zijn vrouw

Quentin Metsys (1466-1530)

1514, Oil on panel/Huile sur panneau,
70 × 67 cm, Musée du Louvre, Paris

VAN GOGH ~ MUNCH

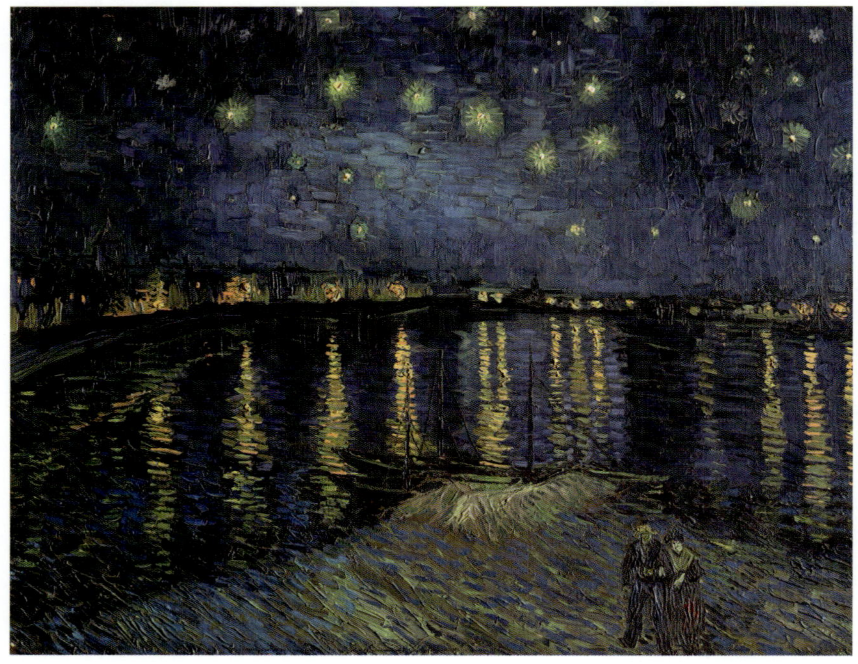

The Starry Night

La Nuit étoilée

Sternennacht über der Rhone

Noche estrellada sobre el Ródano

Noite estrelada sobre o Rhone

Sterrennacht boven de Rhône

Vincent van Gogh (1853-1890)

———

1888, Oil on canvas/Huile sur toile,
73 × 92 cm, Musée d'Orsay, Paris

Starry Night

*Nuit étoilée, paysage nocturne en
Europe du Nord*

*Sternennacht, Nächtliche Landschaft in
Nordeuropa*

*Noche estrellada, paisaje nocturno en el
norte de Europa*

*Noite Estrelada, Paisagem Nocturna no
Norte da Europa*

Sterrennacht

Edvard Munch (1863-1944)

———

1899, Oil on canvas/Huile sur toile,
139 × 119 cm, Munchmuseet, Oslo

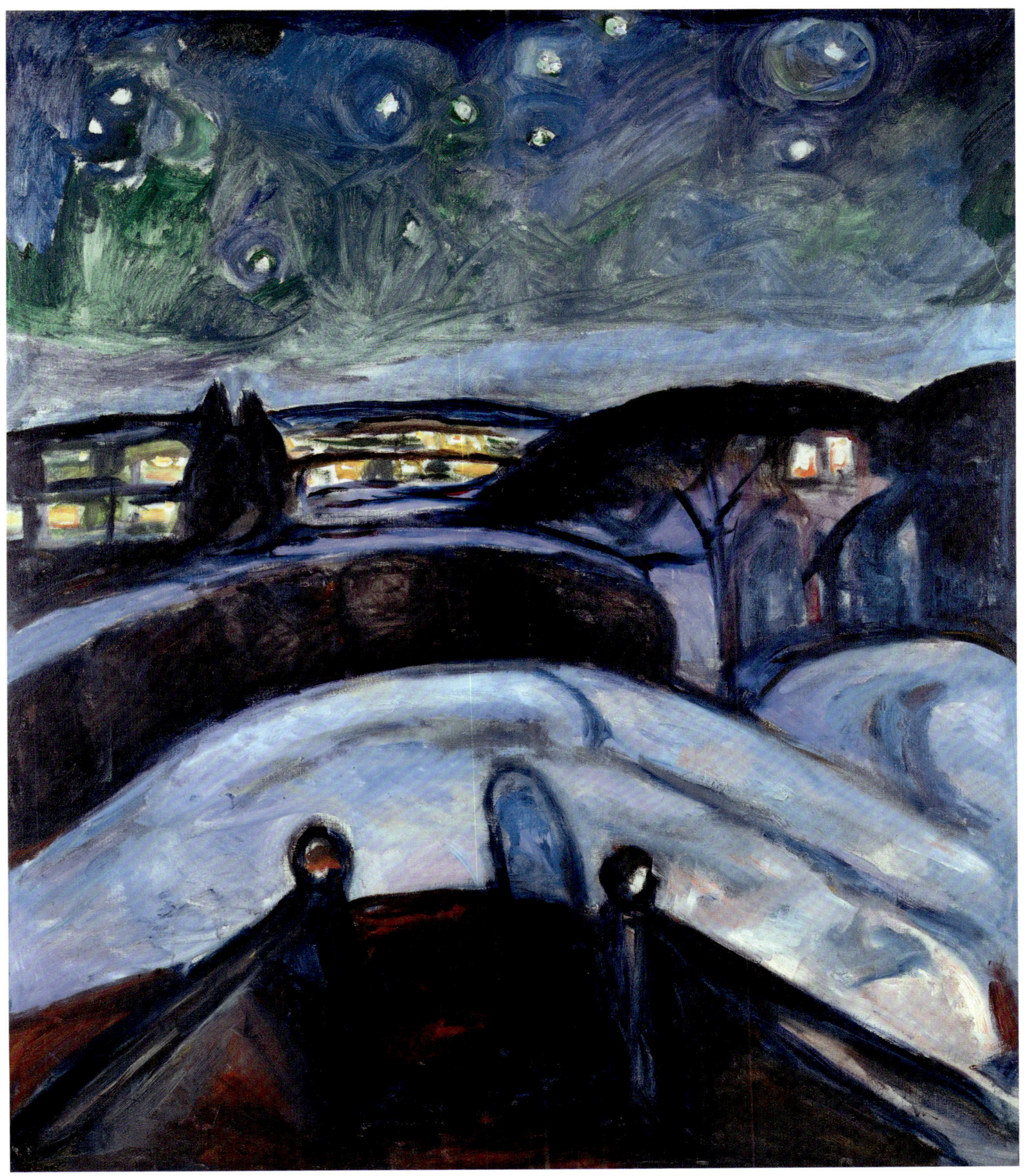

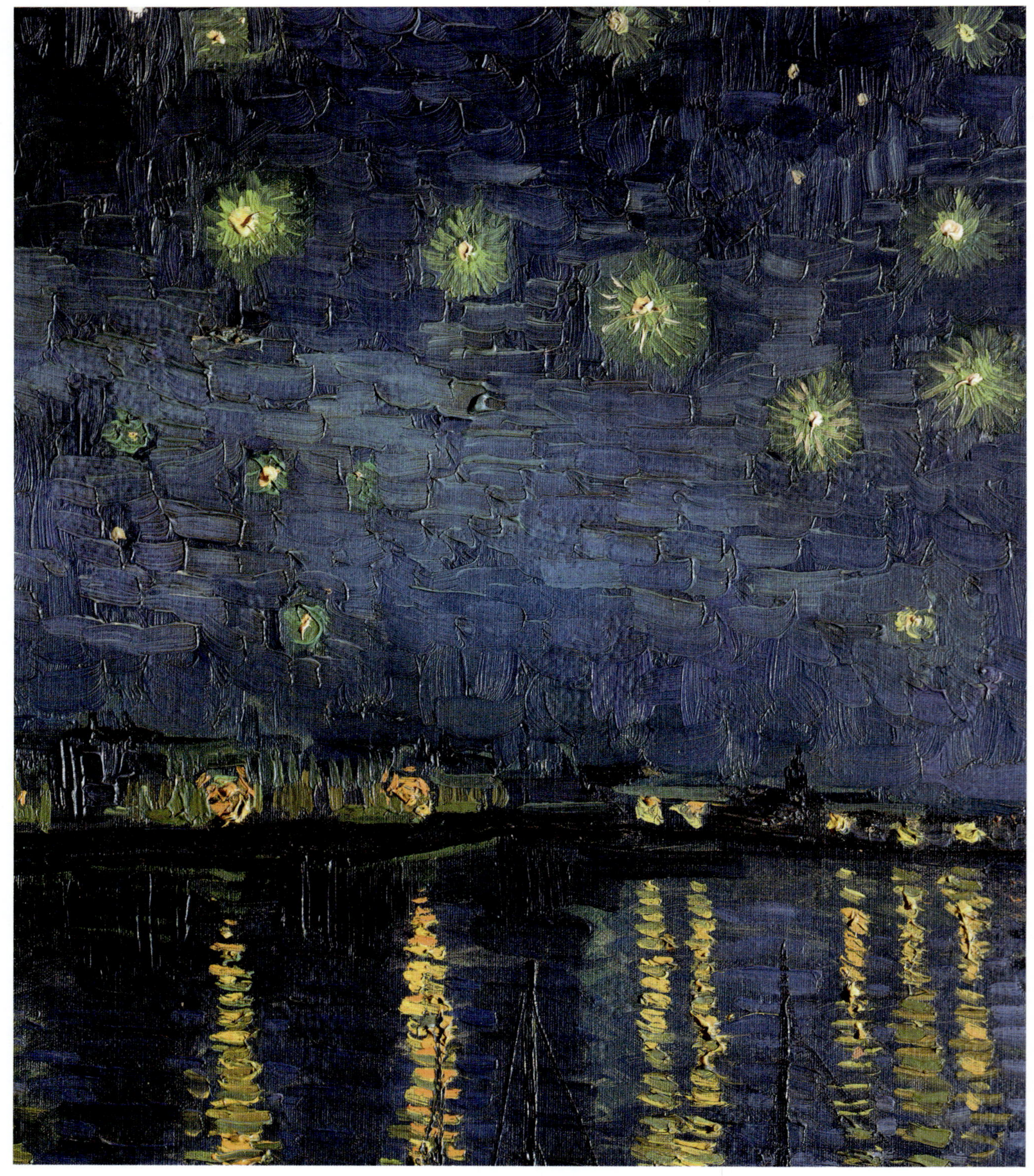

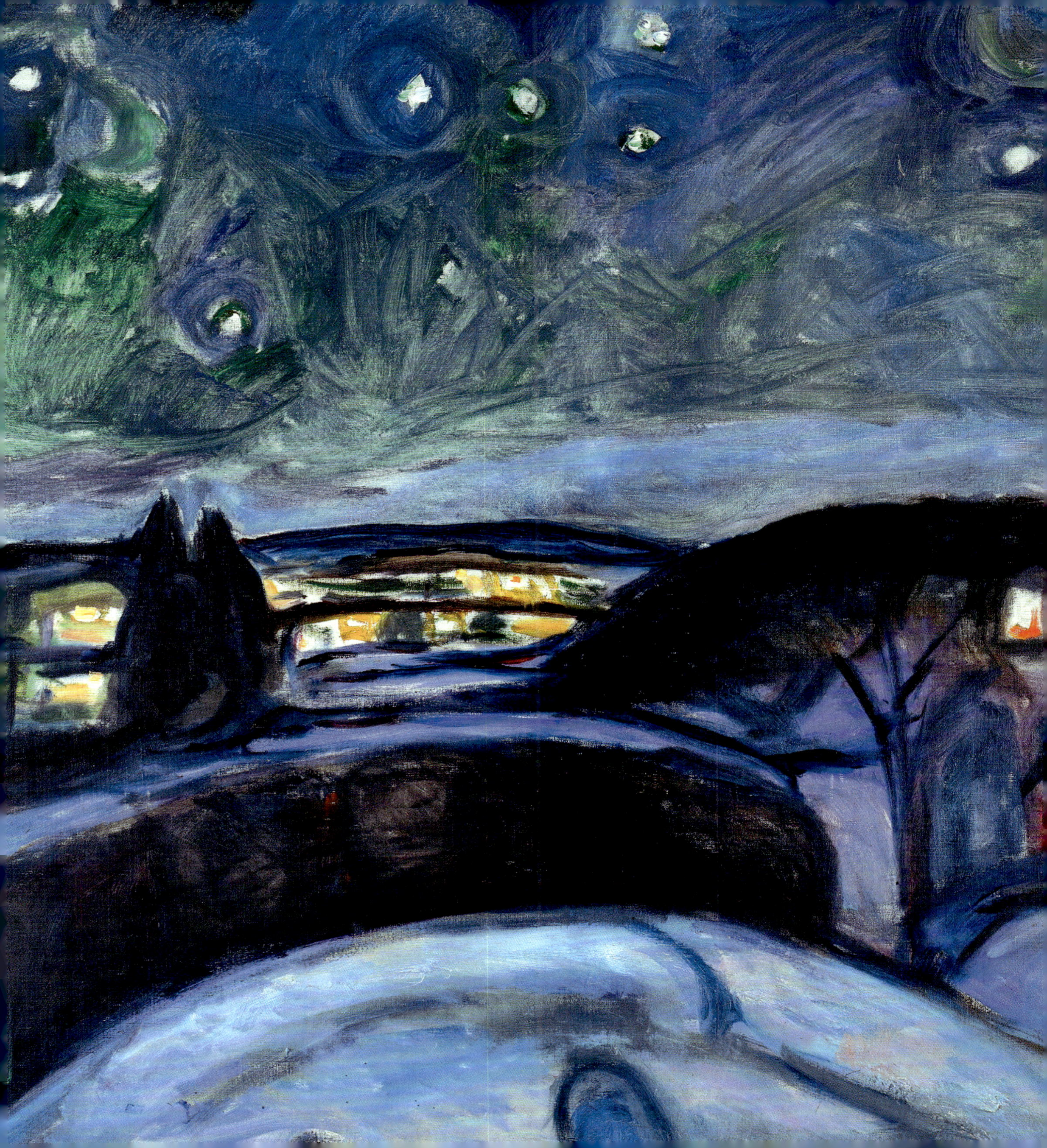

GOYA ~ MANET

In France, under the reign of Louis-Philippe I, there was a keen interest in contemporary or historical Spanish painting. Manet became interested in the Spanish masters at an early age and even undertook a trip to Madrid in 1865. From there he brought back copies of a masterpiece by Goya, *The Third of May 1808 in Madrid*, which was painted about 50 years before Manet's work. The compositions, both constructed in the same way, bear witness to this closeness.

La France sous le règne de Louis-Philippe connaît un engouement pour la peinture espagnole, qu'elle soit ancienne ou contemporaine. Très tôt, Manet s'y intéressera allant même jusqu'à effectuer un voyage à Madrid en 1865. De ce périple, celui que l'on surnomme le père de la modernité rapportera sans doute des images de l'un des chefs-d'œuvre de Goya peint environ cinquante ans avant lui, le *Tres de Mayo*. À bien les regarder, les compositions s'articulent de la même façon !

Im Frankreich unter der Herrschaft von Louis-Philippe I. gab es ein reges Interesse an zeitgenössischer oder historischer spanischer Malerei. Manet befasste sich schon früh mit den spanischen Meistern und unternahm 1865 sogar eine Reise nach Madrid. Von dort brachte er Kopien eines Meisterwerkes Goyas mit, der *Erschießung der Aufständischen*. Das Werk entstand etwa 50 Jahre vor Manets Ausführung. Von der Nähe zeugen die Kompositionen, die beide auf selbe Weise konstruiert sind.

En Francia, bajo el reinado de Luis Felipe I, había un gran interés por la pintura española contemporánea o histórica. Manet se interesó por los maestros españoles desde muy temprana edad e incluso viajó a Madrid en 1865. De allí trajo copias de una obra maestra de Goya, *El tiroteo de los insurgentes*. La obra fue escrita unos 50 años antes de la ejecución de Manet. Las composiciones, ambas construidas de la misma manera, dan testimonio de esta cercanía.

Na França, sob o reinado de Louis-Philippe I, havia um grande interesse na pintura espanhola contemporânea ou histórica. Manet interessou-se pelos mestres espanhóis em tenra idade e até realizou uma viagem a Madrid em 1865. De lá ele trouxe cópias de uma obra-prima de Goya, *O tiroteio dos insurgentes*. O trabalho foi escrito cerca de 50 anos antes da execução de Manet. As composições, ambas construídas da mesma forma, testemunham esta proximidade.

In Frankrijk, onder het bewind van Lodewijk Filips I, was er grote belangstelling voor de eigentijdse of historische Spaanse schilderkunst. Manet hield zich al op jonge leeftijd bezig met de Spaanse meesters en maakte in 1865 zelfs een reis naar Madrid. Vandaar bracht hij kopieën mee van een meesterwerk van Goya: *El Tres de mayo 1808 en Madrid*. Het werk ontstond zo'n 50 jaar voor Manets versie. Van dichtbij is te zien dat de composities op dezelfde manier zijn opgebouwd.

The Third of May,
1808 in Madrid

El Tres de mayo en Madrid

Die Erschießung der
Aufständischen

El tres de mayo en Madrid
o Los fusilamientos

Tres de mayo de 1808
en Madrid ou La carga
de los mamelucos

El Tres de Mayo 1808
en Madrid

Francisco de Goya
(1746-1828)

———

1814, Oil on canvas/Huile
sur toile, 268 × 347 cm,
Museo del Prado, Madrid

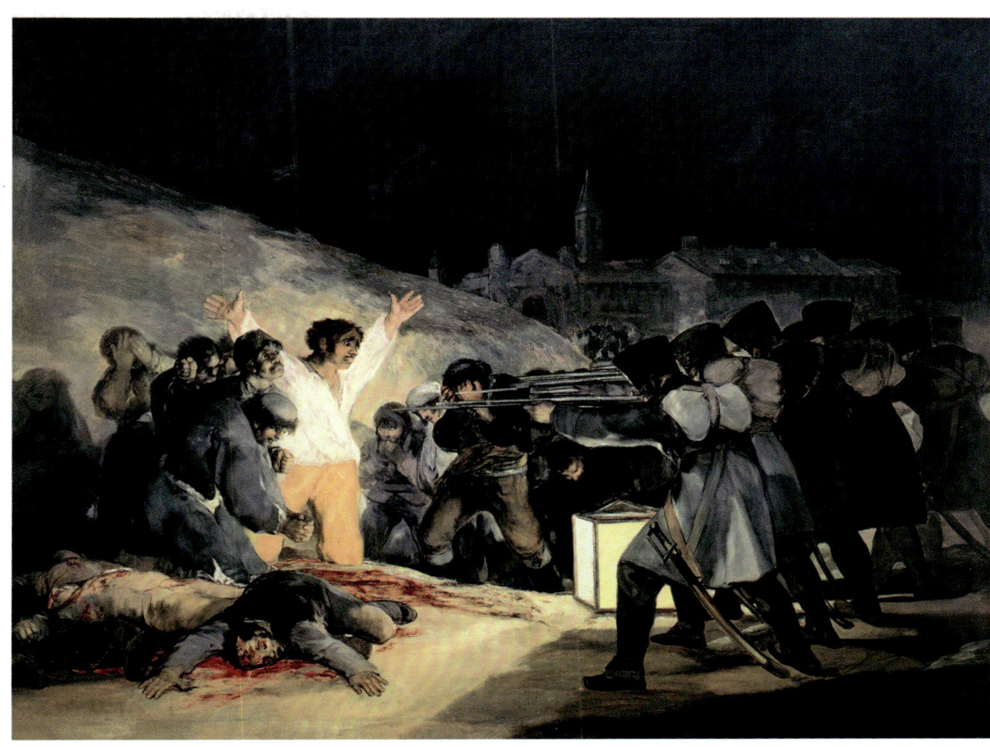

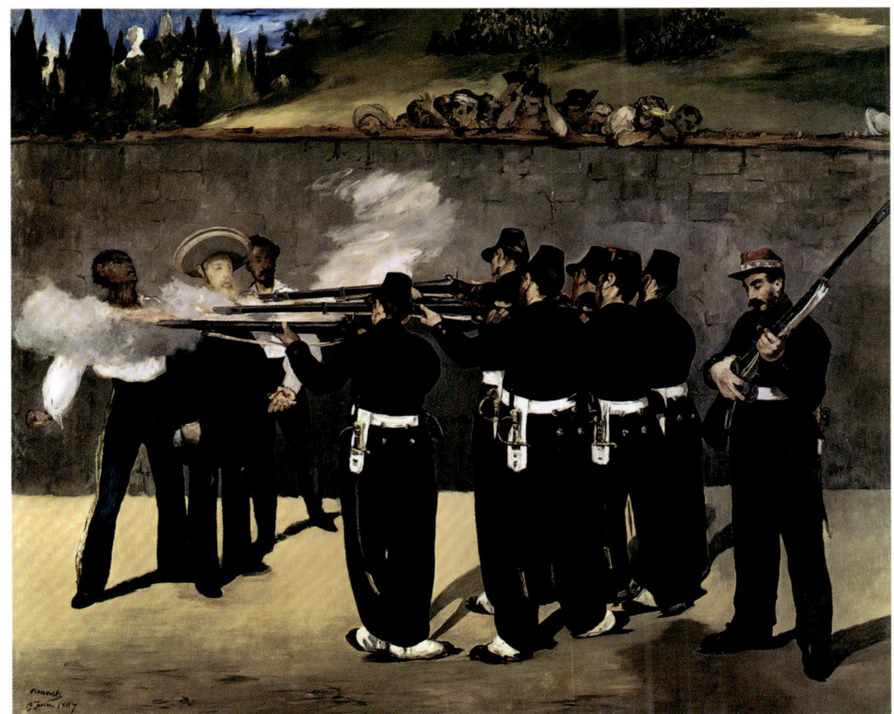

The Execution of Emperor
Maximilian

L'Exécution de l'empereur
Maximilien

Die Erschießung Kaiser Maximilians
von Mexiko

La ejecución del emperador
Maximiliano de México

A Execução do Imperador
Maximiliano do México

De executie van Maximiliaan

Édouard Manet (1832-1883)

———

1868/69, Oil on canvas/Huile sur toile,
252 × 302 cm, Stadtische Kunsthalle,
Mannheim

LIEVENS ~ REMBRANDT

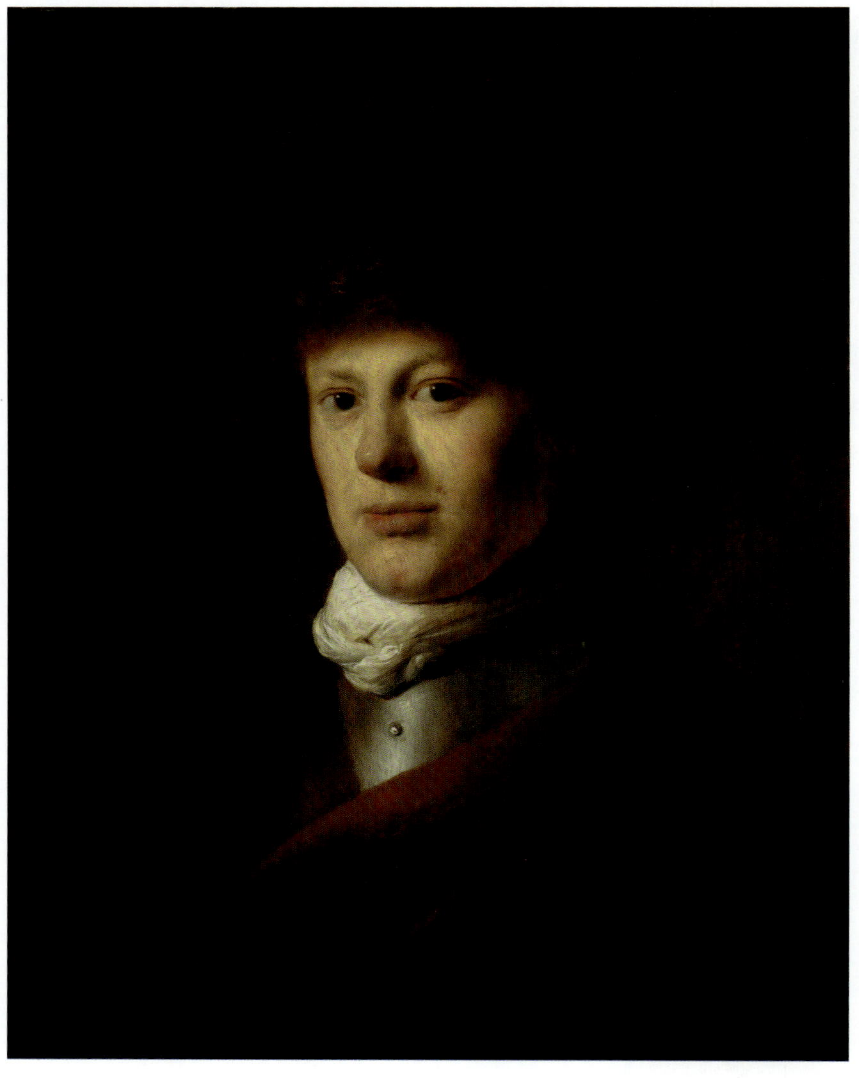

Jan Lievens (1607-1674)

———

c. 1628, Oil on panel/Huile sur panneau, 57 × 44,7 cm, Rijksmuseum, Amsterdam

Rembrandt van Rijn (1606-1669)

———

c. 1629, Oil on panel/Huile sur panneau, 38 × 31 cm, Germanisches Nationalmuseum, Nürnberg

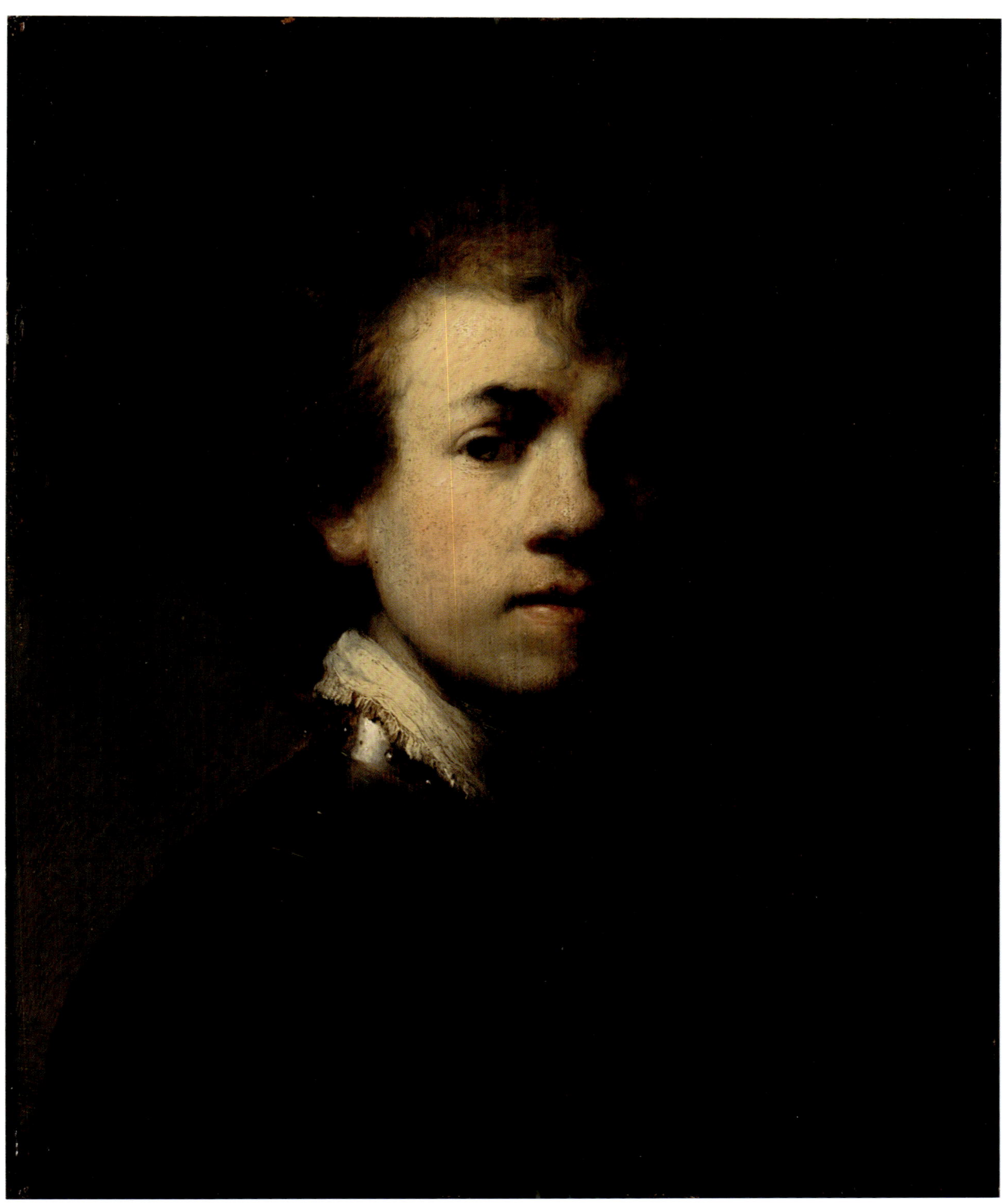

CONSTABLE ~ COURBET

When two nature lovers such as John Constable and Gustave Courbet translate their impressions into a single picture, they not only inspire each other, but also the viewer. The undulating sea under the leaden sky reminds us how difficult it is to depict nature and its power. Like Constable, Delacroix influenced the Romantics just as he inspired the painters of the Barbizon School.

Quand deux amoureux fous de la nature l'observent, la scrutent et la retranscrivent, et qu'ils se nomment John Constable et Gustave Courbet, alors cette dernière tout comme nous s'en voit exaltée. Sous un ciel plombé, cette mer vivifiante nous rappelle combien l'exercice de rendre ce sentiment de nature si puissant est un véritable défi. Constable marqua les romantiques tel Delacroix tout comme il inspira les peintres de l'école de Barbizon.

Wenn zwei Naturliebhaber wie John Constable und Gustave Courbet ihre Eindrücke in einem Bild umsetzen, inspirieren sie sich nicht nur gegenseitig, sondern auch den Betrachter. Das wogende Meer unter dem bleiernen Himmel erinnert daran, wie schwierig es ist, eine derart machtvolle Natur darzustellen. Wie Constable prägte Delacroix die Romantiker, genauso wie er die Maler der Schule von Barbizon inspirierte.

Cuando dos amantes de la naturaleza como John Constable y Gustave Courbet traducen sus impresiones en una sola imagen, no sólo se inspiran mutuamente, sino también al espectador. El mar ondulado bajo el cielo de plomo nos recuerda lo difícil que es representar una naturaleza tan poderosa. Al igual que Constable, Delacroix influyó en los románticos de la misma manera que inspiró a los pintores de la Escuela Barbizon.

Quando dois amantes da natureza, como John Constable e Gustave Courbet, traduzem suas impressões em uma única imagem, eles não só se inspiram mutuamente, mas também o espectador. O mar ondulante sob o céu de chumbo lembra-nos como é difícil representar uma natureza tão poderosa. Tal como o Constable, Delacroix influenciou os Românticos tal como inspirou os pintores da Escola Barbizon.

Wanneer twee natuurliefhebbers zoals John Constable en Gustave Courbet hun indrukken naar een schilderij vertalen, inspireren ze niet alleen elkaar, maar ook de kijker. De golvende zee onder de loodgrijze hemel herinnert ons eraan hoe moeilijk het is om zo'n krachtige natuur uit te beelden. Constable beïnvloedde romantici zoals Delacroix, net zoals hij de schilders van de school van Barbizon inspireerde.

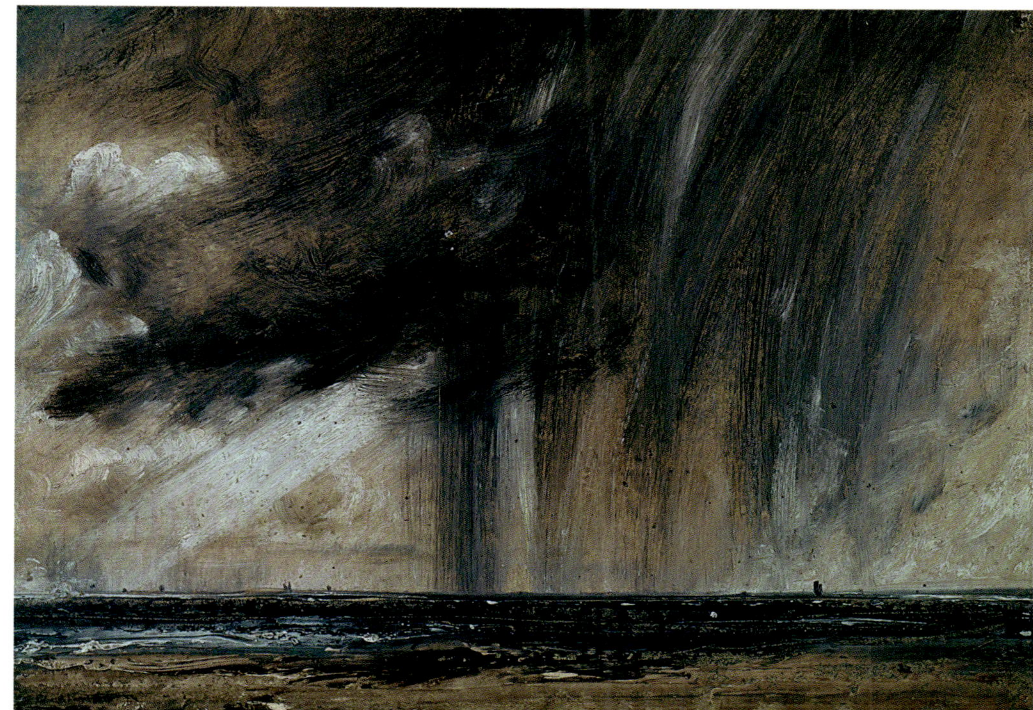

John Constable (1776-1837)

———

c. 1824-28, Oil on paper mounted on canvas/ Huile sur papier montée sur toile, 23,5 × 32,6 cm, Royal Academy of Arts, London

Marine

Marine

Die Wasserhose

Marina

As calças de água

De waterhoos

Gustave Courbet (1819-1877)

———

c. 1866, Oil on canvas mounted on cardboard/Huile sur toile montée sur carton, 43,2 × 65,7 cm, Philadelphia Museum of Art, Philadelphia

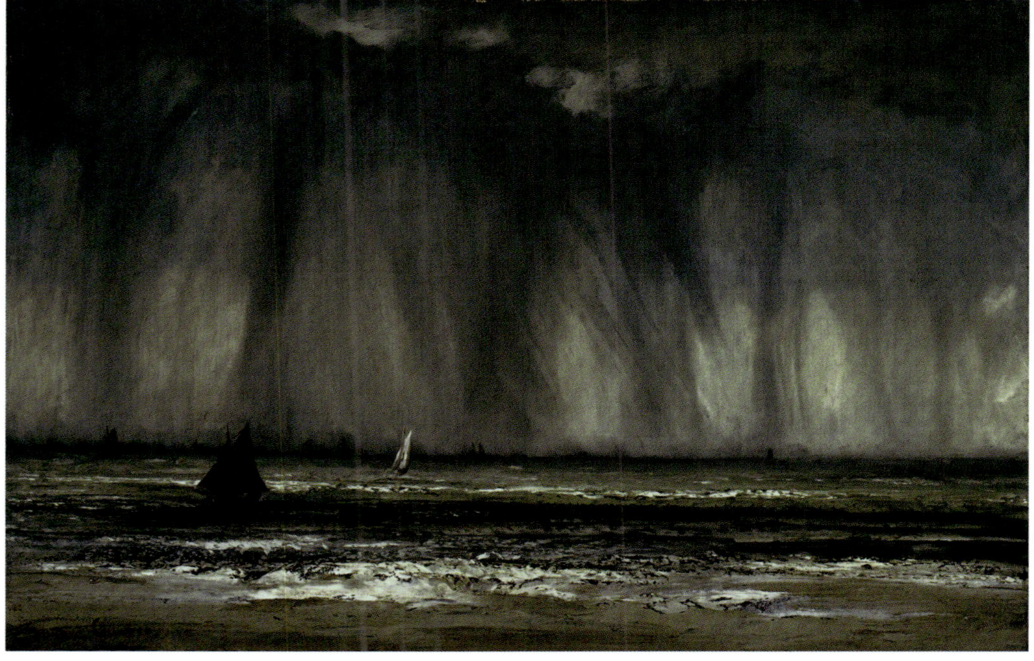

LE NAIN ~ CÉZANNE ~ VAN DOESBURG

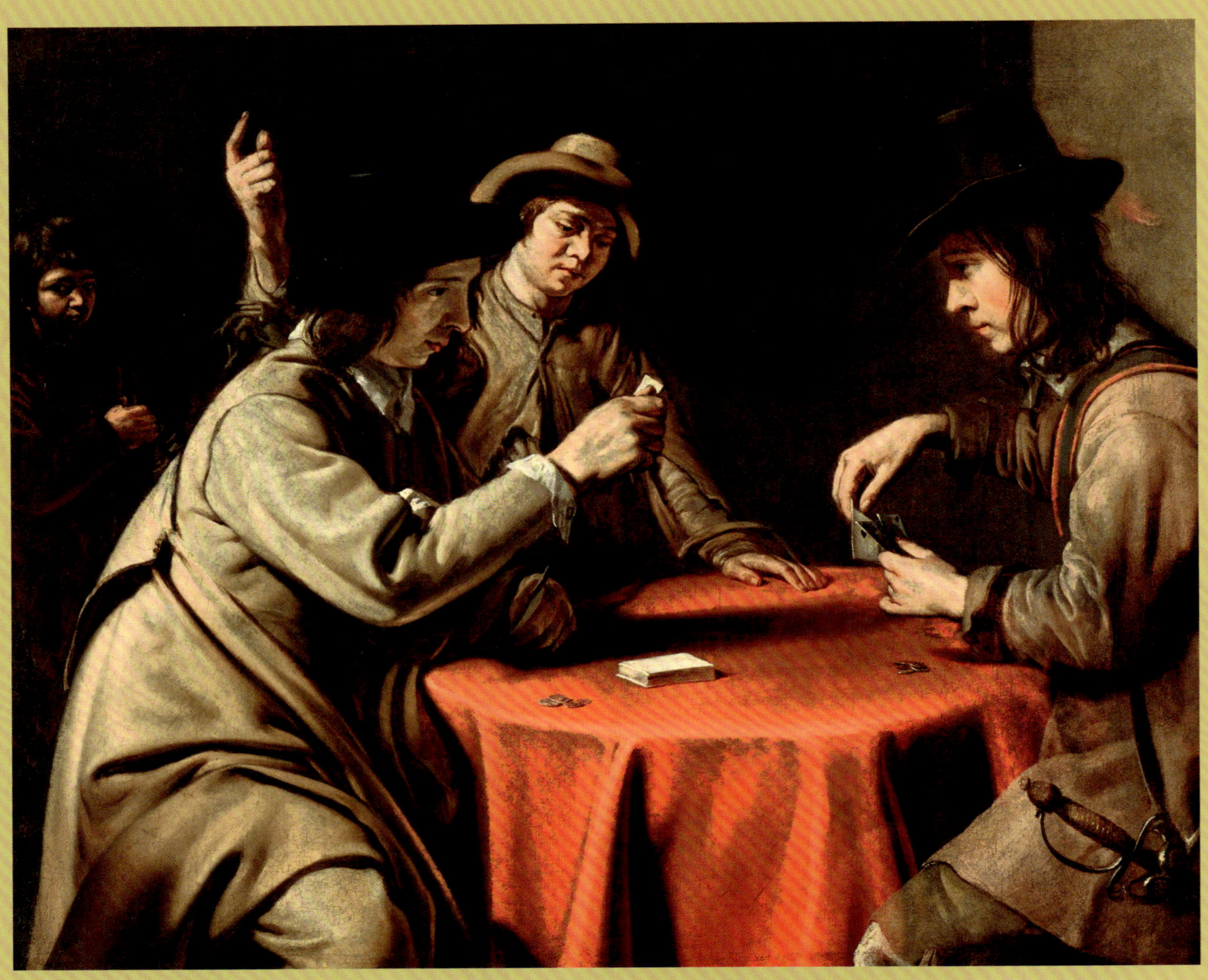

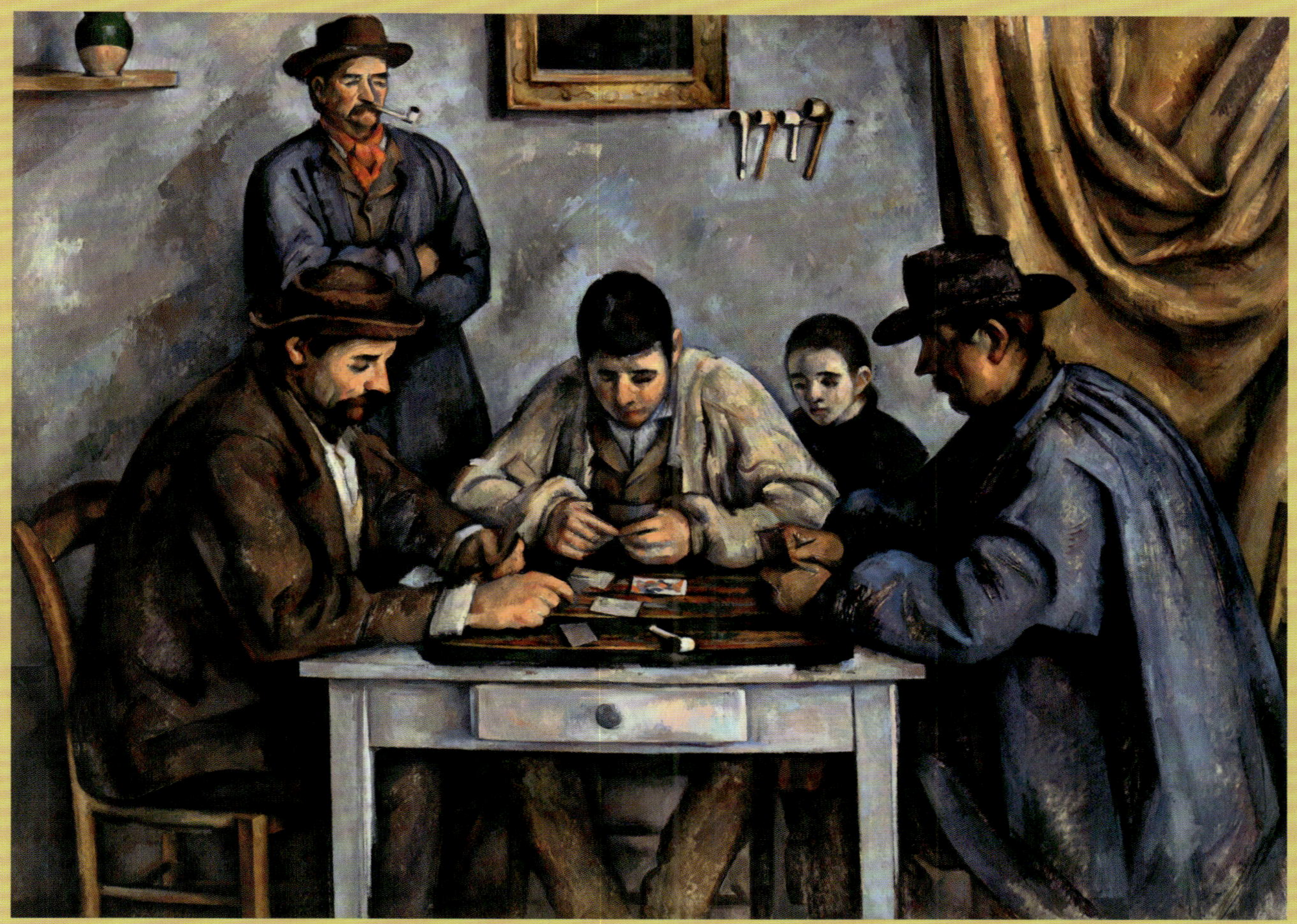

The Cheaters — *The Card Players*
Les Tricheurs — *Les Joueurs de cartes*
Die Falschspieler — *Die Kartenspieler*
Los tramposos — *Los jugadores de cartas*
Os falsos jogadores — *Os jogadores de cartas*
De valsspelers — *De kaartspelers*

Mathieu Le Nain (1607-1677) — **Paul Cézanne (1839-1906)**

———

n. d., Oil on canvas/Huile sur toile,
65 × 81 cm, Musée des Beaux-Arts, Reims

1890-92, Oil on canvas/Huile sur toile,
135,3 × 181,9 cm, The Barnes Foundation,
Philadelphia

LE NAIN ~ CÉZANNE ~ VAN DOESBURG

Card players appear as motifs for the first time in 17th century genre painting in the Netherlands. In addition to card playing at a table, the Le Nain brothers were also interested in playing with light. When Cézanne painted his motif, he concentrated on his ability to arrange the forms in space and dispensed with a background story. Van Doesburg's composition is characterised by the dynamics and rhythm of the colors.

Le thème des joueurs de cartes apparaît en Hollande dans la peinture de genre au XVIIe siècle. Dans un intérieur et autour d'une table se dispute une partie de cartes. Pour les frères Le Nain le jeu est aussi celui de la lumière et quand Cézanne choisit de peindre un tel sujet, il veut déployer son aptitude à organiser les formes dans l'espace en évacuant toute anecdote. Pour Doesburg, sa composition devient par la couleur dynamique et rythmique.

Kartenspieler tauchen in den Niederlanden zum ersten Mal in der Genremalerei des 17. Jahrhunderts als Motiv auf. Neben dem Kartenspiel an einem Tisch ging es den Brüdern Le Nain aber auch um das Spiel mit dem Licht. Als Cézanne sein Motiv malt, konzentriert er sich auf seine Fähigkeit, die Formen im Raum anzuordnen, und verzichtet auf eine Hintergrundgeschichte. Bei Van Doesburg ist die Komposition durch die Dynamik und Rhythmik der Farben geprägt.

Los jugadores de cartas aparecen como motivos por primera vez en la pintura de género del siglo XVII en los Países Bajos. Además de jugar a las cartas en una mesa, los hermanos Le Nain también estaban interesados en jugar con la luz. Cuando Cézanne pinta su motivo, se concentra en su capacidad para organizar las formas en el espacio y prescinde de una historia de fondo. La composición de Van Doesburg se caracteriza por la dinámica y el ritmo de los colores.

Os jogadores de cartas aparecem como motivos pela primeira vez na pintura de gênero do século XVII na Holanda. Além de jogar cartas em uma mesa, os irmãos Le Nain também estavam interessados em jogar com a luz. Quando Cézanne pinta seu motivo, ele se concentra em sua capacidade de organizar as formas no espaço e dispensa uma história de fundo. A composição de Van Doesburg caracteriza-se pela dinâmica e ritmo das cores.

Kaartspelers komen voor het eerst als onderwerp voor in de 17e-eeuwse Nederlandse genreschilderkunst. De gebroeders Le Nain was het niet alleen te doen om het kaarten aan een tafel, maar ook om het spel met licht. Toen Cézanne dit onderwerp schilderde, concentreerde hij zich op zijn vermogen om de vormen in de ruimte te rangschikken en zag hij af van een achtergrondverhaal. Bij Van Doesburg vormen de dynamiek en het ritme van de kleuren de compositie.

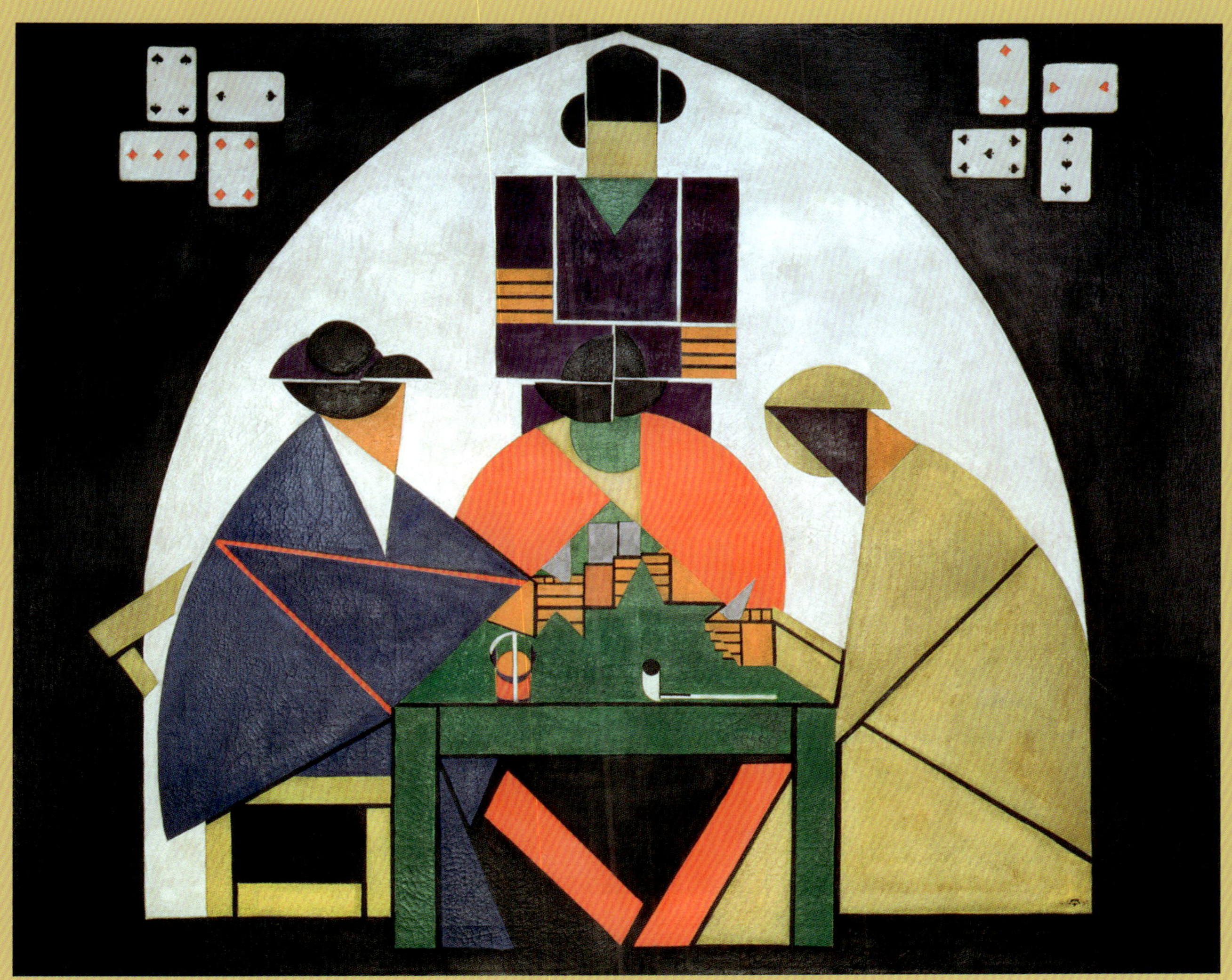

The Card Players
Les Joueurs de cartes
Die Kartenspieler
Los jugadores de cartas
Os jogadores de cartas
De kaartspelers

Theo van Doesburg (1883-1931)

———

1916/17, Oil and tempera on canvas/Huile
et tempera sur toile, 120,2 × 149,8 cm,
Haags Gemeentemuseum, Den Haag

MONET ~ MONDRIAN

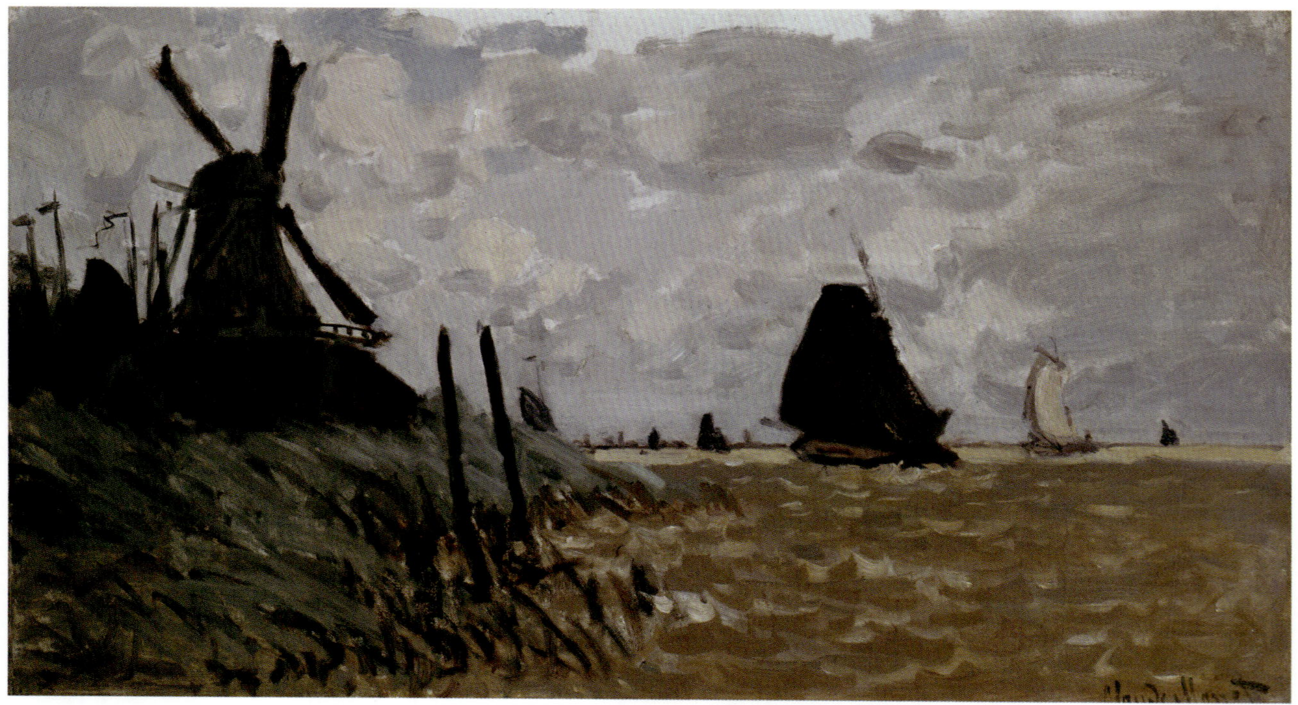

A Windmill near Zaandam

Moulin à Zaandam

Windmühle bei Zaandam

Molino de viento cerca de Zaandam

Moinho de vento perto de Zaandam

Molen bij Zaandam

Claude Monet (1840-1926)

───

1871, Oil on canvas/Huile sur toile,
42 × 73,5 cm, Ashmolean Museum, Oxford

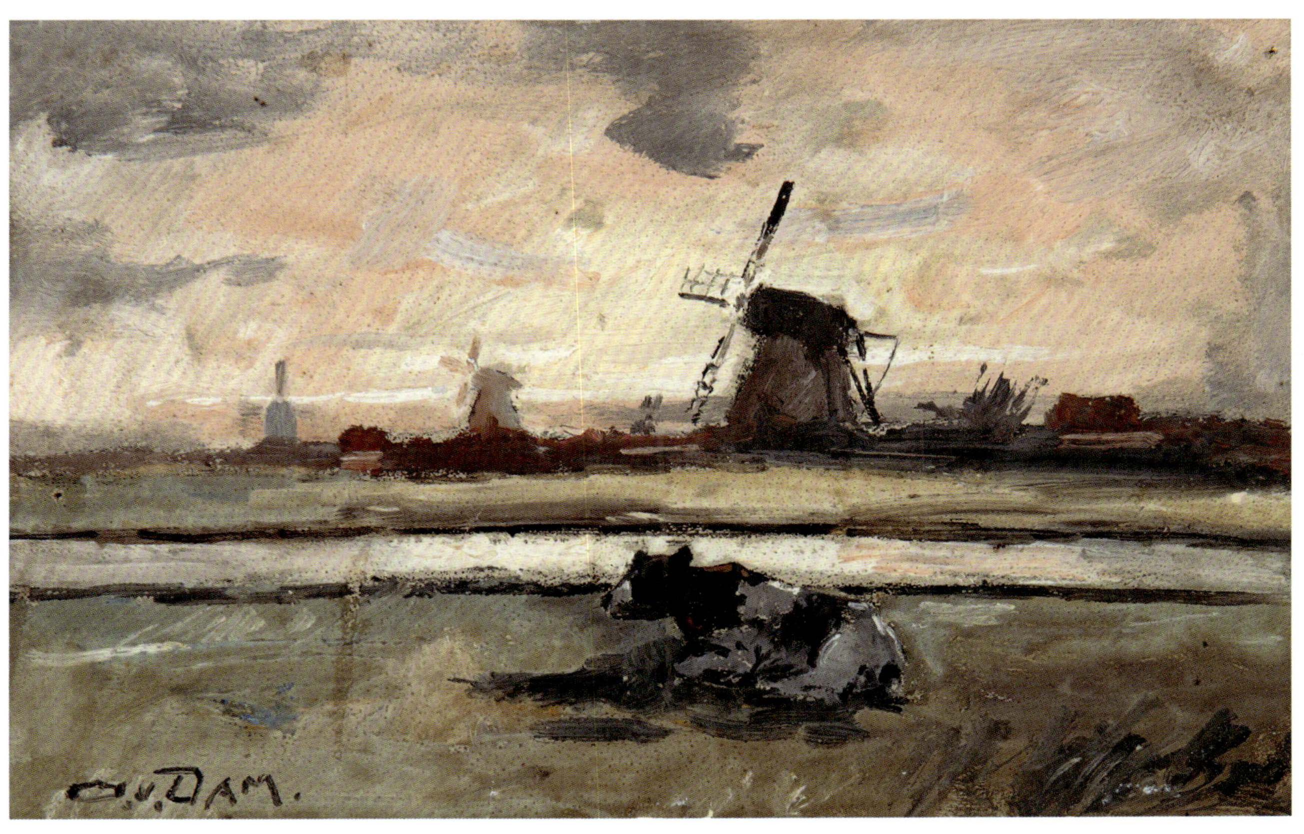

Dutch Landscape
Paysage hollandais
Holländische Landschaft
Paisaje holandés
Paisagem Holandesa
Hollands landschap

Piet Mondrian (1872-1944)

c. 1904, Oil on cardboard paper/Huile
sur papier cartonné, 16,5 × 25,6 cm,
Private collection

CARAVAGGIO ~ GENTILESCHI

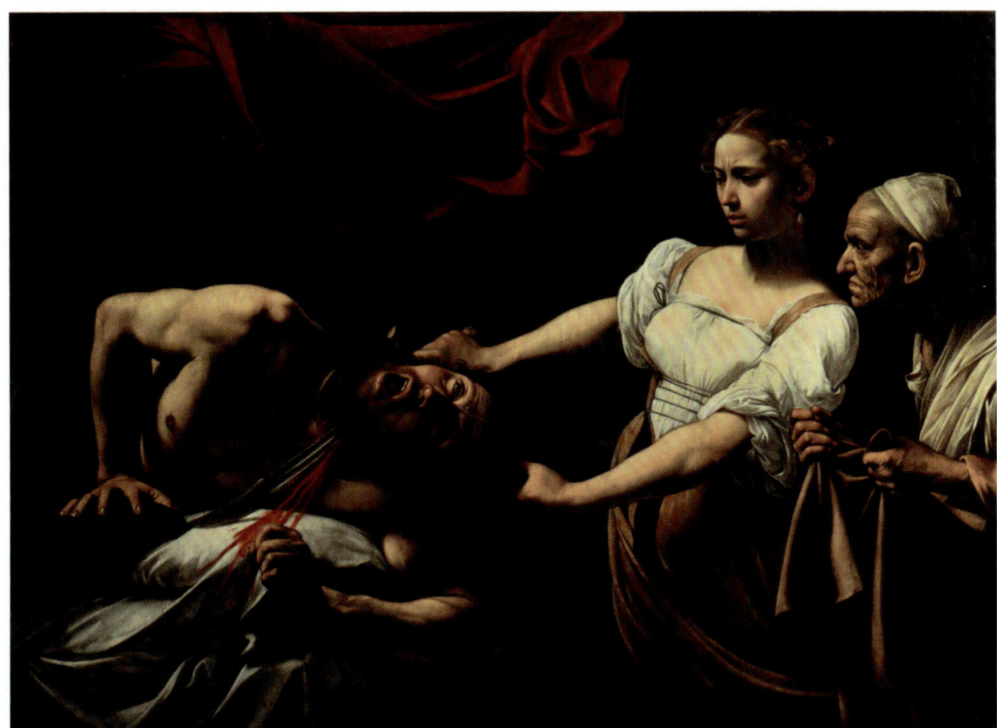

Michelangelo Merisi da Caravaggio (1571-1610)

———

1599, Oil on canvas/Huile sur toile, 145 × 195 cm, Galleria Nazionale d'Arte Antica - Palazzo Barberini, Roma

With Judith, who takes the fate of her people into her own hands, the painter set out to succeed as a woman and artist - and did not hesitate to compete with Caravaggio. Gentileschi not only managed to pass this test with flying colors, but also created an extraordinarily powerful painting.

À l'instar de Judith qui prend en main le destin de son peuple, Artemisia, elle, prend le pari de réussir en tant que femme et artiste. Difficile de rivaliser avec Caravage ? Au regard de la version de Gentileschi on peut décréter que non seulement elle y parvient avec brio mais qu'elle atteint là une puissance singulière.

Mit der Judith, die das Schicksal ihres Volkes in die Hand nimmt, machte sich die Malerin auf, als Frau und Künstlerin Erfolg zu haben – und scheute dabei nicht davor zurück, sich mit Caravaggio zu messen. Gentileschi schaffte es nicht nur, diese Prüfung mit Bravour zu bestehen, sondern schuf darüber hinaus ein außerordentlich kraftvolles Gemälde.

**Artemisia Gentileschi
(1593-1653)**

———

c. 1611, Oil on canvas/Huile
sur toile, 163 × 126 cm,
Museo di Capodimonte, Napoli

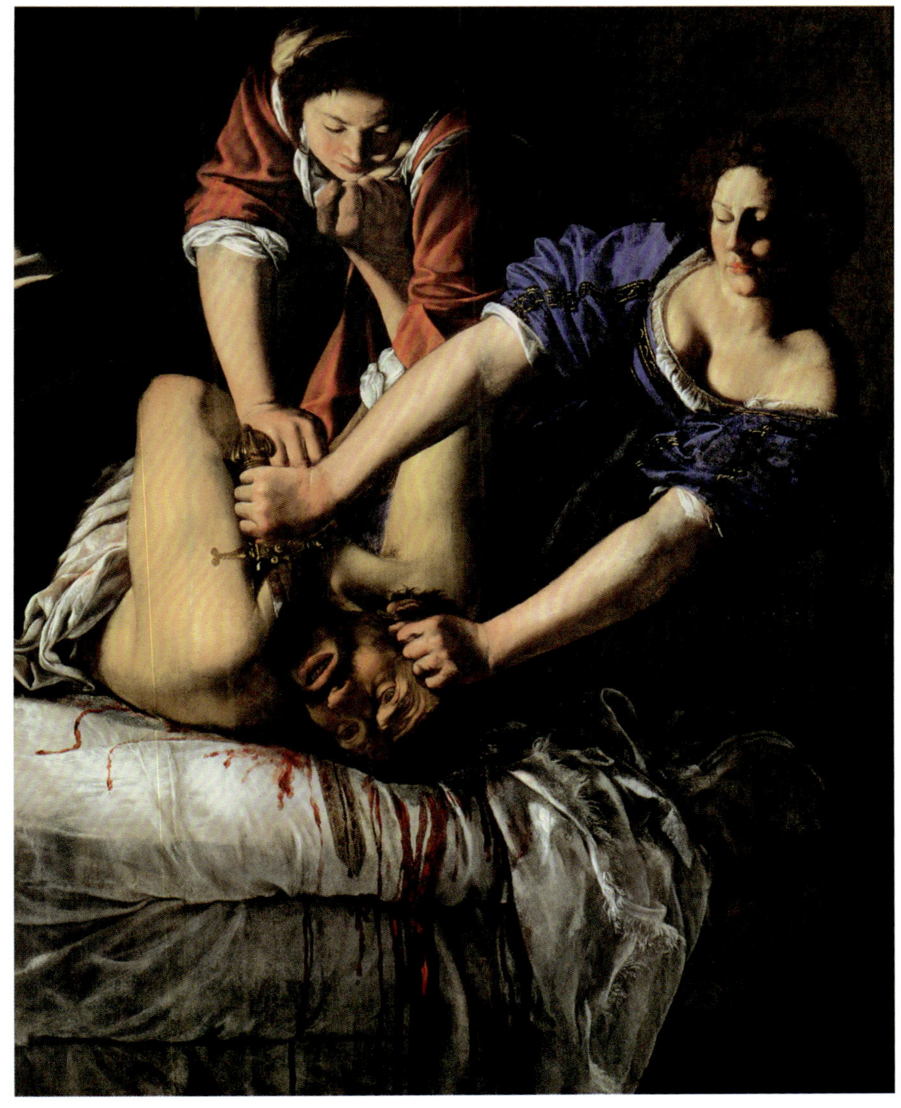

Con Judith, que toma el destino de su pueblo en sus manos, la pintora se propuso triunfar como mujer y artista, y no dudó en competir con Caravaggio. Gentileschi no sólo ha conseguido superar esta prueba con creces, sino que también ha creado una pintura extraordinariamente potente.

Com Judith, que toma nas próprias mãos o destino de seu povo, a pintora partiu para o sucesso como mulher e artista - e não hesitou em competir com Caravaggio. Gentileschi não só conseguiu passar este teste com distinção, como também criou uma pintura extraordinariamente poderosa.

Met Judith, die het lot van haar volk zelf in handen neemt, maakte de schilderes zich als vrouw en kunstenares op voor succes – en schrok ze er niet voor terug om zich met Caravaggio te meten. Gentileschi slaagde er niet alleen in deze test met glans te doorstaan, maar maakte bovendien een buitengewoon krachtig schilderij.

ANONYMOUS ~ SEURAT

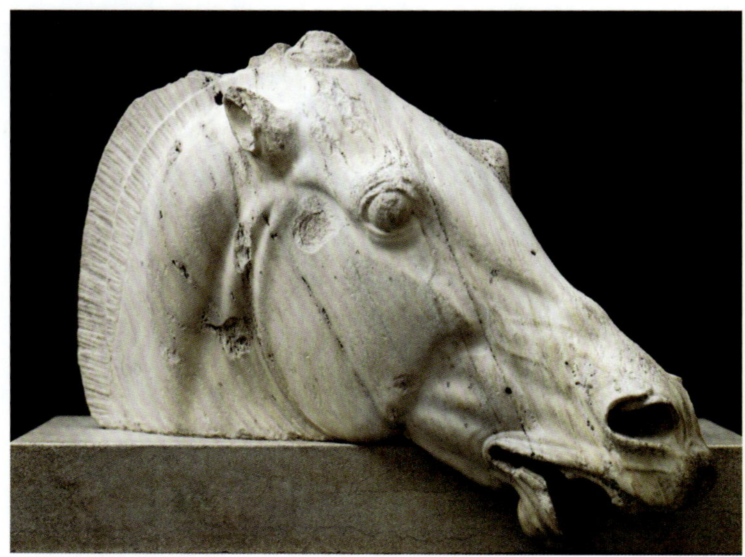

c. 447-432 BC, Sculpture in marble/Sculpture en marbre, British museum, London

Georges Seurat made numerous copies of works by famous painters such as Ingres, but also of numerous sculptures in the Louvre. Although the original work is unknown, this Conté crayon drawing testifies to the fine stroke of the pointillist painter and his ability to represent light.

Georges Seurat fit de nombreuses copies d'après les maîtres comme Ingres, mais aussi d'après de nombreuses sculptures conservées au Louvre. Bien que non retrouvé, ce modèle qui servit au peintre pointilliste démontre l'élégance de son trait et son sens inné à traiter la lumière. Et tout cela au crayon Conté !

Georges Seurat fertigte zahlreiche Kopien von Werken berühmter Maler wie Ingres an, aber auch von zahlreichen Skulpturen im Louvre. Obwohl das Ausgangswerk unbekannt ist, zeugt diese Conté-Zeichnung vom feinen Strich des pointillistischen Malers und seiner Fähigkeit, das Licht darzustellen.

Georges Seurat realizó numerosas copias de obras de pintores famosos como Ingres, pero también de numerosas esculturas del Louvre. Aunque se desconoce la obra original, este dibujo de Conté atestigua el fino trazo del pintor puntillista y su capacidad para representar la luz.

Georges Seurat fez numerosas cópias de obras de pintores famosos como Ingres, mas também de numerosas esculturas no Louvre. Embora a obra original seja desconhecida, este desenho de Conté testemunha o fino golpe do pintor pointillist e a sua capacidade de representar a luz.

Georges Seurat maakte talrijke kopieën van werken van beroemde schilders zoals Ingres, maar ook van talrijke sculpturen in het Louvre. Hoewel het voorbeeld onbekend is, getuigt deze krijttekening van de fijne toets van de pointillistische schilder en zijn vermogen om het licht weer te geven.

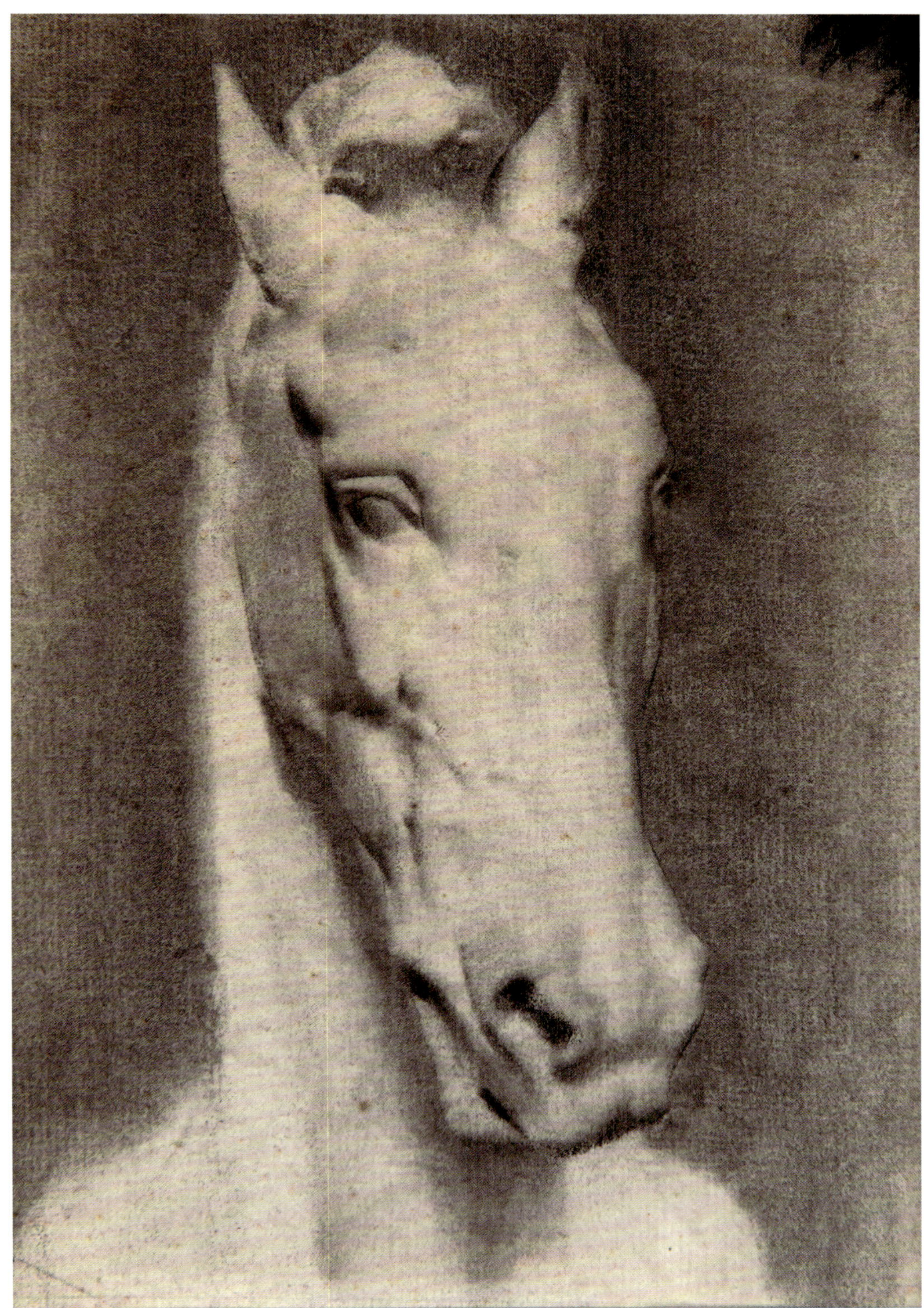

Head of a Horse after an antique marble sculpture

Tête de cheval d'après un marbre antique

Pferdekopf nach einer antiken Marmorplastik

Cabeza de caballo según una antigua escultura de mármol

Cabeça de cavalo depois de uma escultura de mármore antigo

Paardenkop naar een antieke marmeren sculptuur

Georges Seurat (1859-1891)

c. 1876-78, Conté crayon/Crayon Conté, 21,2 × 14,4 cm, Private collection

REMBRANDT ~ SOUTINE

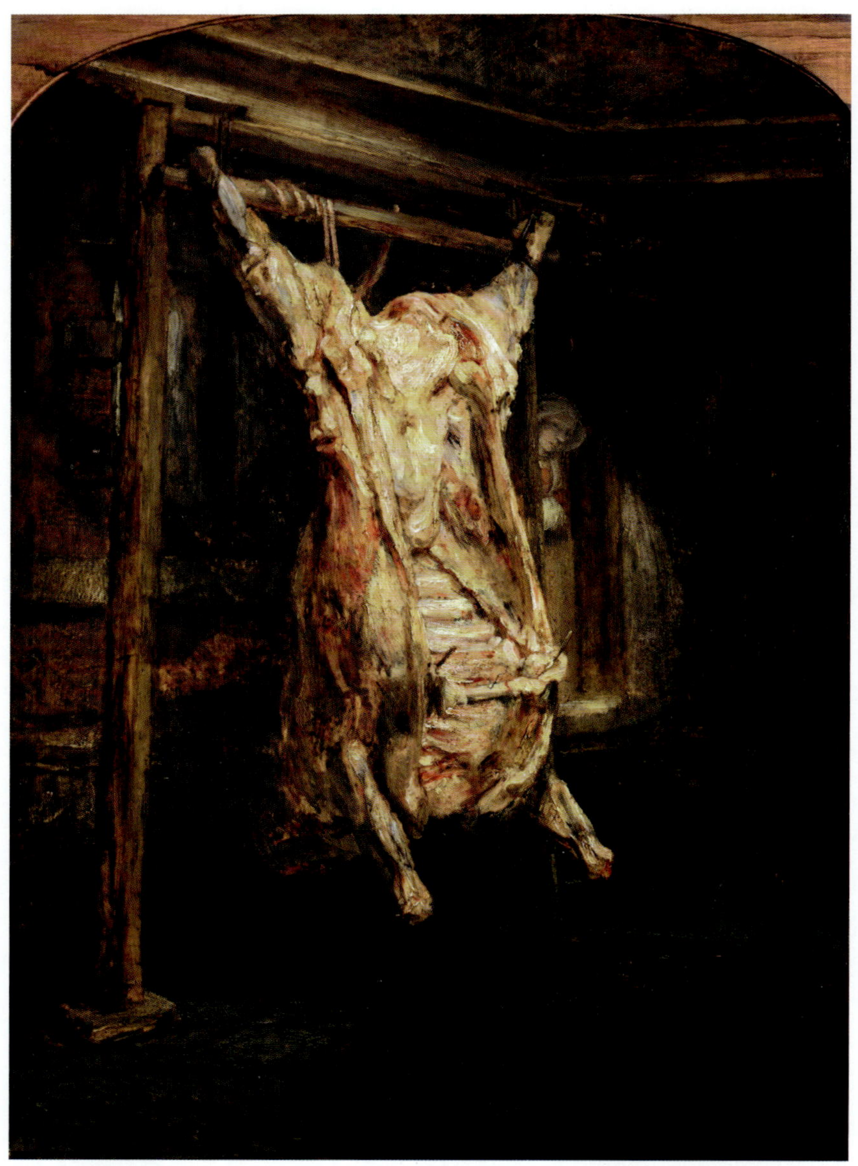

The Slaughtered Ox
Le Bœuf écorché
Der geschlachtete Ochse
El buey desollado
O boi abatido
De geslachte os

Rembrandt van Rijn (1606-1669)

———

c. 1655, Oil on canvas/Huile sur toile,
94 × 69 cm, Musée du Louvre, Paris

Carcass of Beef
Le Bœuf écorché
Abgehäutetes Rind
El buey desollado
Vacas esfoladas
De geslachte os

Chaim Soutine (1894-1943)

———

1925, Oil on canvas/Huile sur toile,
202 × 114 cm, Musée de Grenoble
(copy after/copie)

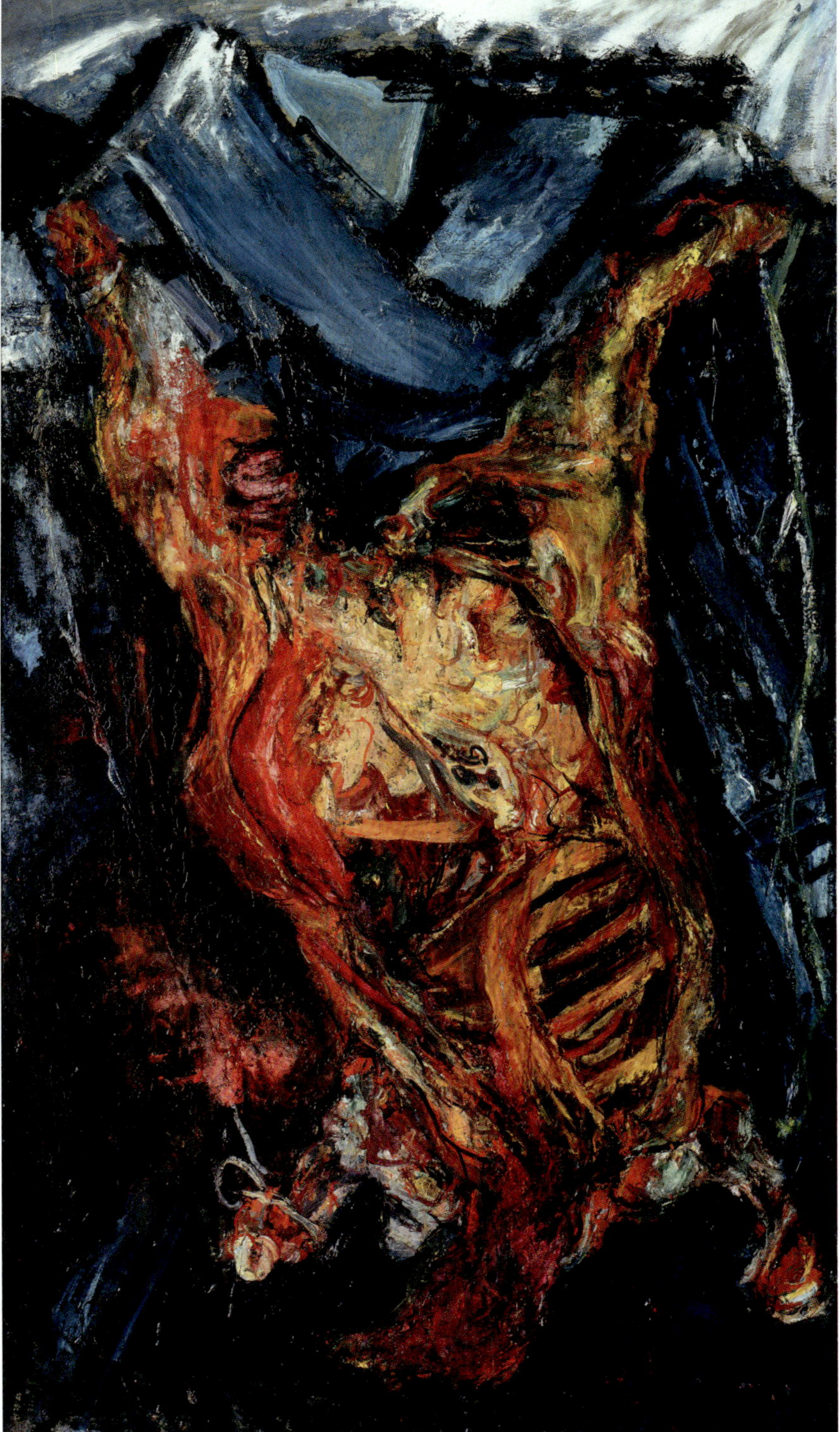

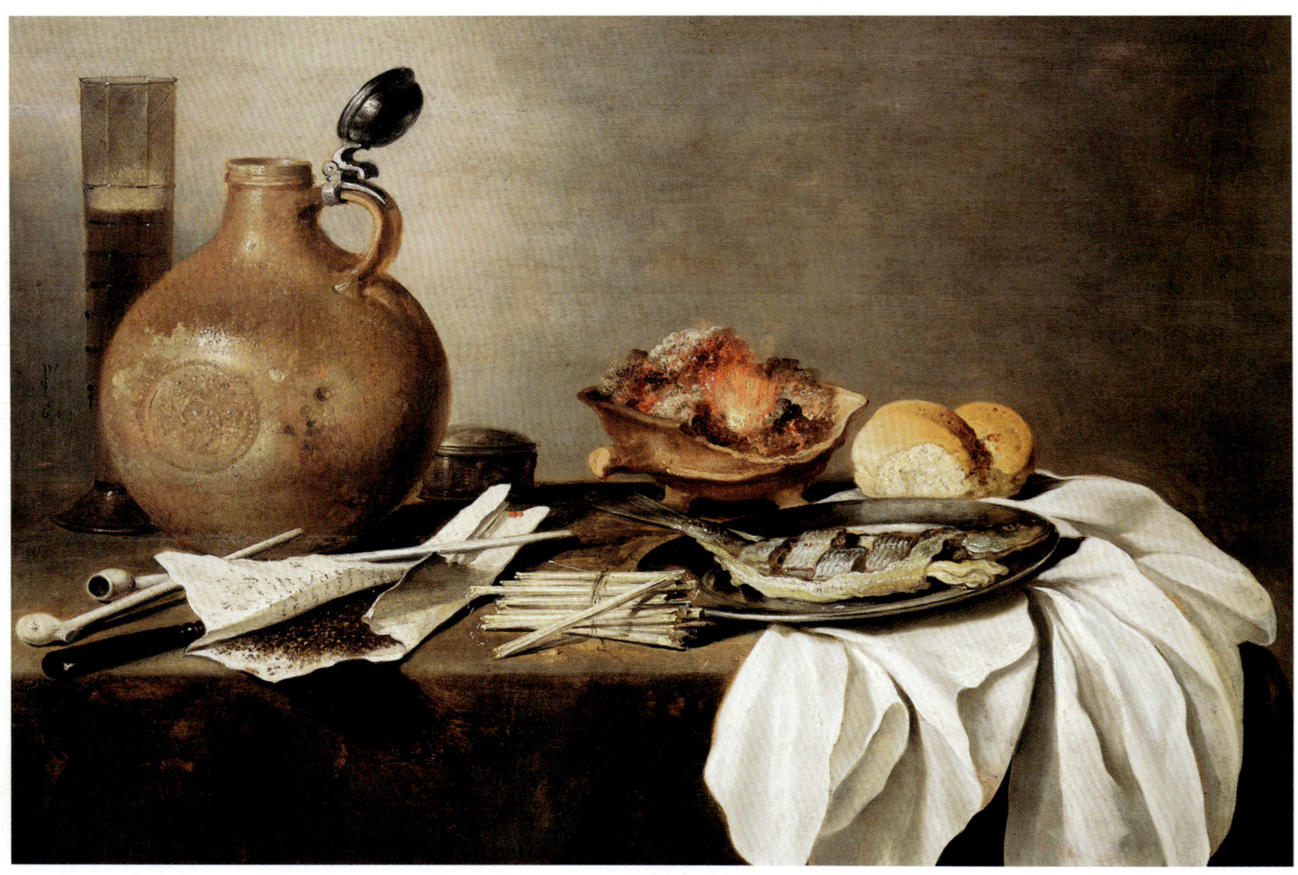

Still life with herring, smoking
equipment, stone mug and beer glass

Nature morte avec hareng, ustensiles
de fumeur, pichet de bière et bock

Stillleben mit Hering, Rauchutensilien,
Bierkrug und Bierglas

Bodegón con arenque, utensilios para
ahumar, jarra de cerveza y vaso de cerveza

Natureza morta com arenque, utensílios
para fumar, jarro de cerveja e bock

Stilleven met rookgerei, haring, bierglas
en baardmankruik

Pieter Claesz (1597-1660)

———

1644, Oil on wood/Huile sur bois,
60 × 83 cm, Suermondt Ludwig Museum,
Aachen

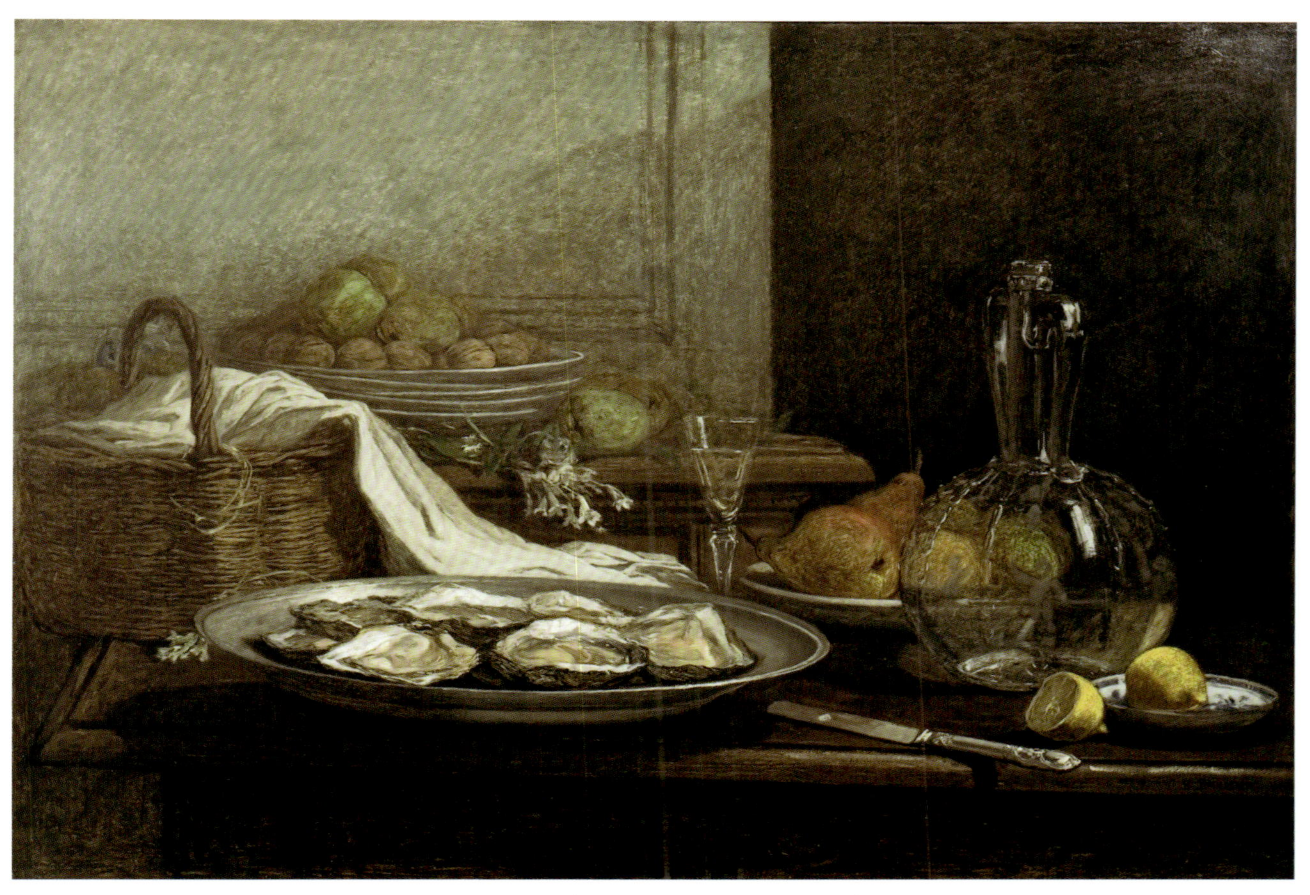

Still life with Oysters

Nature morte aux huîtres

Stillleben mit Austern

Bodegón con ostras

Natureza morta com ostras

Stilleven met oesters

Eugène Boudin (1824-1898)

———

c. 1850, Oil on canvas/Huile sur toile,
56 × 80,5 cm, Bristol Museum and Art
Gallery, Bristol

COROT ~ MORISOT

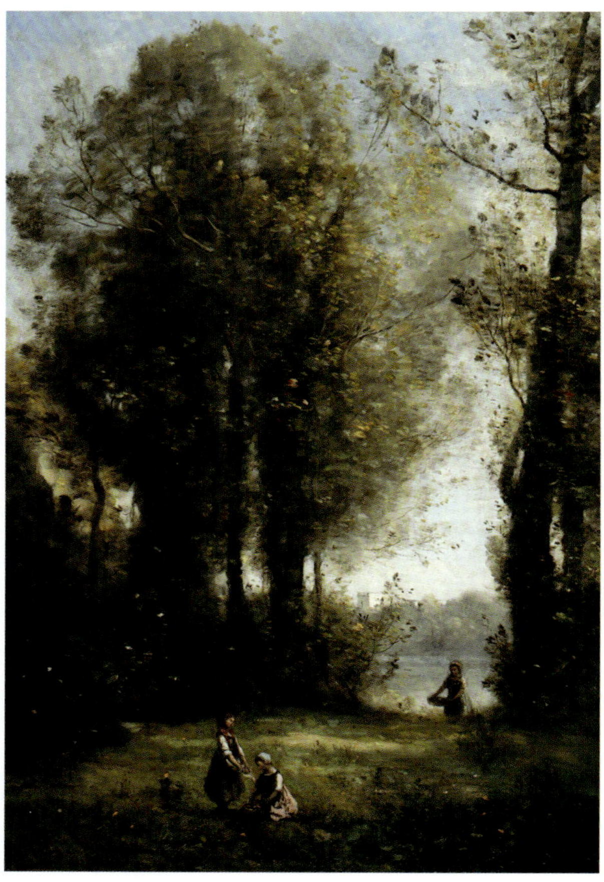

Picking Daisies

La Cueillette des marguerites

Die Margeritenernte

La cosecha de margaritas

A Colheita de Marguerites

Madeliefjes plukken

**Jean-Baptiste Camille Corot
(1796-1875)**

———

c. 1865-1870, Oil on canvas/Huile sur toile,
71,8 × 48,5 cm, Private collection

Morisot was a pupil of d'Oudinot and Corot. In this landscape, the resemblance to the works of her master catches the eye. Not only the way she drew her strokes to paint the branches of the trees, everything about this painting by Berthe Morisot breathes the spirit of Jean-Baptiste Camille Corot.

Morisot fut l'élève d'Oudinot mais également de Corot. Dans ce paysage les ressemblances avec les œuvres du maître sautent aux yeux. La façon de poser ses touches sur la toile pour composer les bouquets d'arbres, mais pas seulement…Tout dans ce paysage de Berthe Morisot respire l'esprit de Jean-Baptiste Camille Corot.

Morisot war Schülerin bei Oudinot und Corot. In dieser Landschaft sticht die Ähnlichkeit mit den Werken ihres Meisters ins Auge. Nicht nur die Art, wie sie ihre Striche setzt, um das Astwerk der Bäume zu malen, alles an diesem Gemälde von Berthe Morisot atmet den Geist von Jean-Baptiste Camille Corot.

Berthe Morisot (1841-1895)

1863, Oil on canvas/Huile sur toile,
45 × 38,8 cm, Private collection

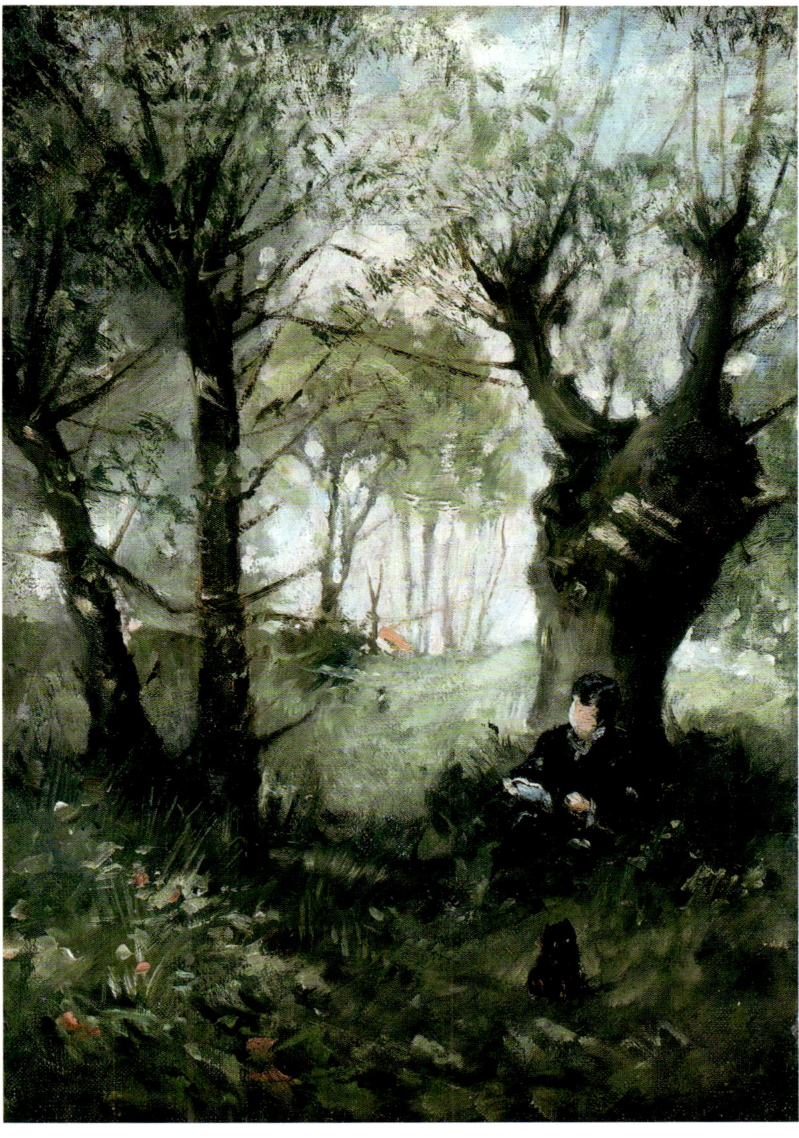

Morisot fue alumno de Oudinot y Corot. En este paisaje, la semejanza con las obras de su maestro llama la atención. No sólo la forma en que dibuja sus trazos para pintar las ramas de los árboles, todo en este cuadro de Berthe Morisot respira el espíritu de Jean-Baptiste Camille Corot.

Morisot era aluno de Oudinot e Corot. Nesta paisagem, a semelhança com as obras de seu mestre chama a atenção. Não só a maneira como ela desenha seus traços para pintar os galhos das árvores, mas tudo sobre esta pintura de Berthe Morisot respira o espírito de Jean-Baptiste Camille Corot.

Morisot was een leerling van Oudinot en Corot. In dit landschap valt de gelijkenis met de werken van haar leermeesters op. Niet alleen de manier waarop ze streken zet om de takken van de bomen te schilderen, maar alles aan dit schilderij van Berthe Morisot ademt de geest van Jean-Baptiste Camille Corot.

REMBRANDT ~ DROST

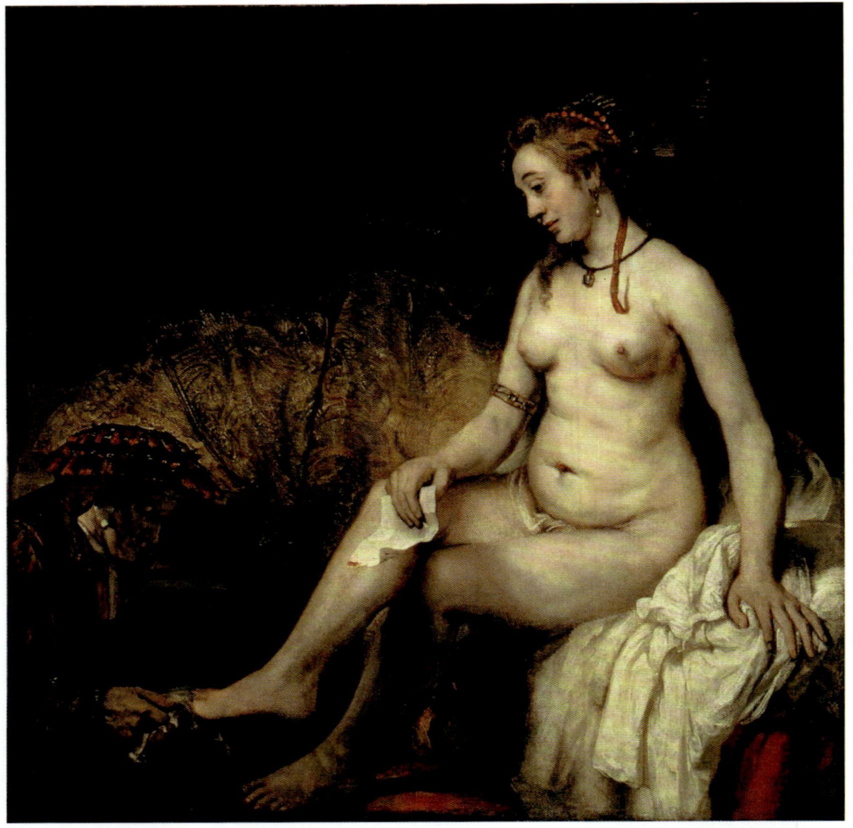

Bathsheba with David's Letter

Bethsabée au bain tenant la lettre de David

Bathseba mit König Davids Brief

Betsabé con la carte de David

Bathsheba a banhar

Batseba met de brief van koning David

Rembrandt van Rijn (1606-1669)

1654, Oil on canvas/Huile sur toile, 142 × 142 cm, Musée du Louvre, Paris

Bathsheba

Bethsabée recevant la lettre de David

Bathseba

Betsabé recibe la carta de David

Bathsheba

Batseba met de brief van koning David

Willem Drost (1633-1659)

1654, Oil on canvas/Huile sur toile, 103 × 87 cm, Musée du Louvre, Paris

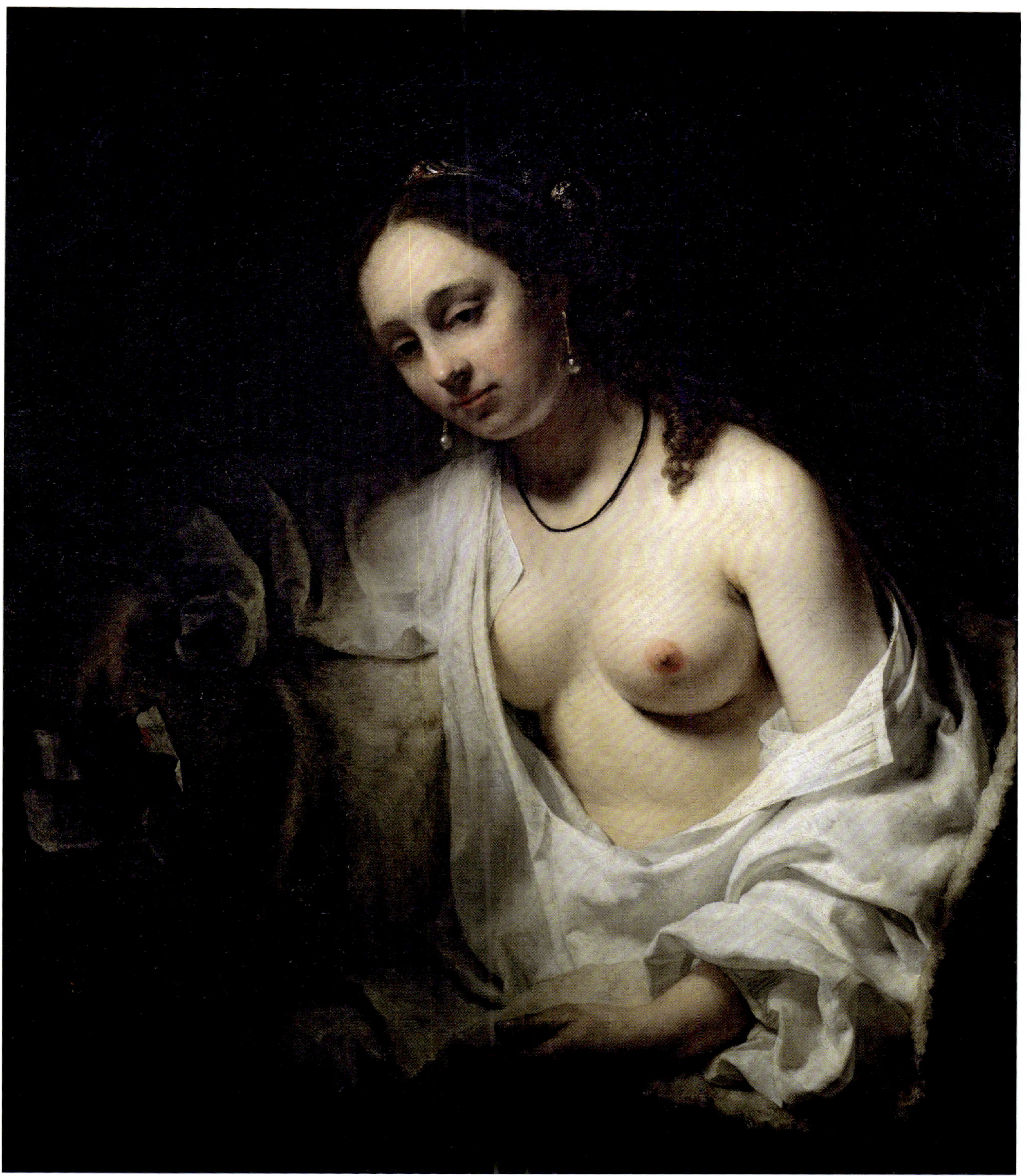

REMBRANDT ~ FRAGONARD

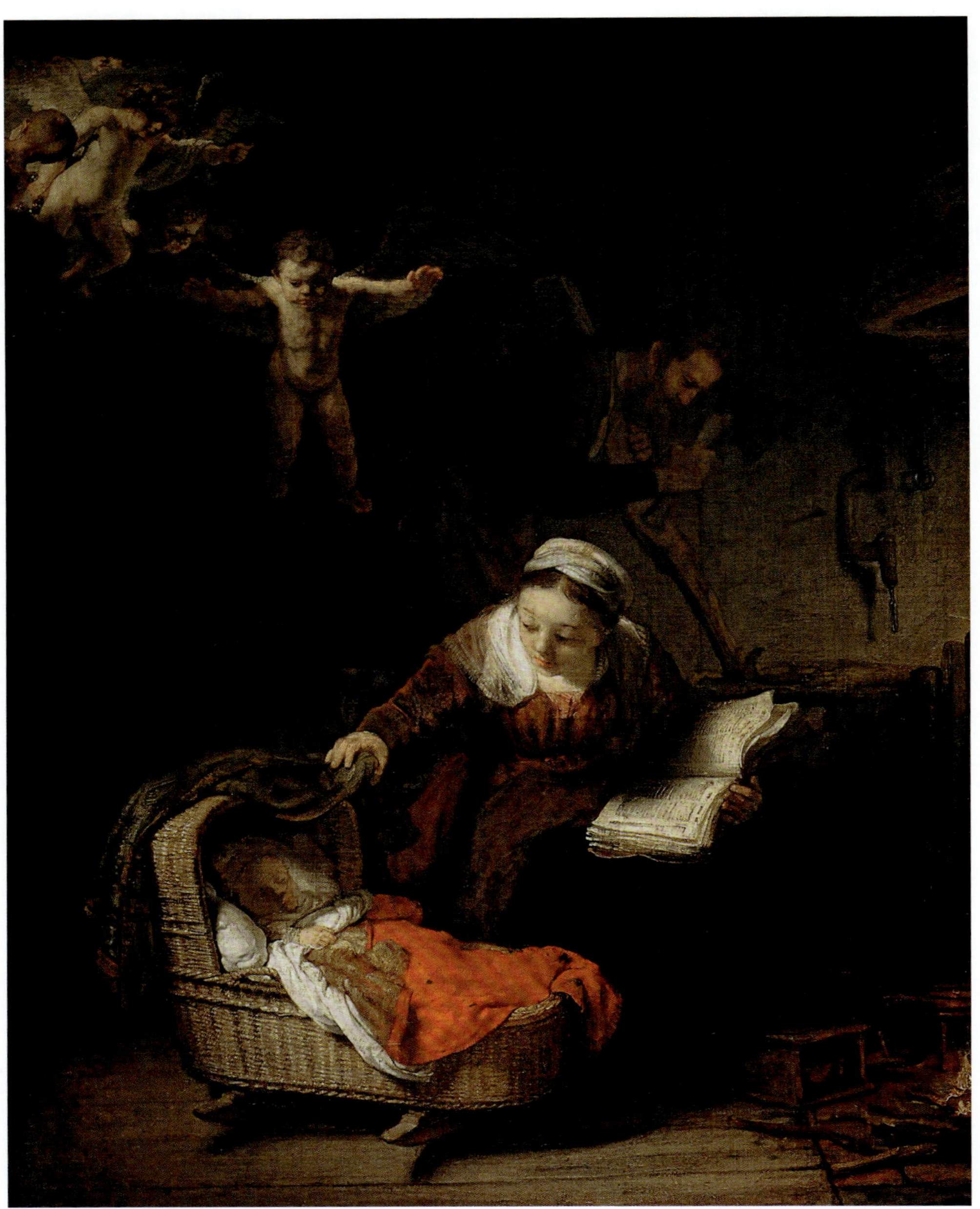

The Holy Family with Angels

La Sainte Famille avec des anges

Die Heilige Familie mit Engeln

La Sagrada Familia con los Ángeles

A Sagrada Família com os Anjos

De Heilige Familie met engelen

Rembrandt van Rijn (1606-1669)

———

1645, Oil on canvas/Huile sur toile, 117 × 91 cm, State Hermitage Museum, St. Petersburg

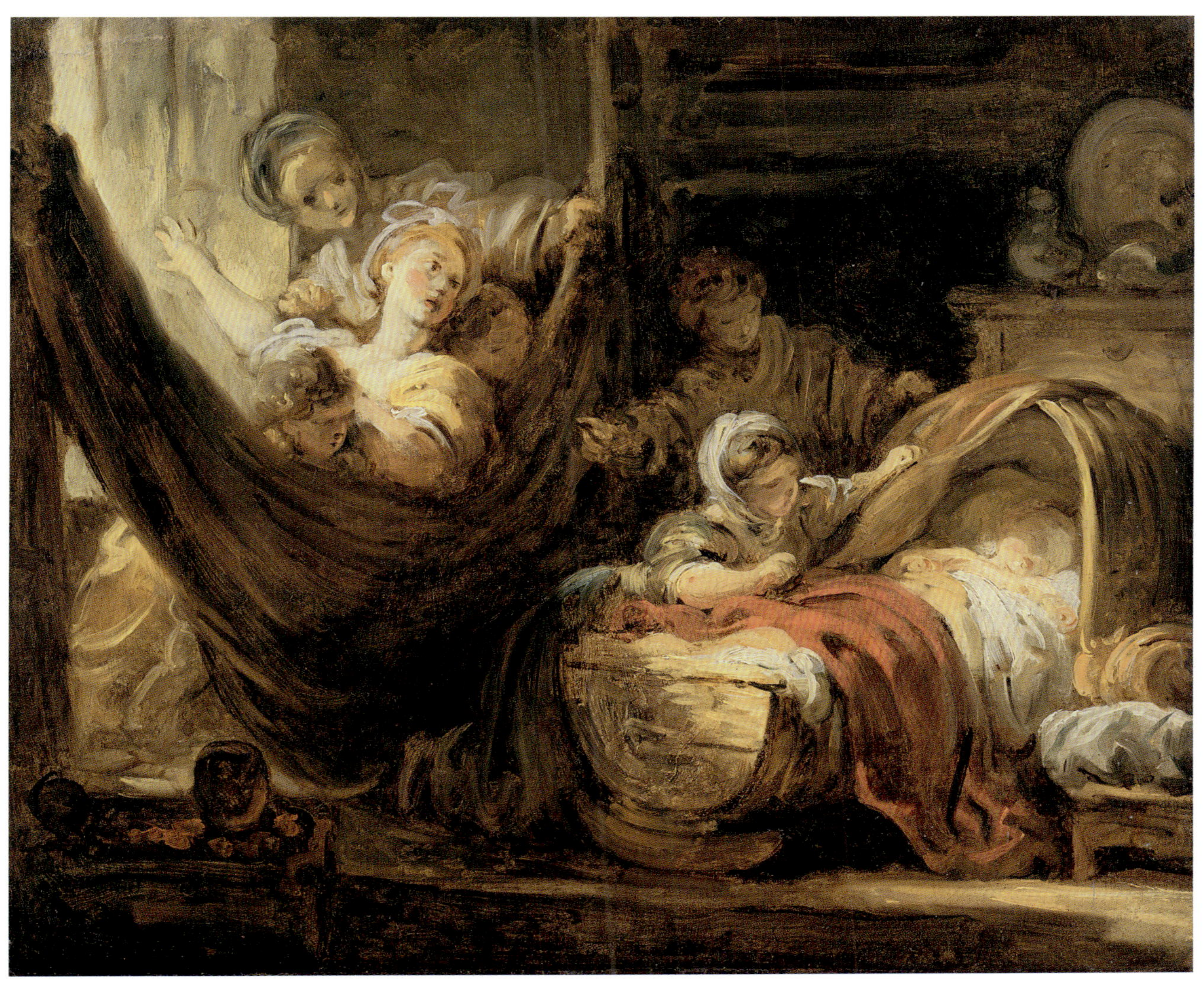

The Cradle

Le Berceau

Die Wiege

La cuna

O berço

De wieg

Jean-Honoré Fragonard (1732-1806)

———

c. 1760-65, Oil on canvas/Huile sur toile,
46 × 55 cm, Musée de Picardie, Amiens

HIROSHIGE ~ LACOMBE

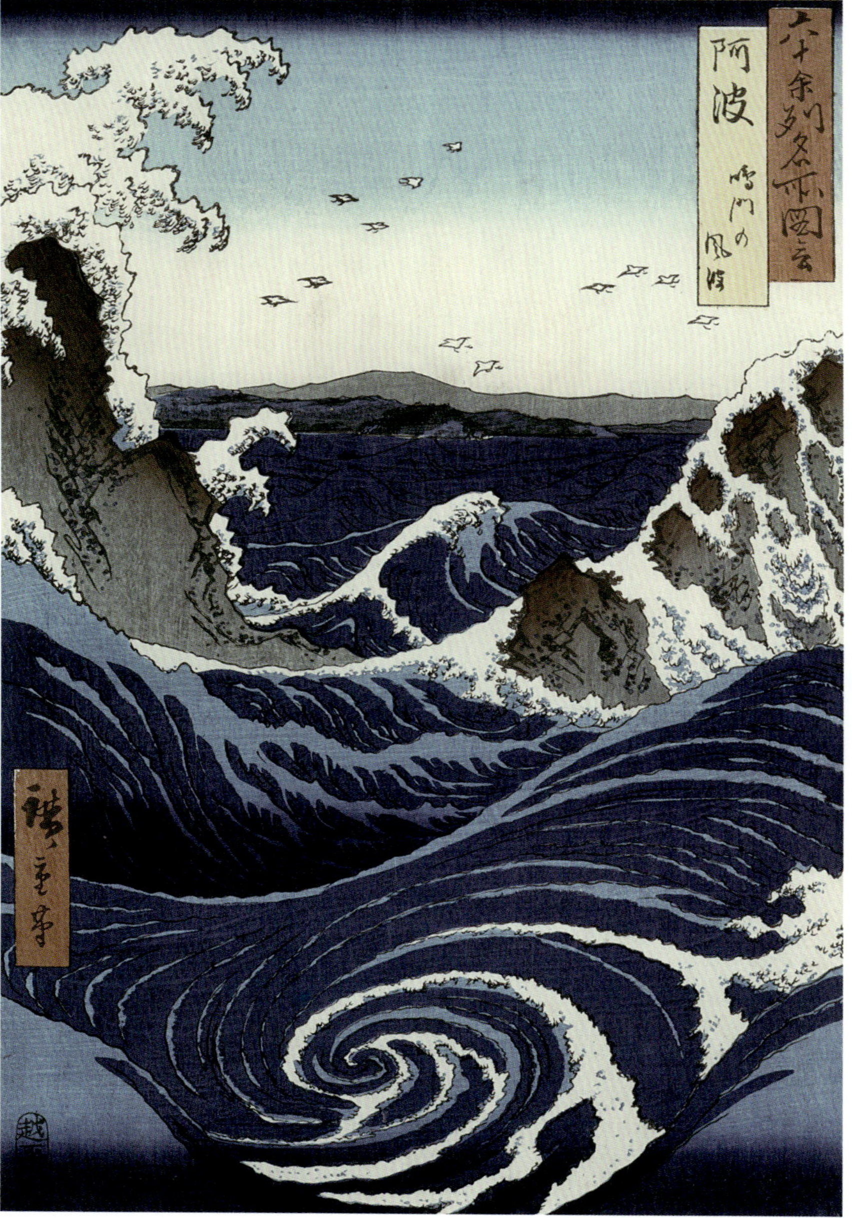

The Naruto Whirlpool in Awa Province

Les Tourbillons de Naruto à Awa

Der Naruto-Strudel in der Provinz Awa

Remolinos de Naruto, Awa

As banheiras de hidromassagem de Naruto a Awa

De draaikolken van Naruto in de provincie Awa

Utagawa Hiroshige (1797-1858)

———

c. 1855, Colored woodblock/Gravure sur bois colorisée, 38 × 25,5 cm, Musée Claude Monet, Giverny

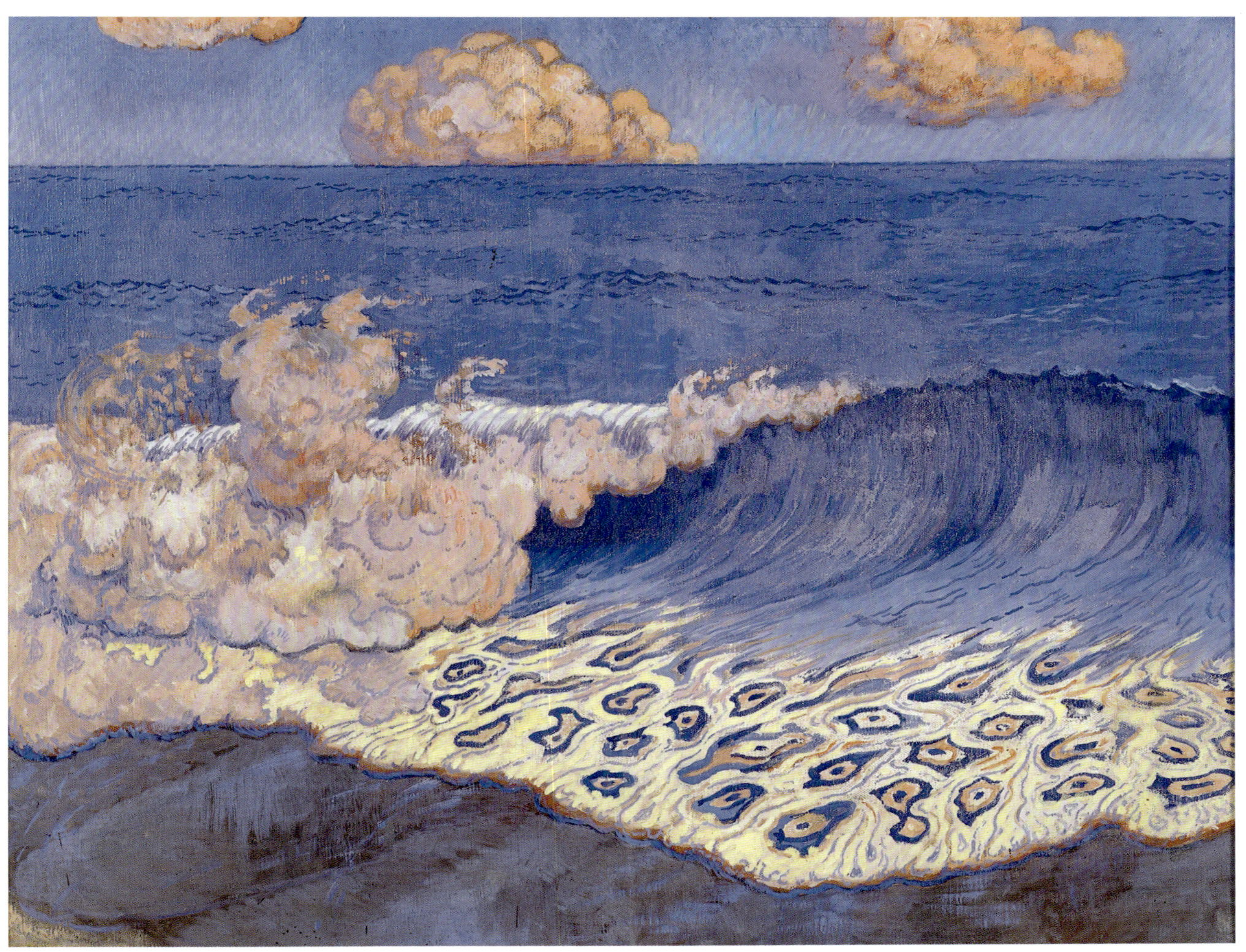

Blue Seascape, Wave Effect
Marine bleue. Effet de vagues
Blaues Seestück, Wellen
Marina azul. Efecto de olas
Marinha azul. Efeito das ondas
Blauw zeestuk, golven

Georges Lacombe (1868-1916)

———

1892-94, Tempera on canvas/Tempera
sur toile, 49,5 × 65,5 cm,
Musée des Beaux-Arts, Rennes

BOTTICELLI ~ INGRES ~ BOUGUEREAU

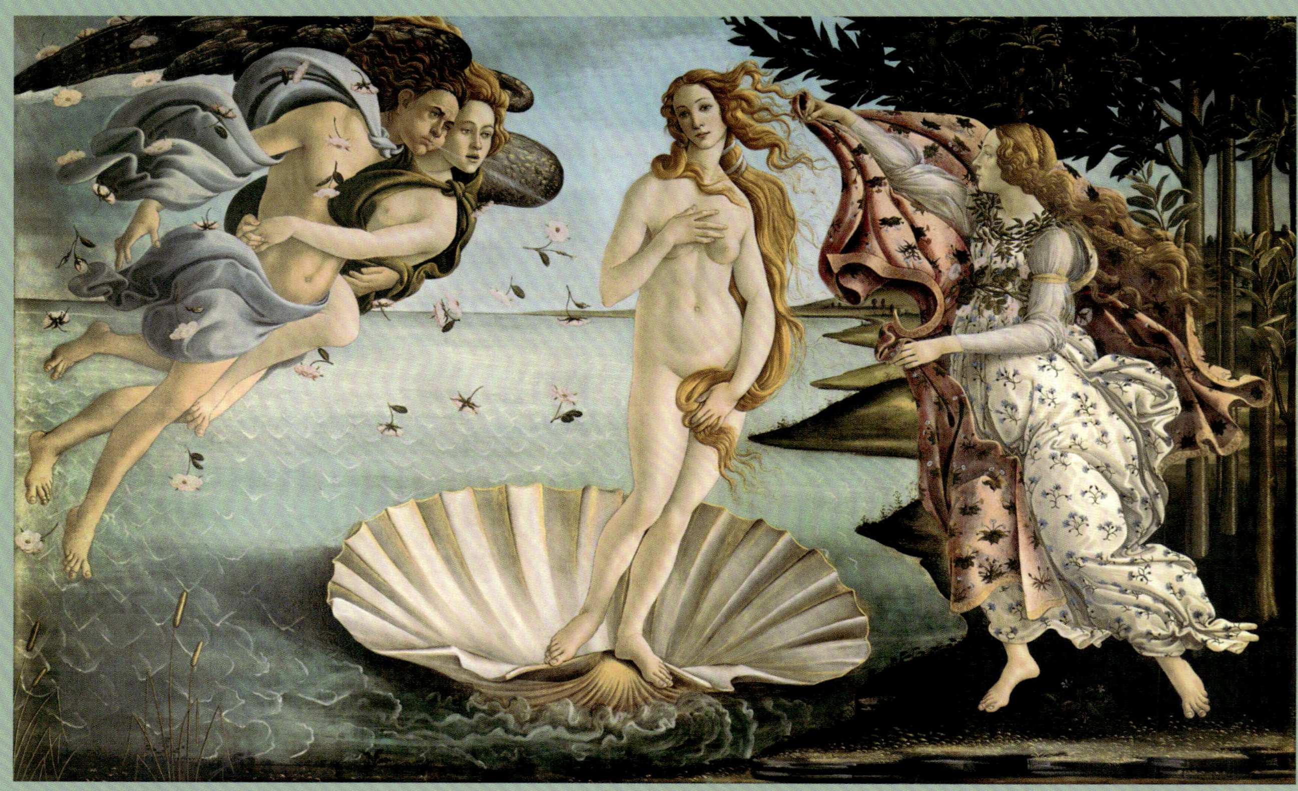

The Birth of Venus
La Naissance de Vénus
Die Geburt der Venus
El nacimiento de Venus
O Nascimento de Vênus
De geboorte van Venus

Sandro Botticelli (1445-1510)

———

c. 1484-85, Tempera on canvas/Tempera
sur toile, 172,5 × 278,5 cm, Galleria degli
Uffizi, Firenze

Venus Anadyome
Vénus anadyomène
Venus Anadyomene
Venus Anadiomena
Vênus Anadyome
Venus Anadyome

**Jean-Auguste-Dominique Ingres
(1780-1867)**

———

1808-48, Oil on canvas/Huile sur toile,
163 × 92 cm, Musée Condé, Chantilly

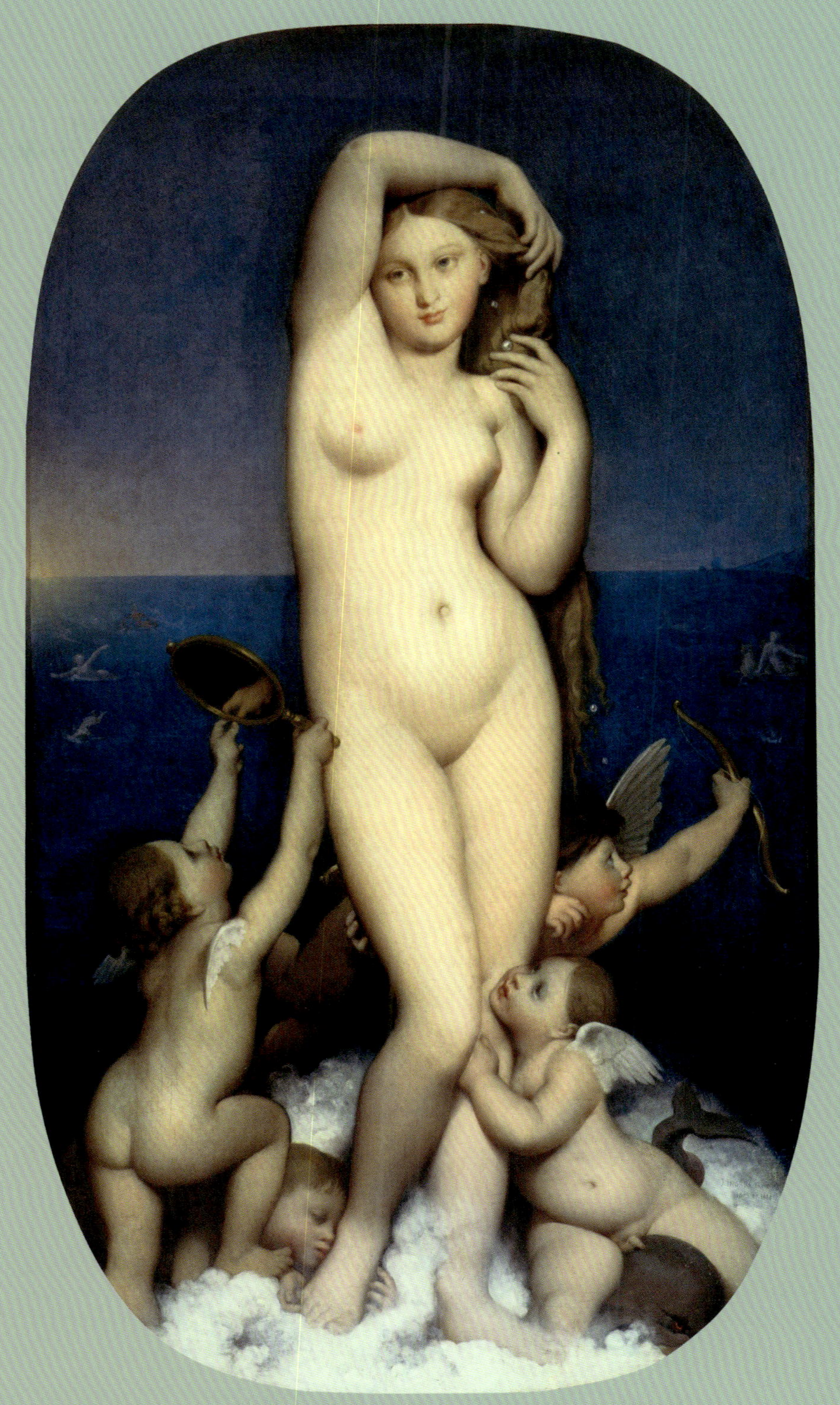

BOTTICELLI ~ INGRES ~ BOUGUEREAU

Mythological subjects have been used by artists since the Renaissance to thematize the female nude under the guise of decency. Both Ingres and Bouguereau knew of Botticelli's masterpiece. Ingres saw it during his stay in Italy in 1805 during a visit to the Uffizi. Both masters of the 19th century created their own image of the goddess.

Ce noble sujet mythologique permet aux artistes, et ce depuis la Renaissance, de traiter le nu féminin en toute décence. C'est une évidence, Ingres comme Bouguereau connaissaient ce chef-d'œuvre classique de l'histoire de l'art, et c'est d'ailleurs en 1805 lors de son séjour en Italie qu'Ingres vit aux Offices *La Naissance de Vénus*. Les deux grands peintres du XIXe siècle créèrent ensuite leur propre vision de la déesse.

Das mythologische Sujet wurde von Künstlern seit der Renaissance genutzt, um den weiblichen Akt unter dem Deckmantel der Anständigkeit zu thematisieren. Ingres sowie Bouguereau kannten Botticellis Meisterwerk. Ingres bekam es bei seinem Italienaufenthalt im Jahr 1805 während eines Besuchs der Uffizien zu Gesicht. Beide Meister des 19. Jahrhunderts schufen ihre eigene Vorstellung der Göttin.

Este noble tema mitológico ha permitido a los artistas, desde el Renacimiento, tratar con decencia el desnudo femenino. Es evidente que tanto Ingres como Bouguereau conocían esta obra maestra clásica de la historia del arte, y fue en 1805, durante su estancia en Italia, cuando Ingres vió en la Galería Uffizi *El nacimiento de Venus*. Los dos grandes pintores del siglo XIX crearon entonces su propia visión de la diosa.

O tema mitológico tem sido usado por artistas desde o Renascimento para tematizar o nu feminino sob o disfarce da decência. Tanto Ingres como Bouguereau conheciam a obra-prima de Botticelli. Ingres o viu durante sua estada na Itália em 1805, durante uma visita aos Uffizi. Ambos os mestres do século XIX criaram a sua própria imagem da deusa.

Het mythologische onderwerp wordt sinds de renaissance door kunstenaars gebruikt om het vrouwelijk naakt onder het mom van fatsoen te schilderen. Zowel Ingres als Bouguereau kende Botticelli's meesterwerk. Ingres zag het tijdens zijn verblijf in Italië in 1805 toen hij de Uffizi bezocht. Beide 19e-eeuwse meesters schiepen hun eigen voorstelling van de godin.

The Birth of Venus

Naissance de Vénus

Die Geburt der Venus

El nacimiento de Venus

O Nascimento de Vênus

De geboorte van Venus

William-Adolphe Bouguereau (1825-1905)

———

1879, Oil on canvas/Huile sur toile, 300 × 215 cm, Musée d'Orsay, Paris

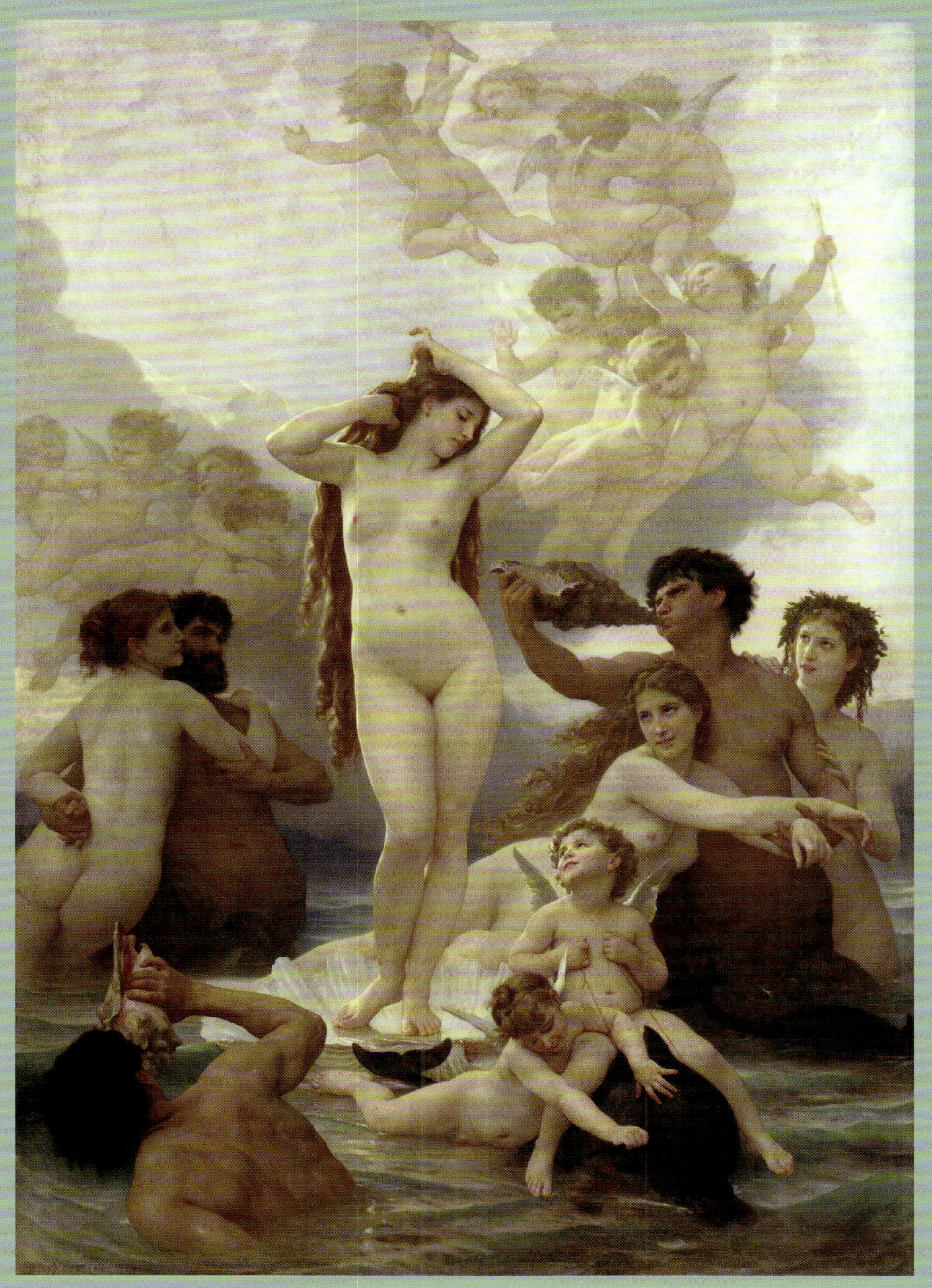

VAN EYCK ~ VAN DER WEYDEN

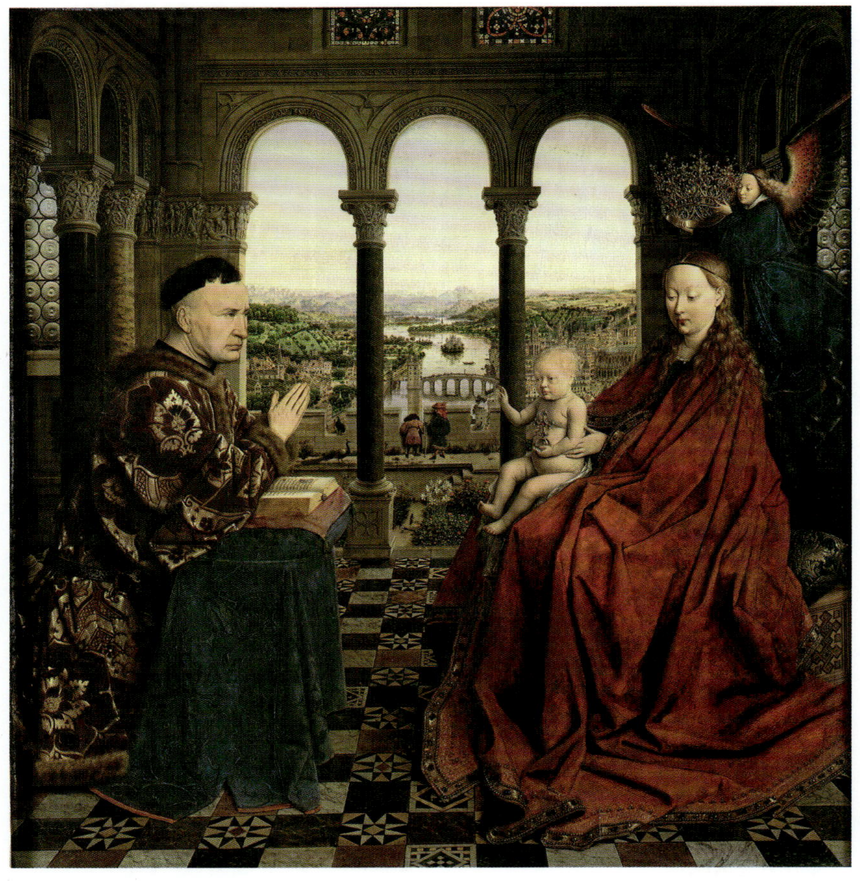

The Virgin and Child with Chancellor Rolin

La Vierge du chancelier Rolin

Die Madonna des Kanzlers Nicolas Rolin

La Virgen del canciller Rolin

Madonna do Chanceler Nicolas Rolin

De Maagd van kanselier Nicolas Rolin

Jan van Eyck (1390-1441)

———

c. 1435, Oil on panel/Huile sur panneau,
66 × 62 cm, Musée du Louvre, Paris

Saint Luke Drawing the Virgin's Portrait

Saint Luc dessinant la Vierge

*Der Heilige Lukas porträtiert die
Madonna*

San Lucas representa a la Virgen

São Lucas retrata a Virgem

De heilige Lucas tekent de Maagd

Rogier van der Weyden (1399-1464)

———

c. 1435, Oil on panel/Huile sur panneau,
137 × 107 cm, Groeningemuseum, Brugge

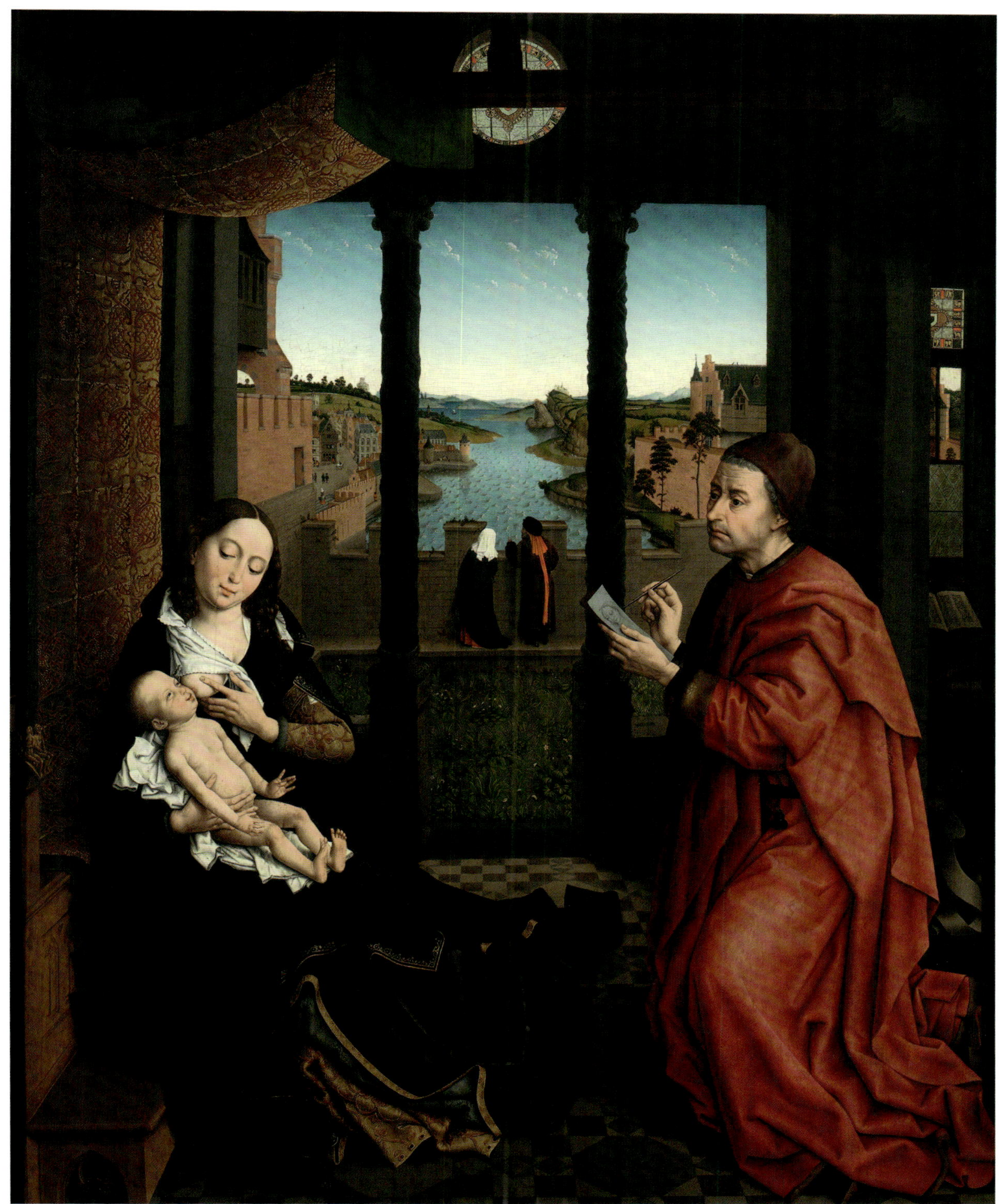

GAUGUIN ~ MUNCH

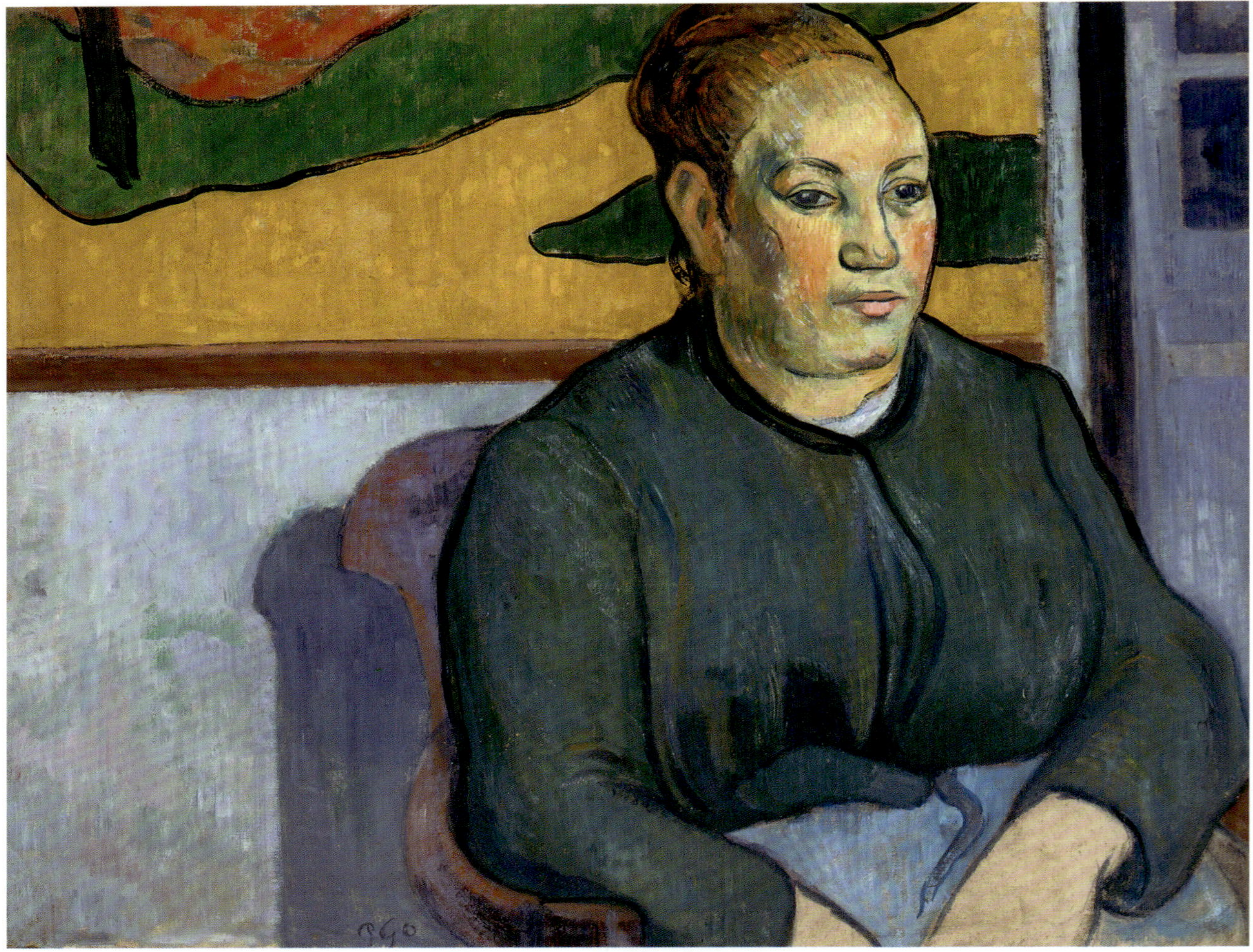

Madame Roulin

Paul Gauguin (1848-1903)

———

1888, Oil on canvas/Huile sur toile,
50,5 × 63,5 cm, Saint Louis Art Museum,
Saint-Louis

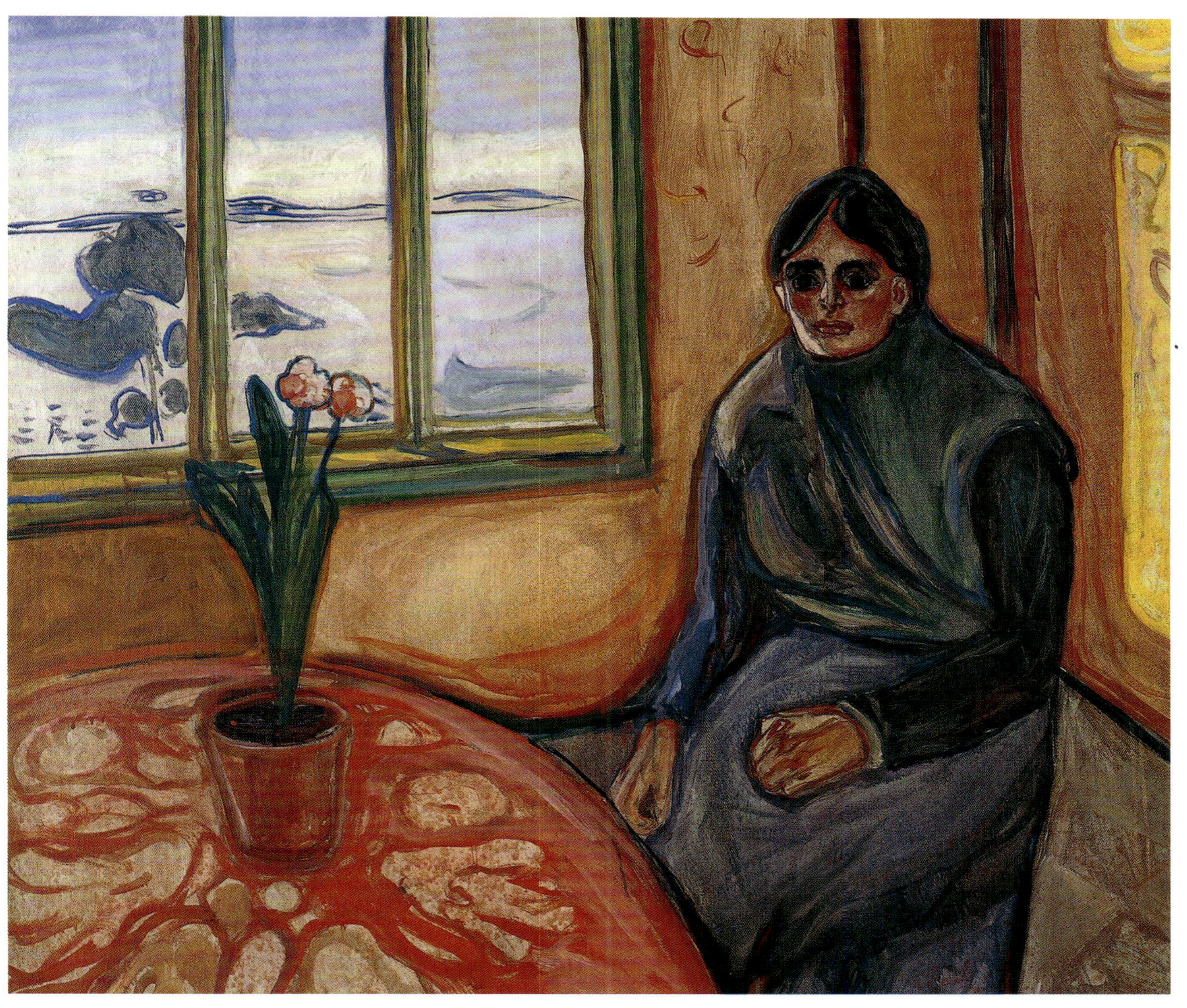

Melancholy or *Laura,* detail
Mélancolie ou *Portrait de Laura,* détail
Melancholie oder *Laura,* Detail
Melancolía o *Laura,* detalle
Melancolia ou *Laura,* detalhe
Melancholie of *Portret van Laura,* detail

Edvard Munch (1863-1944)

c. 1899, Oil on canvas/Huile sur toile, 110 × 126 cm,
Munchmuseet, Oslo

DA VINCI ~ DA VINCI (STUDENT OF/ÉLÈVE DE)

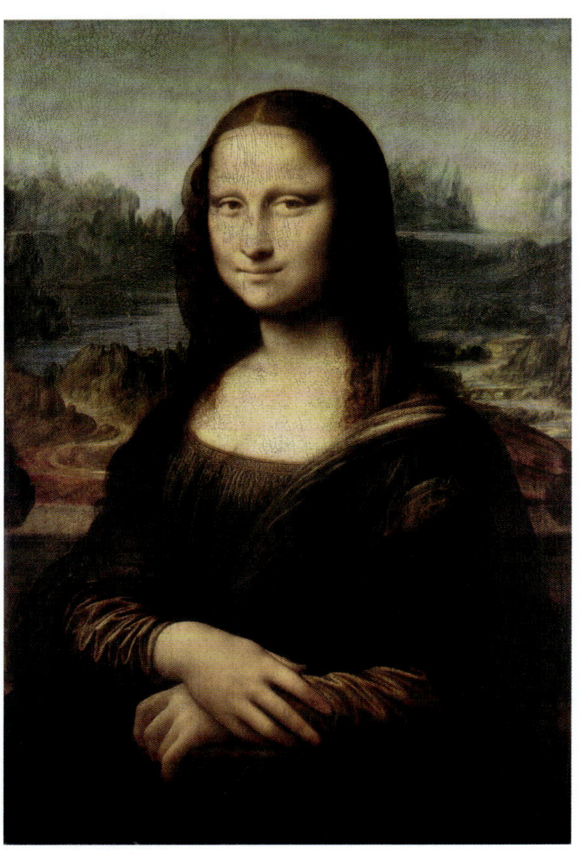

Mona Lisa

La Joconde

Mona Lisa

Mona Lisa (La Gioconda)

Mona Lisa

Mona Lisa

Leonardo da Vinci (1452-1519)

———

c. 1503-19, Oil on panel/Huile sur panneau,
77 × 53 cm, Musée du Louvre, Paris

The clothed *Mona Lisa* comes from da Vinci, the naked version from one of his students. The similarity of the style is easy to see. The paintings differ only in the execution as an oil painting and as a drawing, which shows that the pupil was not only influenced by da Vinci, but took his master as a model.

L'une est habillée, l'autre est nue. L'une est de Léonard, l'autre est d'un de ses élèves. Au-delà de l'exercice que l'on peut aisément qualifier de style, il faut comparer aussi ce qui peut l'être. *La Joconde* est une huile sur panneau, *Mona Vanna* est un grand beau dessin. Ici plus qu'une influence… un modèle !

Die bekleidet *Mona Lisa* stammt von da Vinci, die nackte Version von einem seiner Schüler. Die Ähnlichkeit des Stils ist leicht zu erkennen. Die Gemälde unterscheiden sich nur in der Ausführung als Ölgemälde und als Zeichnung, die zeigt, dass der Schüler nicht nur von da Vinci beeinflusst wurde, sondern sich seinen Meister als Vorbild nahm.

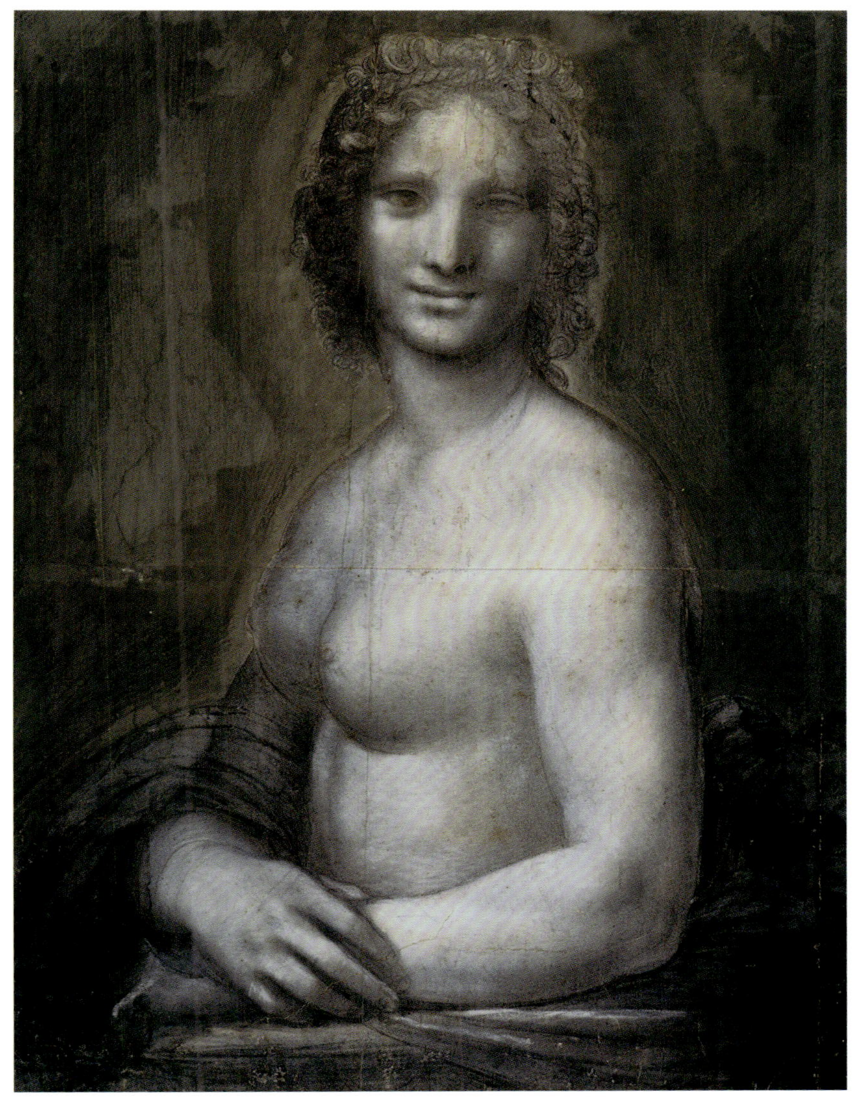

Nude Mona Lisa or *Monna Vanna*

La Joconde nue, dite *Mona Vanna*

Die nackte Mona Lisa oder *Monna Vanna*

La Mona Lisa desnuda o *Monna Vanna*

A Mona Lisa Nua, conhecida como *Mona Vanna*

De naakte Mona Lisa of *Monna Vanna*

**Leonardo da Vinci
(student of/élève de) (1452-1519)**

———

c. 1514-16, Charcoal and lead-white highlights/Charbon de bois et rehauts de blanc de plomb, 72 × 54 cm, Musée Condé, Chantilly

La *Mona Lisa* vestida viene de da Vinci, la versión desnuda de uno de sus alumnos. La similitud del estilo es fácil de ver. Las pinturas se diferencian sólo en la ejecución como óleos y como dibujos, lo que demuestra que el alumno no sólo fue influenciado por da Vinci, sino que tomó como modelo a su maestro.

A *Mona Lisa* vestida vem de Da Vinci, a versão nua de um de seus alunos. A semelhança do estilo é fácil de ver. As pinturas diferem apenas na execução como pinturas a óleo e como desenhos, o que mostra que o aluno não só foi influenciado por Da Vinci, mas tomou seu mestre como modelo.

De geklede *Mona Lisa* is van Leonardo da Vinci, de naakte versie van een van zijn leerlingen. De gelijkenis in stijl is goed te zien. De schilderijen verschillen alleen in de uitvoering als olieverfschilderij en tekening, wat aantoont dat de leerling niet alleen door Da Vinci werd beïnvloed, maar zijn leermeester ook tot voorbeeld nam.

CONSTABLE ~ MONET

The successors to the Barbizon School, the Impressionist painters, of whom Claude Monet is undoubtedly the best known representative, were often inspired by the depictions of the heavens and landscapes of John Constable, an artist who was rightly regarded as a pioneer of open-air painting. Constable's painting contains all the elements Monet loved when he lived in Normandy and made the acquaintance of Eugène Boudin.

S'inscrivant après l'école de Barbizon, le courant impressionniste, dont Claude Monet est sans aucun doute le plus célèbre de ses représentants, ne pouvait qu'être séduit par les compositions atmosphériques et autres paysages de John Constable, artiste considéré d'ailleurs et à juste titre comme un véritable précurseur de la peinture en plein air. On retrouve dans ce tableau de Constable tout ce qu'aimait le jeune Monet à l'époque où il vivait en Normandie et côtoyait Eugène Boudin.

Als Nachfolger der Schule von Barbizon ließen sich die Maler des Impressionismus, deren bekanntester Vertreter ohne Zweifel Claude Monet ist, oft von den Himmelsdarstellungen und Landschaften von John Constable inspirieren – einem Künstler, der zu Recht als Wegbereiter der Freilichtmalerei gilt. Constables Gemälde enthält alle Elemente, die Monet liebte, als er in der Normandie lebte und die Bekanntschaft von Eugène Boudin machte.

Como sucesores de la Escuela Barbizon, los pintores impresionistas, de los cuales Claude Monet es sin duda el representante más conocido, se inspiraron a menudo en las representaciones del cielo y de los paisajes de John Constable, un artista considerado, con razón, como un pionero de la pintura al aire libre. La pintura de Constable contiene todos los elementos que Monet amaba cuando vivía en Normandía y conoció a Eugène Boudin.

Sucessor da Escola de Barbizon, os pintores impressionistas, de quem Claude Monet é sem dúvida o representante mais conhecido, foram muitas vezes inspirados pelas representações dos céus e das paisagens de John Constable, um artista que foi justamente considerado como um pioneiro da pintura ao ar livre. A pintura de Constable contém todos os elementos que Monet amava quando viveu na Normandia e conheceu Eugène Boudin.

Als navolgers van de school van Barbizon lieten de impressionistische schilders, van wie Claude Monet ongetwijfeld de bekendste is, zich vaak inspireren door de luchtweergave en landschappen van John Constable, een kunstenaar die terecht als pionier van de plein-airschilderkunst wordt beschouwd. Constables schilderij bevat alle elementen waar Monet zo van hield toen hij in Normandië woonde en kennismaakte met Eugène Boudin.

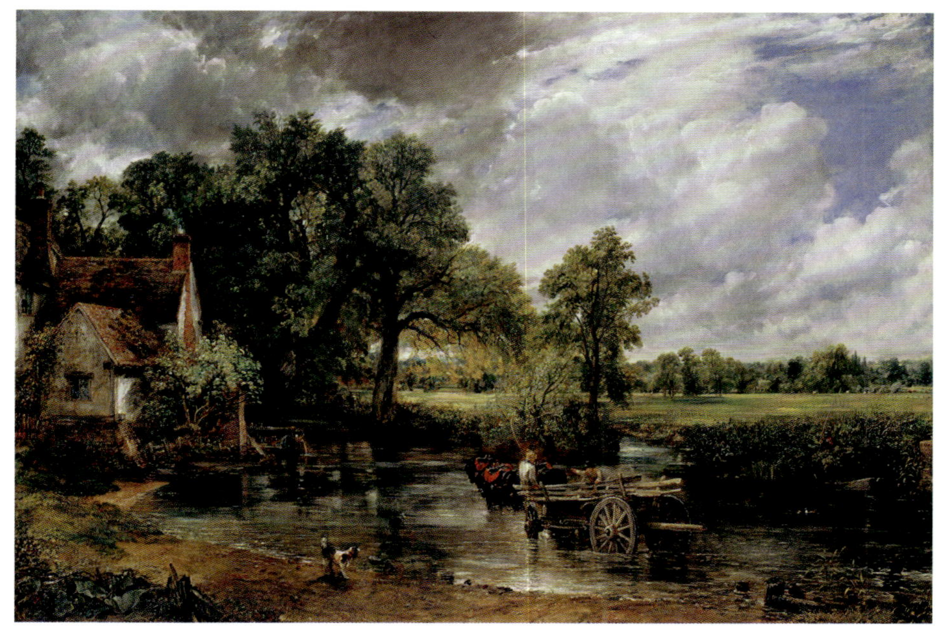

The Hay Wain
La Charrette de foin
Der Heukarren
El carro de heno
A charrete de feno
De hooiwagen

John Constable (1776-1837)

———

1821, Oil on canvas/Huile sur toile, 130,2 × 185,4 cm, The National Gallery, London

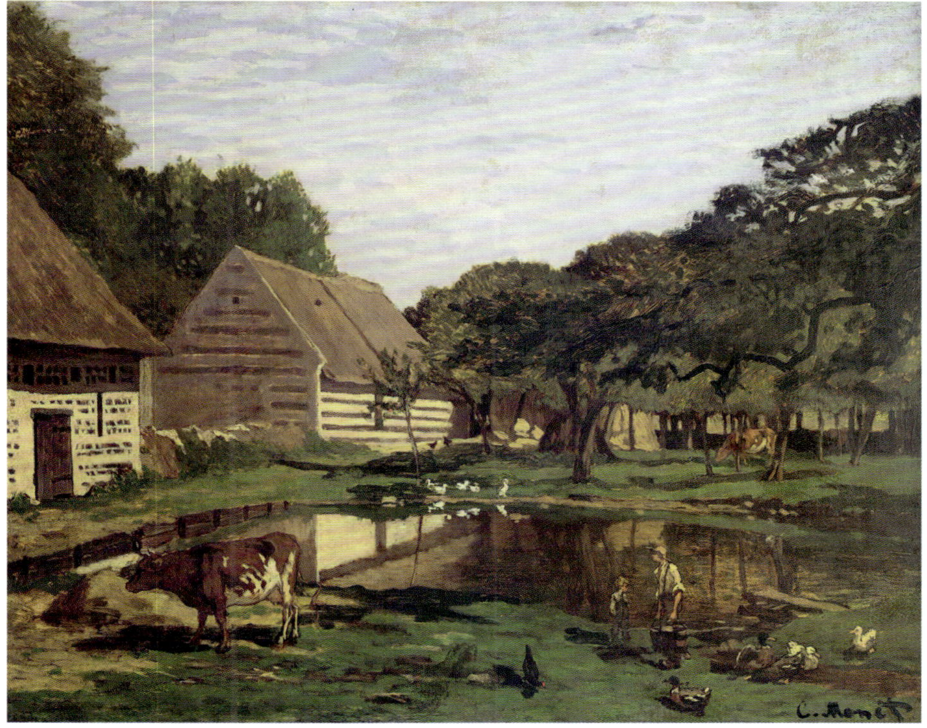

A Farmyard in Normandy
Cour de ferme en Normandie
Ein Bauernhof in der Normandie
Una granja en Normandía
Uma fazenda na Normandia
Een boerderij in Normandië

Claude Monet (1840-1926)

———

c. 1863, Oil on canvas/Huile sur toile, 65,2 × 81,5 cm, Musée d'Orsay, Paris

CHARDIN ~ GAUGUIN

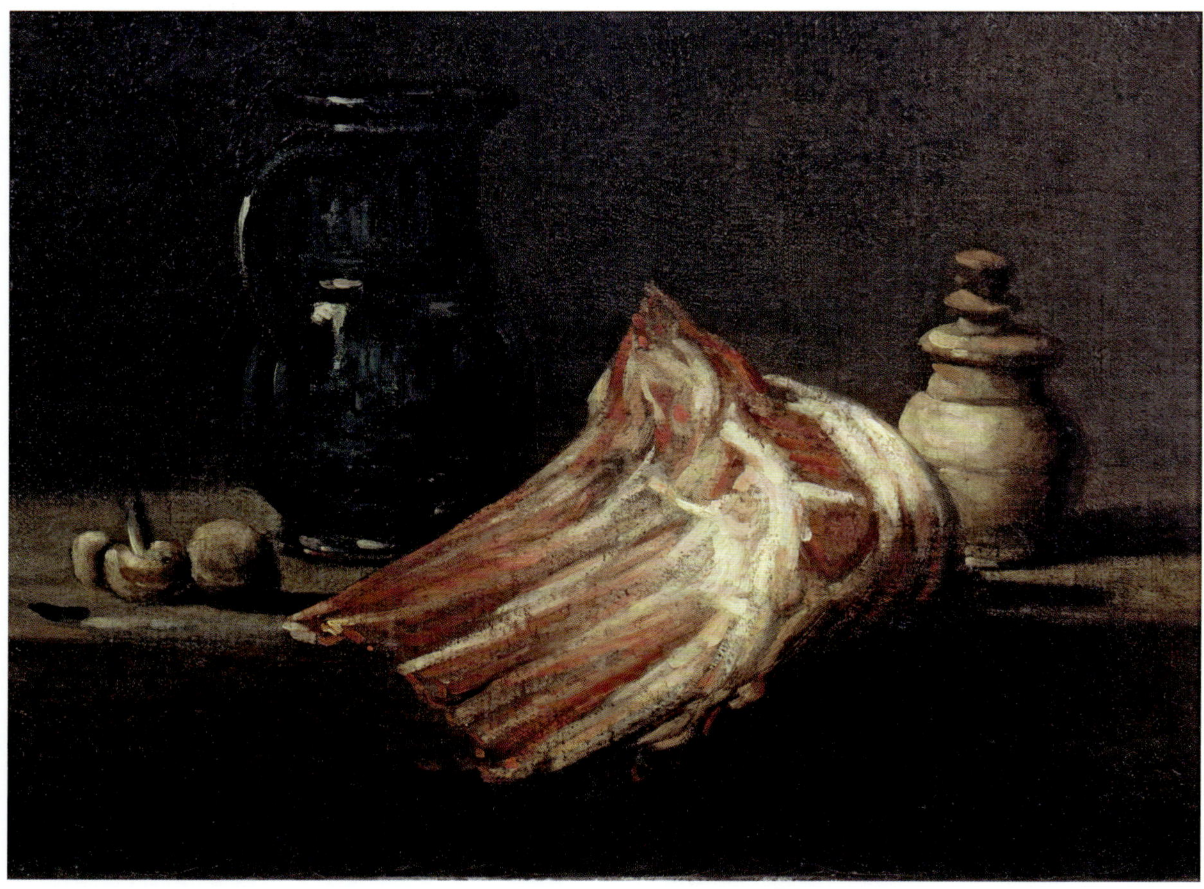

The Kitchen Table with Utensils and
Lamb Rack

Table de cuisine et ustensiles avec un
carré de mouton

Küchentisch mit Utensilien und
Lammkarree

Mesa de cocina con utensilios y paletilla
de cordero

Mesa de cozinha com utensílios e praça
de cordeiro

Keukentafel met keukengerei en
lamscarré

Jean-Siméon Chardin (1699-1779)

———

c. 1740, Oil on canvas/Huile sur toile,
34 × 46 cm, Musée Picasso, Paris

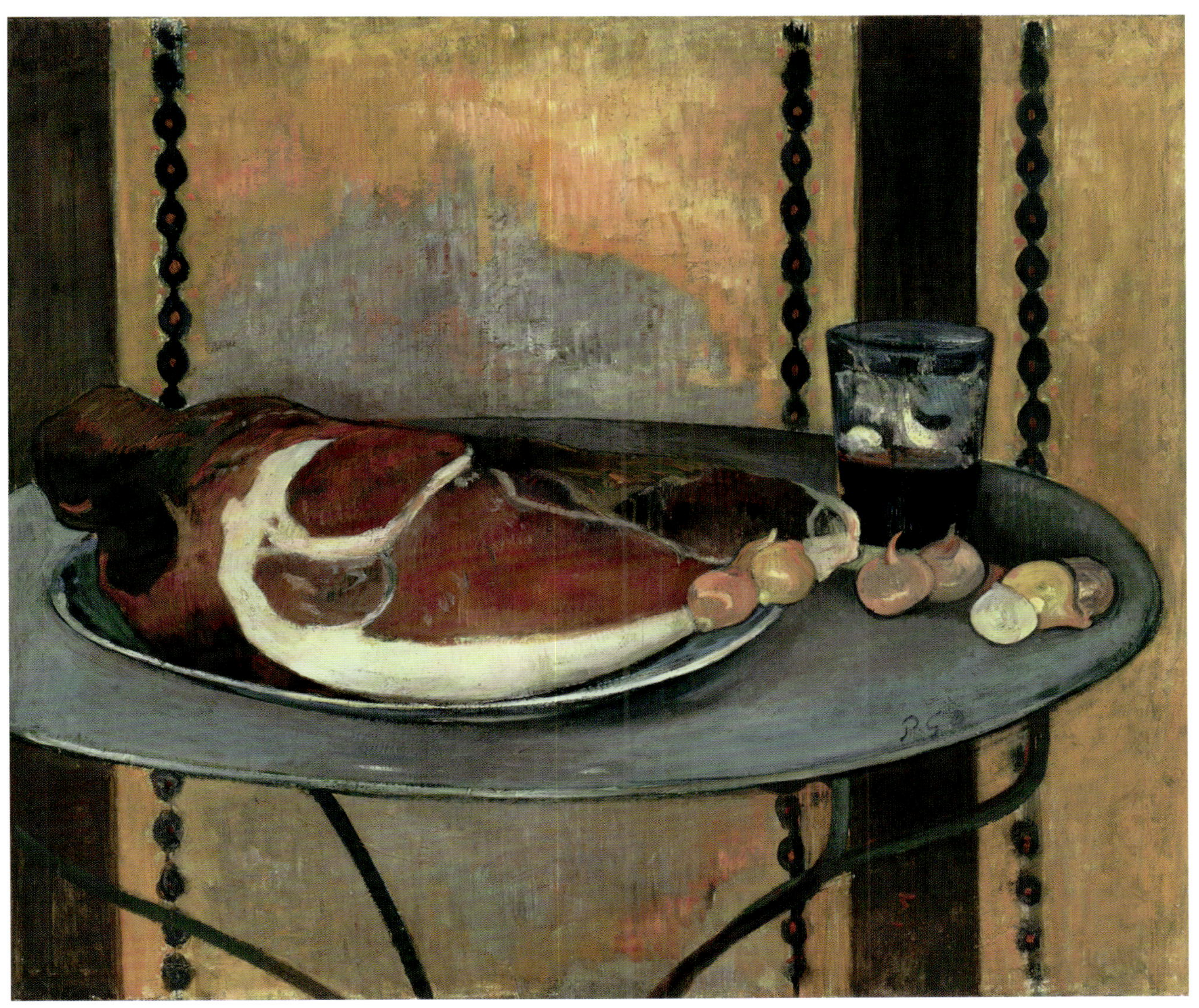

The Ham

Le Jambon

Der Schinken

El jamón

O presunto

De ham

Paul Gauguin (1848-1903)

1889, Oil on canvas/Huile sur toile, 50,1 × 57,7 cm,
The Phillips Collection, Washington

VAN DYCK ~ DAUMIER

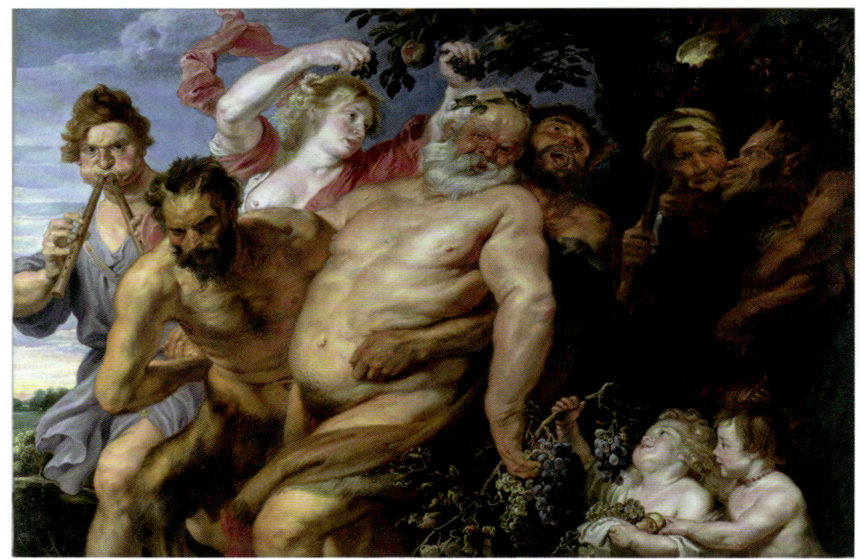

Drunken Silenus Supported by Satyrs

Silène ivre soutenu par des satyres

Triumph des Silen

Triunfo de Sileno

Triunfo do Silêncio

Triomf van Silenus

Anthonis van Dyck (1599-1641)

———

c. 1620, Oil on canvas/Huile sur toile,
133,5 × 197 cm, The National Gallery,
London

It is easy to understand why the French master of caricature was attracted to this painting - not by the style or the way of painting, but by the figure of Bacchus. The exaggerated depiction in many respects inspired Daumier to include the figure in his repertoire.

Il est facile de comprendre ce qui dans cette œuvre attira le regard du maître français de la caricature. Plus que le style ou la façon de peindre, c'est le sujet et sans doute la figure principale de Bacchus. Outrancier à bien des égards, ce dernier se devait de prendre place dans le répertoire des formes de Daumier.

Es lässt sich leicht nachvollziehen, warum der französische Meister der Karikatur von diesem Gemälde angetan war – nicht von dem Stil oder der Malweise, sondern von der Figur des Bacchus. Die in vielerlei Hinsicht überspitzte Darstellung inspirierte Daumier dazu, die Figur in sein Repertoire aufzunehmen.

Es fácil entender por qué el maestro francés de la caricatura se sintió atraído por esta pintura, no por el estilo o la forma de pintar, sino por la figura de Baco. La exagerada representación en muchos aspectos inspiró a Daumier a incluir la figura en su repertorio.

É fácil entender porque o mestre francês da caricatura foi atraído por esta pintura - não pelo estilo ou pela maneira de pintar, mas pela figura de Baco. A representação exagerada em muitos aspectos inspirou Daumier a incluir a figura em seu repertório.

Het is gemakkelijk te begrijpen waarom de Franse meester van de karikatuur werd aangetrokken door dit schilderij – niet door de stijl of manier van schilderen, maar door de figuur van Bacchus. De in veel opzichten overdreven weergave inspireerde Daumier ertoe de figuur op te nemen in zijn repertoire.

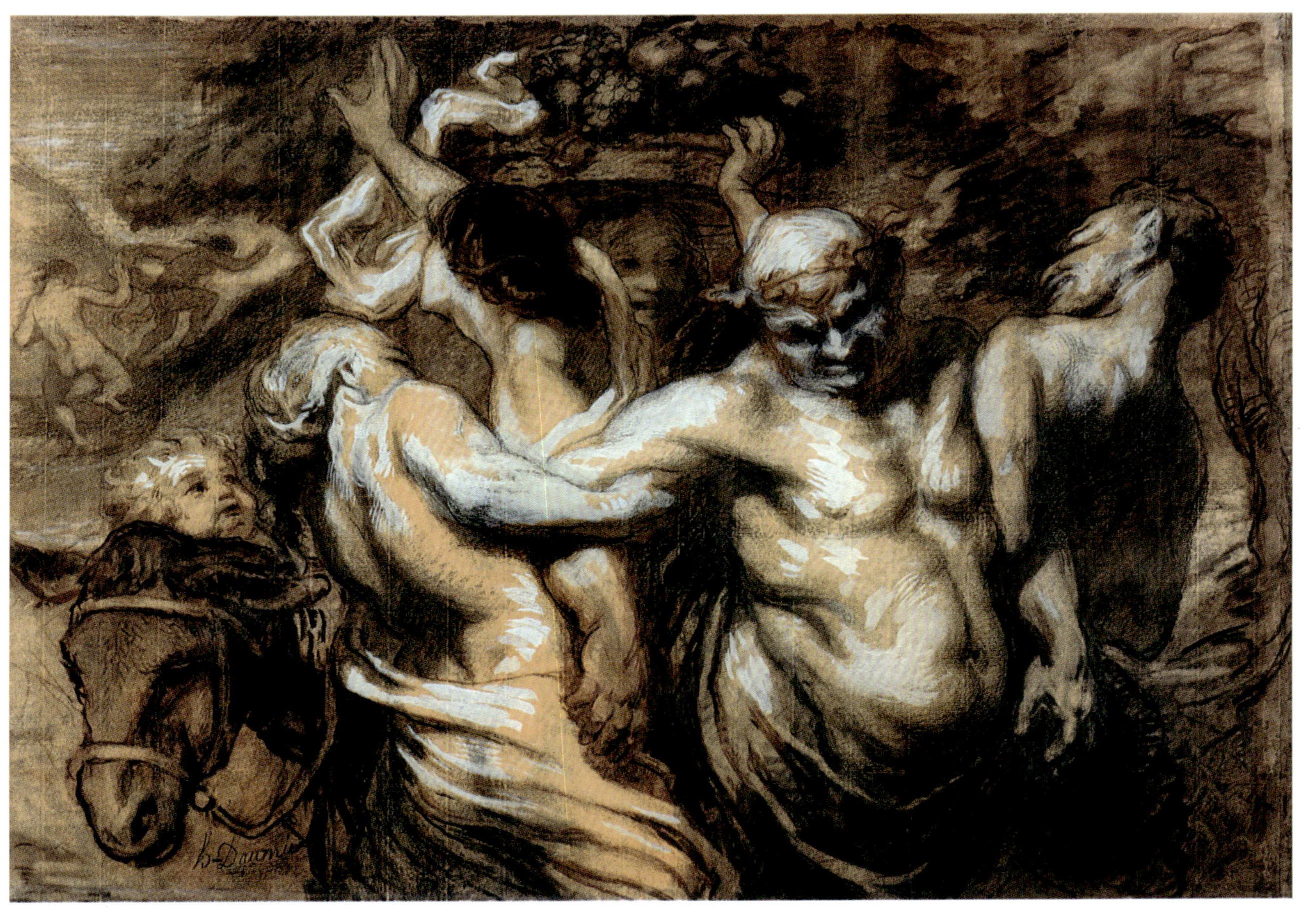

The Drunken Silenus
L'Ivresse de Silène
Trunkener Silen
La embriaguez de Sileno
Silen Bêbado
Dronken Silenus

Honoré Daumier (1808-1879)

c. 1850, Charcoal and bodycolor on paper/
Crayon, fusain et estompe avec rehauts de
gouache blanche sur carton, 43 × 61 cm,
Musée des Beaux-Arts, Calais

IL GUERCINO ~ COURBET

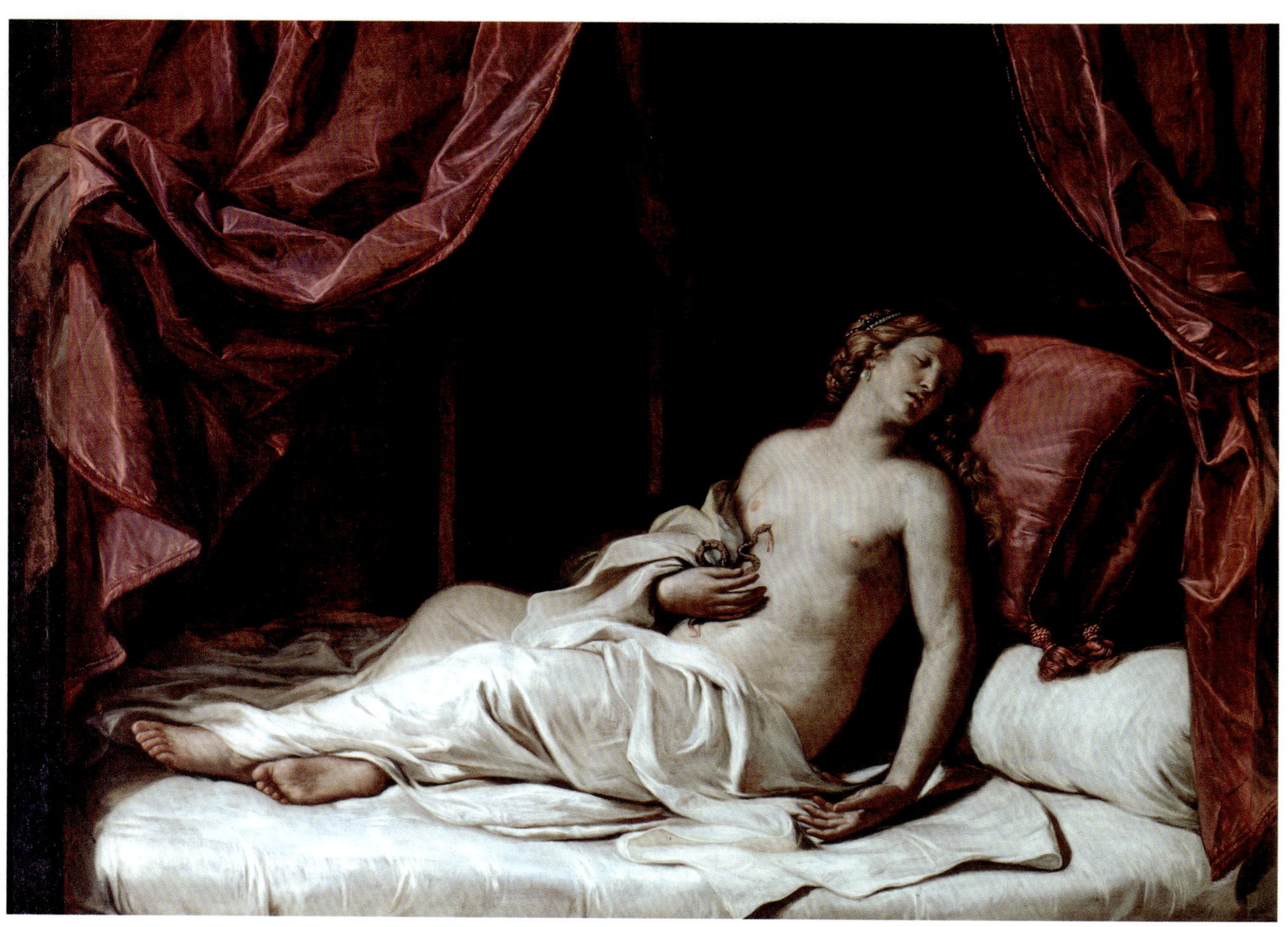

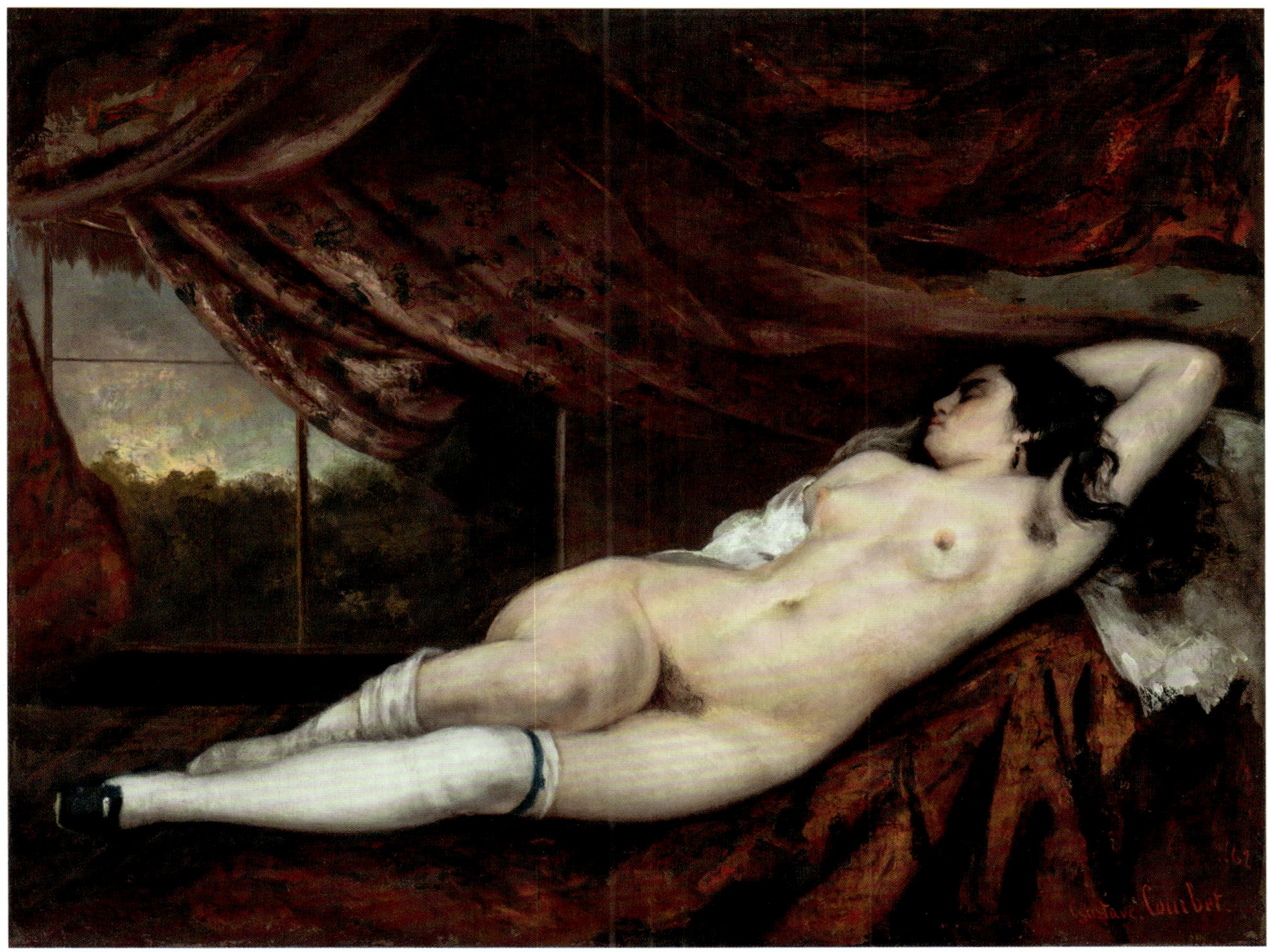

<table>
<tr><td>

The Death of Cleopatra

La Mort de Cléopâtre

Der Tod der Kleopatra

La muerte de Cleopatra

A morte de Cleópatra

De dood van Cleopatra

**Giovanni Barbieri (il Guercino)
(1591-1666)**

———

c. 1648, Oil on canvas/Huile sur toile,
173 × 237 cm, Musei di Strada Nuova,
Genova

</td><td>

Reclining Female Nude

Femme nue couchée

Liegender Akt

Desnudo mujer tumbada

Deitado Nú

Liggend naakt

Gustave Courbet (1819-1877)

———

c. 1862/63, Oil on canvas/Huile sur toile,
74,9 × 97,1 cm, Private collection

</td></tr>
</table>

GÉRICAULT ~ MANET

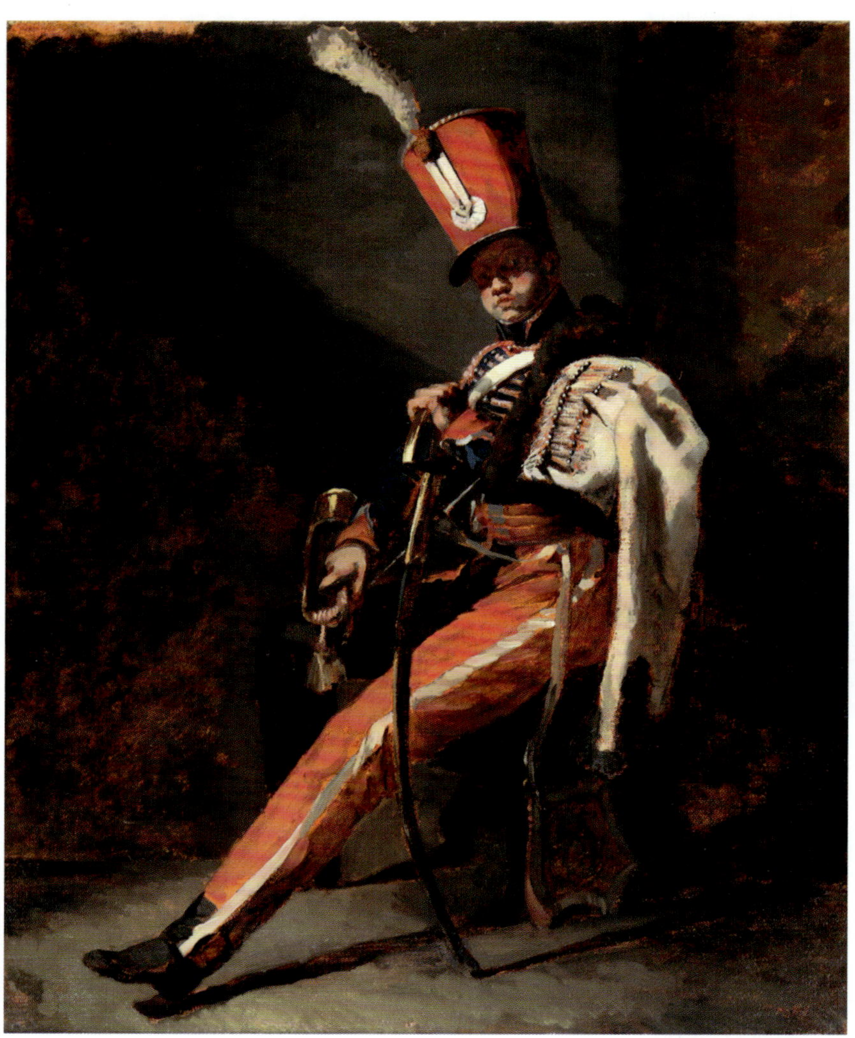

The Trumpeter of the Orleans Hussars

Trompette de Hussards d'Orléans en grande tenue

Der Trompeter der Orleans-Husaren

El trompetista de los húsares de Orleans

O Trompetista dos Hussardos de Orleães

De trompetspeler van de huzaren van Orléans

Théodore Géricault (1791-1824)

———

c. 1814/15, Oil on canvas/Huile sur toile, 47 × 38 cm, Private collection

The Fifer

Le Fifre

Der Querpfeifer

El pífano

O jovem flautista

De fluitspeler

Édouard Manet (1832-1883)

———

1866, Oil on canvas/Huile sur toile, 160,5 × 97 cm, Musée d'Orsay, Paris

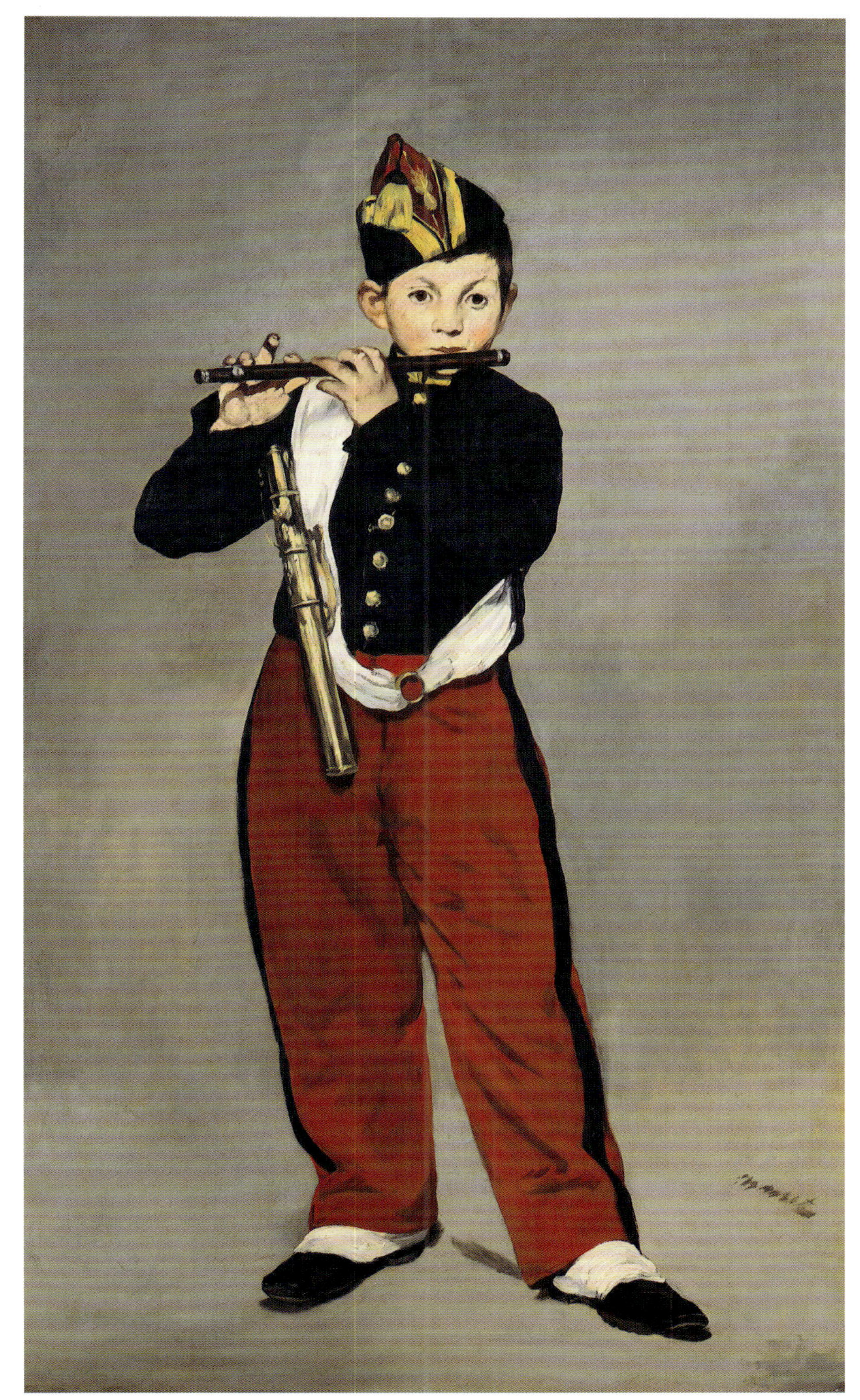

RUBENS ~ VAN DYCK

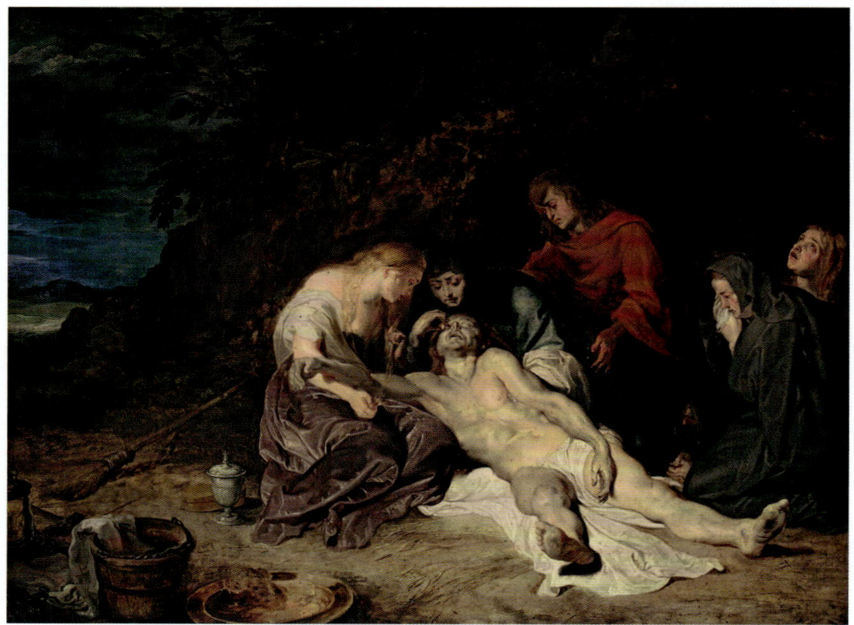

The Lamentation of Christ
La Déploration du Christ
Beweinung Christi
Lamentación sobre Cristo muerto
A Paixão de Cristo
Bewening van Christus

Peter Paul Rubens (1577-1640)

———

c. 1614, Oil on canvas/Huile sur toile,
56 × 75,5 cm, Koninklijk Museum voor
Schone Kunsten, Antwerpen

The Lamentation over the Dead Christ
La Déploration du Christ
Beweinung Christi
Lamentación sobre Cristo muerto
A Paixão de Cristo
Bewening van Christus

Anthonis van Dyck (1599-1641)

———

c. 1629, Oil on canvas/Huile sur toile,
114 × 207 cm, Koninklijk Museum voor
Schone Kunsten, Antwerpen

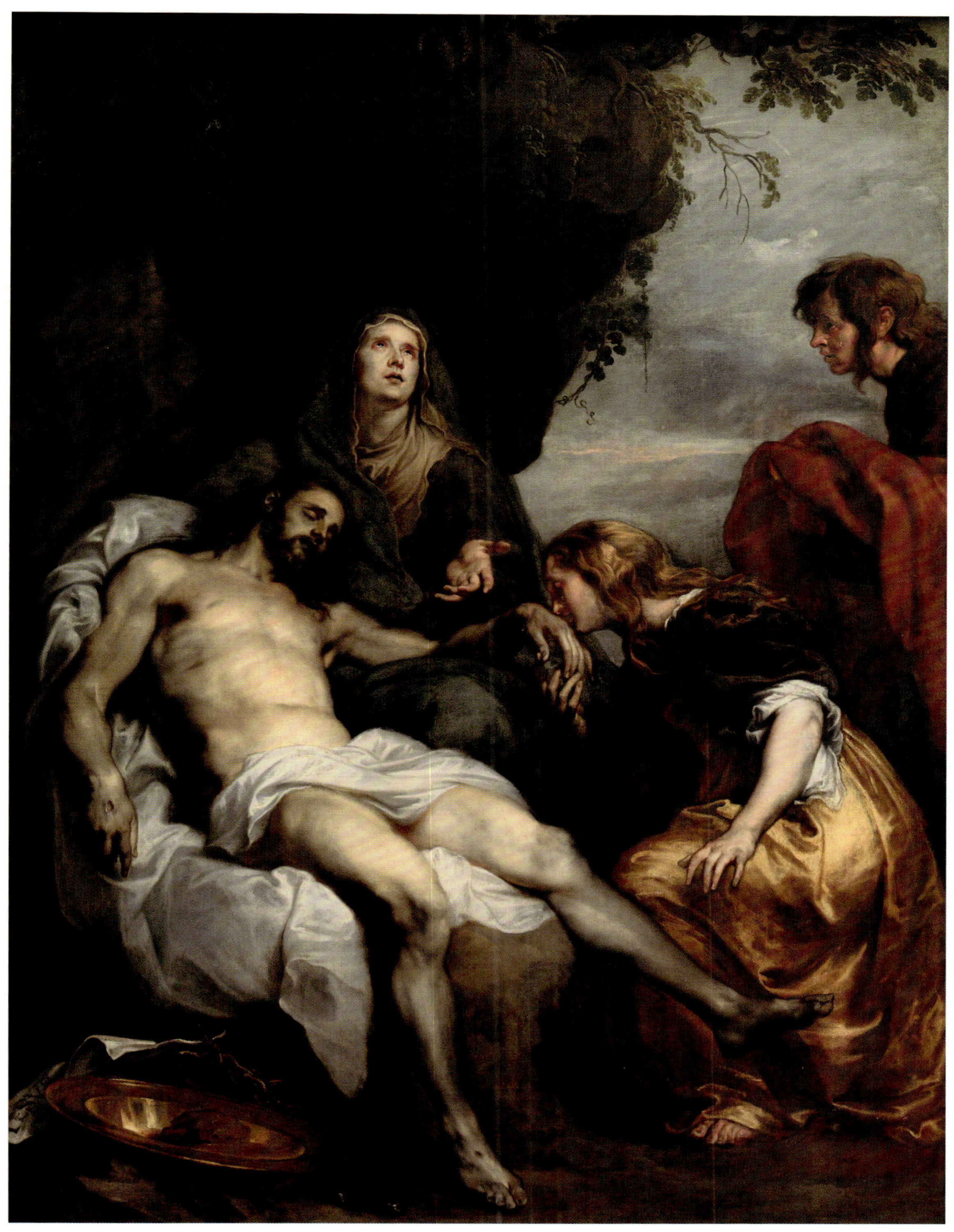

LIEVENS ~ REMBRANDT

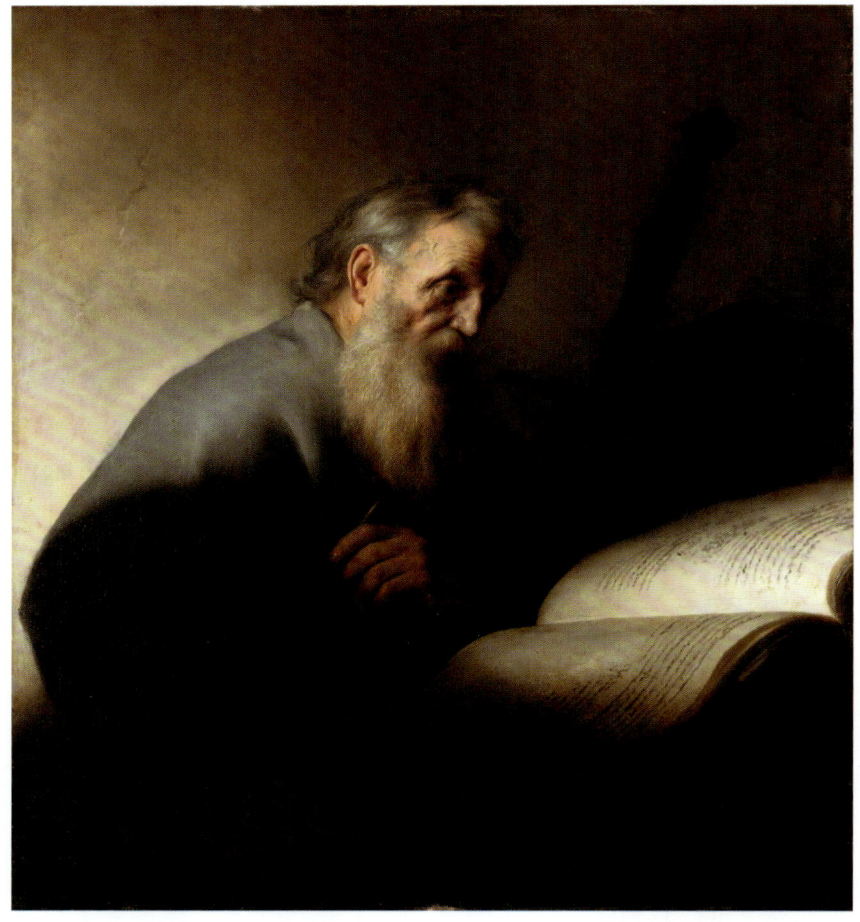

Apostle Paul
Saint Paul
Apostel Paulus
Apóstol Pablo
Apóstolo Paulo
De apostel Paulus

Jan Lievens (1607-1674)

———

1627-29, Oil on canvas/Huile sur toile,
119 × 108 cm, Nationalmuseum, Stockholm

*Jeremiah lamenting the destruction of
Jerusalem*

*Jérémie pleurant la destruction de
Jérusalem*

*Jeremia beklagt die Zerstörung
Jerusalems*

*Jeremías lamenta la destrucción de
Jerusalén*

*Jeremias lamenta a destruição de
Jerusalém*

*Jeremia treurend over de verwoesting
van Jeruzalem*

Rembrandt van Rijn (1606-1669)

———

c. 1630, Oil on panel/Huile sur panneau,
58 × 46 cm, Rijksmuseum, Amsterdam

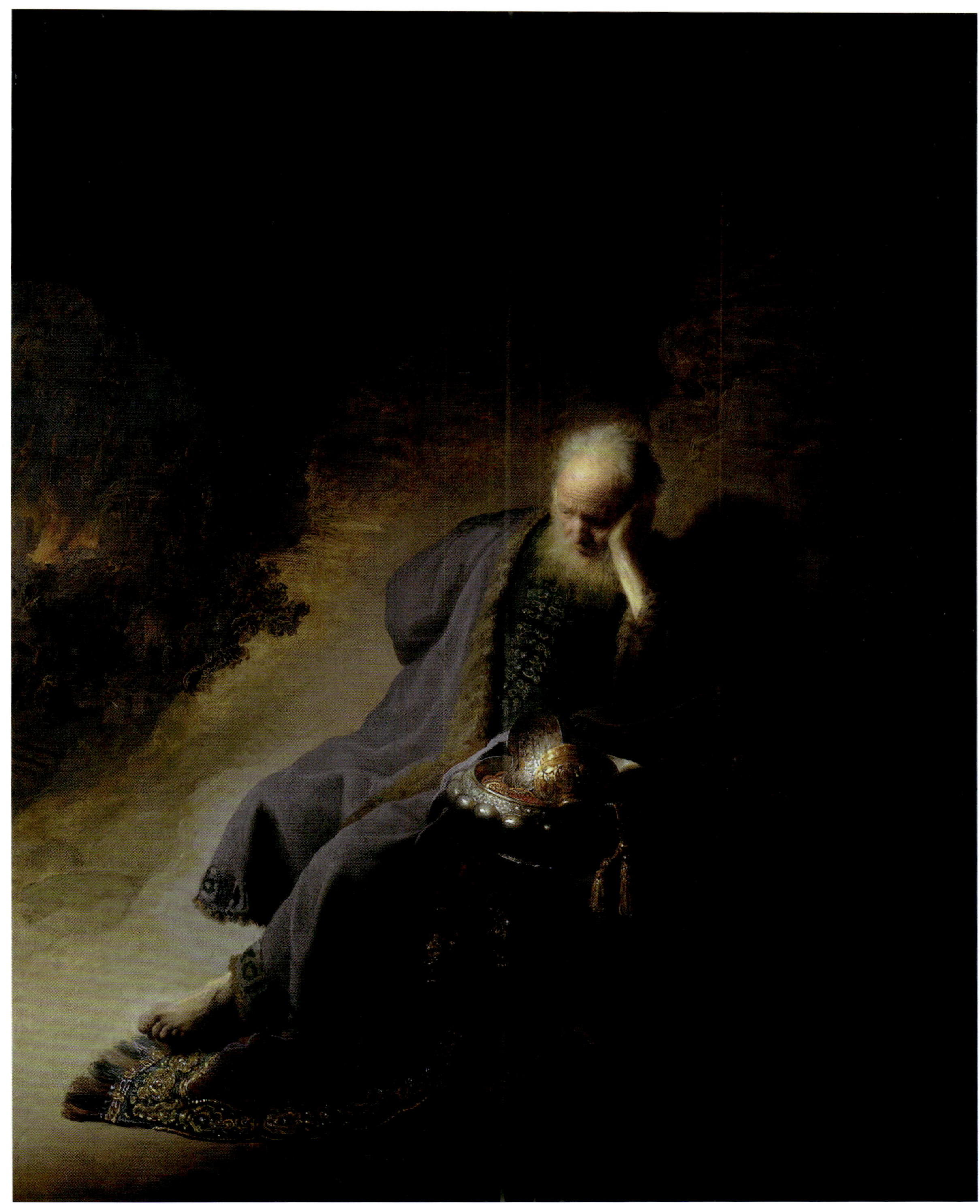

IL VERONESE ~ COUTURE

Large-format paintings were very popular in the 19th century. As a rule, they showed religious, mythological or historical motifs. In this way the painters presented their academic knowledge. Couture refers here to Veronese's painting, in which he adopts the extensive composition of *The Wedding Feast of Cana,* with its frieze of people and the impressive architecture in the background.

Au XIXe siècle on appréciait les très grands formats, appelés « grosses machines », et pour lesquels les sujets nobles étaient de mise – religion, mythologie et Histoire. Il fallait démontrer en une toile l'étendue de son savoir académique. En l'occurrence, Couture se réfère ici à la peinture de Véronèse auquel il a emprunté l'ampleur de la composition des *Noces de Cana* avec ses multiples personnages en frise et cette belle architecture en arrière-plan.

Großformatige Gemälde waren im 19. Jahrhundert sehr beliebt. In der Regel zeigten sie religiöse, mythologische oder historische Motive. Die Maler präsentierten auf diese Art ihr akademisches Wissen. Couture bezieht sich hier auf das Gemälde von Veronese, indem er die weitläufige Komposition der *Hochzeit zu Kana* übernimmt, mit ihren als Fries angeordneten Personen und der beeindruckenden Architektur im Hintergrund.

Las pinturas de gran formato fueron muy populares en el siglo XIX. Por regla general, presentaban motivos religiosos, mitológicos o históricos. De esta manera los pintores presentaron sus conocimientos académicos. Couture se refiere aquí a la pintura de Veronese, en la que adopta la extensa composición de *Las bodas de Caná,* con su friso de gente y la impresionante arquitectura de fondo.

As pinturas em grande formato eram muito populares no século XIX. Como regra geral, mostravam motivos religiosos, mitológicos ou históricos. Desta forma, os pintores apresentaram os seus conhecimentos académicos. Couture se refere aqui à pintura de Veronese, na qual ele adota a extensa composição do *Bodas de Caná,* com seu friso de pessoas e a impressionante arquitetura ao fundo.

Schilderijen op groot formaat waren in de 19e eeuw erg populair. Doorgaans toonden ze religieuze, mythologische of historische onderwerpen. Op deze manier etaleerden de schilders hun academische kennis. Couture verwijst hier naar het schilderij van Veronese, waarin hij de uitgestrekte compositie van *De bruiloft te Kana* overneemt, met de als in een fries geordende personen en de indrukwekkende architectuur op de achtergrond.

Romans during The Decadence
Les Romains de la décadence
Die Dekadenz der Römer
Los romanos de la decadencia
A Decadência dos Romanos
De Romeinen van de decadentie
Thomas Couture (1815-1879)

———

1847, Oil on canvas/Huile sur toile, 472 × 772 cm, Musée d'Orsay, Paris

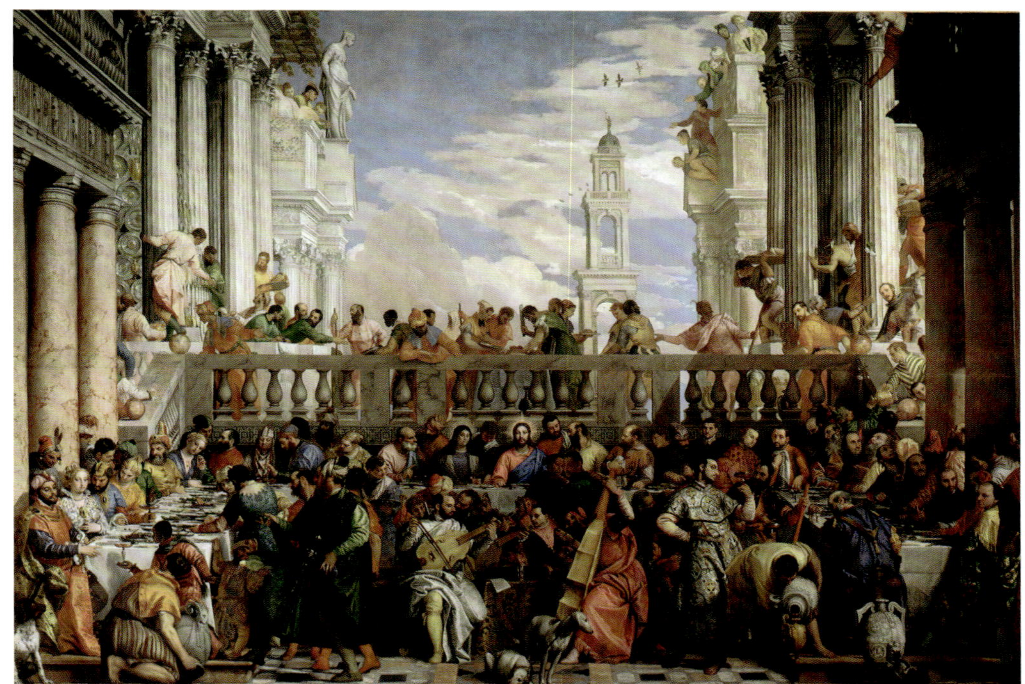

The Wedding Feast at Cana

Les Noces de Cana

Die Hochzeit zu Kana

Las bodas de Caná

Bodas de Caná

De bruiloft te Kana

**Paolo Caliari
(il Veronese)
(1528-1588)**

1563, Oil on canvas/Huile sur toile, 677 × 994 cm, Musée du Louvre, Paris

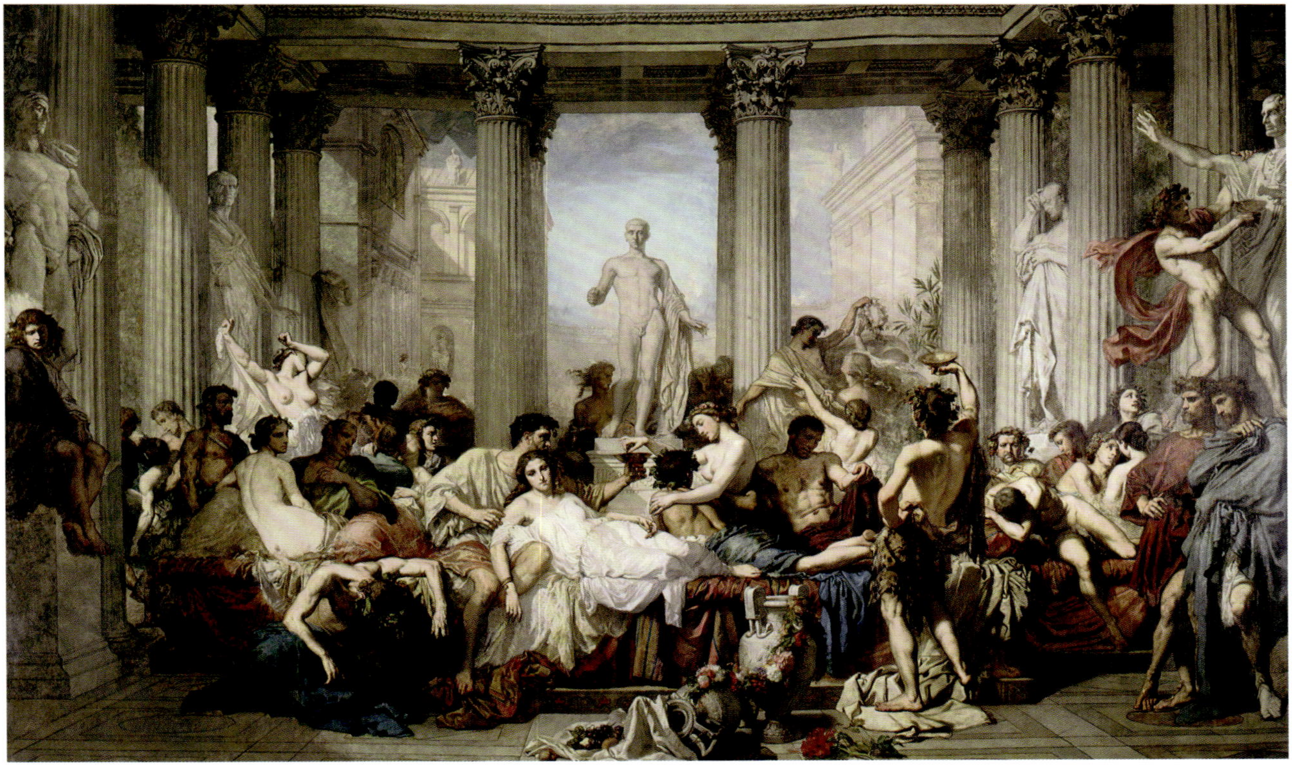

ANONYMOUS ~ DA VINCI (SCHOOL OF/ÉCOLE DE)

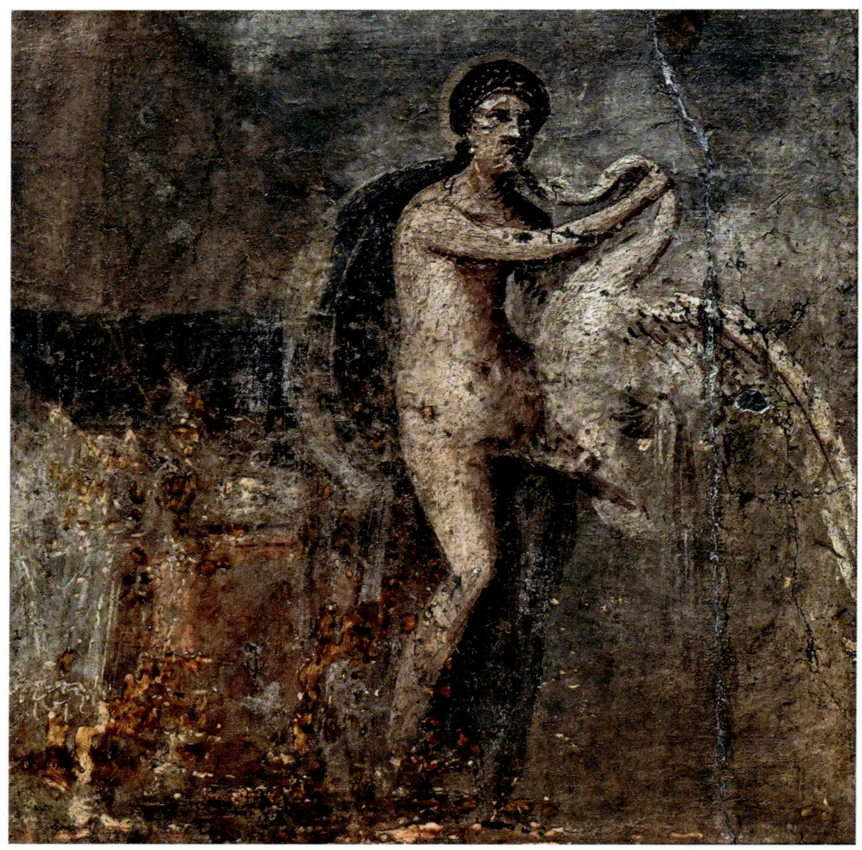

Leda with the Swan
Léda et le cygne
Leda mit dem Schwan
Leda y el cisne
Leda com o Cisne
Leda en de zwaan
Anonymous

———

c. 60-79 AD, Fresco/Fresque, Museo
Archeologico Nazionale, Napoli

Leda and the Swan
Léda et le cygne
Leda und der Schwan
Leda y el cisne
Leda e o Cisne
Leda en de zwaan
**Leonardo da Vinci
(school of/école de)
(1452-1519)**

———

c. 1510-20, Tempera on panel/Tempera
sur panneau, 112 × 86 cm,
Galleria Borghese, Roma

196

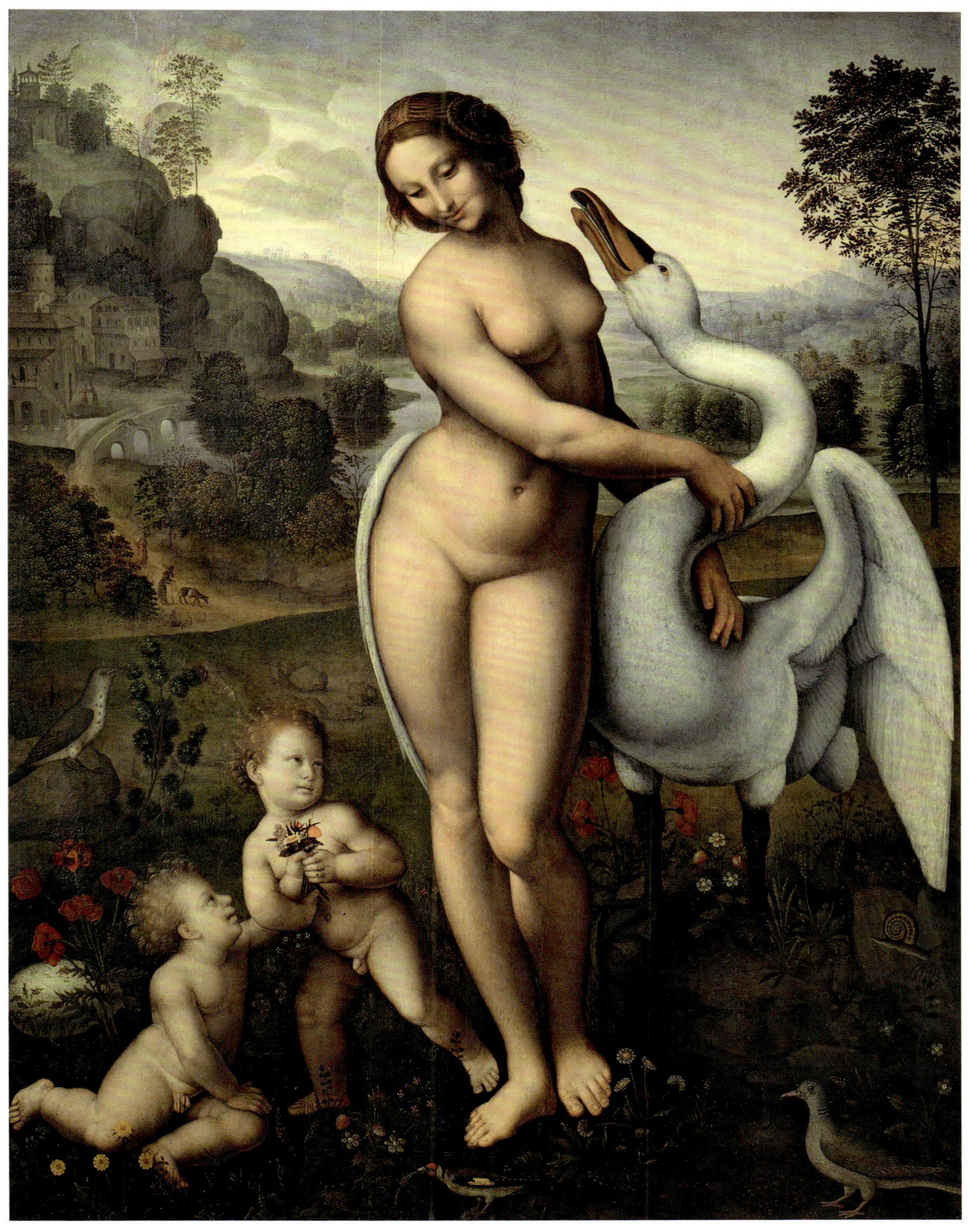

VELÁZQUEZ (WORKSHOP OF/ATELIER DE) ~ MANET

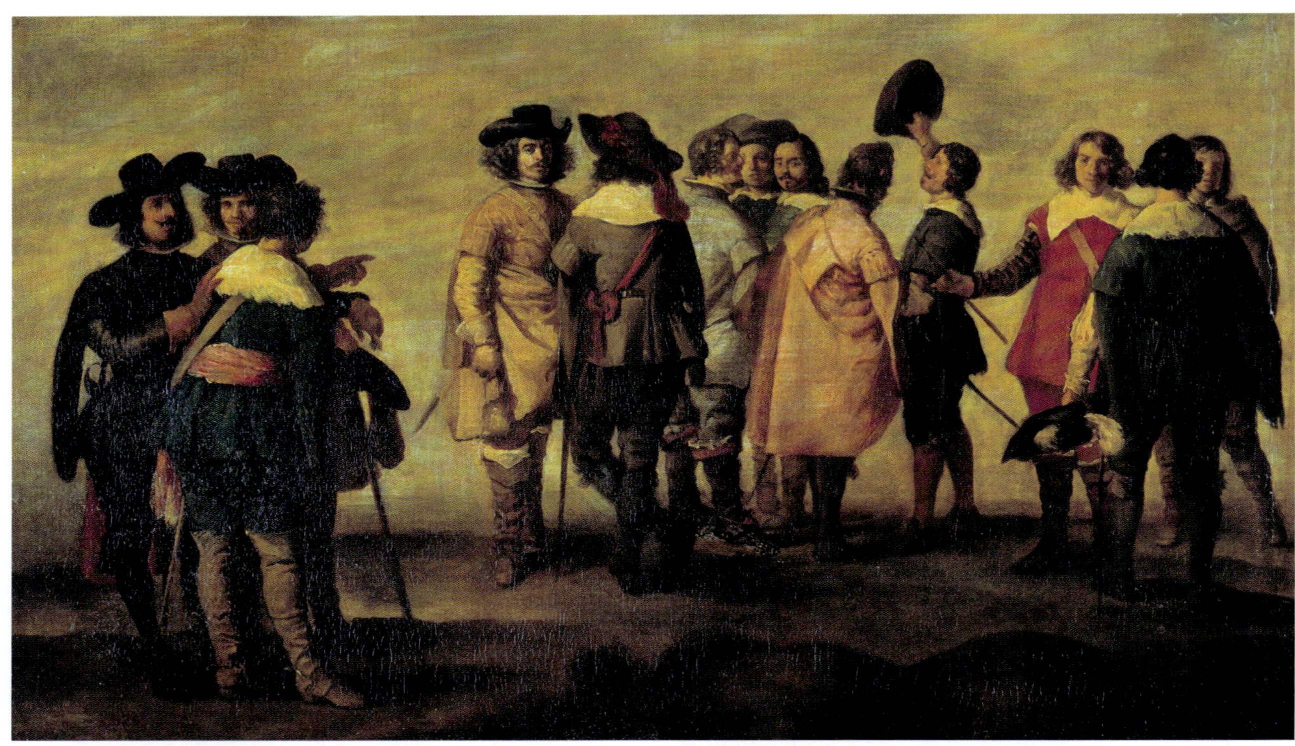

Meeting of thirteen characters

Réunion de treize personnages

Treffen von dreizehn Personen

Reunión de trece personajes

Reunião de treze pessoas

De ontmoeting van dertien personen

Diego Velázquez (workshop of/ atelier de) (1599-1660)

———

c. 1650, Oil on canvas/Huile sur toile, 47 × 77 cm, Musée du Louvre, Paris

Spanish Riders
Cavaliers espagnols
Spanische Reiter
Jinetes españoles
Cavaleiros Espanhóis
Spaanse ruiters

Édouard Manet (1832-1883)

1859, Oil on canvas/Huile sur toile,
45 × 26 cm, Musée des Beaux-Arts, Lyon

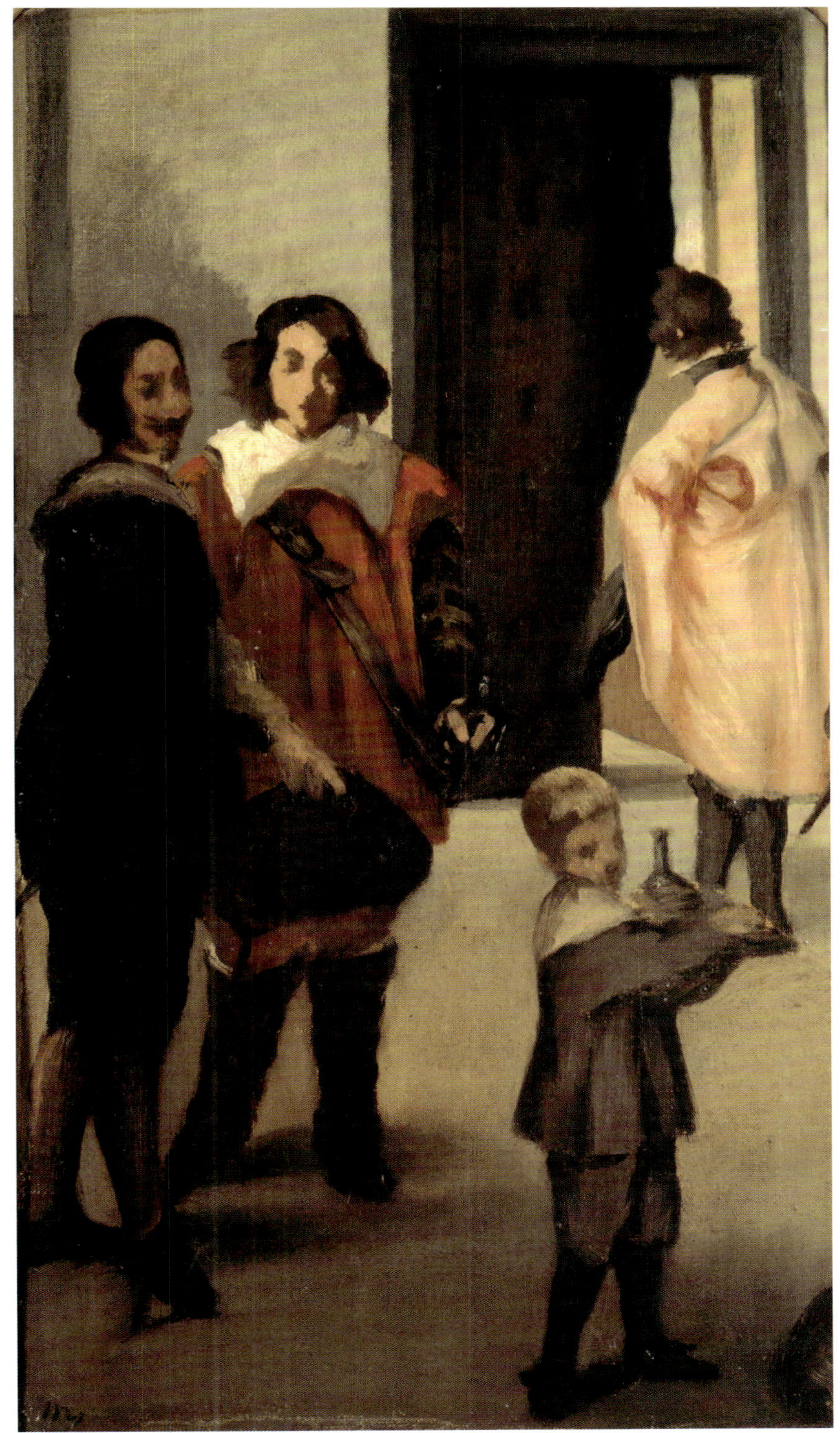

INGRES ~ BONINGTON

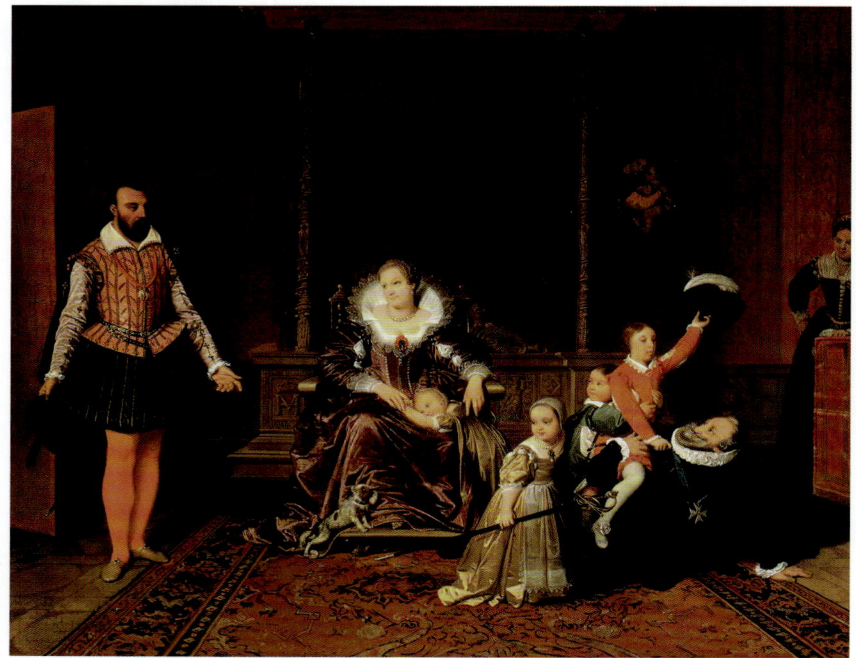

Henry IV Receiving the Spanish Ambassador

Henri IV recevant l'ambassadeur d'Espagne

Der spanische Gesandte überrascht den König beim Spiel mit seinen Kindern

Enrique IV recibe al embajador de España

O enviado espanhol surpreende o rei a brincar com os seus filhos

Hendrik IV spelend met zijn kinderen

Jean-Auguste-Dominique Ingres (1780-1867)

———

1817, Oil on canvas/Huile sur toile, 39,5 × 50 cm, Petit Palais, Paris

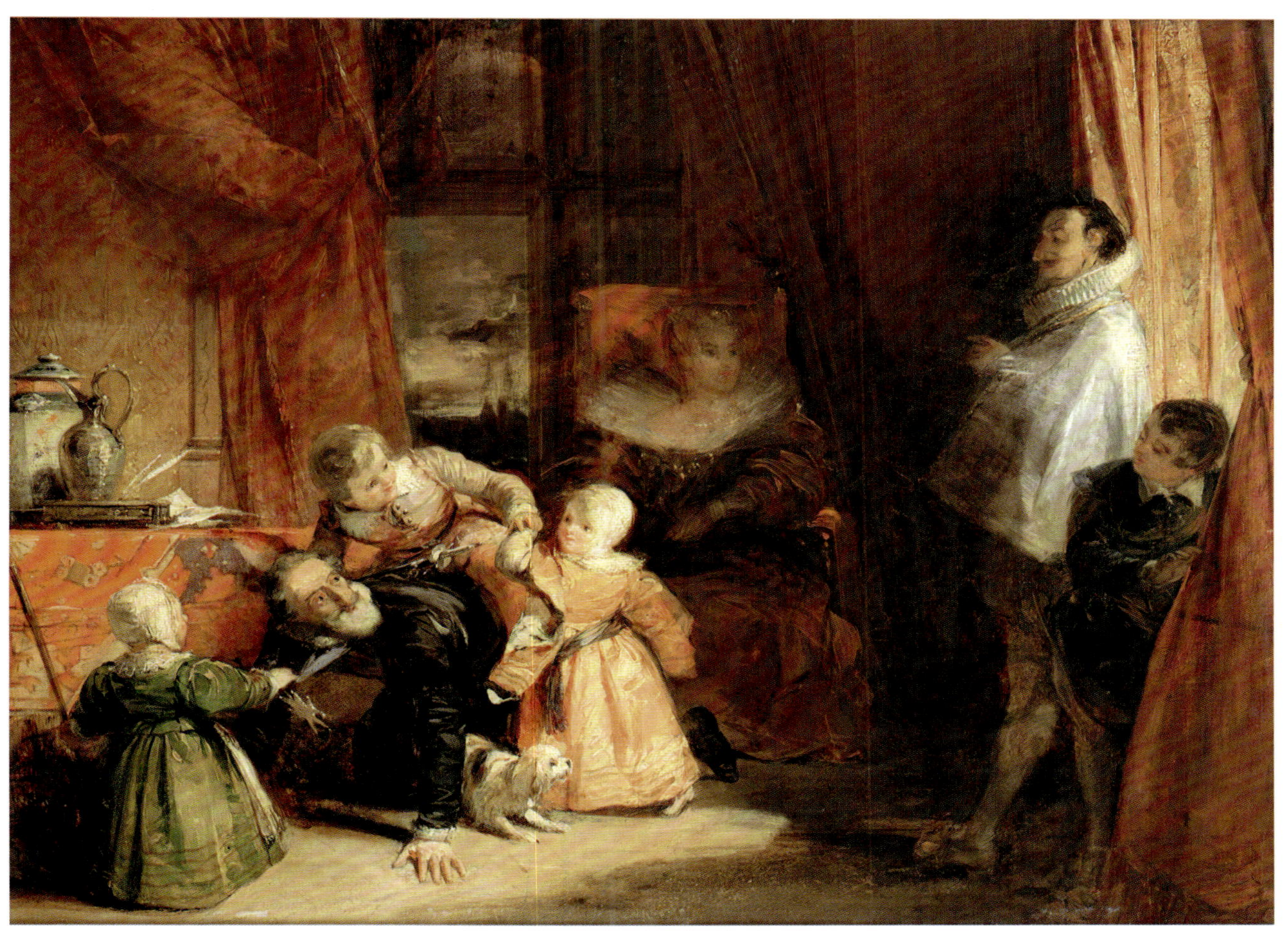

Henry IV and the Spanish Ambassador
Henri IV et l'ambassadeur d'Espagne
Heinrich IV. und der spanische Botschafter
Enrique IV y el embajador de España
Henrique IV e o embaixador espanhol
Hendrik IV en de Spaanse ambassadeur

Richard Bonington (1802-1828)

c. 1827, Oil on canvas/Huile sur toile,
38,4 × 52,4 cm, Wallace Collection, London

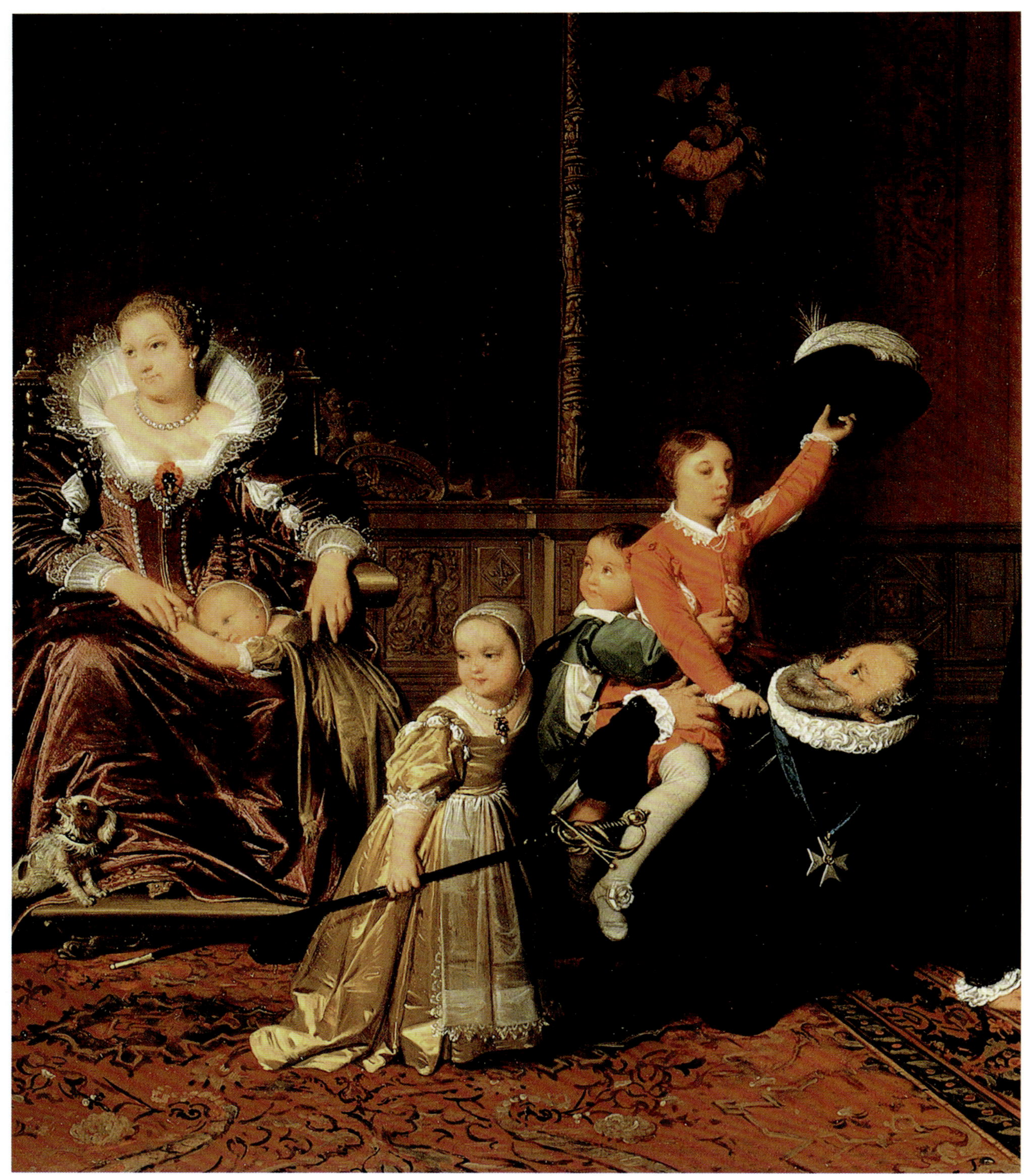

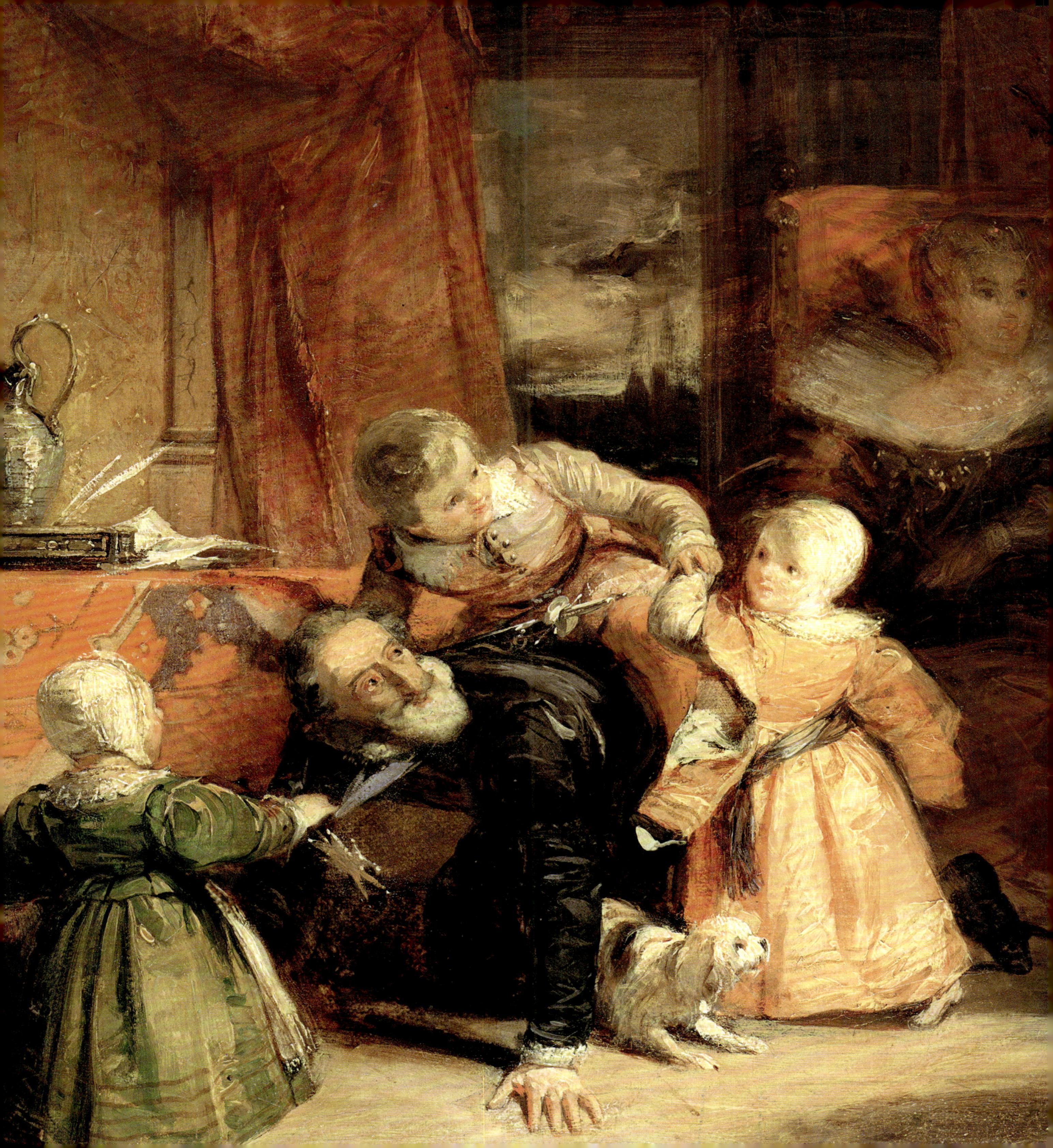

REMBRANDT ~ RIGAUD

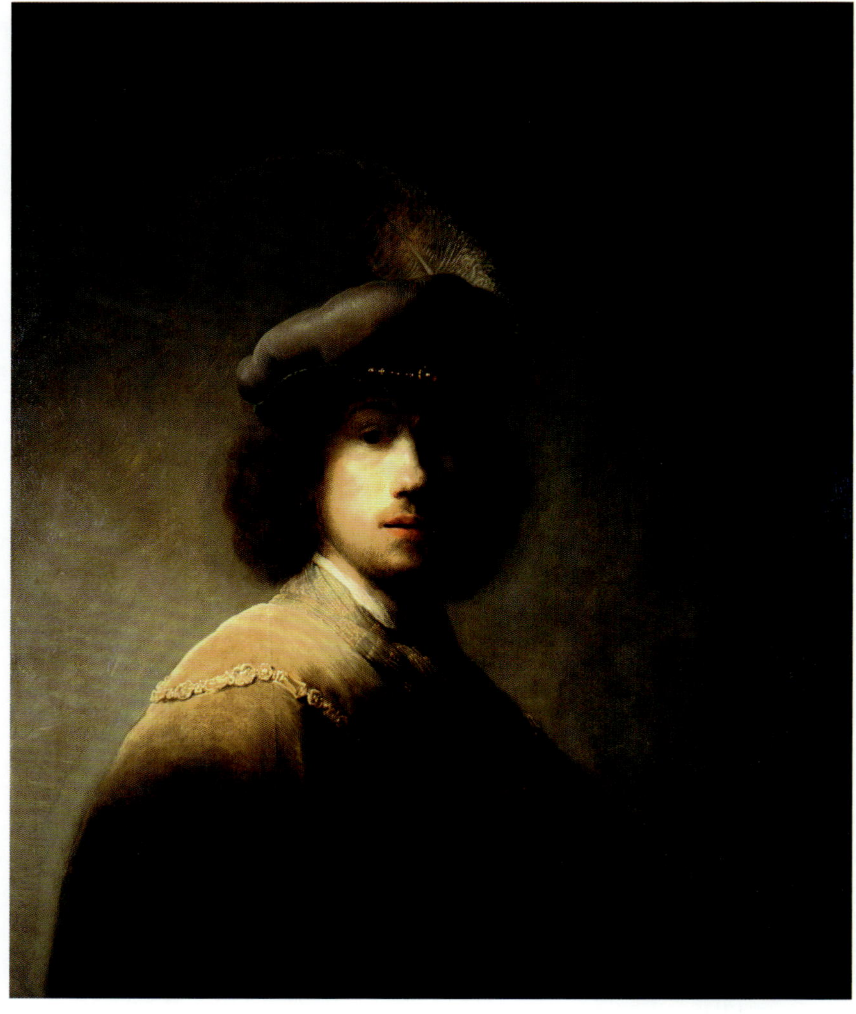

Rembrandt van Rijn (1606-1669)

———

1629, Oil on canvas/Huile sur toile,
89,7 × 73,5 cm, Isabella Stewart Gardner
Museum, Boston

Self Portrait in a Turban
Autoportrait au turban
Selbstporträt mit Turban
Autorretrato en turbante
Auto-retrato em Turban
Zelfportret in een tulband

**Hyacinthe François Rigaud
(1659-1743)**

———

1698, Oil on canvas/Huile sur toile,
84 × 67 cm, Musée Hyacinthe Rigaud,
Perpignan

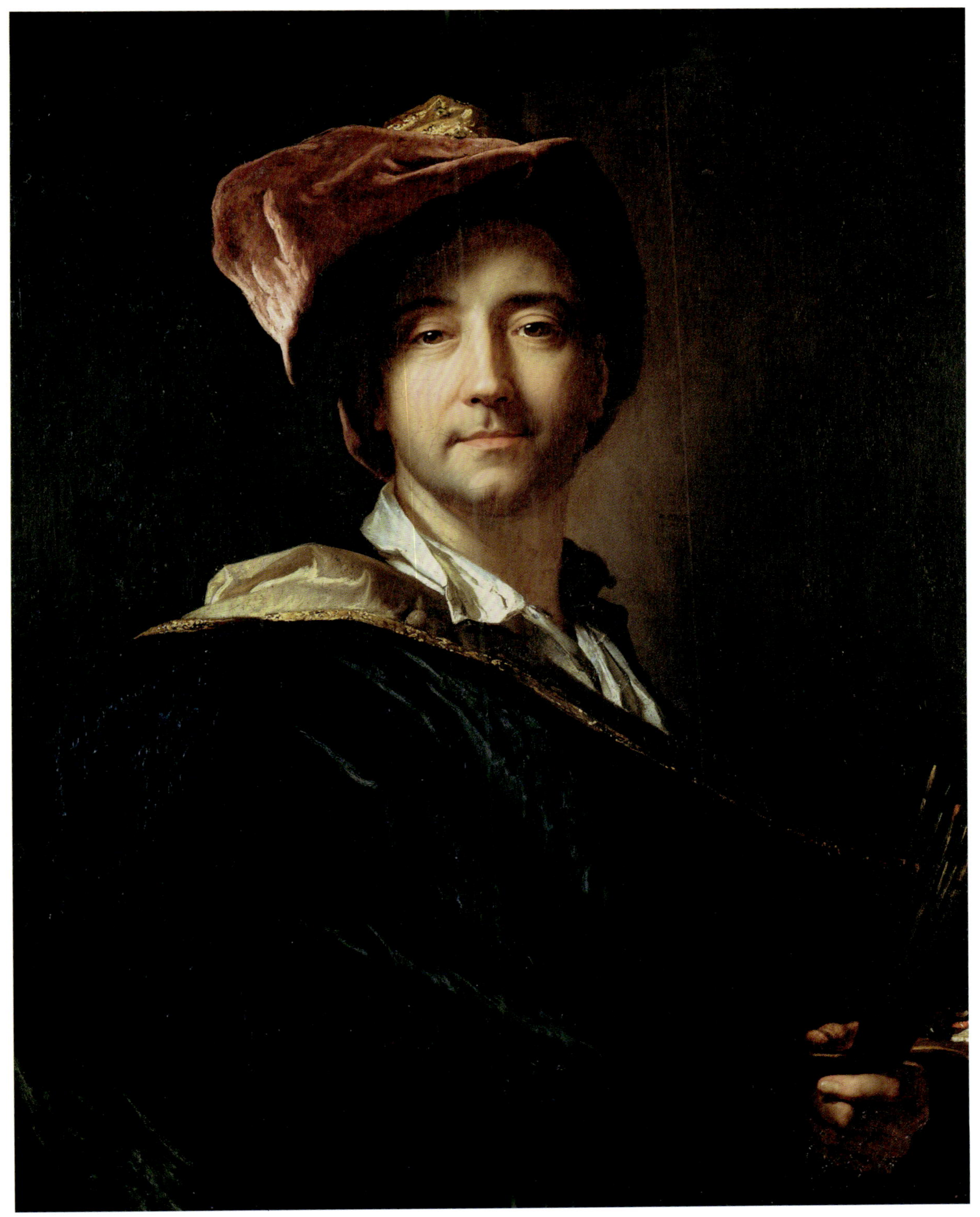

LASTMAN ~ REMBRANDT

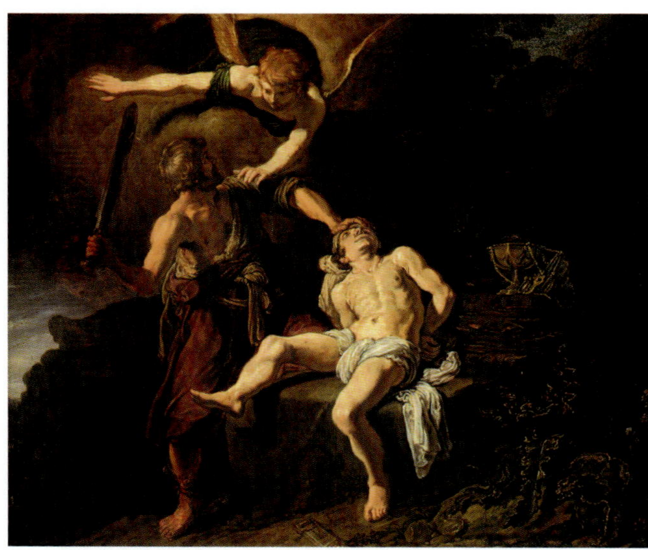

The Sacrifice of Isaac

L'Ange du Seigneur empêchant Abraham de sacrifier son fils Isaac

Die Opferung Isaaks

El sacrificio de Isaac

O Anjo do Senhor impedindo Abraão de sacrificar o seu filho Isaac

Het offer van Abraham: een engel weerhoudt Abraham om Isaak te offeren

Pieter Lastman (1583-1633)

———

1616, Oil on canvas/Huile sur toile, 36 × 42 cm, Musée du Louvre, Paris

Although Rembrandt never visited Italy, he was influenced by Caravaggism through his teacher Pieter Lastman, who had been there. It is therefore thanks to a Dutch caravaggist that the young Rembrandt found a taste for the dramatic play of light and shadow that was to become his speciality.

Si Rembrandt ne visita jamais l'Italie, il fut néanmoins touché par la révolution caravagesque grâce à son maître Pieter Lastman qui lui y avait séjourné. C'est donc un caravagesque hollandais qui transmit au jeune Rembrandt ce goût pour ces jeux délicats de clair-obscur qui deviendront la spécificité de l'artiste.

Auch wenn Rembrandt Italien nie besuchte, wurde er durch seinen Lehrer Pieter Lastman, der sich dort aufgehalten hatte, vom Caravaggismus beeinflusst. Es ist also einem holländischen Caravaggisten zu verdanken, dass der junge Rembrandt Geschmack an dem dramatischen Spiel aus Licht und Schatten fand, das seine Spezialität werden sollte.

Aunque Rembrandt nunca visitó Italia, fue influenciado por el caravaggismo a través de su maestro Pieter Lastman, que había estado allí. Es gracias a un caravagante holandés que el joven Rembrandt encontró el gusto por el juego dramático de luces y sombras que se convertiría en su especialidad.

Embora Rembrandt nunca tenha visitado a Itália, ele foi influenciado pelo caravaggismo através de seu professor Pieter Lastman, que tinha estado lá. Foi graças a um caravagista holandês que o jovem Rembrandt encontrou o gosto pelo jogo dramático de luz e sombra que se tornaria a sua especialidade.

Hoewel Rembrandt Italië nooit bezocht, werd hij via zijn leraar Pieter Lastman, die er wel was geweest, beïnvloed door het caravaggisme. De jonge Rembrandt kreeg dan ook dankzij een Nederlandse caravaggist de smaak te pakken van het dramatische spel van licht en schaduw dat zijn specialisme zou worden.

The Sacrifice of Isaac
Le Sacrifice d'Isaac
Die Opferung Isaaks
El sacrificio de Isaac
O Sacrifício de Isaac
Het offer van Isaak

**Rembrandt van Rijn
(1606-1669)**

———

1635, Oil on canvas/
Huile sur toile,
193 × 132 cm, State
Hermitage Museum,
St. Petersburg

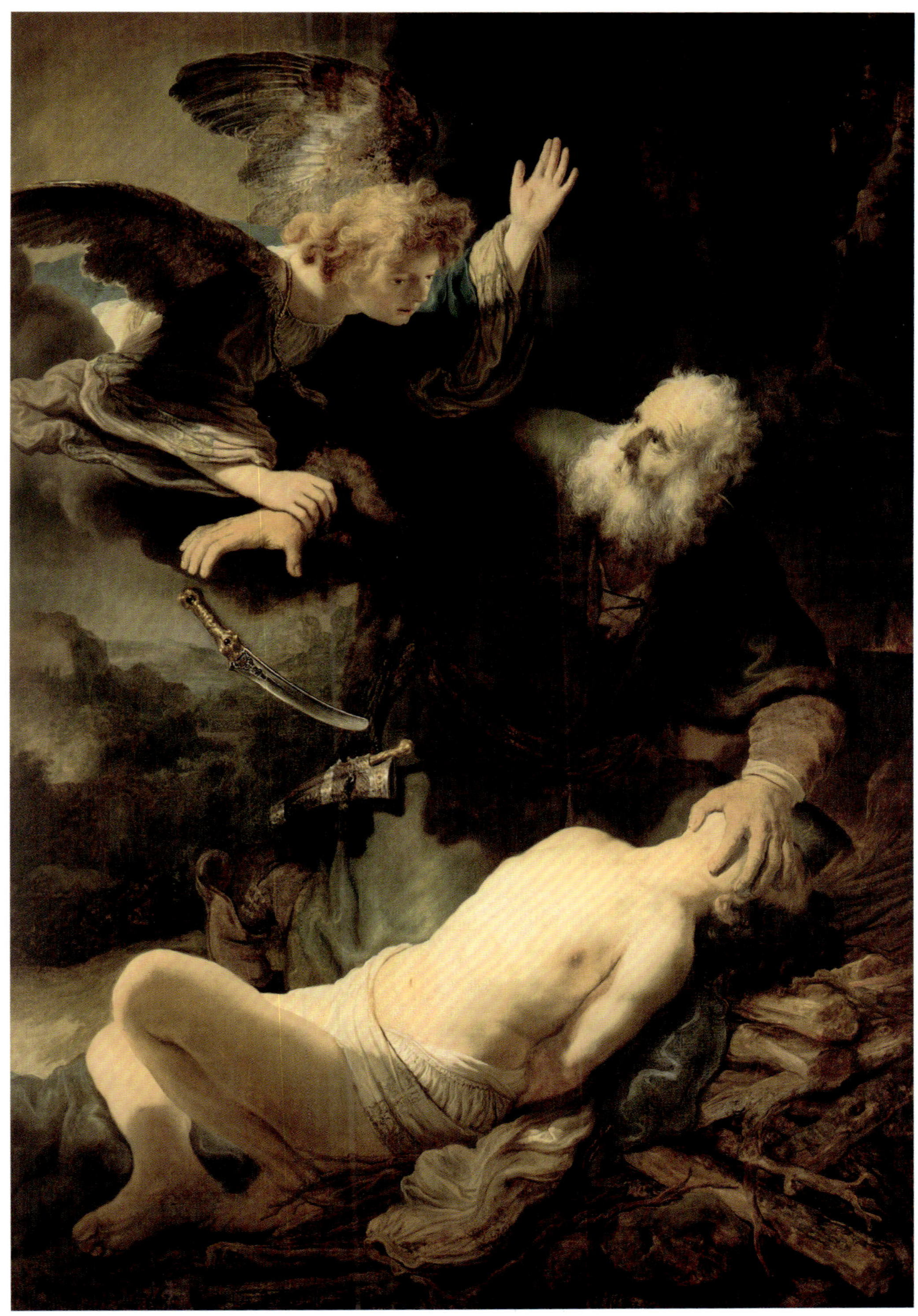

VELÁZQUEZ ~ MANET

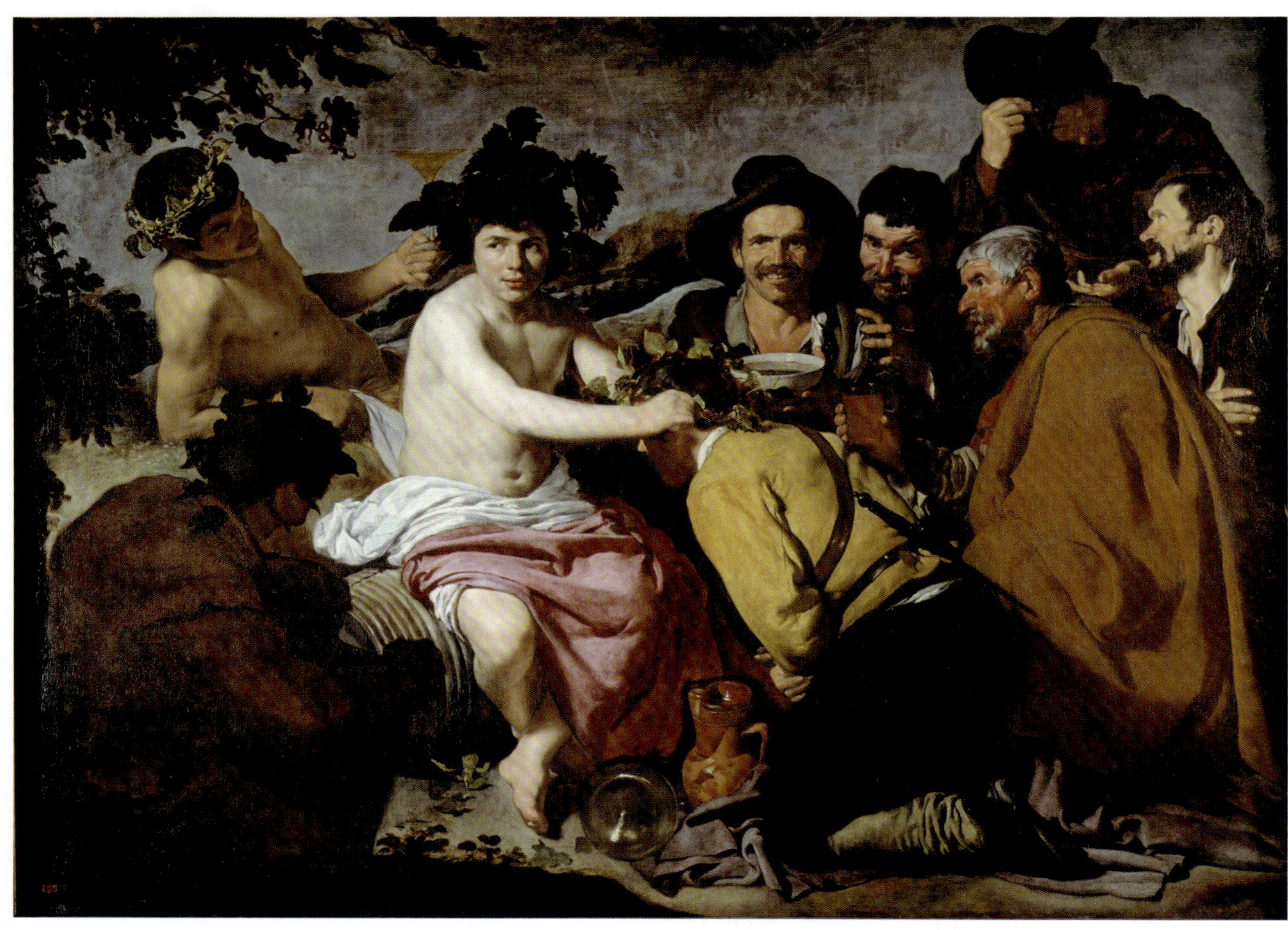

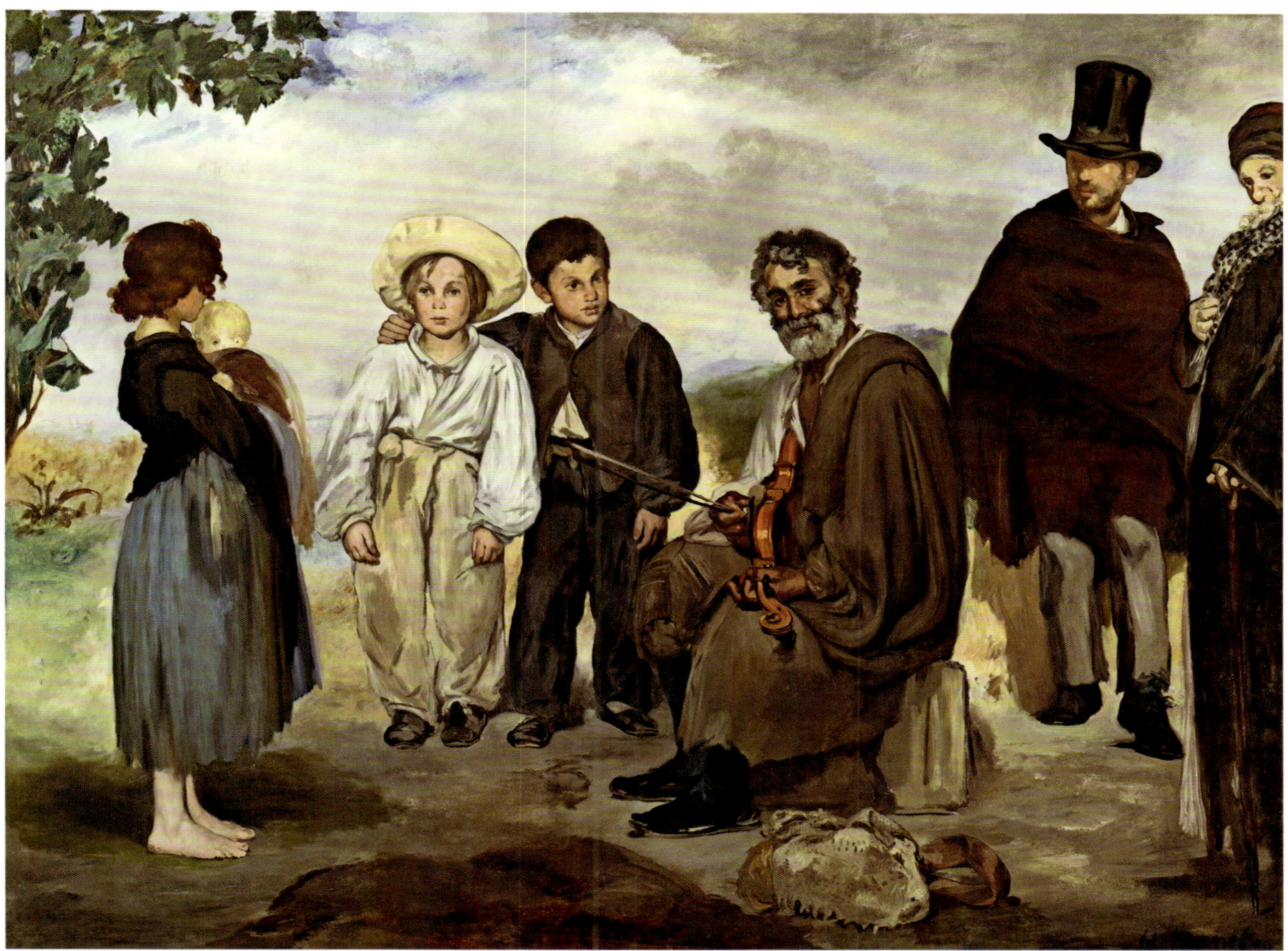

The Triumph of Bacchus
or *The Drunkards*

Le Triomphe de Bacchus,
dit *Les Buveurs*

Der Triumph des Bacchus
oder *Die Trunkenbolde*

El Triunfo de Baco o *Los Borrachos*

O Triunfo de Baco, conhecido
como *Les Buveurs*

Bacchus en de drinkers

Diego Velázquez (1599-1660)

—

1628/29, Oil on canvas/Huile sur toile,
165 × 225 cm, Museo del Prado, Madrid

The Old Musician

Le Vieux Musicien

Der alte Musikant

El viejo músico

O velho músico

De oude muzikant

Édouard Manet (1832-1883)

—

1862, Oil on canvas/Huile sur toile,
187,4 × 248,2 cm, National Gallery of Art,
Washington

IL VERROCCHIO ~ DA VINCI

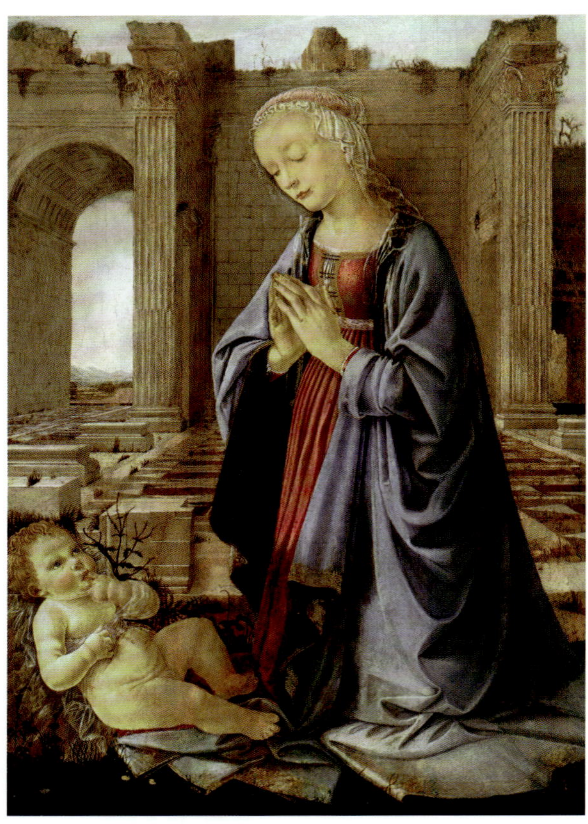

The Virgin Adoring the Christ Child or
The Ruskin Madonna

La Vierge adorant l'Enfant dit *Madone Ruskin*

Anbetung des Christuskindes durch die Madonna oder *Die Ruskin-Madonna*

La Virgen adorando al Niño o *La Virgen de Ruskin*

A Virgem adorando a Criança, segundo *Madonna Ruskin*

Aanbidding van het Christuskind door de Madonna of Ruskin-Madonna

**Andrea del Verrocchio
(il Verrocchio) (1435-1488)**

———

c. 1470, Tempera and oil on canvas/
Tempera et huile sur toile, 106,7 × 76,3 cm,
Scottish National Gallery, Edinburgh

The pronounced drapery clearly reveals Verrocchio's knowledge, which da Vinci acquired as his pupil. After working with him on The Baptism of Christ, he even turned his master away from painting. When Verrocchio recognized the talent of the young Leonardo in their collaboration, he decided to devote himself only to sculpture.

Comme on peut le voir ici dans le rendu des drapés, Vinci était bien l'élève de Verrocchio ! Après avoir contribué avec lui à l'élaboration d'un Baptême du Christ, il supplanta même son maître. En constatant le talent du jeune Léonard sur cette commande, Andréa décida d'abandonner à jamais la peinture pour se consacrer exclusivement à la sculpture.

Der ausgeprägte Faltenwurf lässt deutlich das Wissen Verrocchios erkennen, das da Vinci als sein Schüler erwarb. Nachdem er mit diesem zusammen an der Taufe Christi gearbeitet hatte, brachte er seinen Meister sogar von der Malerei ab. Als Verrocchio das Talent des jungen Leonardo bei ihrer Zusammenarbeit erkannte, beschloss er, sich nur noch der Bildhauerei zu widmen.

Leonardo da Vinci (1452-1519)

c. 1477, Drawing/Dessin,
Galleria nazionali d'arte antica -
Palazzo Corsini, Roma

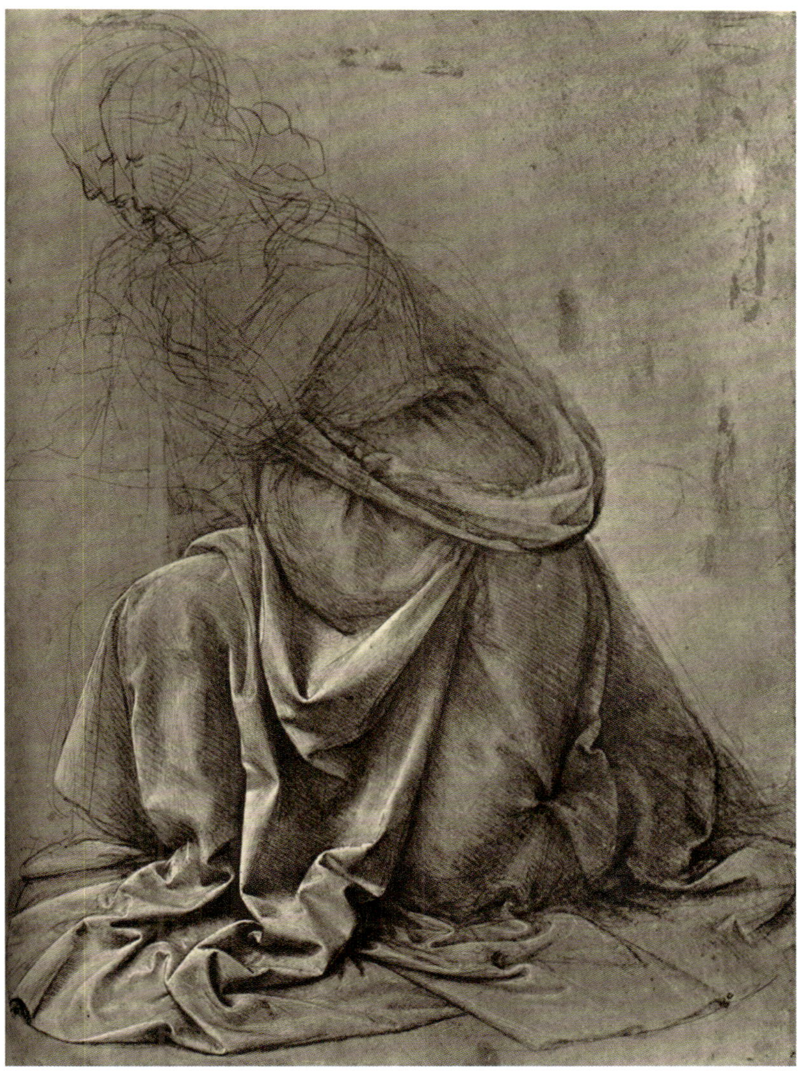

Las cortinas pronunciadas revelan claramente el conocimiento de Verrocchio, que da Vinci adquirió como su discípulo. Después de trabajar con él en El bautismo de Cristo, incluso disoció a su maestro de la pintura. Cuando Verrocchio reconoció el talento del joven Leonardo en su colaboración, decidió dedicarse únicamente a la escultura.

O drapeado pronunciado revela claramente o conhecimento de Verrocchio, que Da Vinci adquiriu como seu aluno. Depois de trabalhar com ele no batismo de Cristo, ele até dissociou seu mestre da pintura. Quando Verrocchio reconheceu o talento do jovem Leonardo em sua colaboração, ele decidiu dedicar-se apenas à escultura.

Het is duidelijk te zien in de weergave van de plooival dat Da Vinci goed is opgeleid door Verrocchio. Nadat hij met Verrocchio aan De doop van Christus had gewerkt, verving hij zijn meester zelfs. Toen Verrocchio het talent van de jonge Leonardo tijdens hun samenwerking herkende, besloot hij te stoppen met schilderen en zich alleen nog aan de beeldhouwkunst te wijden.

ANONYMOUS ~ MODIGLIANI

Modigliani, who was also called the «Black Botticelli», was interested in African art very early on, as were Picasso, Matisse and de Vlaminck. If one compares his head sculpture, of which several versions exist, with the headdress of the Bambara, the similarity immediately catches the eye. The elongated nose confirms the theory that Modigliani must have known the original and copied it or was inspired by it.

Surnommé le « Botticelli nègre », Modigliani à l'instar de Picasso, Matisse ou encore Vlaminck se passionna très tôt pour l'art africain. Lorsqu'on pose côte à côte ce cimier Bambara et son portrait sculpté dont il existe plusieurs versions, on ne peut qu'être sidéré par l'évidente ressemblance. Cette arête de nez immense ne peut que conforter notre idée : Modigliani connaissait ce modèle, le copia peut-être, et s'en inspira très certainement.

Modigliani, der auch der „Schwarze Botticelli" genannt wurde, interessierte sich wie Picasso, Matisse oder de Vlaminck sehr früh für afrikanische Kunst. Vergleicht man seine Kopfskulptur, von der mehrere Versionen existieren, mit dem Kopfschmuck der Bambara, sticht sofort die Ähnlichkeit ins Auge. Die lang gezogene Nase bestätigt die Theorie, dass Modigliani die Vorlage gekannt haben muss und sie kopierte oder sich von ihr inspirieren ließ.

Modigliani, también llamado el «Black Botticelli», se interesó muy pronto por el arte africano, al igual que Picasso, Matisse y de Vlaminck. Si se compara la escultura de su cabeza, de la que existen varias versiones, con el tocado del Bambara, la similitud llama inmediatamente la atención. L a nariz alargada confirma la teoría de que Modigliani debía conocer el modelo y lo copió o se inspiró en él.

Modigliani, que também era chamado de «Black Botticelli», interessou-se muito cedo pela arte africana, assim como Picasso, Matisse e de Vlaminck. Se compararmos a sua escultura de cabeça, da qual existem várias versões, com o toucador do Bambara, a semelhança chama imediatamente a atenção. O nariz alongado confirma a teoria de que Modigliani deve ter conhecido o modelo e copiado ou foi inspirado por ele.

Modigliani, die ook wel de 'Zwarte Botticelli' wordt genoemd, was al vroeg geïnteresseerd in Afrikaanse kunst, net als Picasso, Matisse en De Vlaminck. Als je zijn sculptuur van een hoofd, waarvan verschillende versies bestaan, vergelijkt met de hoofdtooi van Bambara, valt de overeenkomst meteen op. De langgerekte neus bevestigt de theorie dat Modigliani het voorbeeld moet hebben gekend en dat heeft gekopieerd of erdoor is geïnspireerd.

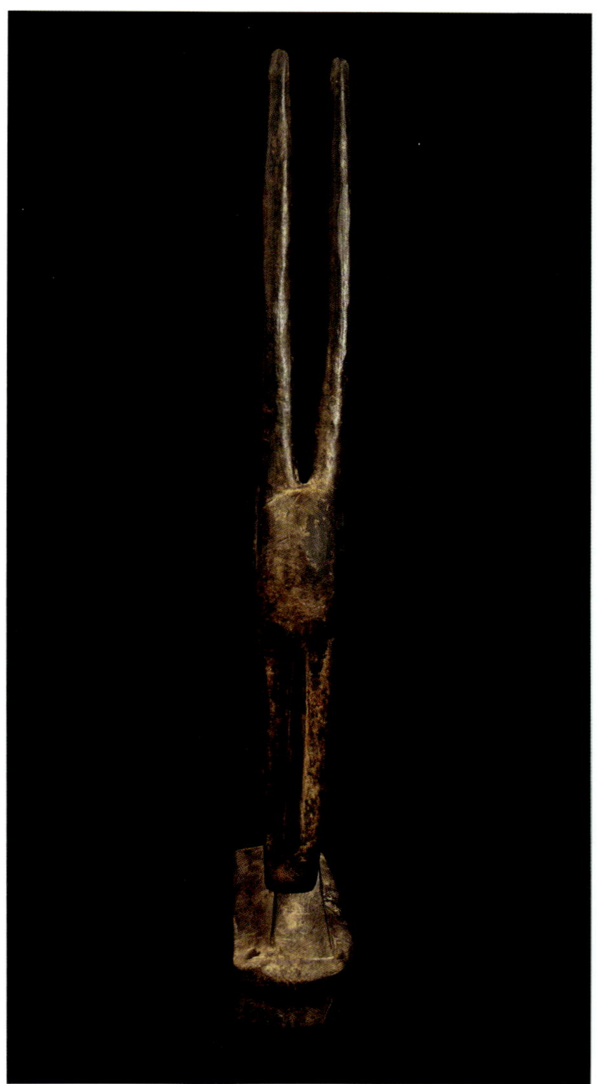

Antelope head
Tête d'antilope
Antilopenkopf
Cabeza de antílope
Cabeça de antílope
Kop van een antilope

Anonymous (Bambara people)

———

19th century, Wood/Bois, 74 × 28 x 10 cm,
Private collection

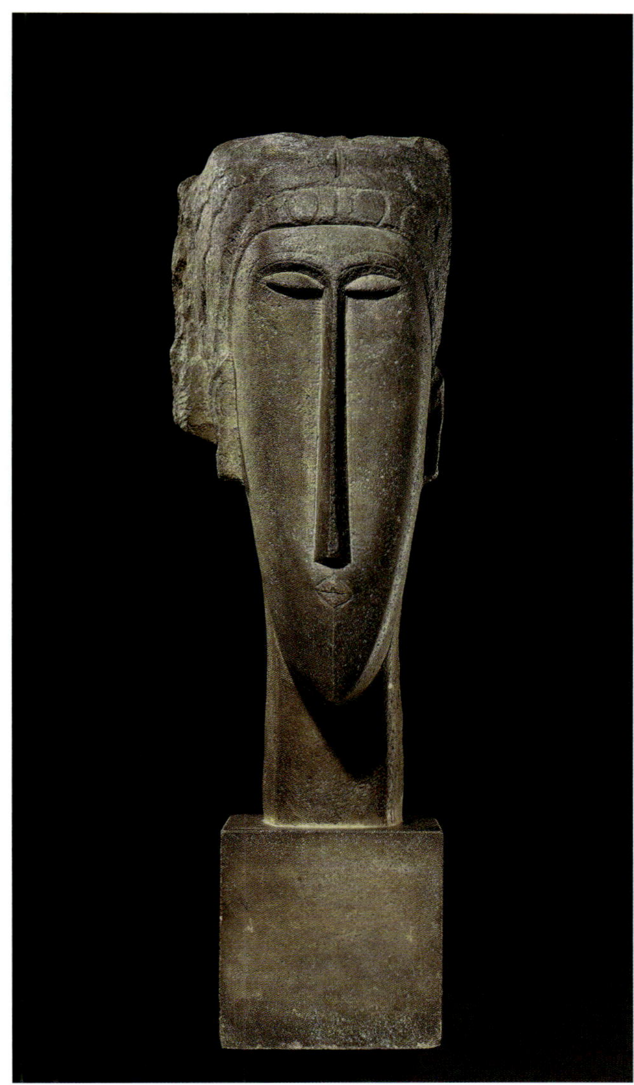

Head
Tête
Kopf
Cabeza
Cabeça
Hoofd

Amedeo Modigliani (1884-1920)

———

c. 1910-12, Limestone/Pierre
calcaire, Private collection

MAUVE ~ VAN GOGH

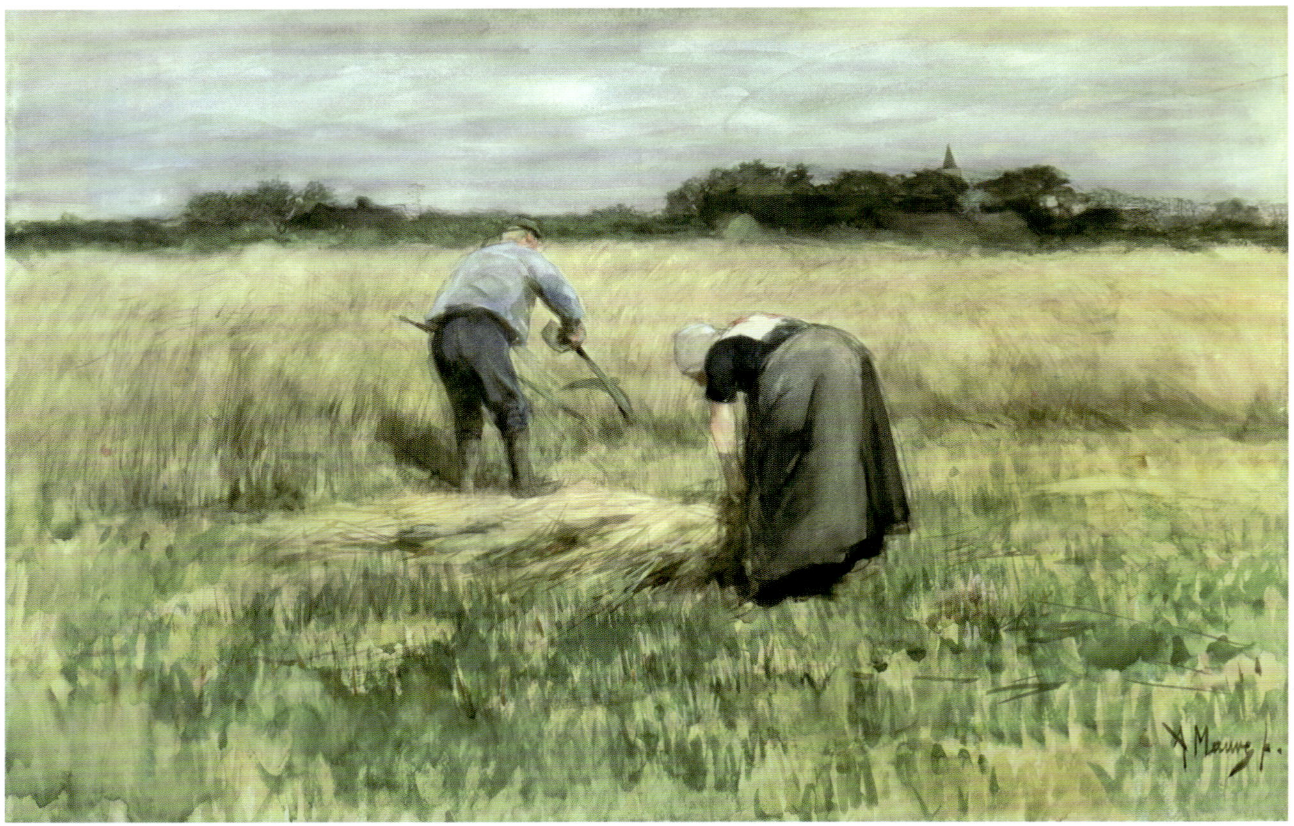

The Harvest

La Récolte

Die Ernte

La cosecha

A colheita

De korenoogst

Anton Mauve (1838-1888)

———

n. d., Watercolor on paper/Aquarelle sur papier,
45,3 × 69 cm, Haags Gemeentemuseum, Den Haag

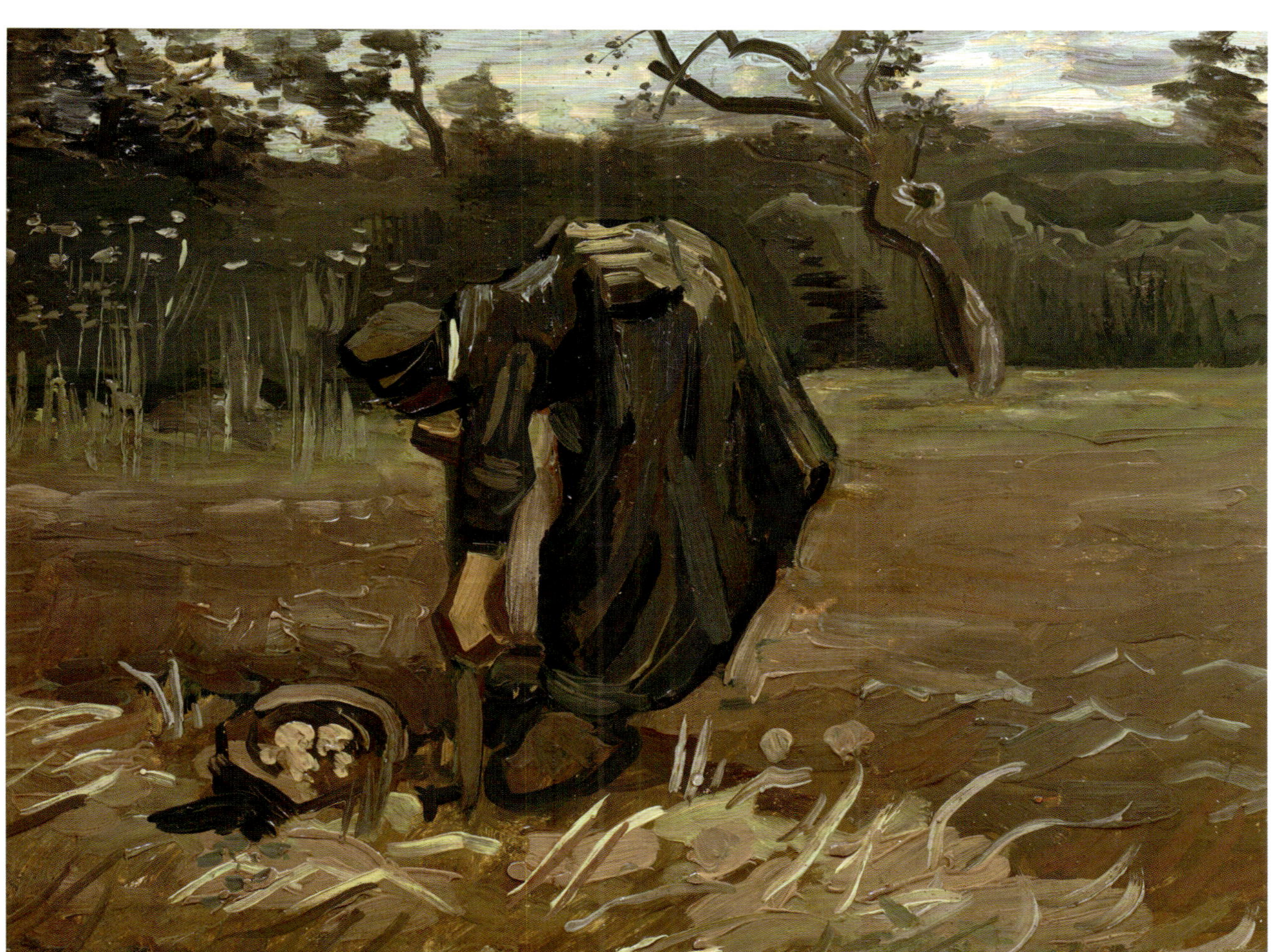

Peasant Woman Digging Potatoes
Paysanne arrachant des pommes de terre
Kartoffelgrabende Bäuerin
Mujer campesina cosechando patatas
Mulher camponesa colhendo batatas
Boerin aardappelen opgravend

Vincent van Gogh (1853-1890)

1885, Oil on paper glued on wood/Huile sur sur papier collée sur bois, 31,5 × 38 cm, Koninklijk Museum voor Schone Kunsten, Antwerpen

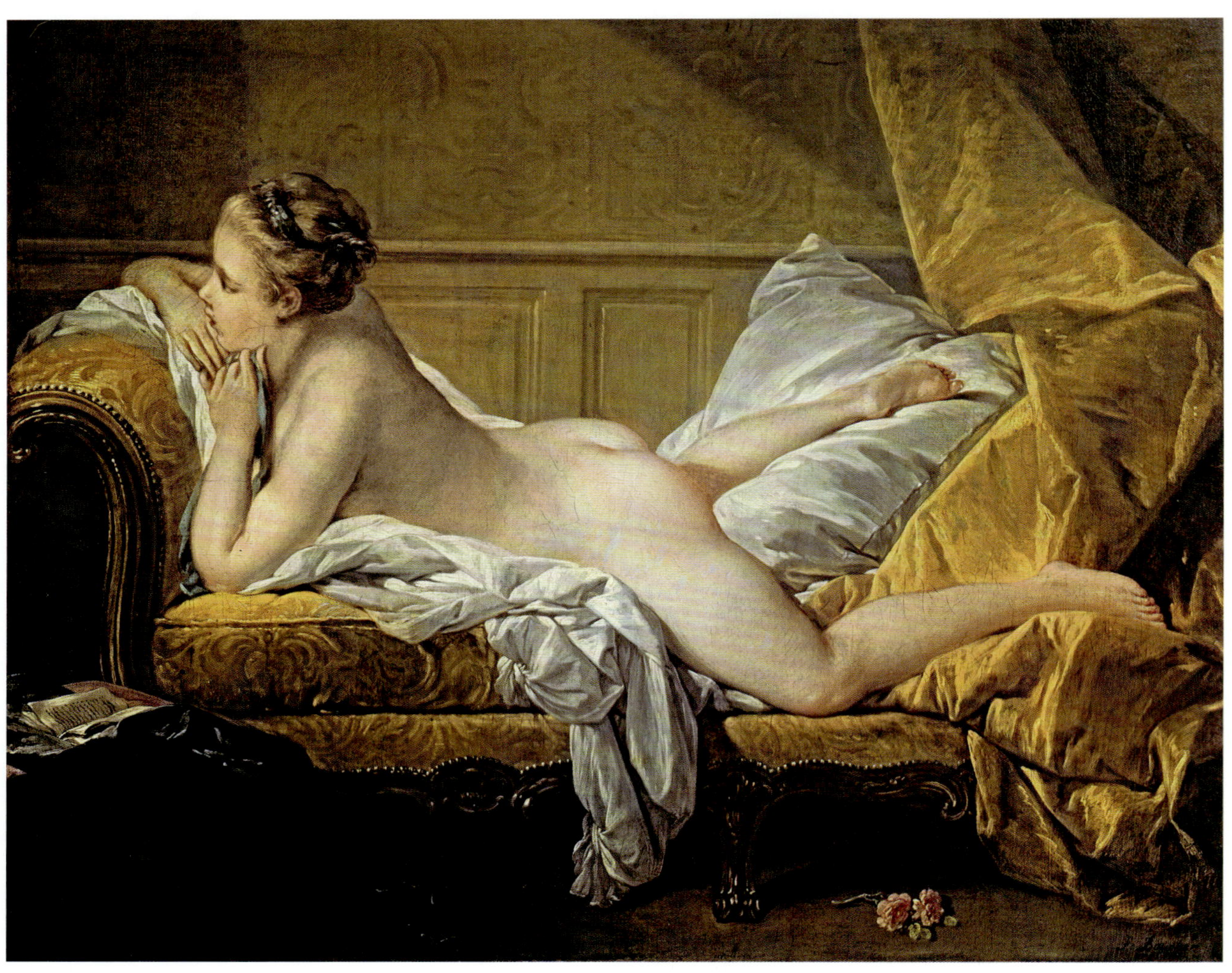

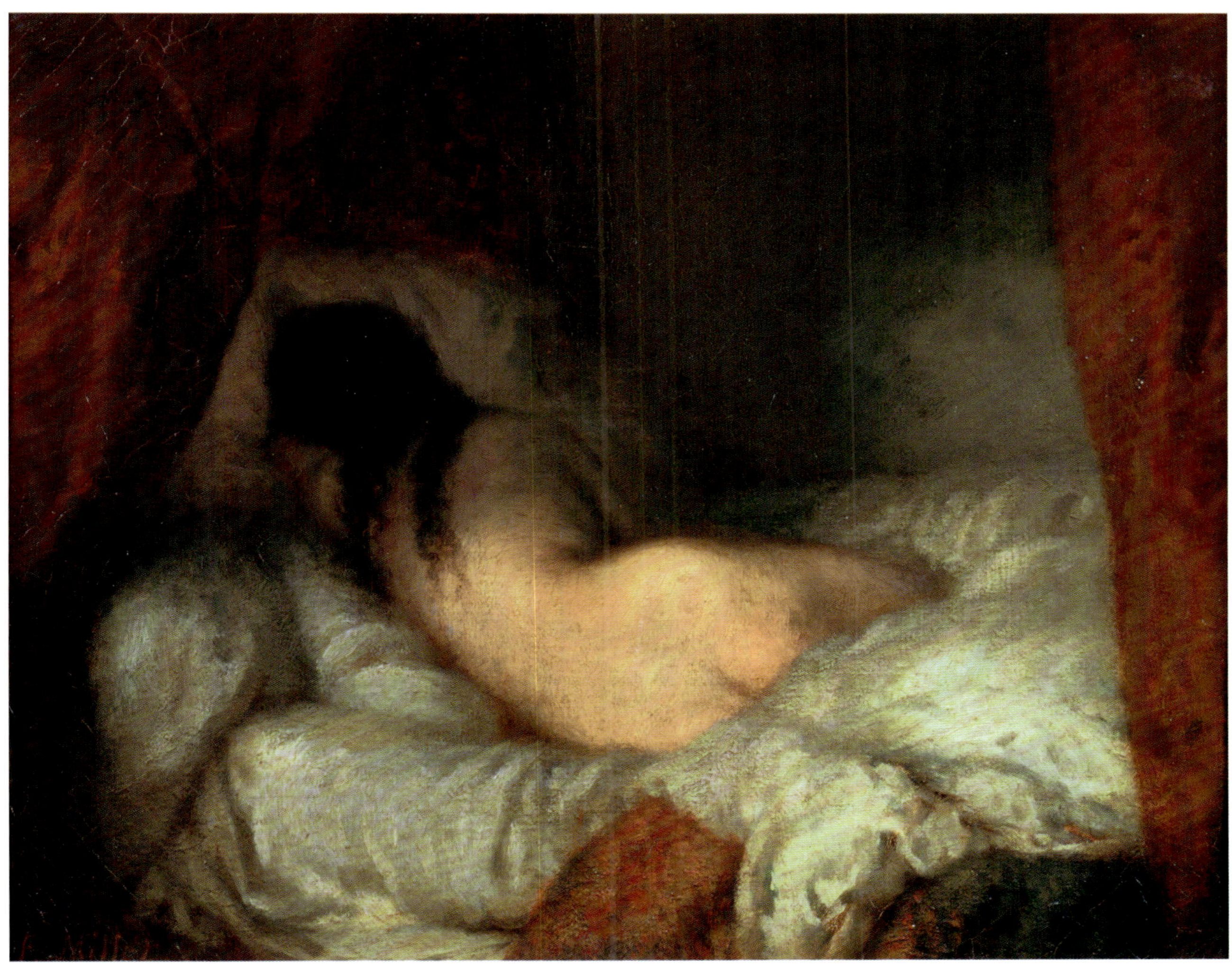

Reclining Nude (Marie-Louise O'Murphy)
Femme nue allongée (Marie-Louise O'Murphy)
Ruhendes Mädchen (Marie-Louise O'Murphy)
Niña descansando (Marie-Louise O'Murphy)
Menina descansando (Marie-Louise O'Murphy)
Rustend meisje (Marie-Louise O'Murphy)

François Boucher (1703-1770)

———

1752, Oil on canvas/Huile sur toile, 59 × 73 cm,
Alte Pinakothek, München

Reclining Female Nude
Femme nue couchée
Liegender Akt
Desnudo mujer tumbada
Mulher nua deitada
Liggend naakt

Jean-François Millet (1814-1875)

———

1844/45, Oil on canvas/Huile sur toile,
33 × 41 cm, Musée d'Orsay, Paris

MONTICELLI ~ VAN GOGH

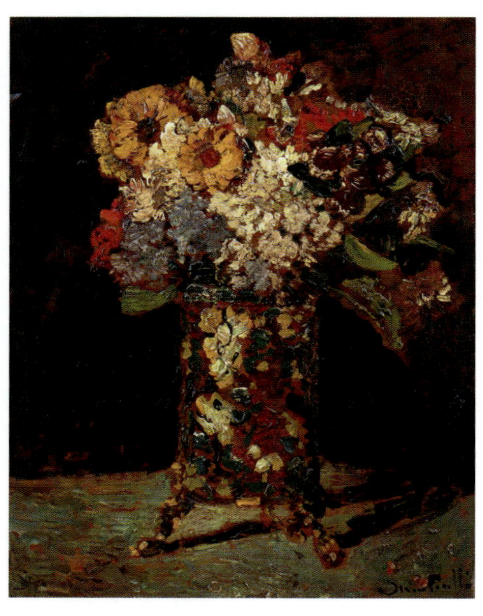

Vase with flowers
Bouquet de fleurs
Stillleben mit Blumen
Bodegón con flores
Bouquet de flores
Vaas met bloemen

**Adolphe Monticelli
(1824-1886)**

———

c. 1875, Oil on panel/Huile
sur panneau, 51 × 39 cm,
Van Gogh Museum, Amsterdam

Bouquet of Flowers
Bouquet de fleurs
Blumenstrauss im Keramikkrug
Ramo de flores en jarra de cerámica
Bouquet de flores em jarro de cerâmica
Vaas met bloemen

**Vincent van Gogh
(1853-1890)**

———

n. d., Oil on canvas/Huile sur toile,
Private collection

Van Gogh was enthusiastic about Monticelli's painting, he even copied the way he painted - the large areas of color and the sometimes garish tones. Unfortunately, the artist's works are rather unknown today, although he has done a lot for modern painting.

Van Gogh fut bouleversé par la peinture de Monticelli auquel il empruntera même sa manière si particulière de peindre, faite de larges empâtements et de couleurs parfois très acides. Aujourd'hui peu de gens connaissent le travail et les œuvres de cet artiste qui apporta pourtant sans le savoir beaucoup à la peinture moderne.

Van Gogh war begeistert von Monticellis Gemälde, bei dem er sich sogar die Art zu Malen abschaute – die großen Farbflächen und die teilweise grellen Töne. Leider sind die Werke des Künstlers heute eher unbekannt, obwohl er viel für die moderne Malerei geleistet hat.

Van Gogh estaba entusiasmado con la pintura de Monticelli, en la que incluso copió la forma en que pintaba: las grandes áreas de color y los tonos a veces chillones. Desafortunadamente, las obras del artista son bastante desconocidas hoy en día, aunque ha hecho mucho por la pintura moderna.

Van Gogh estava entusiasmado com a pintura de Monticelli, na qual até copiou a forma como pintava - as grandes áreas de cor e os tons por vezes berrantes. Infelizmente, as obras do artista são bastante desconhecidas hoje em dia, embora ele tenha feito muito pela pintura moderna.

Van Gogh was enthousiast over Monticelli's schilderij, waarin hij zelfs de manier waarop hij schilderde – met grote kleurvlakken en soms felle kleuren – kopieerde. Helaas zijn de werken van de kunstenaar tegenwoordig nogal onbekend, hoewel hij veel heeft betekend voor de moderne schilderkunst.

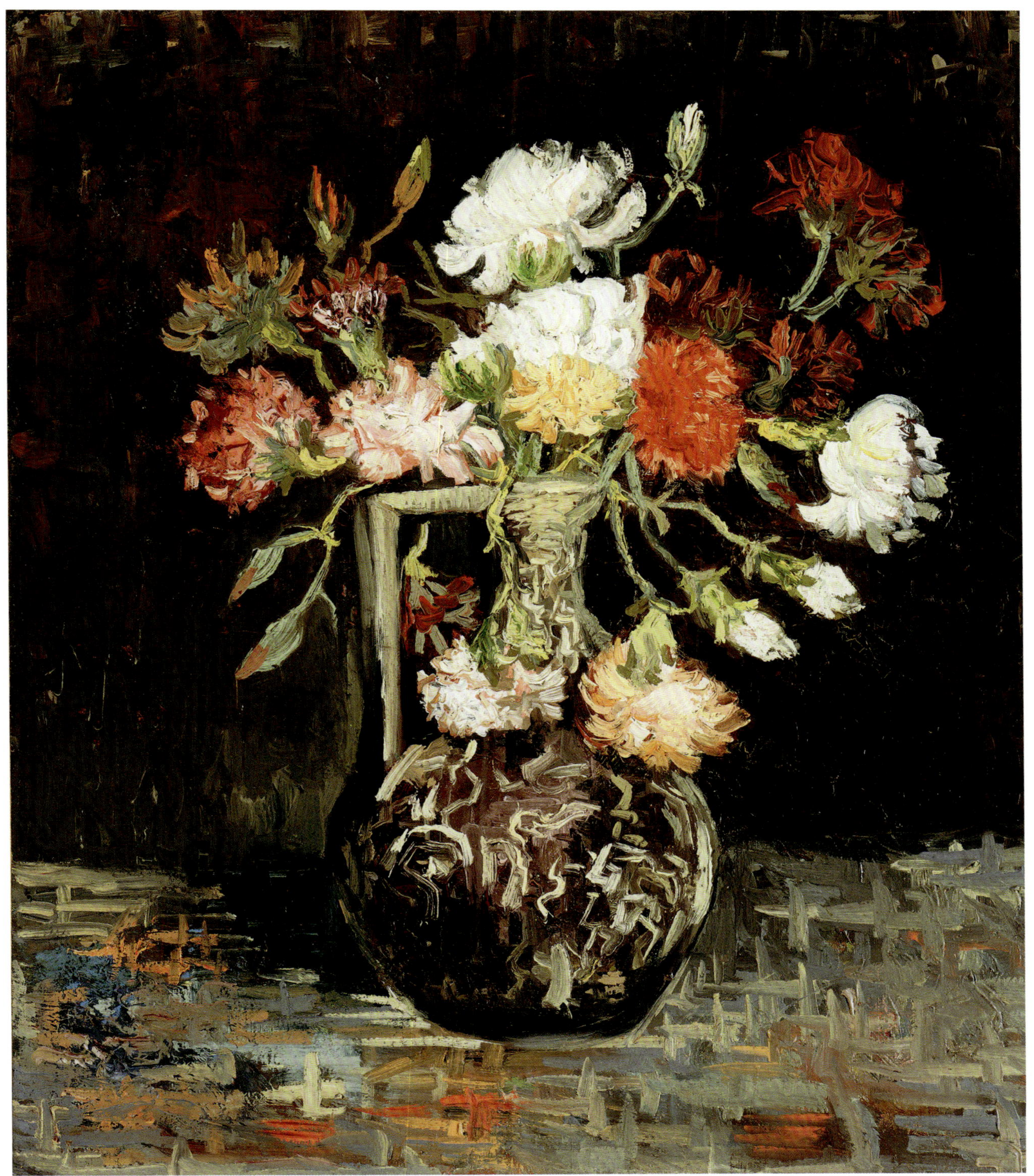

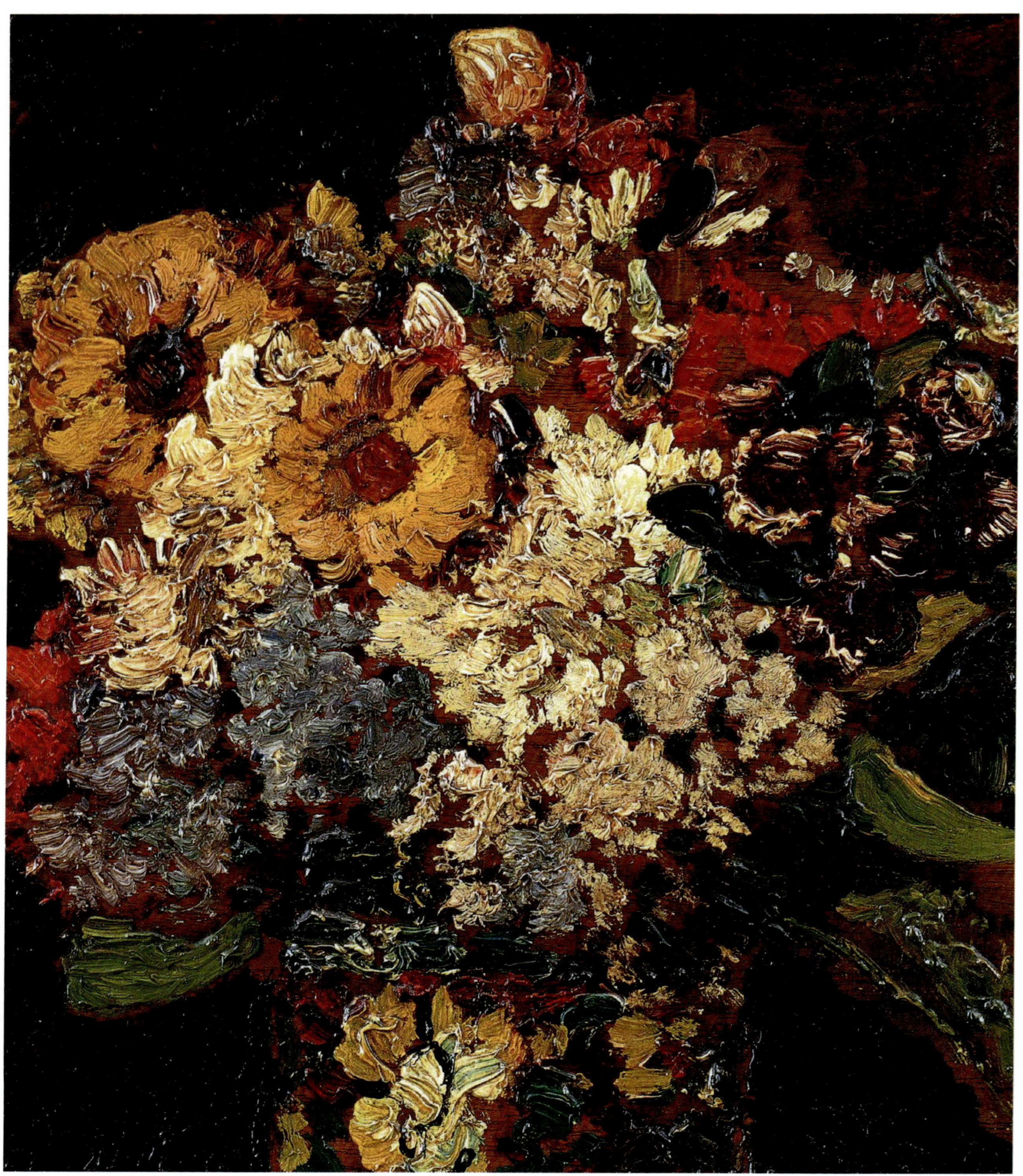

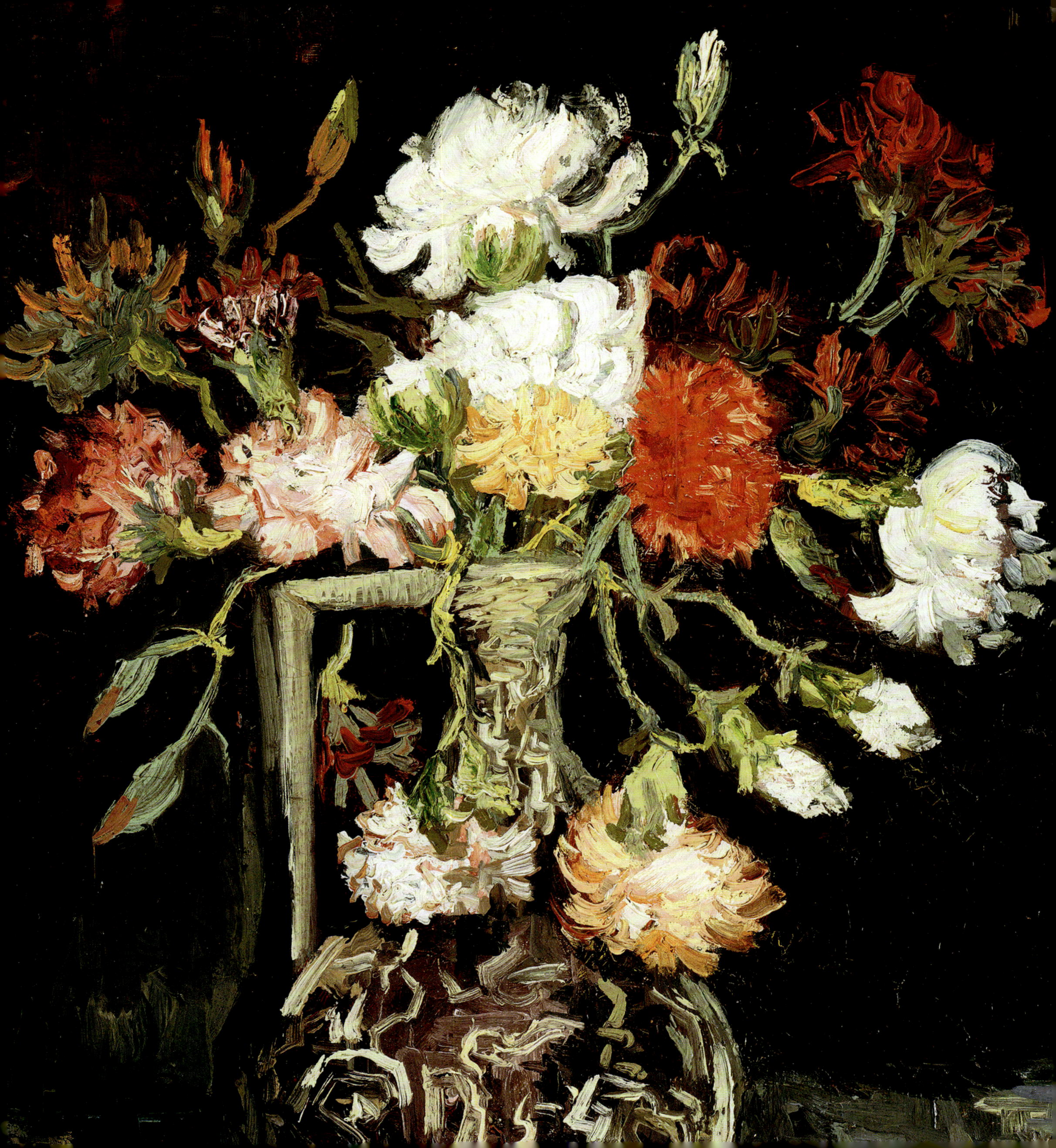

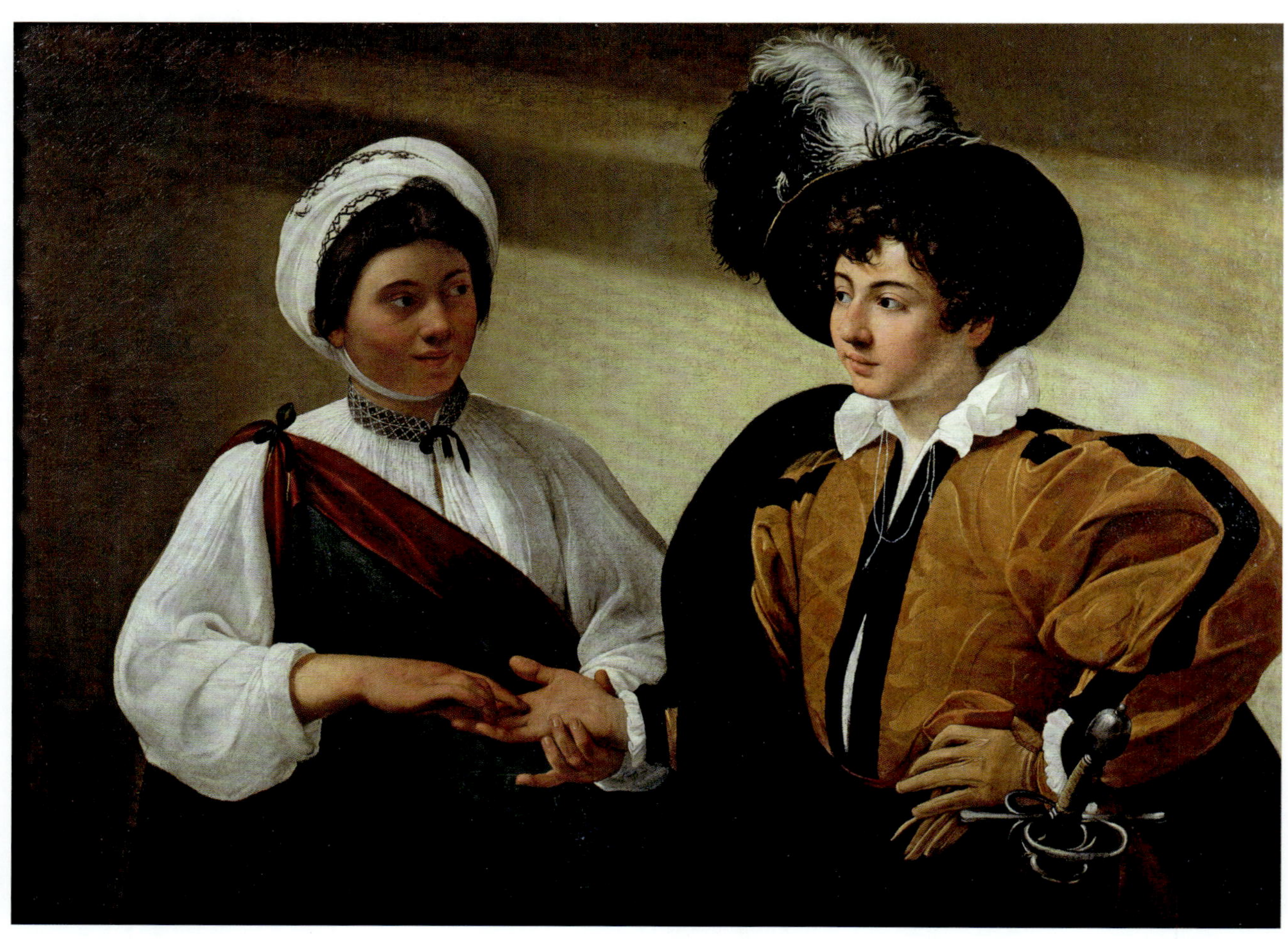

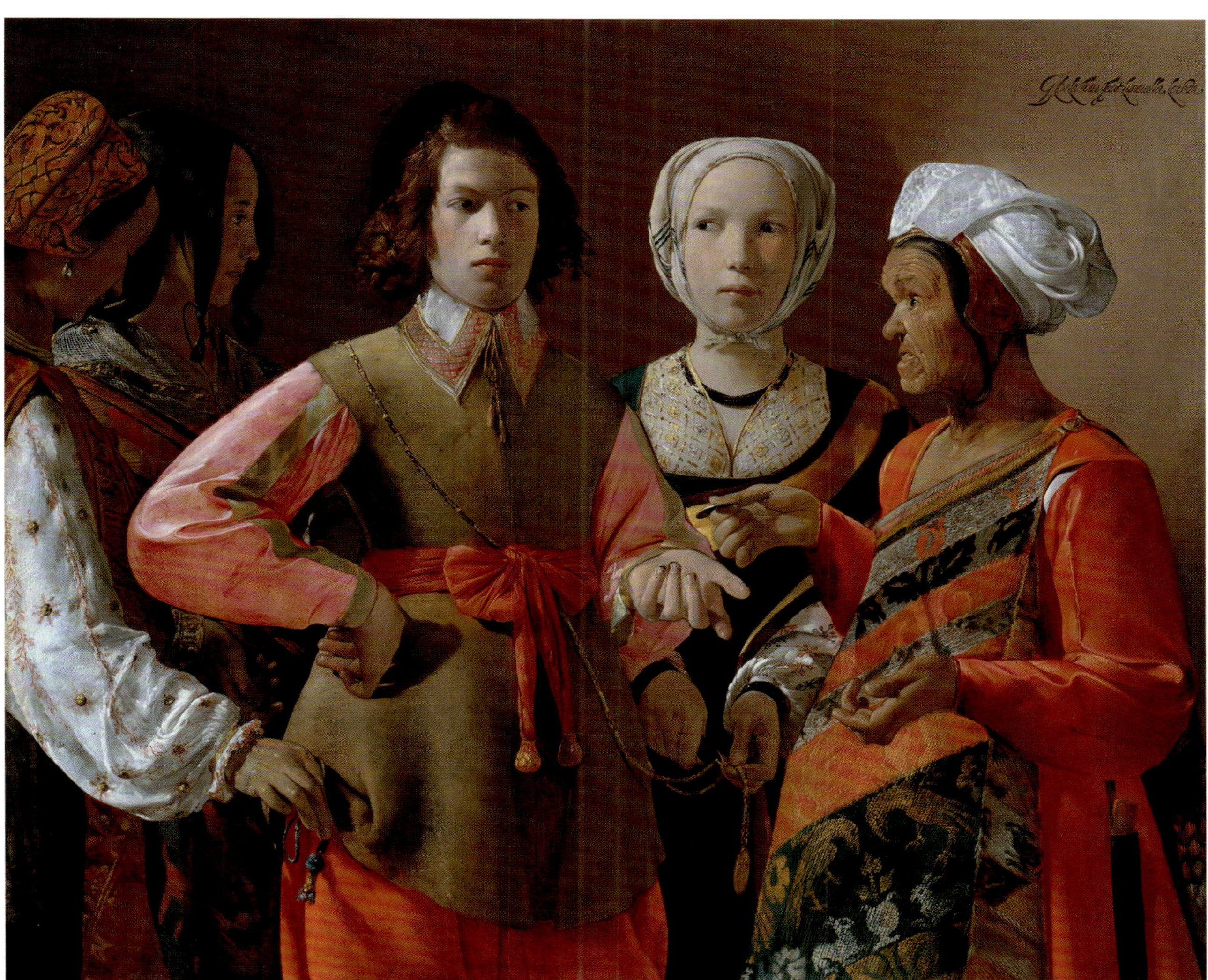

The Fortune Teller

La Diseuse de bonne aventure

Die Wahrsagerin

La adivina

A cartomante

De waarzegster

**Michelangelo Merisi da Caravaggio
(1571-1610)**

———

c. 1595-98, Oil on canvas/Huile sur toile,
99 × 131 cm, Musée du Louvre, Paris

The Fortune Teller

La Diseuse de bonne aventure

Die Wahrsagerin

La adivina

A cartomante

De waarzegster

Georges de la Tour (1593-1652)

———

c. 1635, Oil on canvas/Huile sur toile,
101,9 × 123,5 cm, Metropolitan Museum
of Art, New-York

PRINCETEAU ~ TOULOUSE-LAUTREC

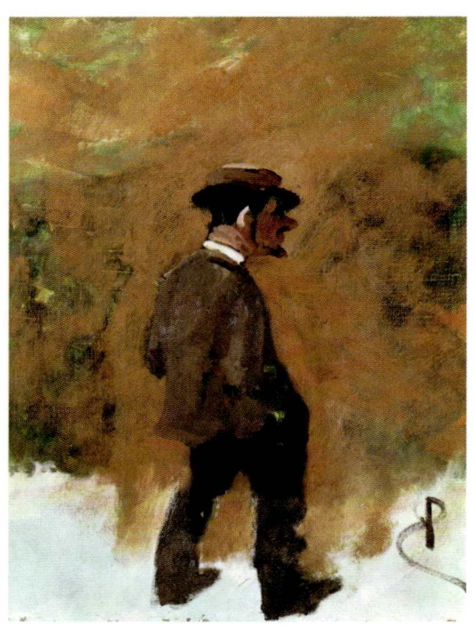

Henri de Toulouse-Lautrec aged 19

Henri de Toulouse-Lautrec à 19 ans

Henri de Toulouse-Lautrec im Alter von 19 Jahren

Henri de Toulouse-Lautrec a la edad de 19 años

Henri de Toulouse-Lautrec aos 19 anos de idade

Henri de Toulouse-Lautrec op 19-jarige leeftijd

René Princeteau (1844-1914)

———

c. 1883, Oil on canvas/Huile sur toile, 45 × 36 cm, Private collection

The painter René Princeteau in his Studio

Le Peintre René Princeteau dans son atelier

Der Maler René Princeteau in seinem Atelier

El pintor René Princeteau en su estudio

O pintor René Princeteau no seu estúdio

De schilder René Princeteau in zijn atelier

Henri de Toulouse-Lautrec (1864-1901)

———

c. 1881, Oil on canvas/Huile sur toile, 54 × 46 cm, Private collection

In 1871, the young Toulouse-Lautrec became a pupil of René Princeteau. The pupil, who was not even ten years old, was already able to draw excellently. His motifs, which he sketched with a pencil or painted in oil on wood, were at that time mainly caricatures or animals, especially horses.

En 1871, René Princeteau devient le professeur du tout jeune Lautrec qui, à 7 ans à peine, a déjà un très joli coup de crayon. À cette époque les sujets principaux de ses croquis ou de ses petites pochades à l'huile sur bois ont essentiellement pour thèmes des caricatures ou des animaux, au premier rang desquels figure le cheval.

Im Jahr 1871 wird der junge Toulouse-Lautrec Schüler bei René Princeteau. Der noch nicht mal zehnjährige Schüler kann bereits ausgezeichnet zeichnen. Seine Motive, die er skizzenhaft mit dem Stift oder in Öl auf Holz malt, sind zu dieser Zeit hauptsächlich Karikaturen oder Tiere, allen voran Pferde.

En 1871, el joven Toulouse-Lautrec se convierte en alumno de René Princeteau. El alumno, que ni siquiera tenía diez años, ya sabía dibujar excelentemente. Sus motivos, que dibuja con un lápiz o pinturas al óleo sobre madera, eran entonces principalmente caricaturas o animales, especialmente caballos.

Em 1871, o jovem Toulouse-Lautrec tornou-se aluno de René Princeteau. O aluno, que não tinha sequer dez anos de idade, já conseguia desenhar de forma excelente. Seus motivos, que ele esboça com um lápis ou tintas a óleo sobre madeira, eram na época principalmente caricaturas ou animais, especialmente cavalos.

In 1871 werd de jonge Toulouse-Lautrec leerling van René Princeteau. De zevenjarige leerling kon al uitstekend tekenen. Zijn onderwerpen, die hij schetste met potlood of olieverf op hout, waren in die tijd vooral karikaturen of dieren, vooral paarden.

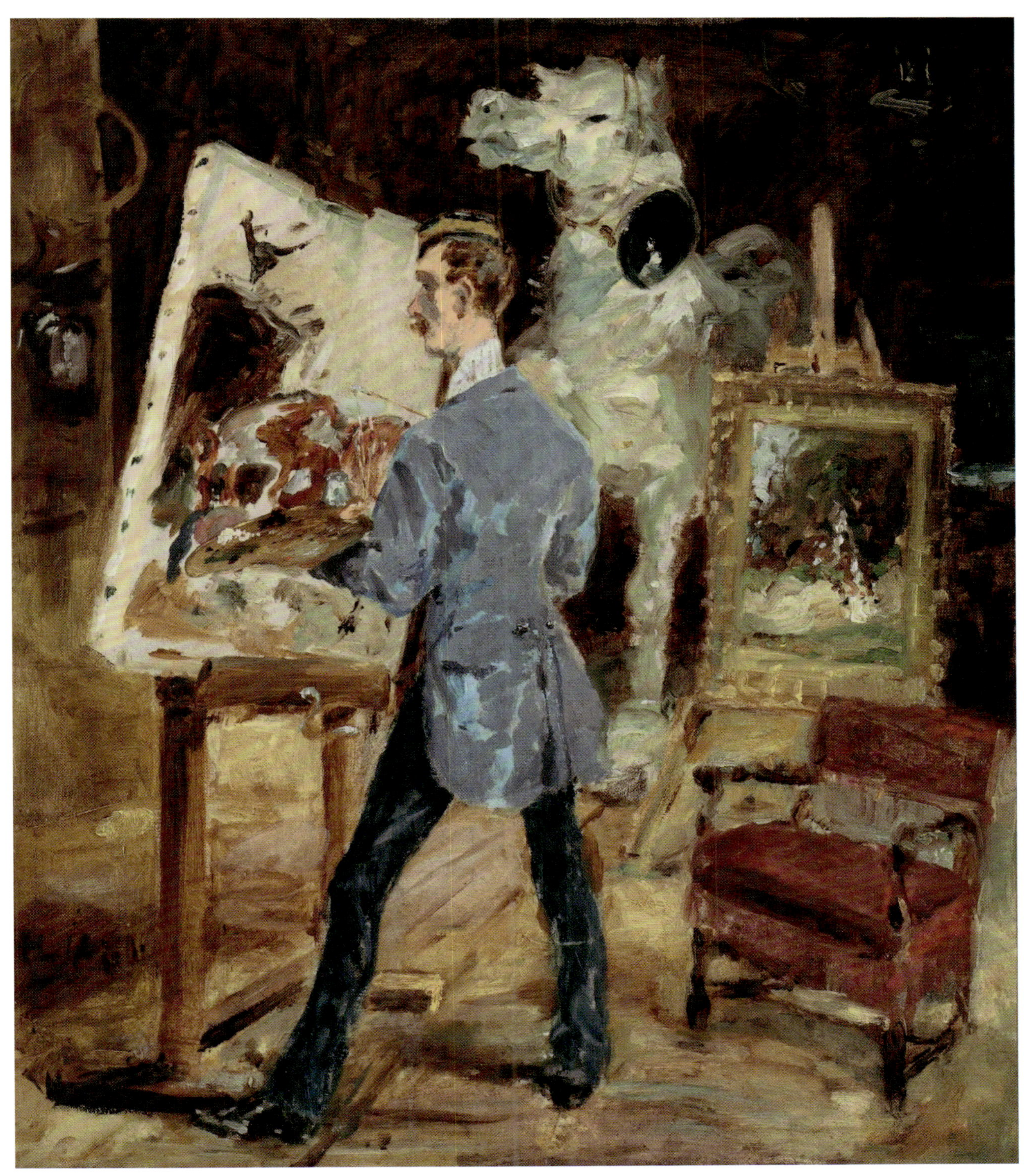

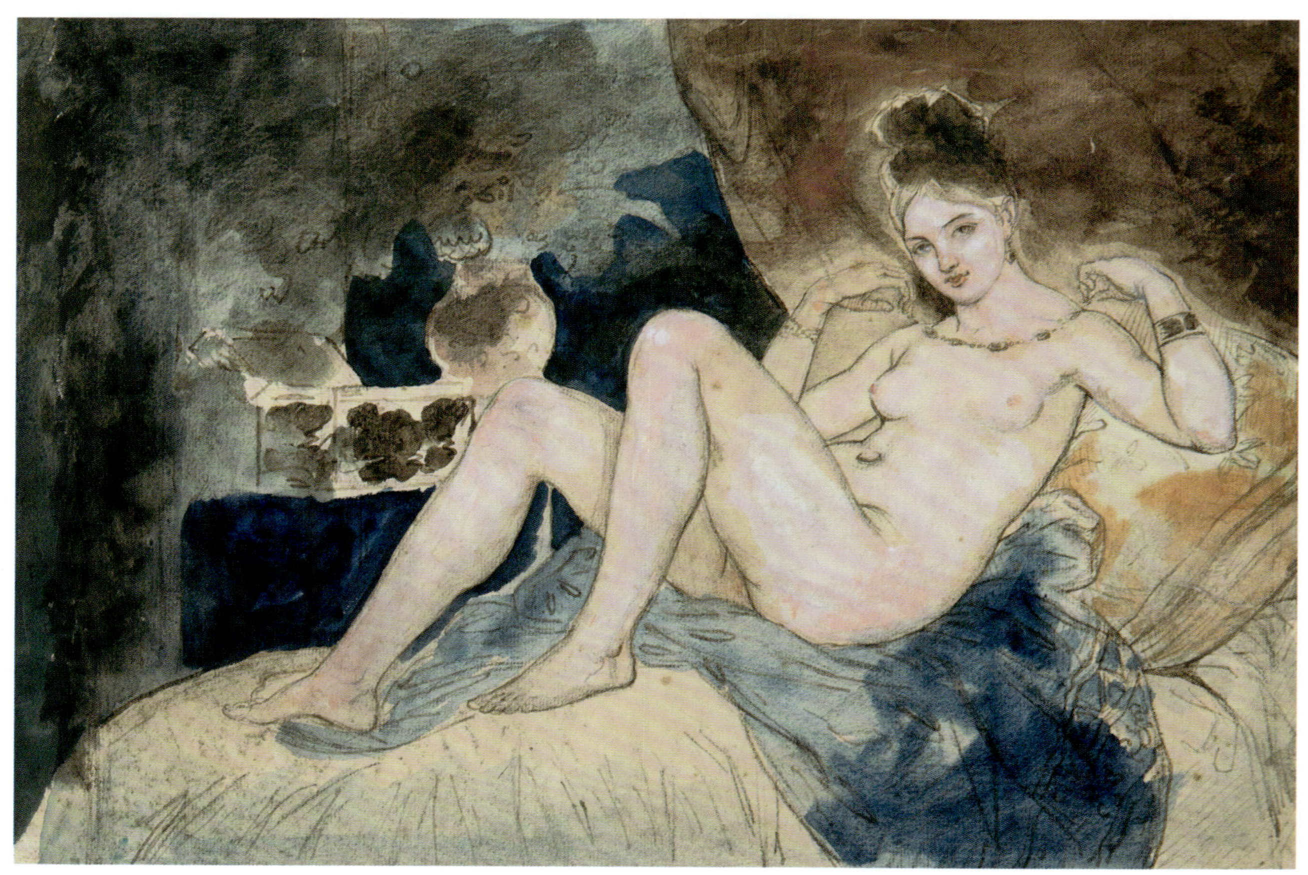

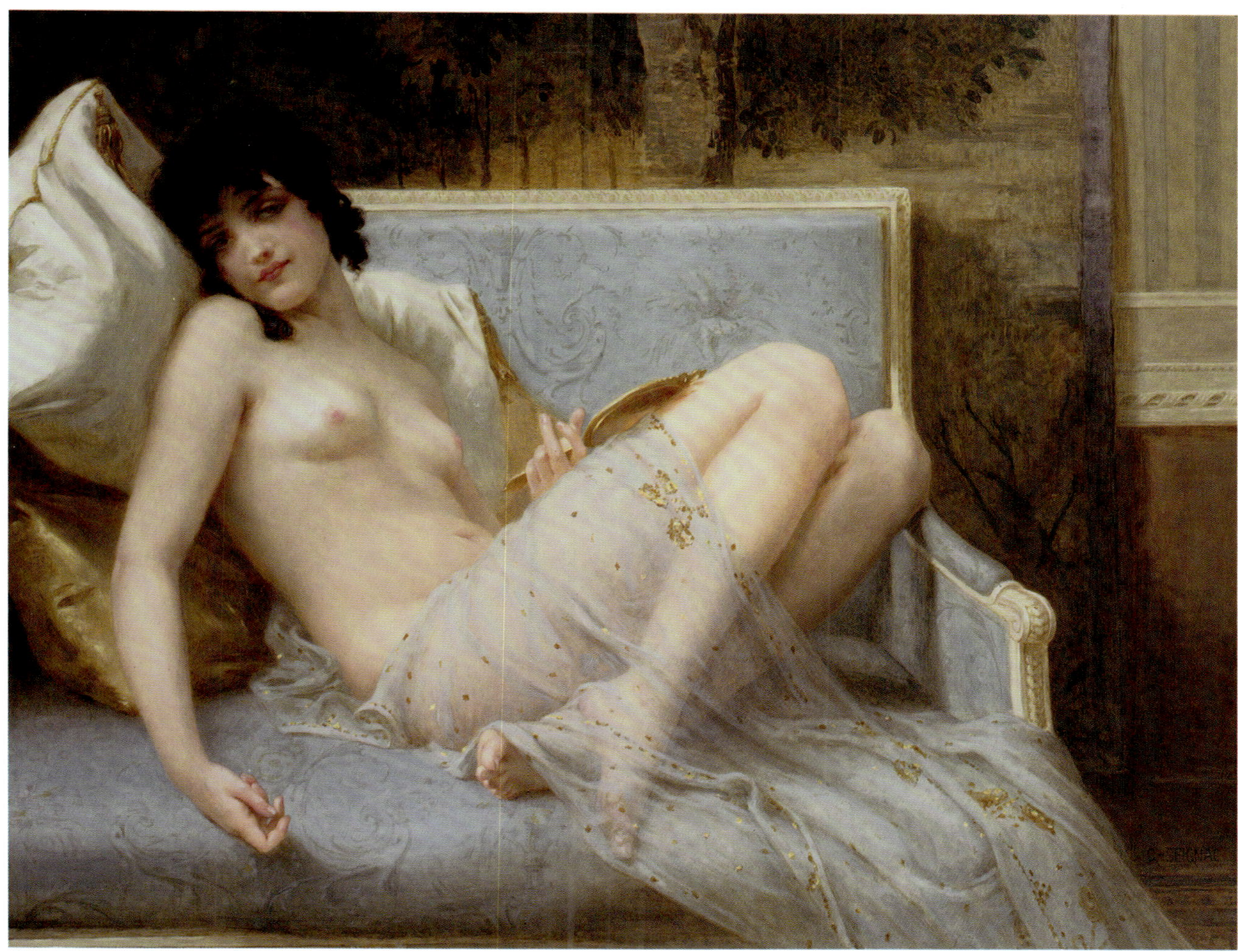

<table>
<tr><td>

Nude on a Divan

Nu sur un divan

Akt auf einem Diwan

Desnudo en un diván

Nua no sofá

Naakt op een divan

Achille Deveria (1800-1857)

———

n. d., Black pencil, pen and brown ink/
Crayon noir, plume et encre brune,
28,5 × 41,4 cm, Private collection

</td><td>

Indolence

Nu au canapé

Die Trägheit

Desnudo en el sofá

A inércia

Jonge vrouw naakt op een canapé

Guillaume Seignac (1870-1924)

———

Before 1914, Oil on canvas/Huile sur toile,
55 × 65 cm, Private collection

</td></tr>
</table>

ANONYMOUS ~ GÉRICAULT

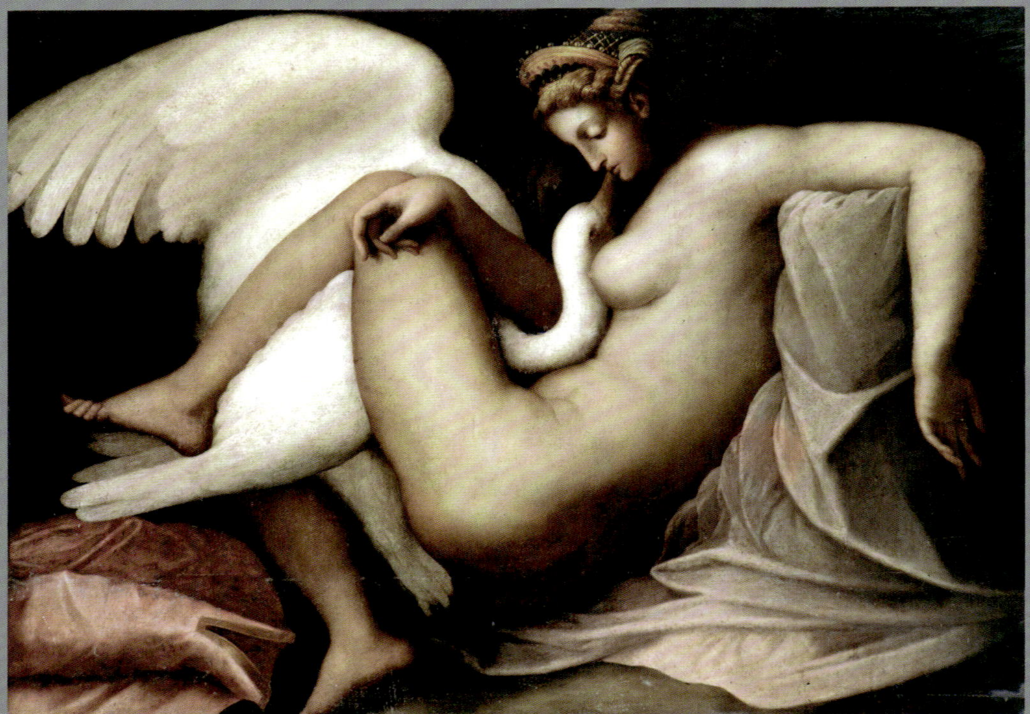

Leda and the Swan
Léda et le cygne
Leda und der Schwan
Leda y el cisne
Leda e o Cisne
Leda en de zwaan

Anonymous (after/d'après Michelangelo)

16th century,
114 × 155 cm,
Museo Correr, Venice

Shortly after his arrival in Rome in 1816, Géricault went to the Sistine Chapel to study Michelangelo's ceiling paintings. During his stay he was not only inspired by the compositional techniques of the Renaissance painter, but also adopted his painting style. This became the basis of his scene of *Leda and the Swan*, based on a lost work by Michelangelo, known through copies.

À peine arrivé à Rome en 1816, la première chose que fit Géricault fut d'aller admirer le plafond de la chapelle Sixtine peint par Michel-Ange. Durant son séjour, il s'imprégna, non seulement des compositions du génie de la Renaissance, mais emprunta aussi son style graphique. Celui-là même qu'il fait courir sur sa feuille pour donner vie à une *Léda au cygne*, reprise d'une œuvre originale de Michel-Ange connue grâce à des copies anciennes.

Kurz nach seiner Ankunft in Rom im Jahr 1816 begibt sich Géricault in die Sixtinische Kapelle, um die Deckenmalereien von Michelangelo zu studieren. Während seines Aufenthaltes lässt er sich nicht nur von den Kompositionstechniken des Renaissancemalers inspirieren, sondern eignet sich auch seinen Malstil an. Dieser wird zur Grundlage seiner Szene der *Leda und der Schwan,* die auf einem verschollenen Werk Michelangelos basiert, das durch Kopien bekannt ist.

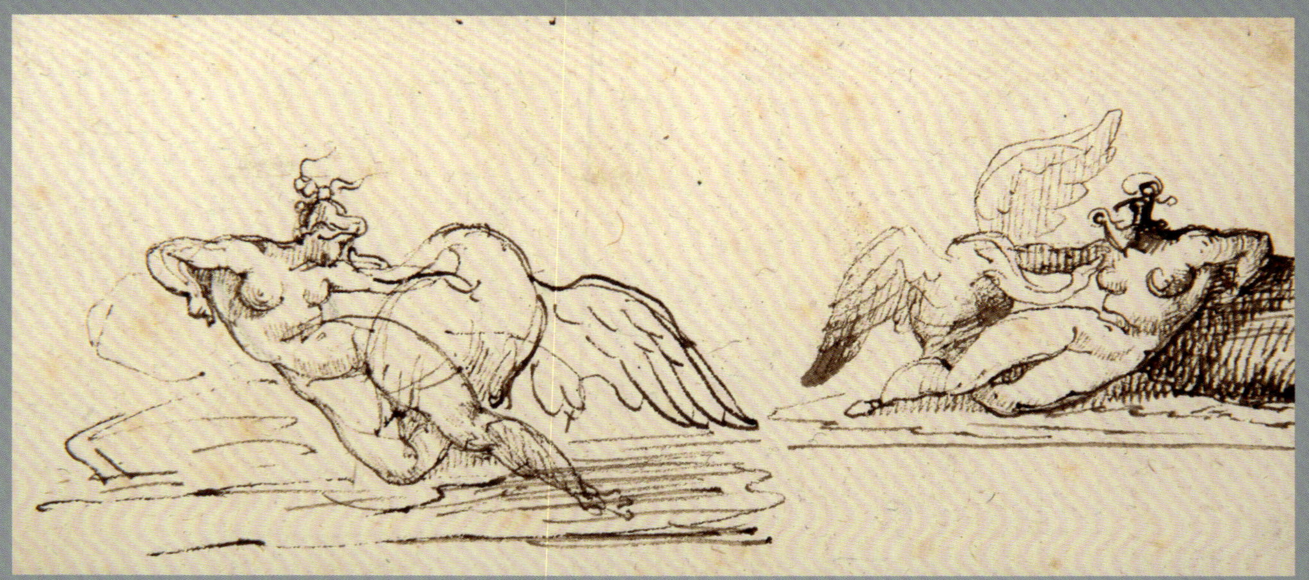

c. 1816/17, Pen and brown ink, black pencil trace/Plume et encre brune, trace de crayon noir, 6,5 × 15 cm, Private collection

Poco después de su llegada a Roma en 1816, Géricault fue a la Capilla Sixtina para estudiar las pinturas del techo de Miguel Ángel. Durante su estancia se inspiró no sólo en las técnicas de composición del pintor renacentista, sino que también adoptó su estilo pictórico. Esta fue la base de su escena de *Leda con el cisne,* basada en una obra perdida de Miguel Ángel, conocida por sus copias.

Pouco depois de sua chegada a Roma em 1816, Géricault foi à Capela Sistina para estudar as pinturas do teto de Michelangelo. Durante a sua estadia, não só se inspirou nas técnicas de composição do pintor renascentista, como também adoptou o seu estilo de pintura. Esta se tornou a base de sua cena da *Leda e o Cisne,* baseada em um trabalho perdido por Michelangelo, conhecido por cópias.

Kort na zijn aankomst in Rome in 1816 ging Géricault naar de Sixtijnse Kapel om Michelangelo's plafondschilderingen te bestuderen. Tijdens zijn verblijf liet hij zich niet alleen inspireren door de compositietechnieken van de renaissanceschilder, maar nam hij ook diens schilderstijl over. Die vormde de basis voor zijn scène van *Leda en de zwaan,* die hij baseerde op een verloren gegaan werk van Michelangelo dat bekend was van kopieën.

ANONYMOUS ~ GÉRICAULT

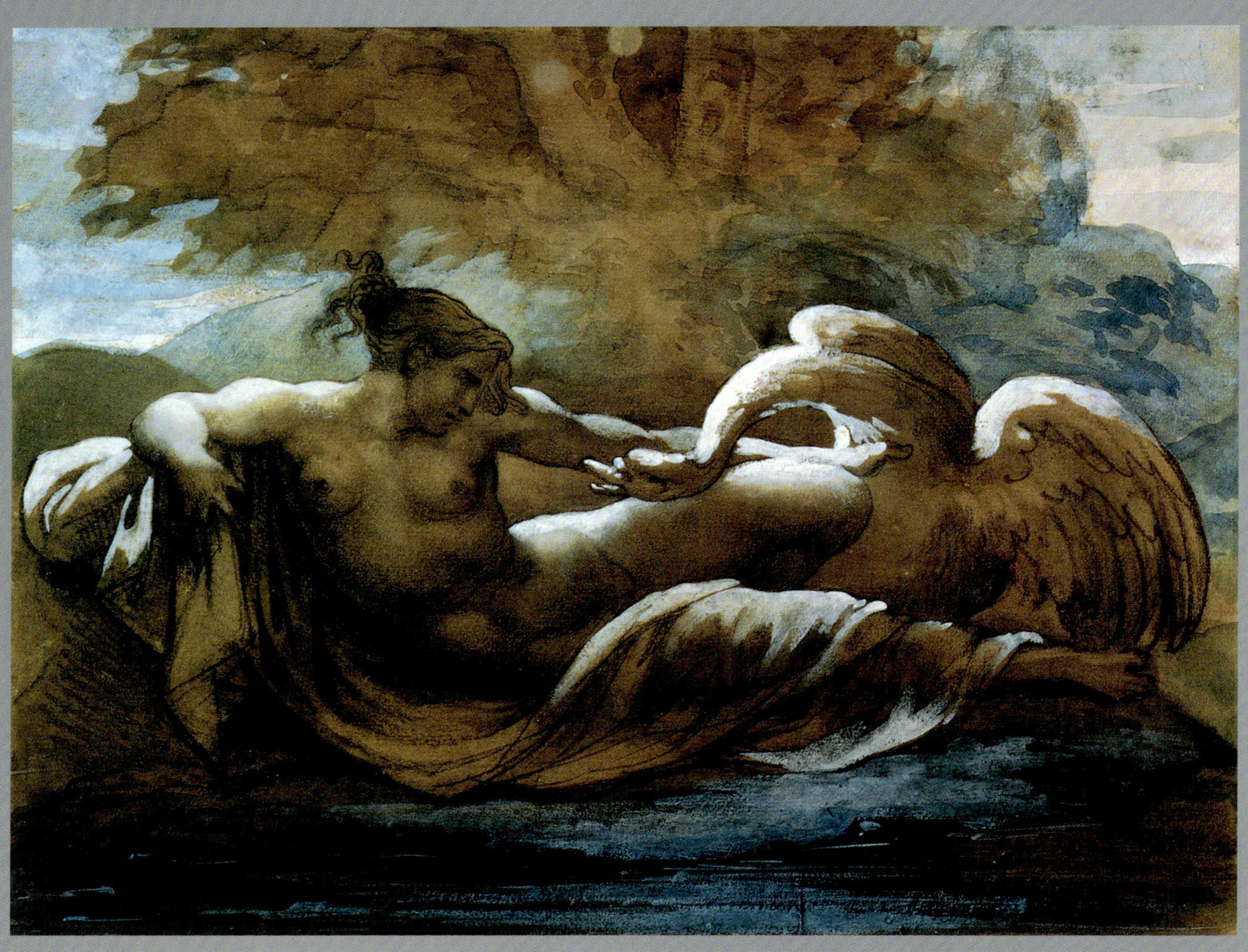

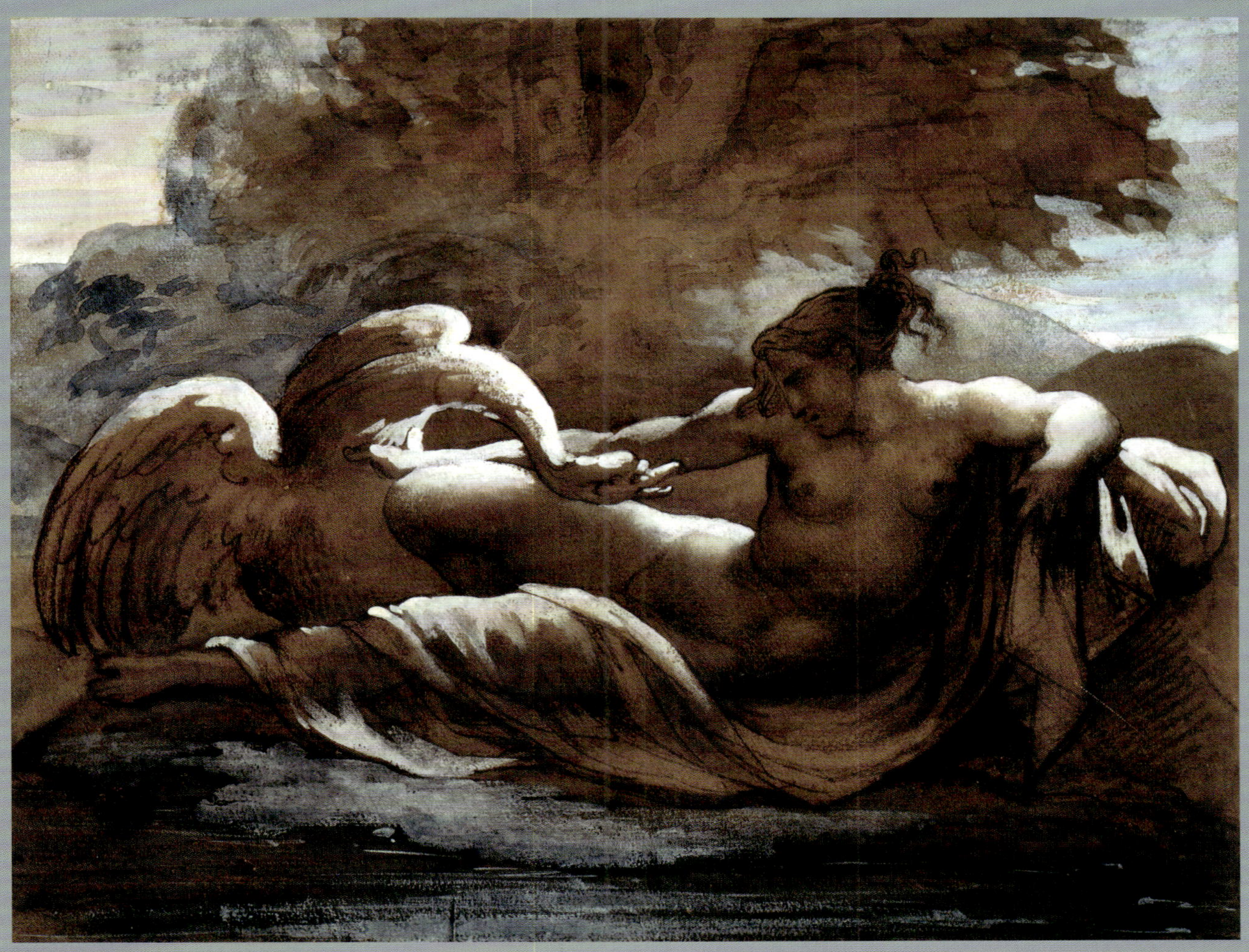

Leda and the Swan
Léda et le cygne
Leda und der Schwan
Leda y el cisne
Leda e o Cisne
Leda en de zwaan

Théodore Géricault (1791-1824)

———

c. 1816/17, Watercolor, brown wash, white
highlights, black pencil on brown paper/
Aquarelle, lavis brun, rehauts de blanc,
crayon noir sur papier brun, 21 × 28 cm,
Musée du Louvre, Paris

Leda and the Swan
Léda et le cygne
Leda und der Schwan
Leda y el cisne
Leda e o Cisne
Leda en de zwaan

Théodore Géricault (1791-1824)

———

c. 1816/17, Watercolor, brown wash, white
highlights, black pencil on brown paper/
Aquarelle, lavis brun, rehauts de blanc,
crayon noir sur papier brun, 21 × 28 cm,
Musée du Louvre, Paris

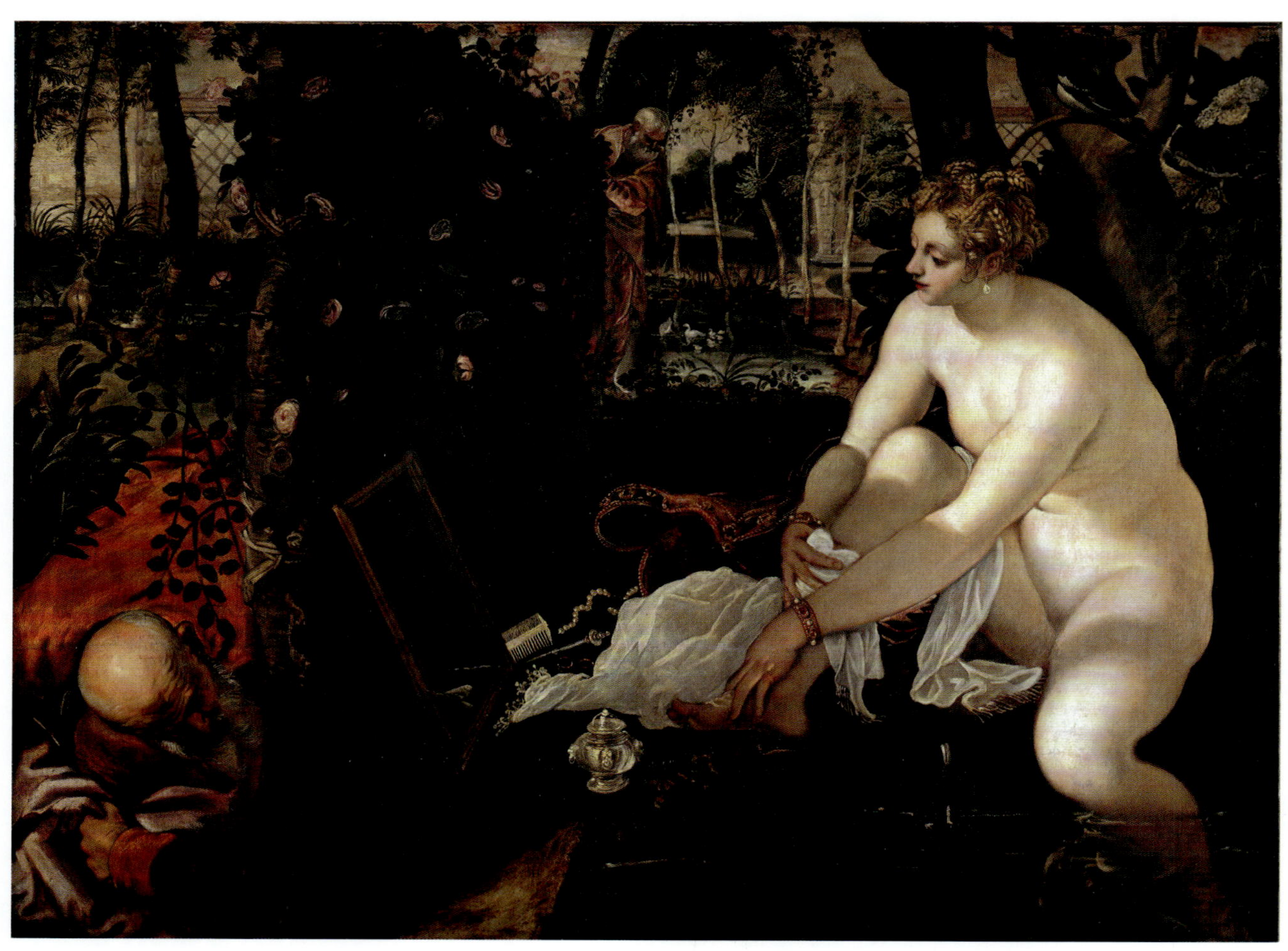

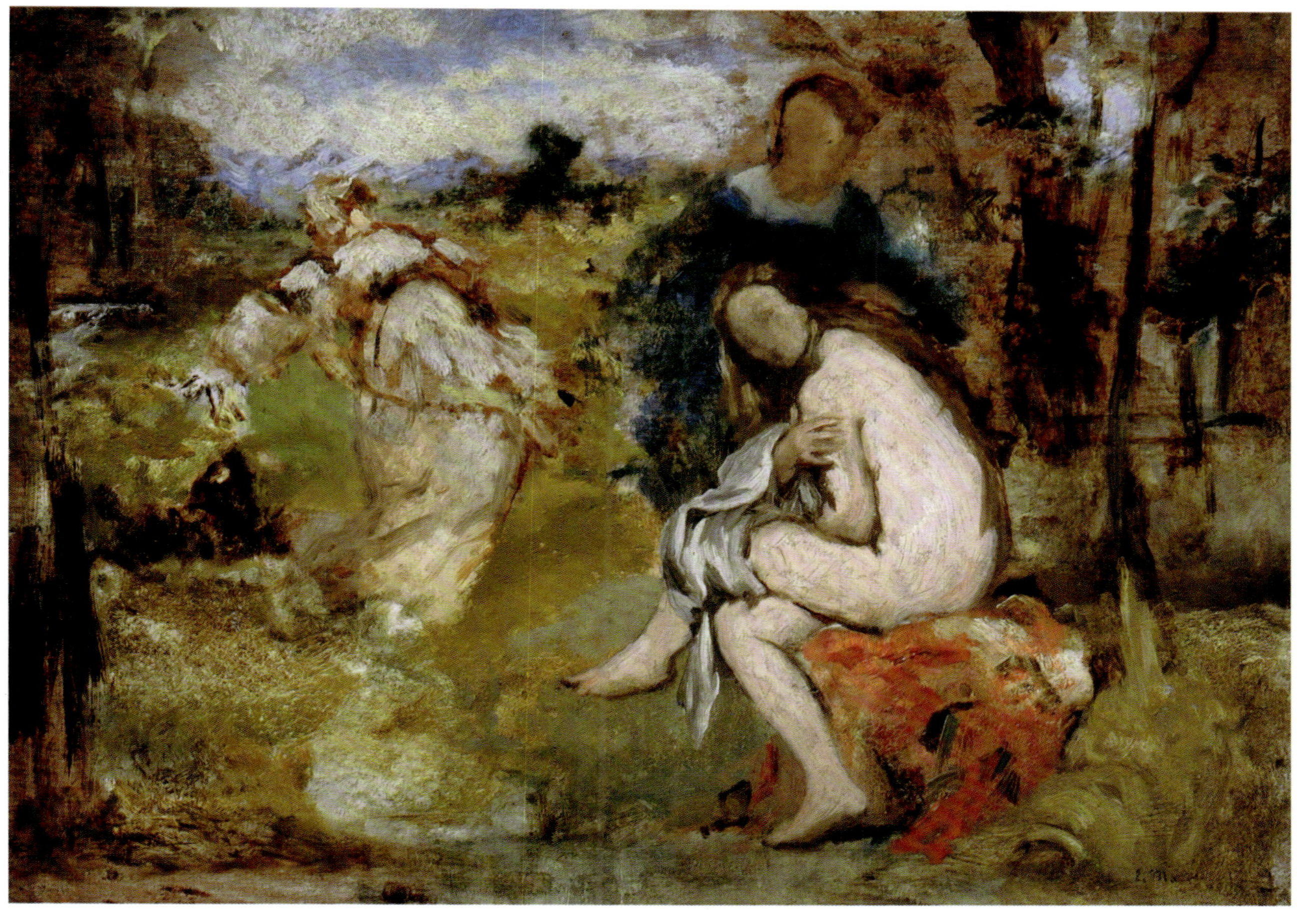

Susanna in the Bath

Suzanne au bain

Susanna im Bade

Susanna en el baño

Susanna no banho

Susanna en de ouderlingen

**Jacopo Robusti (Il Tintoretto)
(1518-1594)**

———

c. 1555/56, Oil on canvas/Huile sur toile,
146 × 193,6 cm, Kunsthistorisches
Museum, Wien

The Surprised Nymph

La Nymphe surprise

Die überraschte Nymphe

La ninfa sorprendida

A Ninfa Surpreendida

De verraste nimf

Édouard Manet (1832-1883)

———

c. 1860, Oil on wood/Huile sur bois,
35,5 × 46 cm, Nasjonalgalleriet, Oslo

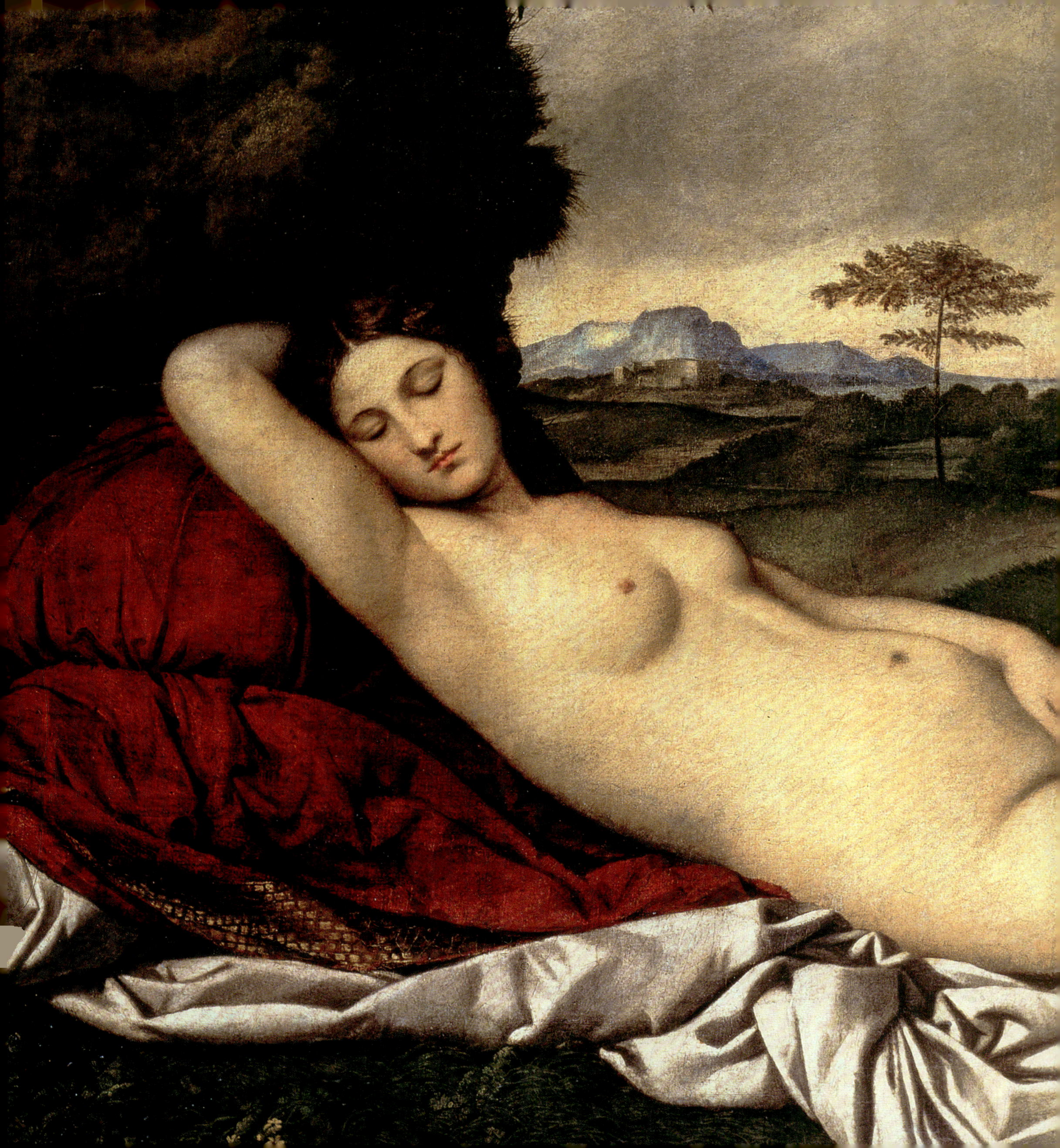

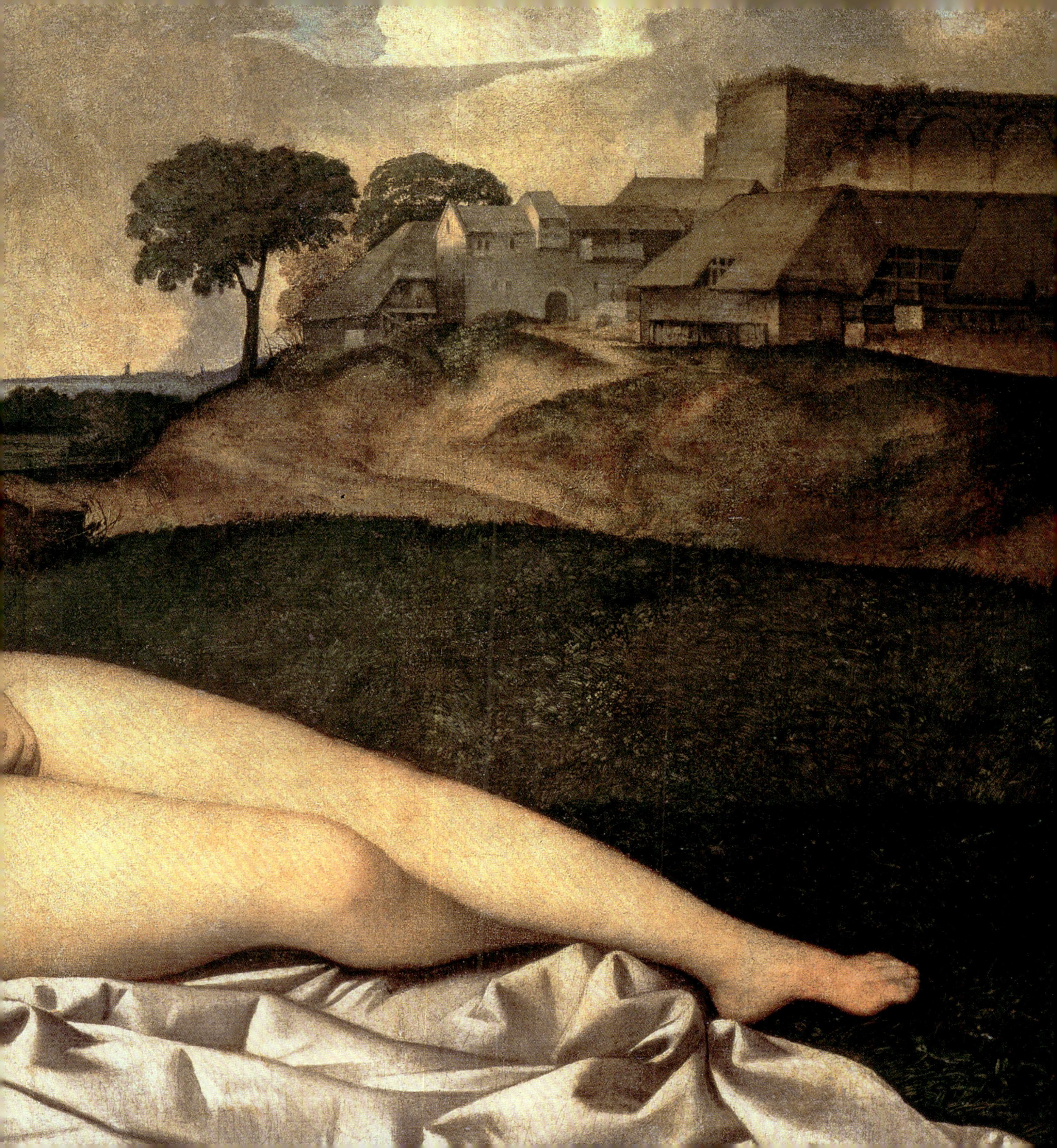

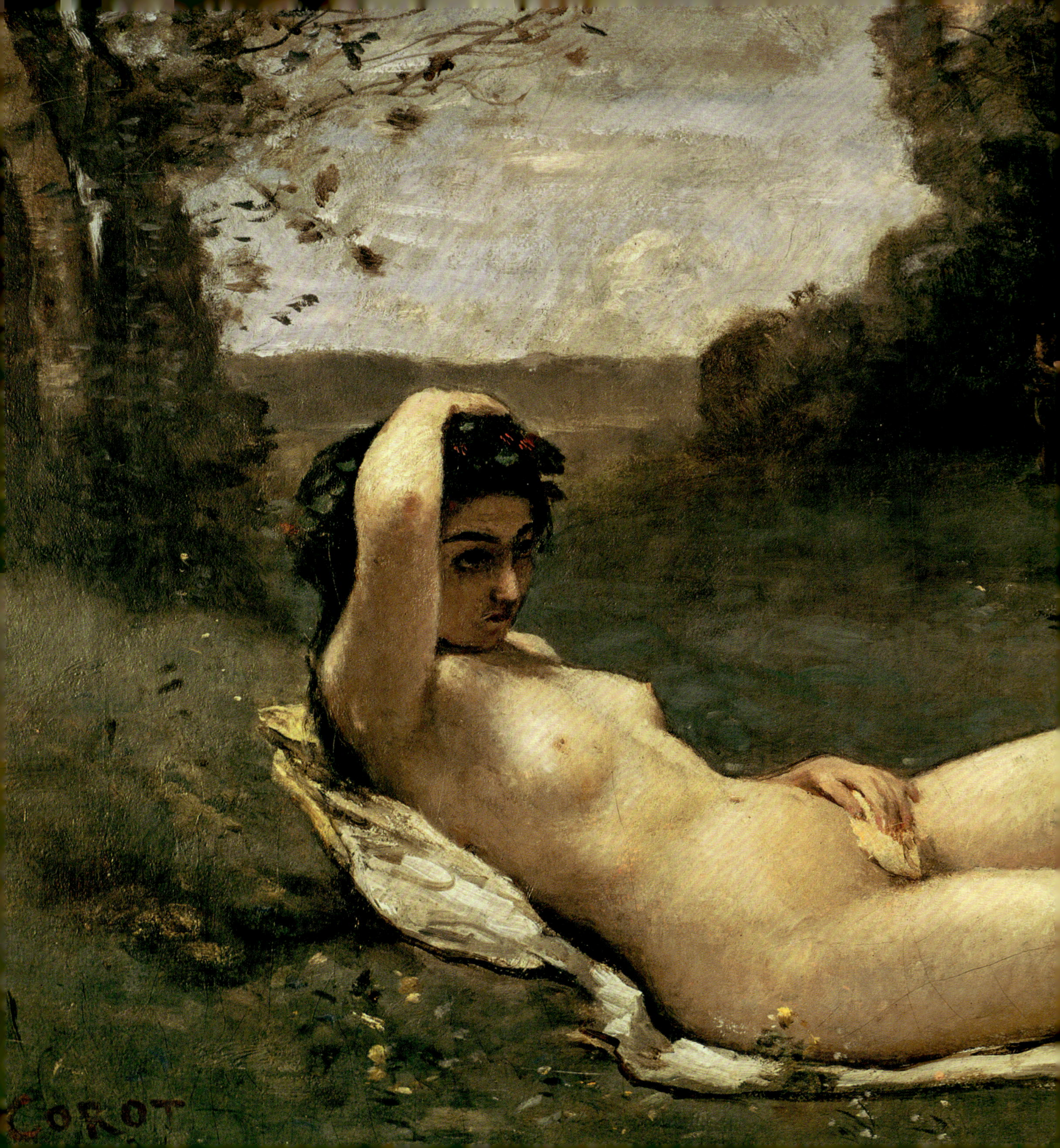

COROT

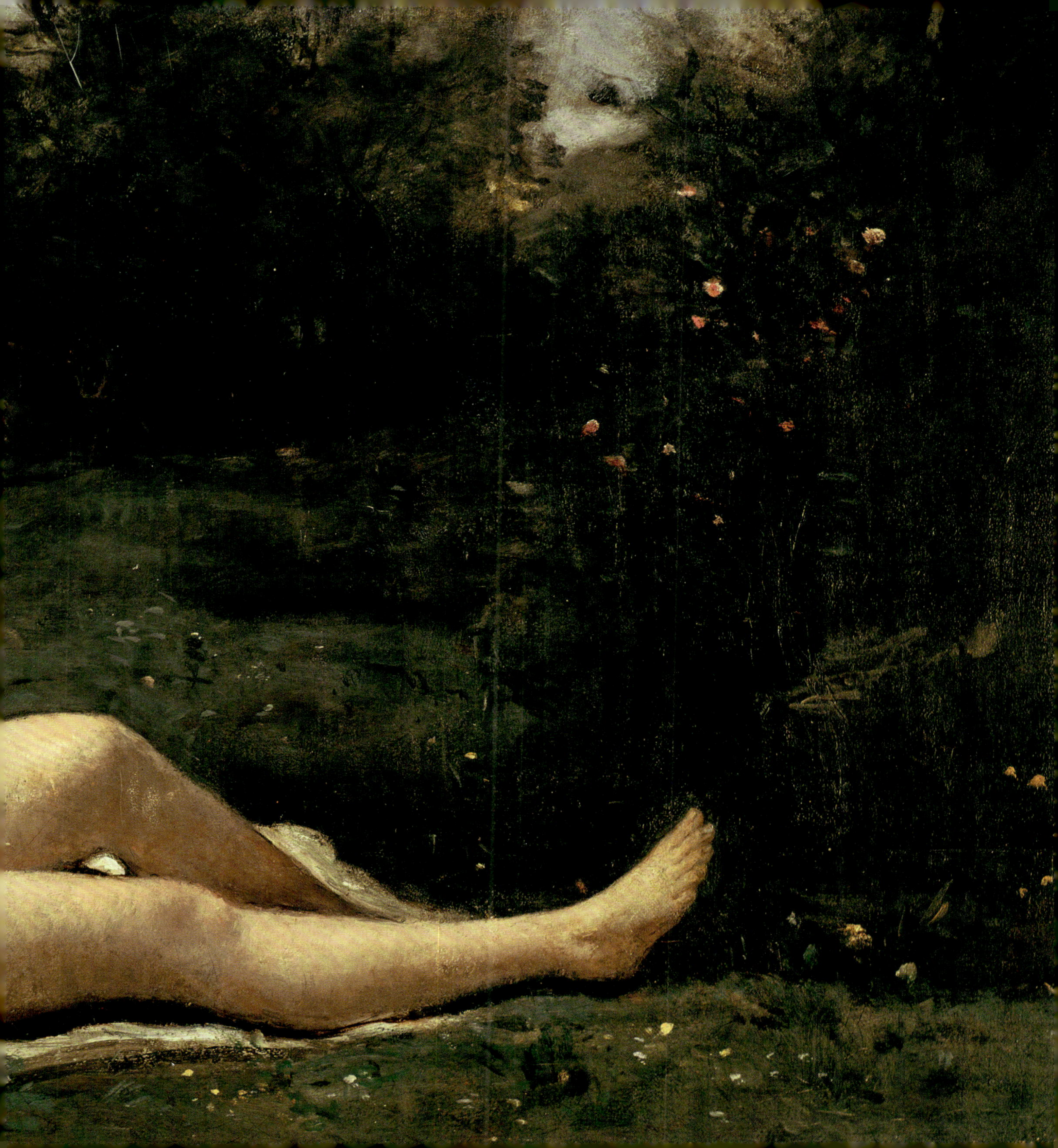

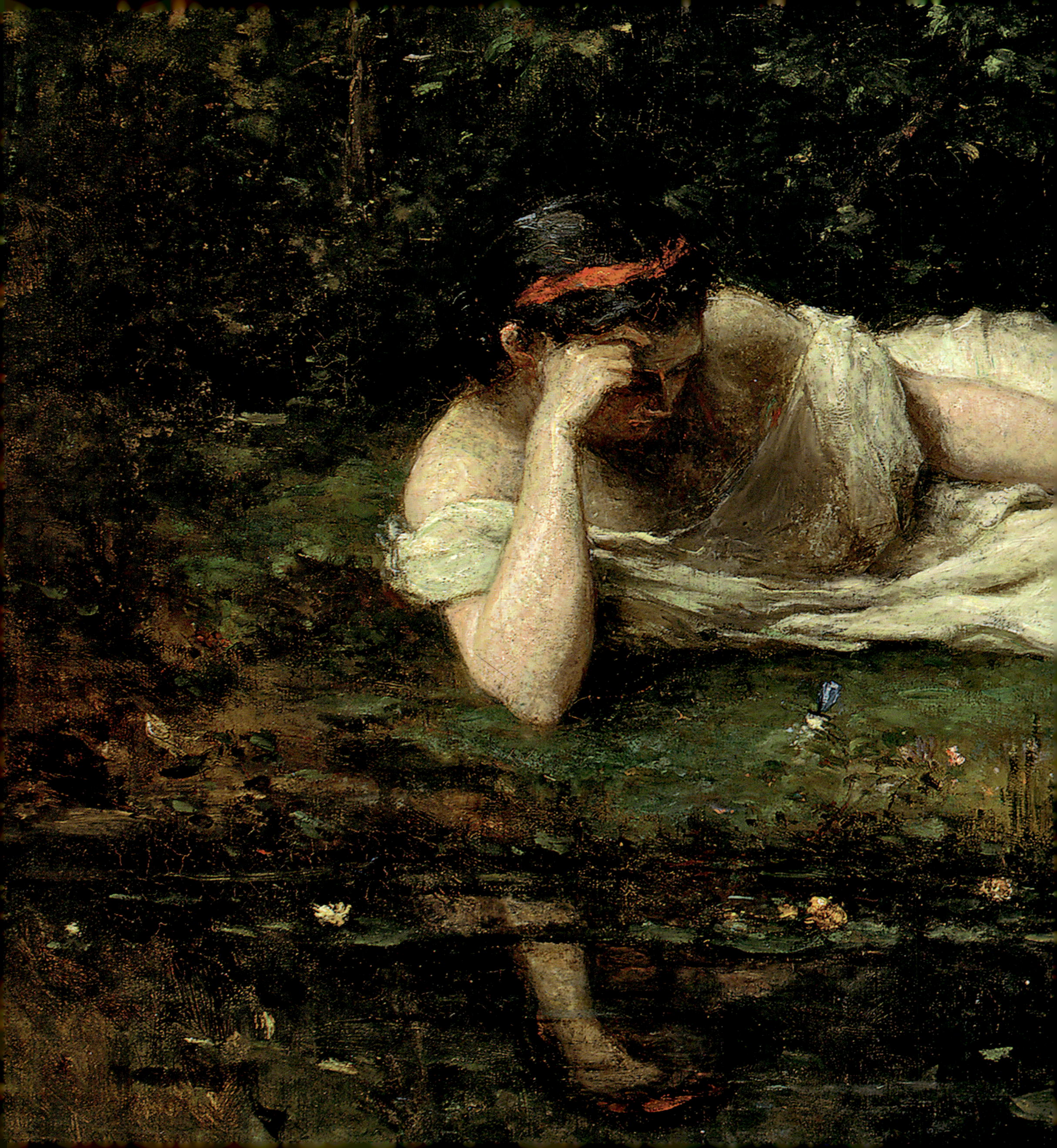

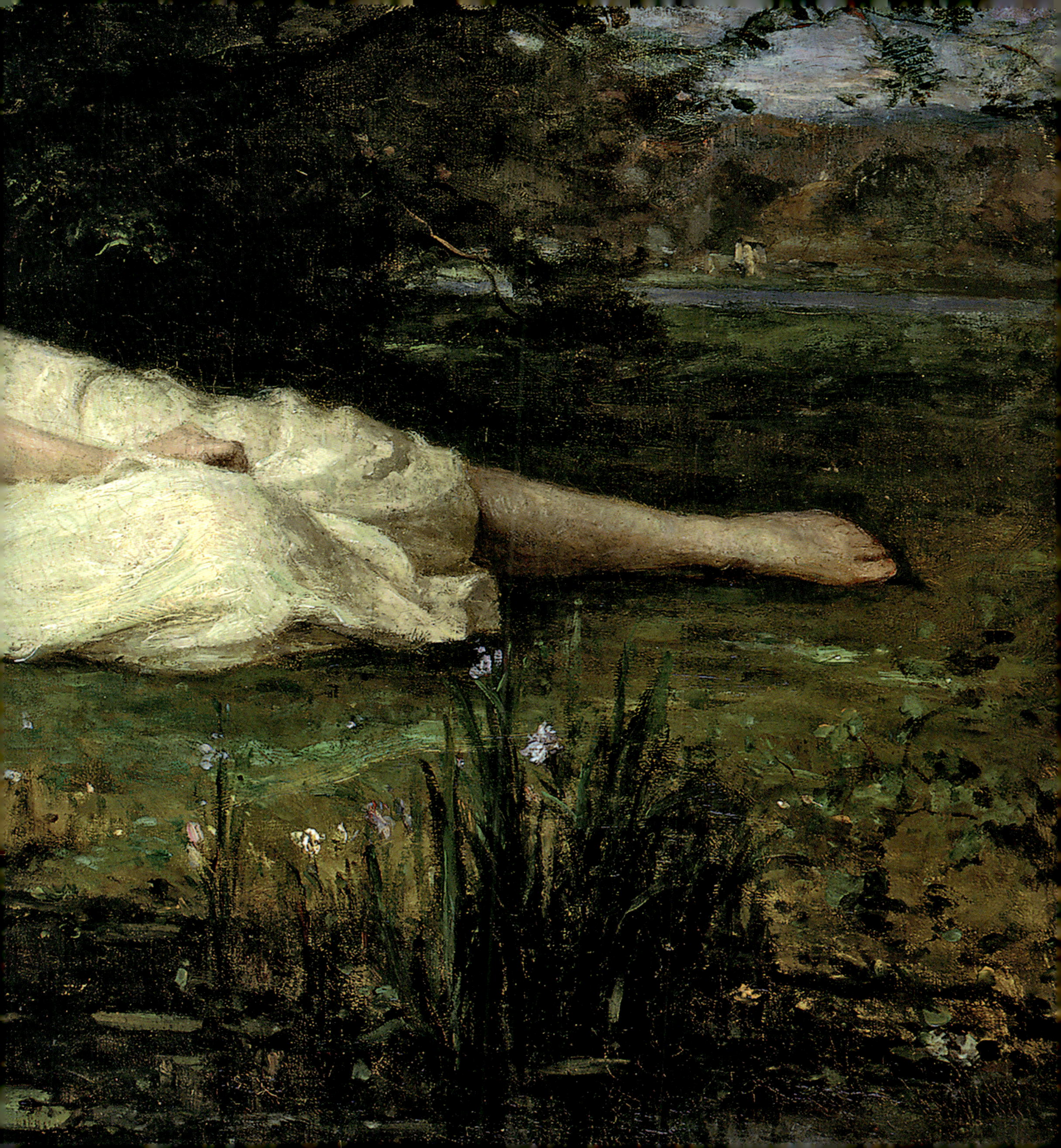

pp. 234-235 :

The Sleeping Venus

Vénus endormie

Schlummernde Venus

Venus dormida

Vênus adormecida

Slapende Venus

**Giorgio de Castelfranco (Giorgione)
(c. 1477-1510)**

——

c. 1508-10, Oil on canvas/Huile sur toile,
108,5 × 175 cm, Gemaeldegalerie Alte
Meister, Dresden

pp. 236-237 :

Reclining Nymph

Nymphe couchée dit aussi *Le Repos*

Liegende Nymphe oder *Die Ruhe*

Ninfa tumbada o *El descanso*

Ninfa mentirosa, também conhecida
como *Le Repos*

Liggende nimf of *De rust*

**Jean-Baptiste Camille Corot
(1796-1875)**

——

c. 1859, Oil on canvas/Huile sur toile,
49 × 75 cm, Musée d'Art et d'Histoire,
Genève

pp. 238-239 :

Study, at The Water's Edge

Étude au bord de l'eau

Studie am Ufer

Estudio en la orilla

Estudo na costa

Studie, aan de waterkant

Berthe Morisot (1841-1895)

——

c. 1864, Oil on canvas/Huile sur toile,
60 × 73,4 cm, Private collection